THE POETRY

Poetry is supposed to be untransl
also translations: Pope's *Iliad*, Po
only the most obvious examples. *The Poetry of Translation* dismantles this
paradox, launching a new theoretical approach to translation, and developing it through readings of English poem-translations, both major and
neglected, from Chaucer and Petrarch to Homer and Logue.

The word 'translation' includes within itself a picture: of something
being carried across. This image gives a misleading idea of what goes on in
any translation; and poets have been quick to dislodge it with other
metaphors. Poetry translation can be a process of opening; of pursuing
desire, or succumbing to passion; of taking a view, or zooming in; of
dying, metamorphosing, or bringing to life. These are the dominant
metaphors that have jostled the idea of 'carrying across' in the history of
poetry translation into English; and they form the spine of Reynolds's
discussion.

Where do these metaphors originate? Wide-ranging literary historical
trends play their part; but a more important factor is what goes on in the
poem that is being translated. Dryden thinks of himself as 'opening'
Virgil's *Aeneid* because he thinks Virgil's *Aeneid* opens fate into world
history; Pound tries to being Propertius to life because death and rebirth
are central to Propertius's poems. In this way, translation can continue the
creativity of its originals.

The Poetry of Translation puts the translation of poetry back at the heart
of English literature, allowing the many great poem-translations to be read
anew.

THE POETRY
OF TRANSLATION

*From Chaucer & Petrarch to
Homer & Logue*

MATTHEW REYNOLDS

OXFORD
UNIVERSITY PRESS

OXFORD
UNIVERSITY PRESS

Great Clarendon Street, Oxford OX2 6DP

Oxford University Press is a department of the University of Oxford.
It furthers the University's objective of excellence in research, scholarship,
and education by publishing worldwide. Oxford is a registered trade mark of
Oxford University Press in the UK and in certain other countries

© Matthew Reynolds 2011

The moral rights of the author have been asserted

First published 2011
First published in paperback 2014

Published in the United States of America by Oxford University Press
198 Madison Avenue, New York, NY 10016, United States of America

British Library Cataloguing in Publication Data

Data available

Library of Congress Cataloging in Publication Data

Data available

ISBN 978–0–19–960571–2 (Hbk)
ISBN 978–0–19–968793–0 (Pbk)

For Robin Kirkpatrick and Edward Williams

Acknowledgements

I am grateful to the Leverhulme Trust for awarding the Fellowship which enabled me to do much of the research for this book and to write it, and to St Anne's College, Oxford, and the Oxford English Faculty for fostering the work. A college is a multilingual and interdisciplinary environment and my friends at St Anne's were in consequence much pestered by enquiries. I am grateful especially to Roger Crisp, Tim Gardam, Peter Ghosh, Howard Hotson, Sian Grönlie, Freya Johnston, Andrew Klevan, Matthew Leigh, Patrick McGuinness, Stefan Talmon, and Sam Thompson. Colleagues elsewhere were no less generous with their expertise, in particular those who read parts or all of the text in draft: Tania Demetriou, Stuart Gillespie, Vincent Gillespie, Stephen Harrison, Jamie McKendrick, and an acute, anonymous reader for OUP; I also owe thanks to Michael Clanchy for constructing the bibliography, and to Elizabeth Stone, Anne Halliday, Kathleen Kerr, and Ariane Petit for their parts in the work of turning the text into a book. My thinking was nourished by discussion at seminars where early samples of my argument were presented: in Glasgow, Manchester, and Oxford; at the Reading and Reception Studies Seminar, London; and at Trinity College, Dublin. Conversations with distinguished translators on the annual occasion of the Oxford–Weidenfeld Translation Prize were a repeated help and provocation; especially those with Anthea Bell, Ciaran Carson, Margaret Jull Costa, and Michael Hofmann. I owe great debts to Peter France, Robin Kirkpatrick, and Christopher Ricks, who supported the research at its beginning; and to Jaqueline Baker at Oxford University Press for welcoming it towards its end. To Kate Clanchy, my debt has no conclusion.

My gratitude to particular written texts is of course indicated in the notes, but I would like to record here my general thanks for two intrepid publishing ventures, the sadly halted Penguin Poets in Translation Series (general editor, Christopher Ricks), and the ongoing *Oxford History of Literary Translation in English* (general editors, Peter France and Stuart Gillespie). Without those books, this book would not be.

Many of my quotations from copyright material are allowed under the provision for fair use for the purposes of criticism. In the cases where they are not, I am grateful to the following for permission to quote: The Random House Group Limited for the extracts from *Men in the Off Hours* and *Autobiography of Red*, by Anne Carson, published by Jonathan Cape; Farrar, Straus and Giroux, LLC, for the extracts from *Ashes for Breakfast* by Durs Grünbein, translated by Michael Hofmann, translation copyright © 2005 by Michael Hofmann; The Random House Group Limited and Wake Forest University Press for the extracts from *Collected Poems* by Michael Longley, published by Jonathan Cape; Carcanet Press Limited for the extract from *Beowulf: A Verse Translation into Modern English* by Edwin Morgan; and New Directions Publishing Corporation for the extracts from 'Sonnet VII', 1910, 'Sonnet VII', 1912, 'Sonnet VII', 1932, and 'Sonnet: Chi è Questa?', 1910 *Provença* version by Ezra Pound, from the original by Guido Cavalcanti, copyright © 1983 by the Trustees of the Ezra Pound Literary Property Trust; © 1983 by Princeton University Press. I have tried hard to trace and contact all relevant copyright holders: I will be glad to make good any omissions brought to my notice.

Contents

PART IV. TRANSLATION AND
THE LANDSCAPE OF THE PAST

PART V. TRANSLATION AS 'LOSS',
AS 'DEATH', AS 'RESURRECTION',
AND AS 'METAMORPHOSIS'

PART I

TRANSLATION AND METAPHOR

1

The Scope of Translation

'Translation' does not happen only between languages. For as long as the word has been in English, other kinds of 'translation' have occurred. In his 1578 bestseller, *Euphues*, John Lyly warned that, if you have a 'crabbe tree', you can 'translate' (i.e. transplant) it as much as you like but it will 'never beare sweete apple'.[1] Two centuries later, Dr Johnson recorded in his *Dictionary* a cutting-edge bit of medical jargon: 'the regimen must be to translate the morbifick matter upon the extremities of the body'.[2] Back in the fourteenth century, when the words 'translate' and 'translation' were just beginning to settle into English, we find in the Wycliffite Bible that Solomon 'translatide' Pharaoh's daughter from the city of David to the house he had prepared for her. 'Translacioun', too, was what jumped Enoch miraculously from earth to heaven—a usage that has just about survived into modern English, thanks to the time-travelling properties of the Bible.[3]

These old, physical senses of 'translation' make visible the word's derivation from the Latin *transferre* (roughly, 'to transfer' or 'carry across' as well as 'to translate'). They have helped keep alive the idea that translation between languages is, like moving an object through space, a process which leaves something fundamentally unaltered, a 'change into another language retaining the sense', as Dr Johnson defined it.[4] The idea of movement, obvious when Lyly talks of the 'translation' of a crabbe tree, lurks within the word when it is used of languages. Just like 'poem' or 'play' or 'novel', 'translation' names a kind of text with a distinguishable role (or rather, cluster of roles) in culture. But, unlike those other words, 'translation' also projects a picture of how the texts it names have come to be the way they are: they must have done some sort of 'carrying across'.

As a linguistic or philosophical description of what happens in translation, 'carrying across' has obvious shortcomings. In 1965 J. C. Catford attacked the idea that translation might involve the 'transference of meaning from one set of patterned symbols...into another'.[5] Jacques Derrida, too, argues sharply against what he calls the 'classical model' of translation as a '"transfer" of pure signifieds'—a conception which, he suggests, underlies the whole endeavour of 'philosophy' in Western culture, and which he claims 'prevailed up until Benjamin perhaps' (i.e. until the publication of Walter Benjamin's essay 'Die Aufgabe des Übersetzers' in 1923).[6] Many other thinkers have followed similar lines, and I will return to their arguments in later chapters. Yet, as we will see, the image of 'carrying across' is remarkably difficult to shake off: even theorists who reject it (even Derrida himself) rely on it at other points in their arguments.

This habit of self-contradiction is not as stymieing as it may seem. For the idea of translation as 'carrying across' needs to be framed, not as a proposition that defines translation, but as a metaphor for it. And metaphors, of course, offer only provisional and angled images of what they are metaphors for. When Andrew Marvell hears 'Times winged Charriot hurrying near' he is not claiming that time is really in a winged chariot, only that that is how it seems to him for the purposes of his poem.[7] Likewise, the picture that lurks within the word 'translation' offers a way of looking at what happens in translation between languages. And that picture is only partial and pragmatic, in some ways illuminating, in others not. The word 'translation', then, includes within itself a metaphor for translation, the metaphor of 'carrying across'.

As we will see, translation between languages is a complex, varied, and unpredictable imaginative enterprise which cannot satisfactorily be reduced to theoretical description. But it can partially and loosely be grasped with metaphors: 'carrying across' is by no means the only one available, though it is the most insistent. Discussions of the translation of literature—and especially of poetry—have, throughout history, been remarkably fertile in metaphors for translation. Derrida's 'classical model' has not been so dominant as, in the fury of argument, he perhaps makes it seem.

For the partial misfit between translation and the image of 'carrying across' has registered even in how the word 'translation' is habitually used. People do not generally speak of 'signifieds' or even 'meaning' being 'translated' out of one text into another; and they never have done. What we say is 'translated' is a 'poem' or a 'book' or a 'speech' or a 'word'. Obviously the whole poem or book or speech or word is not carried across unchanged: this everyday usage, then, rebuts the 'classical model'. Equally, people's flexible way with the word seems to recognize that translation operates on more than Catford's 'meaning' or Derrida's 'pure signifieds'. In the Wycliffite Bible, for instance, 'translatide' and 'translacioun' themselves translate the Latin words 'transtulit' and 'translationem'.[8] What sort of 'translation' has been accomplished here? Perhaps something that might loosely—metaphorically—be called the carrying across of a 'meaning' or 'sense' (I will return to the question); but certainly

also the carrying-across of several letters. A word is transmuted as it is
brought over—in this 'translation'—into a different language, becoming
in some respects but not wholly a different word. And English too is
altered as it is pulled back in the opposite direction and made to mingle a
little more closely with Latin.

In most other European languages, the words for translation include a
similar latent metaphor. In some, however, the sorts of rewriting that
English-speakers call 'translation' are imagined in other terms. Douglas
Robinson points out that, in Finnish, the main idea is of 'turning' between
languages (this thought finds an echo in the English word 'version',
from the Latin 'vertere').[9] Elsewhere in the world—as Maria Tymoczko
has emphasized—many of the 'words indicating the practices and products of translation . . . do not actually mean *translation* as such, in the
sense implied by the English term'.[10] These other terms, she rightly says,
offer new ways of thinking about what translation might be. But the
English tradition can do that too if we open our eyes to the mobility of its
definitions. Those elderly, physical usages of the word 'translation' can
serve, not as illustrations of the 'classical model', but as distinct instances
of meaning, charged with metaphorical possibility. Might translation
between languages be in some way like the development of 'morbifick
matter' through a body, whether as cure or as infection? Dryden sometimes felt it was, as we will see in Chapters 11 and 15. Or could it
somehow resemble translation into heaven? Sir Francis Kynaston thought
so when, in 1635, he hoped that by translating Chaucer's *Troilus and
Criseide* into Latin he had made it 'stable and unmoving . . . throughout all
time' ('per omnia secula . . . stabilem & immotum').[11] Or perhaps translation between languages might involve a sort of marriage (between translator and source, perhaps) like the 'translation' of Pharoah's daughter? Even
Lyly's horticultural usage associates translation with change as much as
with transference: what is exasperating about the 'crabbe tree' is that
when 'translated' it does not alter as one might expect. All these usages
point away from the 'classical model' as much as towards it. The same is
true of that most startling of English literary utterances of the word,
Quince's, in Shakespeare's *A Midsummer Night's Dream* (c.1595), when
his friend Bottom's head (at least) has been changed for that of an ass:
'Bless thee, Bottom, bless thee! / Thou art translated'.[12] How much of the
rest of Bottom is assified—voice? gait? penis?—will depend on the production. This uncertain image of translation reflects searchingly upon
translation between languages, for the play within a play that Bottom
goes on to act in derives from a translation, *The XV Bookes of P. Ovidius
Naso, Entytled Metamorphosis*, done by Arthur Golding (1567)—a text
whose own metamorphic tendencies I will discuss in Chapter 25. In none

of these cases is 'carrying across' all or only or exactly what occurs; in each
of them it is fretted or dislodged by other energies.

The complexities latent in such usages of 'translation' and 'translate'
have long been recognized in discussions of literary translation. The
assumptions identified by Catford, the 'classical model' attacked by
Derrida, never held much sway over this field. Granted, writers did often
describe translations as being 'sense for sense' or, like Johnson, as 'retaining
the sense'; but what was meant by 'for', by 'sense', or by 'retaining' was not
a simple matter. Dryden, for instance, thought that 'sense', could be
'amplified' in translation, though not 'altered': not for him, evidently,
the ' "transfer" of pure signifieds'.[13] But what counted as amplification
and how did it differ from altering? As we will see in Chapter 8, the
distinction could not be sustained. This whatever-it-was that happened
to the 'sense' was, very commonly, felt to be overlaid and intermingled with
other changes. One brief example: when George Granville, in 1697, wrote
a poem 'To Mr. Dryden on his Translations', it seemed to him that more
had gone on in them than marrying or translating into heaven—more even
than in Bottom's metamorphosis. Dryden's 'translations' were resurrec-
tions of the dead, revivals of 'Genius', and transfusions of an alchemical
'nimble Spirit'; they were trading expeditions and 'Flow'rs transplanted';
they were a selection of 'the Noblest Seeds of Foreign Wit'.[14]

In this, Granville's praise of Dryden is typical of discussions of literary
translation. As I have suggested (and as we will see further in chapters to
come), the metaphor of carrying across is only a rough approximation to
what goes on in the translation of any text. But it is especially literary texts
and, among them, especially poems, that give rise to different practices
and images of rewording across languages. To the metaphor of 'carrying
across' that squats within the word 'translation' poet-translators oppose
other metaphors that better describe what they feel themselves to be
doing. These metaphors are not just different ways of describing a single
activity. Arm in arm with the pragmatic business of creating an English
text that somehow stands for a foreign one, and underneath the
corresponding umbrella term 'translation', there flourish different imaginative processes which have been shaped, and can be named, by
different metaphors.

In this book, I trace some of the metaphors that have been most
powerfully operative in the history of poetry translation into English:
'translation as interpretation' and as 'opening'; as 'friendship', 'desire',
and 'passion'; as 'adhesion'; as 'taking a view', as 'moving across
a landscape', and as 'zoom'; as 'loss', 'death', 'resurrection', and 'metamorphosis'. All poem-translations, I will argue, take shape according to
some distinguishable metaphor or metaphors, whether knowingly or

not (almost always, a metaphor plays out through a poem-translation in ways that are not wholly under the translator's control). It follows from my argument—though I do not pursue this implication in detail—that translation in general embraces a range of metaphors, of which 'translation as carrying across'—translation rigidly conceived—is only one. The conventions which govern non-literary translation—of instruction manuals or news articles, for instance—are particular, institutionalized examples.

No more than 'translation as carrying across', none of the other metaphors I will explore offers a perfect model of the process of translation to which it is attached. In consequence, many poem-translations adopt two or more metaphors, each supplementing or contesting or undermining the other: the instances I explore in Chapters 8 to 25 become more involved as the discussion advances. This complexity is a reason for putting poetry-translation at the heart of any understanding of translation in general. Since poetry is routinely taken to be supremely difficult to translate, it can look like a marginal case when people think about translation per se. But in fact it is when translation is most under pressure that it is most self-questioning, and therefore most revealing.

There are historical reasons why some metaphors flourish more at some times than at others: I will endeavour to sketch these in. But there is another, more important limb to my argument. Strangely often, we will discover that the metaphor or metaphors that define an act of translation emerge out of the text that is being translated. Dryden thinks of himself as 'opening' Virgil's *Aeneid* into English because he thinks of the *Aeneid* as showing how destiny is 'opened' into history. Byron, faced with Canto 5 of Dante's *Inferno*, translates after the metaphor of 'translation as passion' because passion is at the heart of the text he is translating. We will explore many other examples of translators seeing 'doubles of translation'—as I call them—in their source texts, and having their practice affected accordingly. This creative interaction between the source text and the way it is translated does not always occur in the translation of poetry: not every 'poem-translation' is a 'poem of translation'. But when it does, it gives rise to texts that have a particular aesthetic charge, and which—for that reason—subject the idea of 'translation' to especially vigorous redefinition. This is what I call 'the poetry of translation'.

Not long after Johnson, the metaphorical energies of 'translation' and 'translate' began to push in a new direction. When Coleridge criticized 'Mr. Pope and his followers' in *Biographia Literaria* (1817), he suggested that their writings were 'characterized not so much by poetic thoughts, as by thoughts *translated* into the language of poetry'. This was part of his and Wordsworth's attack on what they took to be the 'artificiality' of eighteenth-century 'poetic diction'.[15] Coleridge's idea seems to have been that the lesser, unpoetic thoughts first took mental form in plain words— perhaps as prose—and were only then embellished into verse. The fact that Pope was famous, not only as a poet, but as the poet-translator of Homer, has an obvious influence on this conception: it is as though Pope's other verse has been infected by the habit of translation so that it, too, is not pure poetry. For Coleridge, then, 'translation' can describe a kind of writing that involves the transformation of words into other words as part of a continuous, if misguided, process of composition.

Other writers during Coleridge's lifetime used the word for various different ways in which thoughts might come out into language: the trend was fuelled (as Antoine Berman has shown in *L'Épreuve de l'étranger* [1984]) by much speculation on the part of the German romantics.[16] For William Hazlitt, not unusually taking the opposite line from Coleridge, 'translation' was a mark of genius: Shakespeare's language, he says, is 'hieroglyphical. It translates thoughts into visible images'.[17] Thomas Carlyle addressed the same topic twenty years later but took 'translation' to suggest creative compromise. Shakespeare was constrained by having to write for the Globe: he was like a sculptor who 'cannot set his own free Thought before us; but his Thought as he could translate it into the stone that was given'.[18] When Walter Pater adopted the word, in 1889, he used it in a looser sense again: 'translation' was what happened when anyone uttered anything: 'all language involves translation from inward to out-ward'.[19]

Though it loosens as it spreads, the word retains some flavour of translation between languages. But it is hard to judge how much of one. In Pater's case, 'translation' cannot be used so vaguely as to mean just 'change' or 'movement': if it were, the remark would be inane. But neither can it mean exactly the same as when we talk of translation from English to Italian: if it did, it would commit Pater to denying the existence of any difference at all between language and thought. The French word 'traduc-tion' was developing in a similar way at about the same time: Paul Valéry, writing in his *Cahiers* a decade or so after Pater, probed the slippages of meaning which resulted. What we usually call thought, he said, is still only a language, although a very unusual one ('ce qu'on appelle ordinairement *pensée* n'est *encore* qu'une langue. À vrai dire très particulière'). But where does translation in and out of it start? And what is translated? ('mais où commence la traduction? et quoi est traduit?')[20] Valéry's questions are still relevant to cultural theory today, where—as Sherry Simon has re-marked—'translation' is most often used 'as a metaphor...to stand for the difficulty of access to language, of a sense of exclusion from the codes of the powerful'. So, 'migrants strive to "translate" their past into the present', and women to '"translate themselves" into the language of patriarchy'.[21] These recent usages convey an awareness that culture is text and that identity is contructed through language; but they tend not, any more than their nineteenth-century precursors, to hold themselves at all strictly to the model of translation-between-languages. The word 'translate' sometimes means 'express again in different words'—and sometimes just 'express'.

The same metaphorical drift occurs in George Steiner's *After Babel* (1975; third edition 1998). 'Translation is formally and pragmatically implicit in *every* act of communication', he declares: 'to understand is to decipher. To hear significance is to translate'. In short: '*human communication equals translation*'.[22] The phrases sound as though they are announcing a scientific discovery: *water equals H_2O*. But even in these initial formulations the words struggle against the symmetries that Steiner would press them into. He wants us to see no distinction that matters between deciphering—e.g. from the dots and dashes of morse code into the letters that they represent—and translation between languages: but in fact you can know no English whatsoever and still be able to decipher morse code into the letters of English words. If understanding an utterance really 'equals' translating it, then the language of the utterance must be turned into some different language in the mind. Of course, to explain an utterance you have to use other words which in turn have to be explained, etc: in that sense the arrival of the signified is, as Derrida said, endlessly deferred. But the doomed quest for the Final Signified is not the same as the everyday pragmatic apprehension of meaning, the *getting someone's point*, the *seeing what they are on about*. If you think that this kind of understanding is in fact 'translation' you come up against Valéry's problem of how the postulated language-in-the-mind can in its turn be understood. The structure is endlessly recursive.

When Steiner sets out to illustrate his claim, a reservation is silently introduced. It is no longer '*every* act of communication', all 'understanding' and 'hearing of significance' that 'is' translation. Rather, 'when we read or hear any language-statement from the past, be it Leviticus or last year's best-seller, we translate'. Why 'from the past', all of a sudden? Of course, one might claim that by the time any words have travelled through our eyes or ears into our understandings they have reached us 'from the past'; but this turns out not to be Steiner's point. His idea is rather that the passage of some unspecified length of time—more than a nanosecond but less than a year—creates a 'barrier or distance' which is 'exactly the same' as that created by the difference between languages.[23] By way of example he offers readings of some texts 'from the past', including these lines of Shakespeare:

> ... that most venerable man, which I
> Did call my father, was I know not where
> When I was stamp'd.[24]

As Steiner notes, the punctuation and spelling have been adapted to suit modern comprehensions. Nevertheless, someone unfamiliar with Shakespearean English might be puzzled by the word 'which' and, perhaps after a moment's reflection, translate it into 'whom' or 'who'. Here the act of understanding piggy-backs on an act of translation: in the case of this particular word, time has indeed created a 'barrier or distance' so similar to that between (say) the English 'who' and the French 'qui' that it seems true to claim that translation is 'formally and pragmatically implicit' in understanding. But what of the words 'I' and 'know' and 'where' and 'not' and 'when' and 'was' and 'call' and 'father'? Does a speaker of modern Standard English need to go through a process of 'formal and pragmatic' translation in order to understand them? What do we translate them into? Granted, the more you are familiar with Shakespeare's ways with language, the more you know of Renaissance ideas and feelings, and the more sensitively you imagine your way into Posthumus's character and the circumstances in which he speaks, the more nuanced will be your understanding of the words. But it is hardly an accurate description of this deepening apprehension to say that it is 'exactly the same' as translating from one language to another.

As we will see, there are similarities between translation and many other actions and conditions; not only aspects of communication, such as interpretation, but all the sources of the translation metaphors that I have mentioned: 'opening', 'friendship', 'desire', 'passion', 'adhesion', 'taking a view', 'moving across a landscape', 'zoom', 'loss', 'death', 'resurrection', and 'metamorphosis'. All these can become doubles of translation: they all offer metaphors through which to comprehend translation between languages; and translation between languages, in return, becomes a powerful means of writing about them. Any of them could be, and indeed have been called 'translation'. In fact you can call anything at all a 'translation' if you would like: eating is 'translation'; seeing is 'translation'; even a stone lying still on the ground is being 'translated' through time. But there is a crucial difference between thinking that you are making a literal statement—a proposition—when you say that any of these things 'is' translation, and realising that you are coming out with a metaphor. In the first case, difference collapses and the word 'translation' becomes so loose as to be meaningless. In the second, the differences between translation and the other term of the metaphor continue to matter. Translation-between-languages and—say—passion do not disintegrate into one another but 'interact' (to borrow a word from Max Black).[25] Passion exerts a pull on the practice of translation, reshaping it into one of the range of varieties which I mentioned before. Equally, the example of translation-between-languages alters how passion is conceived. If we are to trace and make sense of these imaginative and semantic interminglings we must not lose sight of the differences they cross.

The word 'translation', then, veils distinctions that metaphors reveal and define. 'Think how many different kinds of thing are called "description" ', wrote Wittgenstein (as translated by G. E. M. Anscombe): 'description of a body's position by means of its co-ordinates; description of a facial expression; description of a sensation of touch; of a mood':[26] translation can happen in at least as many ways. As we have begun to see, translation does more than 'transfer significance'. Steiner's definition, in one sense too vast, is in another respect too narrow. Translation stretches words, bridges times, mingles personal identities, and unsettles national languages. As it does so, it creates a distinctive medium in which connections between different places, times and people can be imagined, thought over, and felt through.

My next three chapters survey some theoretical ground which may be unknown to readers who are at home in English literature but are less familiar with discussions of translation. For those who are expert in such discussions, the territory will not be new; but I hope the line I take across it will be sufficiently distinctive to sustain interest. The aim is to recalibrate established understandings of translation somewhat, so that when we rejoin the main trajectory of my argument (which happens in Chapter 5) its ramifications can be more readily traced.

2

Translating within and
between Languages

Languages do not have boundaries. 'The entities we label as the "English language" or "Flemish dialect"'—as Suzanne Romaine puts it—'are not . . . discrete.' They have separated and merged over time and they typically intermingle in the present. 'Ciao' can be said in English, as can 'soupçon' and 'schadenfreude': 'any variety is part of a continuum'. Along this continuum of utterance, the gatherings of usage we call languages are separated by factors that are, not inherently linguistic, but 'geographical and social'.[1]

Similar divisions exist within each language too, variegating it into dialects which are not only regional but social and generational, and into registers which accord to profession or activity. Families, and even individuals, can have their own distinctive words, syntactic structures, and ways of using them. Communication between these varieties may call for translation. A doctor may have to translate 'coronary thrombosis' or 'abdominal haemorrhage' for an English patient as much as for a visiting foreigner; a child may have to explain what she means by 'sick' or 'lol' to her teacher no less than to her French exchange. For Natalia Ginzburg, in *Lessico famigliare* (1963), the family of her childhood possessed its own 'lexicon': 'those phrases are our Latin', it strikes her, looking back ('quelle frasi sono il nostro Latino'). Her father had a store of words—'sbrodeghezzi', 'potacci', 'fufignezzi'—which only he would use.[2]

Given this landscape of utterance, in which languages are at once continuous with one another and internally divided, it looks as though there can be no distinction of kind between translation that happens within what we think of as a single language and translation that bridges two such languages. In *Mouse or Rat?* (2003), part way through an argument generally—and rightly—oriented against the assumptions of *After Babel*, Umberto Eco endeavours to fend off this conclusion. He seeks help from Gertrude's cry in Hamlet:

What wilt thou do? thou wilt not murder me? Help, help, ho!

Translated into other English words with the help of a dictionary, he says, this might come out as:

> What wilt thou cook? Thou wilt not remove me from life? Do a favour, do a favour, ho!

Eco says this is 'something that no publisher would pay for as a translation';[3] and he is absolutely right. It is, however, the sort of thing that many hotels and restaurants pay for as translation all the time, as any traveller's personal experience will attest. 'Our wine list leaves you nothing to hope for' and 'measles not included in room charge' are but two of the instances collected in a recent droll anthology.[4] Granted, these are bad translations; but Eco's humorous example is also a bad rewording. Take this instead:

> What are you up to? You're not going to kill me? Guards! Guards! Help!

And compare the French translation by André Gide:

> Que veux-tu faire? Tu ne vas pas me tuer? Au secours! Au secours! Oh![5]

It would be hard to prove which is the closer.

Nevertheless, the translation of English into English does feel like an awkward thing to do. In part this is because it is unusual: if a text is in your language already there is no need to translate. But it is also because sufficiently close synonyms seem hard to find, especially for common basic words like 'I', 'yellow', 'bread', 'milk'. Think of another language, and 'io' (say), and 'giallo', 'pane', 'latte' slot into place with an ease that, well, 'one', er... 'the colour of jaundice', um... 'crust', and—what, 'weak cream?'—distinctly lack. Yet, on a moment's reflection, these Italian words have their own particularities which pull them away from what at first felt like their English twins. 'Io' is less frequent and more emphatic than 'I'. 'Giallo' is marked by that final 'o' as agreeing only with masculine nouns (and it does not have the sense of 'cowardly'; and when said of a novel it means 'detective'). 'Pane' and 'latte' generally denote substances that are rather different from English bread and milk and are used differently too: not so often toasted, not typically added to tea. The Italian stabs at synonymy suddenly seem no better than the English. Turn to a language that is more distant both culturally and in structure, and the difficulties of course proliferate. Here is the anthropologist A. L. Becker:

> When we confront a distant language, we are compelled to give full attention to the fact that saying, for instance, 'I am' is something we do with words in English, for in that distant language there is no *I* like our *I*, and no *am* at all. To put one's speaking self into words in Burmese, Javanese, or Malay is to

make claims of status (high or low) that alienate our very selves, and in none of those languages is there either a verb like *be* (a copula) or a distinction between present and past tense.[6]

This is obviously a more drastic non-equivalence than the difference between 'I' and 'io' let alone the lack of English synonyms for 'bread'. The gap between the two ways of living-and-meaning that belong to the two languages has become so vast as almost to establish separate worlds.

These considerations will be familiar to any translator, and indeed to anyone who knows a foreign tongue. But the strange thing is that non-synonymy remains more obvious within a language than between two languages. Near-synonyms in the same language function as alternatives. Their difference from one another is part of what they signify: when you speak, you continually choose one rather than another, and so have your awareness of their particularities refreshed. But a word's difference from a near-synonym in another language is not usually part of its significance. Italian words (and words in Burmese even more so) are pulled away from English by a multitude of factors: grammatical form, semantic structure, habitual referents, and the clutter of associations which cultures gather around their words, and which linguists call 'encyclopaedic knowledge'.[7] But this very comprehensiveness of difference creates a linguistic and cultural landscape which is largely (though not, as we have seen, wholly) distinct from that of English, and which can therefore seem, albeit roughly, to map onto it. The correspondences seem the more persuasive because, when a language is foreign to you, you have (by definition) a less sharp command of the detail of its meanings and of how they vary from the forms of meaning you are used to. As the linguist John Lyons has pointed out, 'bilingual dictionaries encourage us to believe' in a greater degree of synonymy than actually exists between languages.[8] Our general use of translations as stand-ins for their originals exerts the same pressure, as does the whole enterprise of trying to communicate across language barriers which is primarily a matter of discovering what is or can be shared, that is, what can be made to pass as synonyms (something of this has to happen even if the aim is to assert the difference of one culture from another). An array of institutional structures, from school textbooks to international courts, underpins this sufficiently functional degree of simi-larity—'pragmatic equivalence' as it is called in theories of translation.[9] And much of the time it all works adequately well.

Nevertheless, we must resist the pressure, put on us by these observa-tions, to say that there is something called 'translation', translation 'proper' (to borrow the Derridean label), which is translation between languages, and which is different in kind from rewording within a language. If you define translation in that way, you conceal the fact that what translation does, and therefore is, varies according to the pairs of languages involved: translating between English and Burmese poses different challenges and asks for different solutions from translating between English and French. In the history of English literature, most translation of poetry has been from languages and cultures with which English writers can feel a fair degree of continuity: Latin, Greek, Italian, French, German. Many of the tactics for understanding and reimagining that we will encounter in the following chapters are dependent on that proximity. The two major exceptions I will explore, Edward FitzGerald's *Rubáiyát of Omar Khayyám* and Ezra Pound's *Cathay*, both find distinctive shapes for translation in order to make sense of the unusual linguistic and cultural distances that separate them from their sources. The recognition of loss in translation, and the frank failure to translate, become part of what they express and explore (Robert Browning did something similar with Aeschylus's Greek, as we will see in Chapter 5; but he was avowedly bucking a trend).

Equally, to say that what happens within a language is never 'translation' is to attribute a specious transparency to people's everyday endeavours to be understood and to understand. As we have established, the claim that '*human communication equals translation*' is unsustainable. Nevertheless, communication is always shadowed by the possibility of having to translate. When you are faced with a language that is foreign to you, the necessity of translation—whether by you or someone else—is obvious: having to be translated is part of what being 'foreign' means. Even within a language, the need to translate is sometimes similarly taken for granted: part of what it is to be a doctor or a lawyer, for instance, is to be allowed to speak in a way that other people cannot understand without translation. But you may also just be surprised by a word or way of speaking that is new to you. You may decide to wonder about the meaning even of terms you usually use without hesitation and perhaps turn to a dictionary where a series of possible translations can be found. In conversation you may realize you are not making yourself clear, or puzzle out what someone else must be trying to get across. When translation ambushes people who had not thought they needed it a fissure opens up. Translation draws attention to difference even as it overcomes it: it formalizes the gap it simultaneously endeavours to cross.

In such cases, the feeling of reaching out, of bridge-building, can predominate, as it does when, in *Oliver Twist* (1837–8), the Artful Dodger encounters the wandering Oliver. ' "Beak's order, eh?" '—he asks. ' "But," he added, noticing Oliver's look of surprise, "I suppose you don't know what a beak is" '—and proceeds to translate.[10] But translation can also emphasize division, as it does when Oliver has become better versed in the Dodger's dialect, though no more at home in it:

> 'I suppose you don't even know what a prig is?' said the Dodger, mournfully.
> 'I think I know that', replied Oliver, looking up. 'It's a th-; you're one, are you not?' enquired Oliver, checking himself.[11]

Why does Oliver interrupt his translation? Because completing it would aggravate the difference between the Dodger's world of words, where 'prigs' are proud, and Oliver's, where 'thieves' are hanged.

To recognize that you need to translate, then, is to split your language off from the language of the people around you. In fleeting ways this happens all the time. But it can be done with focused and consistent design. When, in 1844, William Barnes translated his *Poems in the Dorset Dialect* into 'the dialect which is chosen as national speech', he not only bridged but reasserted the difference between the 'pure', 'broad and bold shape of English' spoken in Dorset and 'common English' with its 'so-thought...elegance', its '*rouge*'.[12] And when (to turn from regional to chronological difference) Dryden, in 1700, modernized parts of *The Canterbury Tales*—or, as he put it, 'translated Chaucer into English'— he signalled that Chaucer's way with words had come to seem a different tongue.[13] Even with languages already felt to be foreign, the estrangement effected by translation can be made expressive. In Chapters 15 to 17 I explore the work of some poet-translators who are entrammelled in the metaphor of 'translation as desire'. They recognize, with especial rage, that translation inevitably shuts them off from what they nevertheless keep trying to grasp—by translating.

3

Translation and Paraphrase

Beyond translation there are other degrees on the scale of rewording: paraphrase, précis and interpretation. All of these can be done across languages; but they are more commonly thought of as happening within a language where the rewording and the source can readily be compared. In fact, 'paraphrase' is often used to refer to instances of translation within a language such as those we have just touched on. But the word has a divergent connotation. With a 'paraphrase', just as with a 'précis' or an 'interpretation', the emphasis is generally on its difference from the original. These kinds of rewriting are meant to be clearer or shorter or more persuasive, otherwise what would be the point of them? With translation, on the other hand, the endeavour is to achieve as much similarity as possible. Eco puts it nicely: 'if to interpret always means to respect the spirit (allow me this metaphor) of a text, to translate means to respect also its body'.[1] In consequence, texts are often 'quoted' in translation. If you call a work a 'paraphrase' or 'précis' or 'interpretation' you distinguish it from 'copies' and 'quotations'; but we merrily talk of people 'quoting' Tolstoy or Barthes even when the words they offer are in English. One sign of translation happening within a language is when you feel you are 'quoting' someone even though your words are different from what was actually said. This is usually thought of as a variety of indirect speech: 'the doctor said I'd had a heart attack', for instance, when the doctor really said 'you've had a coronary thrombosis'. Of course in some formal contexts (such as this book) the distinction between direct and indirect quotation is strictly enforced. But everyday conversation—not to mention literature—is more permissive.

Translation shades into these other modes of rewriting. 'I call it "translation" but it's more like an interpretation really'—you might say, excusing a loose version; or you might denounce a slack performance by someone else: 'this so-called translation is no more than a paraphrase'. Back in the sixteenth and seventeenth centuries the distinctions were even less secure. For Dryden, the word 'translation' stretched (as it has done for us) to include rewordings of texts in the same language; and they did not always have to be as distant from their translator as Chaucer was from him. Persius, Dryden wrote, brought into his own poems a 'multitude of... translations from Horace'; Donne would always lack 'dignity', even 'were he translated into numbers, and English' (a catty addition, those last two words!).[2] Correspondingly, Dryden adopted the word 'paraphrase' to mean translation—especially in his own preferred style, a middle road between the 'servile, literal translation' that he called 'metaphrase' and the 'libertine way' of those, like Cowley, who practise something that is better called 'imitation': they risk losing the 'name' of 'translator'. In 'paraphrase', the source's 'words are not so strictly followed as his sense, and that too is admitted to be amplified, but not altered' (an assertion I touched on in Chapter 1, and to which I will return in Chapter 8). Paraphrase also assumes a 'liberty to be allowed for the expression': this is necessary if the source is to be adapted to the 'proprieties' of the English language and its poetry.[3]

I will explore the tensions created by this layering of translation and paraphrase in Part II. But already we can see that, more than our current way with 'translation' and 'paraphrase', Dryden's usage takes the weight of the obvious fact that no translation is exactly the same as its source. 'I' is not the same as 'io', so metaphrase, with its ambition of word-on-word equivalence, will always fail: some sort of re-creative loosening is inevitable. The metaphrast, Dryden says, 'is encumbered with so many difficulties at once, that he can never disentangle himself from all'; but in paraphrase, 'thought' is 'translated truly', and 'the spirit of an author may be transfused'.[4] Translations have to be paraphrases too. Dryden's argument leaves us no choice—it would seem—but to agree with the statement, much reiterated in recent theory and criticism, that a 'translation is never a substitute for the original', as Donald Carne-Ross put it in 1996; and perhaps to accept even Clive Scott's more daring reformulation: 'no translation ever sets out to be a substitute for the original text, even when the reader of the translation has no knowledge of the original or its language'.[5]

Yet there is something peculiar about the phrasing which Scott and Carne-Ross—both learned, brilliant scholars—find themselves having to adopt. Usually it is taken for granted that a 'substitute' is different—and often crucially—from what it replaces. The whole point of saccharin is to have fewer calories than sugar; in football, the whole point of a substitute is to be fresher or faster or a better defender than the player coming off. But this is the opposite of what Scott and Carne-Ross appear to want the word to mean. They both set up a polarity between thinking of translations as 'substitutes' and being interested in 'a translator's enlargements, his liberties ... and additions' (Carne-Ross), all ways in which translations 'measure a difference' (Scott). There is nothing wrong with the general thrust of the recommendation; but there must be something askew in the argument if the statements it is meant to knock down—translations are or set out to be substitutes—already accept that there are differences between translation and source.

In fact translations have always been taken as substitutes, that is, as texts that in some circumstances can be read instead of their originals. In the preliminary 'chat'—as he calls it—which prefaces his version of Aeschylus's *Agamemnon* (1877), Robert Browning imagines readers who wish 'to acquaint themselves' with Aeschylus's tragedy, and can 'only do so by the help of a translator'.[6] Dryden addresses his volume of Juvenal and Persius's *Satires...Made English* (1693) to 'those gentlemen and ladies' who have not 'been conversant in the original' or at least not 'made Latin verse so much their business as to be critics in it'.[7] But the point hardly needs illustrating: it is everywhere taken for granted in reviews and introductions. Of course, translation can be done for other reasons too: as a stylistic exercise; as a step towards learning the language; as a way of illustrating different possible interpretations in a scholarly edition; as a catalyst of literary innovation. And then any translation can be read alongside its source as a work of criticism and interpretation: as Dante Gabriel Rossetti remarked in the Preface to his versions of early Italian poets, 'translation remains perhaps the most direct form of commentary'.[8] Scholars will always be attracted to this way in which translations can be used: in *Translating Baudelaire* (2001), Scott himself deploys translation to open up the ambiguities in the French sources, to map their contours and make hearable their rhythms. But criticism of translations as translations cannot simply ignore the mode of being they largely have in culture: to be made and used as substitutes for their originals.

It is, though, crucial that a substitute is not a substitute in every possible circumstance. Saccharin is no good if what you want is calories; a manager can freely substitute a player on the pitch but not, for instance, in a transfer deal. In such instances, we tend to say, the putative replacement 'is no substitute for the original': what this means is that it might be offered as a substitute but it will not do for me, or not on this occasion. A substitute that was acceptable in every possible circumstance would be identical with its original: it would be no longer a substitute, but the same.

In his *Linguistic Theory of Translation* (1965), J. C. Catford proposed that what is really meant when people say that a translation 'means the same as' or 'is equivalent to' its source is that the two texts 'are *interchangeable in a given situation*', that is, one can be substituted for the other. Translation, he says, is 'a process of substituting a text in one language for a text in another'.[9] This account, which develops the contextual semantics launched by J. R. Firth, supplies a good explanation of why it is that translation can be done—much of the time—perfectly satisfactorily despite the disparities of meaning we have touched on. Take, for example, John Lyons's description of how translation deals with the particular non-synonymy of 'denotational non-equivalence' (e.g. that 'the cat' does not denote the same class of animals as 'le chat'):

> What we do when we translate is to determine, as best we can from the context, how the objects being referred to would be categorized in terms of a more or less similar, but frequently incongruent, system of distinctions; and very often it is of little consequence that, in default of any information in the context which would decide the question one way or the other, we are forced to decide arbitrarily between alternatives.[10]

On Catford's account, the best new categorization is the one that functions best in the new context of use, or 'situation'. Peter Fawcett has observed that 'the concept of sameness of situation' is difficult to elaborate theoretically;[11] but there are many instances where it is sufficiently plain in practice. When we buy a microwave, the instructions are adequately translated from Japanese if they enable us to make the oven work. It does not matter that 'yellow' is not in every respect the same as 'giallo' because all a word's possible meanings and connotations are never simultaneously brought into play. What matters for a translation, most of the time, is that 'yellow' should do enough of the same job as 'giallo' on this occasion here. The same principle governs my own crib translations from foreign texts in this book.

As these examples show, the purpose a text is designed to fulfil, and the purposes that readers bring to it, are crucial elements of its 'situation'. They need to be taken into account by translators wondering how to set about their work and by critics judging whether a translation has been a success—that is, whether it has achieved the requisite kind of partial 'equivalence', given that the absolute equivalence of sameness is impossible. Eugene Nida put the point clearly three decades ago:

> When the question of the superiority of one translation over another is raised, the answer should be looked for in the answer to another question, 'best for whom?' The relative adequacy of different translations of the same text can only be determined in terms of the extent to which each translation successfully fulfils the purpose for which it was intended.[12]

A group of German scholars have elaborated this view into a theory of translation-purpose, or *Skopostheorie*. Hans Vermeer sums it up: 'what the

Skopos states is that one must translate, consciously and consistently, in accordance with some principle respecting the target text'.[13]

This approach has the virtue of emphasizing that translation includes a range of kinds of activity. But it is limited for two simple reasons: translators are people; and what they produce are verbal texts. As Douglas Robinson has been most vigorous in pointing out, translators' ideas and feelings of what they are up to are complex and variable: they can get tired or bored; they use their intuitions; they inevitably have mixed motives, including ones that are unconscious.[14] Not only that, but the texts they produce are liable to be taken by different readers in different ways. To some extent, readers' responses are shaped by genre, by the shared expectations which texts cultivate and to which they adapt themselves. The genre of an instruction leaflet is pretty straightforward; but with more complex texts the concept is more shifting and conflicted. Take, for instance, the genre of the news report. Expectations are signalled strongly by the sorts of publication in which news reports appear; and they are evident also in the structure of news stories and the sort of language they typically employ: these norms are partially consistent across cultures. Translating such a text for publication in a newspaper, you are likely to have a purpose which, though inevitably complex, is in many respects well defined: for instance, it is likely to include the wish to be clear and impartial. The pursuit of those aims may lead you to neglect aspects of the source text—for example, peculiarities of phrasing—which might be relished by a literary translator. So far, so comparatively straightforward. But imagine that you then come up against a very sensitive term such as the Arabic '*shaheed*', which—Mona Baker points out—might be translated as 'martyr', 'victim', or 'freedom fighter' (or indeed as 'terrorist').[15] There is no translation that does not establish an ideological affiliation. What seems impartial to one reader will strike another as biased. It is not possible to hold your translated text to a principle of impartiality.

The 'situation', 'purpose', and 'genre' of literary texts are all generally more complex still. In part this is due to the varieties and relatives of translation that are typically involved in their genesis: not only the reworkings of Homer in Virgil, say, or North's Plutarch in Shakespeare, or Shakespeare in Dryden or Dickens or Joyce, but the myriad momentary repetitions enacted by allusion and echo, and the freer layerings of imitation, indebtedness, and influence. And then each new work will, if it establishes itself as literary, be read and rewritten across time in its turn. This liberty in the practice of rewording is part of what distinguishes texts called literary from those not. It collaborates with other kinds of linguistic complexity: the 'movement...between different languages and speech types' characteristic of novels;[16] the patterning of words established by verse form; the glitter of meanings released when a word is transposed into an unusual context to create a metaphor—all factors which dislodge language from its usual communicative functions, focusing our attention on the words for their 'own sake' (as Jakobson put it),[17] and opening the text to multiple re-readings, each of which will connect it to a different cluster of assumptions and relevancies, so placing it in a different 'situation'. The reason the translation of a literary text can never be adequate to the same degree as the translation of a book of instructions, the reason it can never 'do the job', is that the 'situation' of a literary text, what matters in it, what job it does, can never finally be defined.

This finally ungraspable nature of the literary text is of course well known. But it is oddly difficult to keep in focus when discussing translation. It gets lost sight of, for instance, in a recurrent line of argument which conjures up a fantasy of perfect translation—of a work that is miraculously the same as its source despite existing in the changed circumstances of a different language and culture—so as then to say it is impossible. Carne-Ross and Scott both fall into this pattern with their talk of a 'substitute': they want that word to mean 'a substitute in every respect'—that is what it makes sense to say translations never are, and were never meant to be. This rhetorical structure exerts a distorting pressure on how the source text is imagined: it has to be presented as something that can be grasped—something that it is at least theoretically conceivable (if impossible in practice) to reproduce in other words. Carne-Ross:

> Pope does not give us Horace. No translator does that; translation is never a substitute for the original...

But Horace's texts do not 'give us Horace' either: Horace is an idea constructed out of them by a process of interpretation. The desire to emphasize the difference between translation and source pushes Carne-Ross into ignoring the source's difference from itself, its openness to multiple readings, its final ungraspability. Scott is alert to this danger and points out that 'too often, translation translates an interpretation' rather than attempting to do justice to the source's multiplicity.[18] He is right that translations sometimes do seem too narrowly confident about what the source must mean. But his phrasing downplays the fact that interpretation plays a part in everything that is done in a translation. Even the apprehension of a rhythm includes an element of interpretation; even the noticing of a rhyme.

This habit of conceiving what literary translations are not—something that no literary text ever is anyway—has a ricochet effect on the description of what they are. Carne-Ross again:

> ... translation is never a substitute for the original but rather a parallel text which brings to the fore new aspects of a poem while playing down others.

Translation may not 'give us Horace' but it does apparently give us something of the source, 'aspects' which, for all that they are said to be 'new', are also assumed to have been carried over: if they are now pushed freshly 'to the fore' they must have been present in the 'original' somewhere, even if obscured. Notice how 'poem' blurs together translation and source: are the 'aspects of the poem' being pointed to after or before they have been brought to the fore? It seems not to matter: they are the same aspects, and translation and source are, to the degree that they share the same 'aspects', the same poem. Even Scott, so sensitive to the difficulties that crowd this form of argument, cannot but make the same move:

> No translation ever sets out to be a substitute for the original text... Translations are re-embodiments of the original, whose principal function is to measure a difference.

'Re-embodiments'? In the midst of asserting that what matters in translations is how they differ from their sources, Scott finds himself using a word that says the opposite. If something is 're-embodied' it is the same thing that is in the second body as in the first. Yet nothing can be carried over wholly unchanged between languages, not even an 'aspect'. 'Bread' does not mean the same as 'pane'. Even a proper name will take on new connotations, even a rhythm, even the letter A. The structure of argument which contrasts what really happens in literary translation with an ideal that is obviously impossible, allows a less obvious version of the same impossibility to slip back into the definition unnoticed.

The predicament recurs everywhere in discussions of translation. Introducing his comprehensive history of the subject, *The True Interpreter* (1979), L. G. Kelly contrasts 'linguists' models' which 'assume that translation is exact transmission of data' with 'hermeneutic theorists' who 'take it to be an interpretive recreation of text'.[19] Yet 'recreation' must include some element of 'transmission': it must be the same thing, or at least some of the same thing, that is being created again. Derrida offers 'transformation' as a word that recognizes better than 'translation' the fact that 'we shall not have and never have had to deal with some "transfer" of pure signifieds'. But, as Robert J. Matthews points out, 'the notion of transformation carries with it precisely the same suggestions of determinacy and presence to mind' as are implicit in 'translation'.[20] The same difficulty afflicts Philip Lewis, a Derridean theorist whose idea of 'abusive fidelity' is explicitly oriented against the bad old conception of 'translation rigidly conceived'. An abusively faithful translator will allow the source text's 'most insistent and decisive effects . . . to resurface in the translated text' ('resurface'?); and aim 'to rearticulate analogically the abuse that occurs in the original text' ('rearticulate'?).[21] Maria Tymoczko's *Translation in a Postcolonial Context* (1999) is an exemplary study of the differences introduced by translation; but even she cannot wholly jettison the idea of sameness: 'some but not all of the source text is transposed'.[22]

The same oscillation of attitudes is evident in everyday talk about translations, and in the way they are printed. Even scholars can slip into saying 'oh yes I have read Proust' when they know fine well that what they have really read is the approximation to Proust by Scott Moncrieff. A book jacket that offers us '*The Door*' by 'Magda Szabó' sends out completely contradictory signals: 'this a novel by Szabó' and 'this is a novel in English'. Or take the following wholly usual headline for some passages of verse in the *London Review of Books*:

Four Poems by Valerio Magrelli
Translated by Jamie McKendrick[23]

Does this mean that Magrelli composed four poems in Italian which are the source for the English translations McKendrick has written? Or is it that the translations should still be thought of as poems by Magrelli? The sequence of words encourages the first interpretation; the different font sizes suggest the second. The ambiguity is inseparable from our usage of the word. 'Here is a translation of Manzoni's *The Betrothed*': no, 'here is a text called *The Betrothed* which is a translation of Manzoni's *I Promessi sposi*'. Or again: 'I read Kafka's *Die Verwandlung* in translation'; no, 'I read a text called *Metamorphosis* which is a translation of Kafka's *Die Verwandlung*'. These peculiarities of phrasing point to the same paradox as the reading practices I have described and the rhetorical structure we observed in critical arguments. Translations are accepted as departing from their sources and also as being identical to them. They are taken to be both different and the same.

This paradox allows us to draw a distinction, although not a watertight one, between translation and paraphrase. As we have seen, paraphrases are acknowledged to be different from their sources and translations are similarly different from their originals. But, with translations, the recognition of difference is overlaid by the flickering possibility of identity: they can be said have the same author as the source text; they can be used as quotations. This does not happen to paraphrases except in borderline cases, such as Dryden's Chaucer, which are in any case being offered as translations. The disparity between the two modes, as well as their continuity, are brilliantly made plain in a scene from Brian Friel's *Translations* (1981) where the imperialistic re-mapping of the Irish landscape is being explained by Captain Lancey. His English is translated by the bilingual Owen into Irish so it can be understood by his listeners; but Owen's Irish is represented in the play by English words so it can be understood by the audience:

> LANCEY: This enormous task has been embarked on so that the military authorities will be equipped with up-to-date and accurate information on every corner of this part of the Empire.
>
> OWEN: The job is being done by soldiers because they are skilled in this work.
>
> LANCEY: And also so that the entire basis of land valuation can be reassessed for purposes of more equitable taxation.
>
> OWEN: This new map will take the place of the estate-agent's map so that from now on you will know exactly what is yours in law.[24]

Owen's words, though obviously misrepresentative, could still just about count as paraphrase; yet they are being offered to their hearers as translation. The scene's black humour is sparked by the clash of two assumptions with which we are familiar: 'all translations differ from their sources' and 'they are, or at least ought to be, the same'. Friel's scene asks for a double response of resignation and outrage: 'this is the sort of thing all translations do' and 'this is no translation!'

4

Translating the Language of Literature

Perhaps we might escape the difficulties in which we are becoming entangled if we are, simply, more resolute than Scott or Carne-Ross or Lewis or Tymoczko or Derrida in abandoning any idea of sameness, transmission or carrying across. Theo Hermans has recently taken this line. In international diplomacy, he points out, versions of the same treaty in different languages are sometimes thought of, not as original and translation, but as 'parallel authentic versions'.[1] Even if one of them has in fact been drafted first and the others translated from it—that is, even if there are original and translations in a 'genetic' sense—the parallel texts are accepted as being all equally authoritative. This, he thinks, is the blueprint that allows us to understand how any translation comes to be taken as a substitute:

> A translation cannot double up with its parent text. It uses different words, which issue from a different source, in a different environment. A translation cannot therefore be equivalent with its prototext, it can only be *declared* equivalent by means of a performative speech act.[2]

This 'performative speech act' occurs when lawyers and politicians agree that the different versions in different languages all embody the same treaty. In literary culture, the relevant speech acts tend to be less binding than those of international law: they consist in publishers' blurbs, reviews, and readers' reactions. Nevertheless, Hermans sees them as having the same magical power:

> I regard a translation as initially being merely another text until it is declared to be a translation. At that moment, provided the speech act succeeds, a change takes place: the translation continues to look as it did before, but its nature has altered because somehow it is now another work.[3]

As we saw in Chapter 2, institutional structures play a crucial part in defining and policing different kinds of 'equivalence'. But Hermans magnifies their role to a startling degree. One does have to wonder what (in his account) translators can all along think they are up to while they are producing these 'other texts' which only turn out to be translations when they have been institutionally accepted. What is missing from Hermans's argument is the recognition that his validating speech acts have to have grounds.[4] All the difficulties that have been exercising us are swatted away with his swift subordinate clause, 'provided the speech act succeeds'. But what determines whether it succeeds? The institutional assertion that a text is a translation will only work if that text already possesses qualities that are amenable to counting as translation. We are thrown right back into the problem of describing what these are.

The stubborn fact remains that no translation can accomplish the perfect reproduction of any element of the source. But we established in Chapter 3 that, for non-literary texts, this largely does not matter. There is such a thing as a sufficient degree of equivalence; what counts as 'sufficient' will depend on a text's situation, purpose, and genre. The roughness of fit between translation and source-text is the more tolerable because there is already only a rough correspondence between the source text and how people interpret it in its own language. The text is full of potential for meaning which readers realize in different ways. Even in the simplest texts, and with the most basic categories of meaning, there is variability between speakers of the same language. Take for instance Lyons's category of 'descriptive meaning', which is taken to be the same in two expressions if 'nothing is entailed by one expression that is not entailed by the other'. The expression 'person' entails 'is warm-blooded', 'needs to blink', and so on: the accumulation of such entailments gives support to the idea that 'person' has the same descriptive meaning as 'rational biped'. It is a rough and ready sort of synonymy. Yet even for this straightforward kind of meaning there is, as Lyons points out, much pragmatic flexibility in ordinary language use:

> Different speakers may hold partly different beliefs about the meaning and applicability of words, so that the set of implications that one speaker will accept as following from a given utterance may differ, to a greater or less degree, from the set of implications that another speaker will accept as following from the same utterance. But there will commonly be considerable overlap.[5]

A translation, then, gives a loose approximation to a source text which is already entrammelled in loose approximations in its own language. And the translation will itself be subjected to a similar congeries of loose approximations when it is read. Given this bagginess in the way we generally use language it is quite reasonable for us to settle for translations that create enough overlaps of meaning with the overlaps released by the source—enough to explain how to use the microwave, commit different countries to sufficiently similar treaty obligations, or refer to the same news events in broadly the same way.

In literature—as we have seen—the controlling factors of 'situation', 'purpose', and 'genre' are comparatively indeterminate. Nevertheless, literary texts do of course have much in common with texts that are not considered literary; and in these respects our usual tolerance of the approximate continues to apply. Even though their function cannot finally be pinned down, there are some things they often indisputably do: they engage your attention, for instance, or make you think. Their words have everyday 'descriptive meaning' as well as the more subtle meanings that literary writers cultivate. Finally, they have formal features that can be matched: a beginning and an end; shifts from (say) description to direct speech and back again; a number of chapters or cantos of verse; and often a narrative structure. As more of these formal correspondences match up, confidence that translation is happening will grow. This is why it may often seem possible to give a better translation of a sentence than of a word; and a better one still of a whole poem or play or novel. Susanne Langer's remark about visual representation, in her *Philosophy in a New Key* (1942), can extend towards translations:

> The only characteristic that a picture must have in order to be a picture of a certain thing is an arrangement of elements analogous to the arrangement of salient visual elements in the object.[6]

With a text, no less than with an object, there is room for disagreement as to what counts as a 'salient element': Carne-Ross's perception that translations (like interpretations) establish new saliencies by bringing aspects 'to the fore' must be kept in mind. Nevertheless, a piece of writing that matches a fair number of plausibly salient elements, and that achieves substantial overlap of descriptive meaning, while also being readable in something like a literary way, has a good chance of being accepted as a translation.

Still, for literary texts this rough degree of similarity is often felt to be not enough. And it is especially often felt to be not enough for poetry. The reasons are familiar, though we can rephrase them so as to connect them to the line of argument we are pursuing. In prose fiction or drama, the most salient formal elements (paragraphs, chapters) can readily be matched without damage to descriptive meaning; not so those of poetry (metre, rhyme, and the complex rhetorical patterns which are often spun across them). Much poetry does not have a strong narrative structure (though much of course does); prose fiction is less readily divorced from narrative. And then poetry, more than prose, relies on kinds of significance that are more subtle than descriptive meaning, and to which the everyday approximation of an 'overlap' seems not enough. 'It is the rhythm that matters here, no it is the syntax, no it is the particular heft of this word, no it is the

word's echo in this other word over here, no it is all these things together'—
translators might find themselves thinking before screaming and throwing
their originals against the wall. Then comes the reaction: well actually I can
catch this, or reproduce that; actually, this nuance, at least, will leap across.[7]
The rhetorical structure we identified in criticism— rejection followed by
reassertion of the possibility of translation—is evident also in the behaviour
of translators. There is a feel of inwardness, of personal recognition, in
Dryden's description of the 'verbal copier' who is 'encumbered with so
many difficulties at once, that he can never disentangle himself from all':
''tis much like dancing on ropes with fettered legs'. In his case, the reaction
leads to paraphrase which, of course, is not a perfect reproduction of
the source, yet still (he thinks) brings something across: 'the spirit of an
author may be transfused'.[8] Vladimir Nabokov thinks this is nonsense: 'it is
when the translator sets out to render the "spirit" . . . that he begins to
traduce his author'. But what can be caught, he thinks, is 'exact contextual
meaning. Only this is true translation.'[9] For T. S. Eliot, discussing Pound,
'good translation is not merely translation, for the translator is
giving the original through himself, and finding himself through the
original':[10] the way to translate well, really to give readers the original, is
by not doing mere translation. The same pattern of assertion is widespread
among contemporary poets endeavouring to enforce a distinction between
the 'versions' written by them and translation as it is otherwise practised.
For Christopher Reid, the 'Accounts' of Homer by Christopher Logue are
not 'translations'; but still they 'take Homer's unsentimental, pre-humanis-
tic vision, and . . . make it as immediate . . . as the original must have been to
its first listeners'.[11] And Derek Mahon's *Adaptations*, the blurb announces,
are 'not translations, properly speaking, but *versions*' which allow 'their
sources to remain audible'.[12] The reflex is everywhere the same. The text
being described does something different from translation, and therefore
translates all the more effectively. Translation is not translation.

These contrasting claims all point to the same conclusion. The complexity and therefore the indeterminacy of literary texts are what make
ordinary or 'mere' translation inadequate. And yet those same qualities are
what make the vaunted 'true' or 'good' or 'audible' or 'immediate' translation possible. The explanation lies in an obvious fact: that it takes the
mind's ear of a reader to determine what a text is saying; the mind's eye of
a reader to limn its spirit or visualize its vision. What literary translation
captures is not simply in the source text but is brought into being by
the continuous process of reading-and-making-sense-and-translating.
Translators, no more than readers, do not simply 'read things in' to
their sources; but neither do they simply 'read off' from them. Theory
founders before the process by which sense—or whatever we should call

it, 'sense' seeming too narrow a word—emerges from a text in collaboration with its readers. But it is indisputable that the collaboration occurs.
This whatever-it-is, brought into being by the process of reading-making-
sense-translating, is what translators can feel that they are making 'immediate', or 'audible', or 'giving', or 'carrying across'.

This is why Walter Benjamin, in the 1923 essay 'Die Aufgabe des
Übersetzers' that I mentioned in Chapter 1, said that literary translations
should not aim for 'Ähnlichkeit' ('alikeness' or 'similarity') with their-
sources, but rather for a deeper connection which allows dissimilarity:
'Verwandtschaft' ('kinship').[13] The desire for alikeness stops short of what
most matters in a literary text: it refuses to bite the lure to interpret which
the literary by definition holds out. Let us look at a small example, from
Paul Muldoon's translation of Montale's 'L'anguilla', 'The Eel':

> that self-same eel, a firebrand now, a scourge,
> the arrow-shaft of Love on earth
> which only the gulches or dried-out
> gullies of the Pyrenees might fetch and ferry back
> to some green and pleasant spawning-ground, . . . [14]

> l'anguilla, torcia, frusta,
> freccia d'Amore in terra
> che solo i nostri botri o i diseccati
> ruscelli pirenaici riconducono
> a paradisi di fecondazione; . . . [15]

'Ähnlich' translations can be found in the dictionary: for 'torcia', not
'firebrand' but 'torch'; for 'frusta', not 'scourge' but 'whip'; for 'freccia',
not 'arrow-shaft' but plain 'arrow'. Muldoon's 'firebrand' humanizes the
eel a little since firebrands can be people, especially historical figures like
Luther or Cromwell. 'Scourge' then brings in a hint of narrative, for
firebrands sometimes set about scourging places, as Cromwell did to
Ireland. But 'shaft', attached to 'arrow', pulls 'scourge' back towards the
kind of scouring that sometimes has to be done to pipes or well-shafts; and
it hints at the salacious meaning of 'shaft'. These changes respond to the
vigour which pulses in the alliterative beat of: 'torcia, frusta, / freccia' but it
is hard to know how much the meanings of the two passages overlap. We
might say that Muldoon helps nuances to emerge from the Italian via a
collaborative reading, just as I have helped nuances to emerge from his
English. But collaboration verges into creativity as the English words
inevitably bring with them something new: an Italian reader of Montale's
poem is unlikely to have the fleeting thought of Cromwell.

Muldoon has suggested that translators reach through the source to
'some ur-poem' of which 'both "original poem" and "poetic translation"
are manifestations'. He does not know, he says, of 'another single meta-

phor that's equal to the complexity of the activity of translation'.[16] This metaphor allows him to feel that what is fundamentally the same energy from the 'ur-poem' can manifest itself in different ways: primarily as sound in Montale's lines; and as more of a semantic sparkle in Muldoon's. In what happens next, the phantasm of the ur-poem licenses even greater change: Montale's 'riconducono' becomes, not 'bring back', but 'fetch and ferry back'; and his 'paradisi di fecondazione', not 'paradises of fertilization', but 'some green and pleasant spawning ground'. Muldoon must see in the ur-poem here a hint of life after death: it comes through in Montale's 'paradisi' but emerges in the English via 'ferry' (since Charon has one). And he must think that what really matters in the ur-poem is, not a mention of paradises in themselves, but the reminiscence they bring with them of a major literary figure, Dante, the author of *Paradiso*. So in his English he supplies an analogous recollection, of Blake's 'Jerusalem', via 'England's green and pleasant land'.[17] The ur-poem is coming through, not only into English, but into English poetry; not only into English poetry but into English poetry as Muldoon can write it. Hence the trace of his weighty immediate predecessor, Seamus Heaney, in the word 'spawning'. 'If I dipped my hand the spawn would clutch it', go the last words of Heaney's 'Death of a Naturalist'.[18] The line must itself have clutched Muldoon's hand when he read it; and so the stain of it is allowed to gleam here, in 'spawning-ground', even though the new context has an almost opposite emotional heft. Since Montale's lines are doing more than flagging up descriptive meaning, they require a more searching interpretation. They draw on particular areas of literary knowledge and linguistic sensitivity; and they ask you to collaborate with them in building an imaginative understanding. You have to do this: it is what the poem asks of you. But in doing it you are building a meaning which is inescapably in part your own. This is all you can know of the 'ur-poem'. And this is what you then endeavour to fetch and ferry back into your poem-translation.

There are, then, two kinds of process in literary translation that might be thought of through the metaphor of 'carrying across'. One is the everyday lining-up of salient elements, rough similarity of function, and overlapping of descriptive meaning which operates in all translation. The other is this bringing-across that is inseparable from seeing in the first place, this reading-making-sense-translating all in one, this re-rendering of an 'ur-poem'. It is only by moving away from 'Ähnlichkeit' that the poetry to be felt or heard or transfused or given can be discovered. This is why literary translators can think of themselves as 'giving' the original, or transfusing its spirit, or making it audible or immediate. And this is how a translation can in fact claim to 'give us Horace': just as much, and just as little, as any other piece of writing.

5
Words for Translation

Translations can emerge from their sources in a multitude of ways. But in many areas of language (as we have seen) those processes are disciplined by 'situation', 'purpose', and 'genre'; in some contexts, such as education and international law, approved practices of translation are enforced by institutional structures. But literary translation—especially the translation of poetry—operates in wilder territory. Here, translation can flaunt its variety: in consequence, it has attracted many adjectives and been given many names. Translations can be 'free' or 'close' or 'literal' or 'creative'. A translation can be an 'Englishing', a 'rendering', a 'traduction', a 'gloze', a 'crib', a 'version', or a 'conversion'; to translate can be, not only to 'paraphrase' and 'interpret', but to 'turn', to 'render', or 'reduce'. Browning called his intently literal *Agamemnon* a 'transcript'; Nabokov thought of himself as 'transposing' *Eugene Onegin* into English.[1] Attaching an adjective to a noun is of course an everyday defining or clarifying move; but to choose a whole new noun or verb for what you are up to is more disruptive. It would be odd for a playwright, for instance, to deny that what she does is write plays; but many writers (in the literary field) of what one might think to be translations have rejected or at least displaced the idea that what they are doing is translating. The words they have preferred signal the different tactics that can be followed in the process of reading-making-sense-translating; they register the varieties of imaginative work which are, broadly speaking, translation, but which strive for something other than 'Ähnlichkeit', and therefore pull away from the corresponding image of 'translation as carrying across', that is, translation rigidly conceived.

Take Robert Browning's attachment to the word 'transcript'. The title page of his *Agamemnon of Aeschylus* (1877) announces that it has been *'transcribed by Robert Browning'*: in the explanation that follows it emerges that, though he is still ready to call himself a 'translator', he thinks of himself as a translator of an unusual kind. He will be 'literal at every cost save that of absolute violence to our language' and will attempt to 'furnish... the very turn of each phrase in as Greek a fashion as English will bear'.[2] The word 'furnish', near 'turn' and 'fashion', sparks a suggestion of woodcarving, of language as a material to be shaped. The implications of 'translate'—of something carried across—are being narrowed and partially displaced by those of 'transcribe'—of something written across—as though the physicality of the Greek words could be copied as precisely through translation as it might be by a clerk transcribing a legal document.

A century earlier, the Edinburgh lawyer Alexander Tytler had reached for the same word in his compendious *Essay on the Principles of Translation*. The first of his three 'laws of translation' was 'that the Translation should give a complete transcript of the ideas of the original work'.[3] But Tytler's usage, as it turns out, is very loose: he is an advocate of the Augustan tradition of 'translation as paraphrase', and in consequence does not himself 'transcribe' the idea of a 'transcript' at all fully into his own argument. Browning, though similarly determined that readers should be presented with the 'ideas of the poet', has a more particular understanding of that phrase. These are not 'ideas' in the sense of paraphrasable meaning. Not for Browning the model of translation adopted by a slightly earlier translator of Aeschylus, F. A. Paley, whose version he had in his library. Paley had thought of himself as concentrating on 'the author's meaning' more than on 'his mere words'.[4] For Browning, words are never 'mere'. And so he takes the word 'idea' as though it had itself been transcribed via transliteration from the Greek 'ἰδέα' meaning form or look. For him, here, ideas are inseparable from their shapes which are made visible in language.

Browning's distinctive understanding of 'transcription' is everywhere apparent in his *Agamemnon of Aeschylus*, with its transliterated names, its mimickings of Greek syntax, and its reconstructed compounds. 'Klutaimnestra', for instance, is said by the watchman to have 'the man's-way-planning hoping heart of woman'.[5] Looking at the Greek, one can see how it is that, for Browning, the 'idea' of a phrase like 'γυναικὸς ἀνδρόβουλον ἐλπίζον κέαρ' is the particular clinch of its compaction. As the great classical scholar Eduard Fraenkel notes in his edition of the *Agamemnon* (1950), the compound 'ἀνδρόβουλον' was probably coined for this occasion, and the whole strange concatenation is 'forceful both in sound and sense'.[6] Browning's response to the phrase shows how his 'transcript' differs from word-for-word cribbing, for in fact it is Paley who here (and often) keeps the closer to the sequence of Aeschylus's words: 'a woman's manly-counselling hopeful heart'.[7] What drives Browning to translate differently? If—as he surely did—he read this version, he must have flinched at 'manly', Victorian cliché as it already was; and he must have felt that 'counselling' was too mild. One way of describing this reaction is to reach for August Schleiermacher's geometry, outlined in his 1813 lecture 'Über die verschiedenen Methoden des Übersetzens', in which the translator has a choice of moving the 'author' towards the 'reader' or of moving the 'reader' towards the 'author'.[8] In those terms, Browning must have felt that Paley had brought Aeschylus too close to home, too much 'domesticated' him in our contemporary jargon of 'domestication' versus 'foreignization'. There is an intuitive plausibility to this description. But when you try to prove the matter, it turns out to be impossible to say whether Paley or Browning takes us further towards the 'author'. Paley keeps the shock conjunction of 'woman' and 'manly'; Browning thinks it more important to avoid 'manly's' Victorian connotations. Each feels his way into the Greek differently and imagines a different 'author', with the result that different English emerges. The distinctive trajectory of Browning's imagining-in and translating-out is named by his word 'transcript'.[9]

Can we say that this 'transcript' is 'very literal', one extreme of a cline from 'literal' to 'free'? The trouble is that, within the word 'literal', there lurks an ambiguity. Louis and Celia Zukofsky, in their translations from Catullus, took the word 'literal' almost literally: they focused on the letters of the text, reproducing as much as they could of the source's sound. 'Amabo, mea dulcis Ipsitilla' becomes 'I'm a bow, my dual kiss, Ipsithilla'.[10] But for another vigorous 'literalist', Vladimir Nabokov, 'literal' translation meant 'rendering, as closely as the associative and syntactical capacities of another language allow, the exact contextual meaning of the original'. The opening line of *Eugene Onegin* could be rendered word for word or, as he puts it, 'lexically' like this: 'my uncle [is] of most honest rules [:]'. But the 'literal' translator will discern that 'rules' is not the best equivalent for what Pushkin must mean in this context: after adjusting for 'syntactical capacities' he will produce 'my uncle has most honest principles'.[11] At one point Nabokov reaches for the word 'transposing' to clarify his variety of literalism.[12] This word sticks closer to the usual implications of 'translation' than Browning's 'transcript'; but it still narrows and adjusts them. The meaning is not merely 'carried over' from the source; rather, you uncover it when you imagine your way into a particular context in the source; and you then re-pose it on the new stage-set of English.

The Zukofskys' kind of literalism, then, takes the word 'literal' literally, focusing on the materiality of words, their letters, sound, and order. But Nabokov uses 'literal' metaphorically: he thinks of himself as capturing a variety of what people call 'the literal meaning'—a phrase which is, when you think about it, a startling oxymoron. The two ways of being literal each cling close to a different aspect of the source: there is no single scale of greater or lesser proximity on which both can be located. And what of Browning's 'transcript'? It shares with the Zukofskys an attachment to word order and rhythm, but not their aim to reproduce phonetic values. Yet we cannot simply call it 'less literal' (in the literal sense), for it goes further than the Zukofskys in its imitation of foreign syntactic structures. Again, its aim of rendering Aeschylus's 'ideas' sounds a bit like Nabokov's commitment to 'exact contextual meaning'; but there turns out to be a difference. What (yet another ambiguity!) is the meaning of 'literal meaning'?

The *OED* shows that this phrase originated in medieval theories of the Bible, where it meant 'that sense or interpretation (of a text) which is obtained by taking its words in their natural or customary meaning, and applying the ordinary rules of grammar'. Nabokov stretches the phrase further: for him, the 'literal meaning' is the sense a word has in its current communicative context which he thinks—sure of his own powers of imagining-in—can be pinpointed 'exactly'. But in Browning 'literal' takes on yet another sense. His search for the 'idea' whose 'turn' can be 'transcribed' reaches beneath the meanings most alive in the usage of Aeschylus's time, down towards the etymological origins from which they have derived. For instance, Browning's contemporaries and modern scholars all agree that, at the crucial moment when Agamemnon sets off along the ceremonial pathway laid out by Clytemnestra in a show of welcome, what he treads on, 'ἀλουργέσιν' are 'purple cloths' (or, as Fraenkel calls them, 'draperies').[13] But Browning digs to the word's roots, which mean 'sea' and 'to do work', and chooses to transcribe them: 'sea-products'.[14] It is as though 'television' were rendered 'far-sight', or 'football' translated into Italian as 'piede-pallone'. In cases such as these, 'literal meaning' comes to mean 'root meaning'; and Browning's translation is in the paradoxical position of being more 'literal' than its original.

I will explore Browning's ways with translation further in Chapters 21 and 23. But what we can see already is the potential of words such as 'transcript' and 'transposing' to flower into significance and to unveil, by naming them, some of the many distinguishable imaginative processes which are hidden under the umbrella term 'translation'. Browning's 'transcript' is different from Nabokov's 'transposing', and different again from the phonetically oriented literalism practised by the Zukofskys.

Attention to such words can begin to open a way past 'the old binary concept of translation' (Susan Bassnett's phrase), with its imagining of the translator as a sort of 'black box' which, as Maria Tymoczko put it in her essay 'Reconceptualizing Translation Theory' (2006), 'decodes a given message to be translated and recodes the same message in a second language'. Tymoczko goes on to observe that 'although this classic representation of the process of translation has been criticized by many scholars as being too simple, nonetheless the model continues to operate implicitly in many, even most, formulations of translation theory'. In Chapter 3 we saw that thinkers who set out to combat this notion nevertheless had to rely on it somewhere in their arguments, even if what is carried over is not 'meaning' but an 'aspect' or an 'effect' or an 'abuse': Tymoczko herself put a foot in the black box with her assertion that 'some but not all of the source text is transposed'.

The model endures because the enterprise of 'translation theory' is strongly oriented towards doing something which might at first seem quite reasonable: defining an activity called translation and classifying its sub-varieties. Tymoczko's own study of Englishings of the Irish tale *Táin Bó Cúailnge* is a work of exemplary detail and precision; yet even she announces, at its outset, that 'translation *theory* . . . should apply to *practice* in general': 'it is a betrayal of the very enterprise of theorizing and model-making to fail to test conclusions for their . . . applicability to the *arbitrary* case'. The assumption, then, is that particular translations should serve as examples of established theories, or else as counter-examples which will prompt the construction of new models. In a later book, *Enlarging Translation, Empowering Translators* (2007) Tymoczko takes the pressure of an obvious objection to this approach: that, worldwide, rewriting across languages is done in too many different ways for them all to be subjected to the dominion of a single theory. Hence her observation which I quoted in Chapter 1: 'words indicating the practices and products of translation in languages throughout the world . . . do not actually mean *translation* as such, in the sense implied by the English term'. In consequence, she admits, there can be no 'rigid, one-size-fits-all theory'.[15]

Nevertheless, she takes it for granted that a theory does still have to be constructed. It must recognize variety by adopting a 'branching structure': 'if translation occurs in an oral culture, then it will probably have the characteristics m, n, o . . . ; if translation occurs in a highly computer literate culture, then it will probably have the characteristics p, q, r'. Even this is at once—and rightly—seen to be too simple: '"a multiplicity of complex conceptual structures"' (Clifford Geertz's phrase) are going to be required. And not only that: 'a comprehensive theory of translation . . . will have . . . indeterminacies caused by cultural singularities and, notably, indeterminacies related to the translators themselves who can decide to flout rules, invent translation strategies, and inject all sorts of unpredictable elements into translations'.[16] This observation is incontrovertible; but Tymoczko does not (I think) quite see its force. Pretty much everything I discuss in this book is in the realm of 'indeterminacies related to the translators themselves' (or, more precisely, translators in collaboration with particular source texts). And those 'indeterminacies' go a long way to explaining why poem-translations are the way they are. How might a 'branching structure' account for Browning's transcript of the *Agamemnon*? Done in a literate culture, that reverenced the classics, and in which Aeschylus had a particular status (which could be specified at great length). Done by a poet—but so far we have got nowhere near the particularities of the text we are trying to describe, since many poets at that time translated similar material quite otherwise: even exactly the same play was translated by Edward FitzGerald in a wholly different way, as we will see in the next chapter. Only when we get to 'done by Browning' do we reach a statement that has much predictive force. So: done by Browning, of a play—but hang on, Browning translated other plays in other styles at other times (as we will see in Chapter 23). We reach 'done by Browning, of Aeschylus's *Agamemnon*, in 1879'—at which point the 'theory' becomes as complex as the field it set out to describe, and so ceases to have any explanatory power. Tymoczko's 'indeterminacies' release cracks that shatter the whole theoretical edifice. As we have seen, even what looks like the fundamental category of 'literal translation', restricted to writing in a single language over less than a hundred years, takes on three incompatible definitions.

The self-destructiveness of Tymoczko's 'branching structure' reveals the difficulty, for someone engaged in an enterprise called 'translation theory', in accepting that the texts that interest them may not be very satisfactorily reducible to an abstract explanatory scheme. Even though she so vividly sees the great variety of rewritings across languages, the metaphor with which she chooses to arrange them implies that there is an essence of translation—a trunk—from which the branches ramify; and the texture of her discussion in general comes under the sway of the same assumption. All those texts that are first said to be not '*translation* as such' are soon being referred to as 'divergent types of translation'.[17] And Tymoczko's is a uniquely complex and sensitive attempt: the usual way of accounting for the many texts that could be thought of as translations is to align them along a single scale. They are pinned up between the poles of 'faithful' and 'free', or 'formally equivalent' and 'dynamically equivalent', or 'of the letter' and 'of the spirit', or 'adequate' and 'acceptable', or 'overt' and 'covert', or 'foreignizing' and 'domesticating'.[18] Each of these pairs has connotations slightly different from the others; but the overriding feature they all share is that they are locked in coupledom, with an implicit one-dimensional axis connecting the two partners. The assumption is that what is fundamentally a single activity—translation—is happening all the way along each scale, only to a different degree. But this is a simplification so brusque as to falsify the material it is endeavouring to comprehend. As we have seen, the Browning *Agamemnon* and the Zukofskys' Catullus and the Nabokov *Eugene Onegin* cannot be metred on a scale of more or less

'literal'. They are all equally 'faithful', though they understand fidelity in
different ways; all would, I suppose, have to be labelled 'formally equivalent';
and one could argue forever about which to call the more 'foreignizing'. We
can label them all 'translations' for the pragmatic reason I identified in
Chapter 3: they offer themselves, and can be used as, 'substitutes' in that
sense of being obviously different from their sources while also making a
flickering claim to sameness. But, beyond that, it is not at all obvious that
they are best understood by being viewed as surface variants of what is
fundamentally a single process. They are the products of distinct imaginative
encounters with their source texts. If we are to grasp their particularity, we
need to approach them, not as 'examples' that prove or disprove a theory,
but as texts that ask to be read.

That is what I endeavour to do in the bulk of this book. Following
Wittgenstein, I do not assume that the 'many different kinds of thing' that
may be called 'translation' need have some theorizable essence in common
just because they can be given the same name. The image latent in
the word 'translation'—of 'carrying across'—has always helped fix those
binary models whose persistence Bassnett and Tymoczko have regretted.
As I try to draw out the distinctivenesses of the writing I am reading I will,
in consequence, be alert to other words for the closenesses of texts in one
language to texts in others, and to the metaphors that have always
clustered under and around translation. As we have seen, apparently placid
terms like 'transcribe' and 'transpose' can flower into metaphorical life,
taking on descriptive richness and power. Metaphors too can assume
consistency and precision, and come to define with some fullness processes
that, although they may be referred to as 'translation', do not follow the
assumptions of translation rigidly conceived. Before we begin this exploration, though, I need to give some more attention to metaphor.

6

Metaphors for Translation

The 'black box' is in a venerable tradition, for discussions of translation have long had recourse to metaphor: as Lieven d'Hulst put it in 1992, 'les métaphores sont une caractéristique durable des théories traductives'.[1] Through the centuries, translation has been said to give a work new clothes or place a jewel in a different casket; to conquer, or enfranchise or bring home. It has infused, transfused, refined; and mirrored, and copied, and opened the window. It has been thought of as preserving fire, or suffering from disease, or bringing the dead to life. It has always been, and is still, 'carrying across'. For Charles Tomlinson it is 'metamorphosis';[2] for Christopher Reid it is a making 'immediate'; for Derek Mahon it is a keeping 'audible'.[3] For Jean Starr Untermeyer, translator of Hermann Broch, '*The Death of Virgil* was musically conceived and executed, and it needed to be musically interpreted'.[4] For Gayatri Chakravorty Spivak, the translator must 'enter' and 'direct' the 'staging of the subject' in the source text, 'as one directs a play, as an actor interprets a script'.[5] Many of the everyday words for describing translation have an obvious metaphorical charge: 'faithful', 'free', 'close'; as do many of the jargon terms of translation studies: 'domesticate', 'dynamic', 'formal'.

In Chapter 1, we saw how the word 'translation' has wandered into different semantic fields, and how this has in some respects narrowed and in others clouded understanding of translation between languages. Correspondingly, other terms and images have been pulled in to describe those kinds of textual closeness across languages which are, of course, broadly speaking 'translation' but do not seem quite to be 'translation rigidly conceived'. As Max Black has argued, people reach for metaphors when 'the available literal resources of the language' are 'insufficient'.[6] Writers who find themselves in the predicament of wanting to say 'translation is not translation' can save themselves by adopting a different image. It may be merely fleeting or ornamental; but it may also extend far into their practice of translation, animating and defining it.

For instance, Browning's contemporary Edward FitzGerald also produced an *Agamemnon*, in 1865, not 'transcribed' but—as the title page

announces—'taken' from Aeschylus. The Preface explains that Aeschylus's verses, and in particular the choruses, 'are so dark and abrupt in
themselves, and therefore so much more mangled and tormented by
copyist and commentator, that the most conscientious translator must
not only jump at a meaning, but must bridge over a chasm'. 'Jump' implies
liberty—and the translation is certainly 'free', to use the familiar loose
word: FitzGerald has had, he says, 'to break the bounds of Greek tragedy'.
But these images of release and fracture are balanced by images of reconstruction and re-enclosure: of the chasm being bridged, and of 'one license
drawing on another to make all of a piece'.[7] If we read on into FitzGerald's
Agamemnon Taken from Aeschylus, we can see how this compound metaphorical pattern, not of 'free translation' but of 'freedom in order to bridge
gaps', inheres in his practice. Chasms are everywhere bridged in front of us
as we walk. If we need assistance with references, it is supplied: Aeschylus
writes 'Hephaistos'; FitzGerald adds 'the lame God, / And spriteliest of
mortal messengers'. Stage-directions are written into speeches to help us
imagine the scene (Clytemnestra on Cassandra: 'she keeps her station still,
her laurel on, / Disdaining to make answer').[8] Motivations are explained;
and lassos of sympathy are thrown out from the characters towards their
implied readers. Here, for instance, are lines written by FitzGerald for the
watchman near the end of his opening speech:

> . . .—might I but,
> But once more might I, see my lord again
> Safe home! But once more look upon his face!
> But once more take his hand in mine!—[9]

The swell of sentiment owes something to Tennyson's *In Memoriam*, and
more to FitzGerald's own rhetoric in personal letters to absent friends. Its
effect seems meant to be a general bridging of chasms—between the
watchman's peculiar circumstance and more familiar experiences of absence; between Aeschylus's abrupt, hermetic text and Victorian shapes of
feeling. As we will see in Part II, the behaviour of FitzGerald's imagination
here is not dissimilar to the modes of 'translation as paraphrase' widely
practised in the seventeenth century. But a fuller description is supplied by
his own metaphors.

FitzGerald's talk of breaking bounds sends a flicker of acknowledgement towards another of Aeschylus's tragedies, *Prometheus Bound*, whose
best-known translator in the mid-nineteenth century was Elizabeth Barrett Browning. In the Preface written for her first attempt at the work,
published in 1833, the then Elizabeth Barrett suggests that translation
continues the inspiration that had given rise to the original. Translations,
she writes, are like mirrors 'held in different lights by different hands':

'according to the vocation of the artist, will the copy be'. Usually there is an element of dismissiveness in calling a translation a copy. But not here, for Aeschylus's writings too, like 'all beauties, whether in nature or art', are themselves 'reflections, visible in different distances, and under different positions, of one archetypal beauty'. In this chain of reflections reflected there seems to be at least the possibility that a translator might capture 'archetypal' beauty no less well, and perhaps even better, than the first mirror off which it has bounced: a reflection reflected is after all the right way round. A similar implication is latent in the Preface's other prominent pattern of images, according to which Aeschylus 'stands . . . forward' to demonstrate that the ancients were not coldly classical but 'felt passionately, and thought daringly'—that is, were just like his character Prometheus, who 'stands eminent and alone . . . original, and grand, and attaching'. Prometheus in his turn is offered as an emblem of the present 'original age' with its 'noble dreams'.[10] Translation takes its place in a relay of inspiration, a visionary chain reaction.

Although Barrett seems at this time not to have known anything of Shelley's beyond *Queen Mab* and *Adonais* there are tantalizing similarities between her Preface and his justification of his utter reworking of Aeschylus in *Prometheus Unbound* a decade before. Yet Barrett's own 1833 translation is at odds with the libertarian fanfare that has preceded it. 'To the literal sense I have endeavoured to bend myself as closely as was poetically possible', she says at the end of her Preface, now aligning herself, not with Prometheus's undaunted spirit which 'nothing will bend', but with his body, shackled at Zeus's command.[11] This subjugated version was not well received, and as the years passed she came to be ashamed of it: by the mid 1840s, in her correspondence with Robert Browning, she was calling it 'cold stiff & meagre, unfaithful to the genius if servile to the letter of the great poet'.[12] It was 'a Prometheus *twice* bound'. So she set about rewriting, this time allowing her practice as a translator to be energized by the theory she had long espoused. Here is part of one of Prometheus's speeches:

First version:
           . . . Rather hear
What crimes I perpetrated touching man;
How from his idiot state I made him wise
And mind-possessive. Blaming him in nought,
But making clear my gifts' beneficence,
I will describe them. In the olden time,
Men seeing, saw in vain, and did not hear

Hearing; but similar to shades of dreams

Later version:
           . . . List rather to the deeds
I did for mortals; how, being fools before,
I made them wise and true in aim of soul.
And let me tell you—not as taunting men,

But teaching you the intention of my gifts,
How, first beholding, they beheld in vain,
And hearing, heard not, but, like shapes in dreams,
Mixed all things wildly down the tedious time,

Long mingled all things in confusedness;   . . .
. . .   . . . There, came to them
To them, of winter shone no certain sign,   No steadfast sign of winter, nor of spring
Nor yet of flowery spring, nor fruitful   Flower-perfumed, nor of summer full of
    summer;   fruit,—
But all things did they void of sapiency—   But blindly and lawlessly they did all things,
Until I show'd the rising of the orbs,   Until I taught them how the stars do rise
And mystic setting. . . .   And set in mystery[13]

In 1833 Prometheus makes humans 'mind-possessive' and redeems them from being 'void of sapiency': both phrases are transcripts, of 'φρενῶν ἐπηβόλους' and 'ἄτερ γνώμης', such as might later have been penned by her husband.[14] What is it, exactly, that results in their transformation, in 1850, into 'true in aim of soul' and 'blindly and lawlessly'? Not a wish to translate more accurately—or even more fluently—the descriptive meaning that Aeschylus must have meant to convey: that would have produced something like 'implanted . . . the capability of knowledge' and 'without discernment'—both renderings from a prose translation that Barrett Browning might have known.[15] Rather, a determination to look through the angled reflection of Aeschylus's writing to the conditions of humanity it describes; and to redefine those conditions in her own words. Like one of the mortals Prometheus is talking about, she at first 'seeing, saw in vain'; but then made a leap into understanding: now she looks through Aeschylus's words to the 'archetypal beauty' she takes them to reflect, as though she were at last seeing that a 'flower' is a sign of 'spring'. Of course, the second version stays shackled to its source in the sense of having that analogous 'arrangement of elements' and overlap of descriptive meaning which we saw to be crucial to the definition of a translation: the same things happen and are referred to in the same order in pretty much the same proportions (the 1850 translation is a couple of hundred lines longer than the first, and than the source). But Barrett Browning stands forward to display her own originality in her confident rephrasings. Asserting liberty of spirit within the restraints of structural fidelity, the work asks to be taken, not only as a translation of *Prometheus Bound*, but as a Promethean act of translation.

Two kinds of 'liberty': FitzGerald's breaking of bounds for the sake of building bridges; and Barrett's Promethean unbinding of the spirit within structural fidelity. As she worked on the second version, Barrett was exchanging letters with Robert Browning: between the two of them, Prometheus leaps in different figurative directions. '*I* feel it delicious to be free when most bound to you, Ba', he wrote to her at one point, signalling a connection between translation and passion which we will explore further in Part III.[16] The metaphors adopted by FitzGerald and Barrett are more than ornamental flourishes. Neither do they look like detached analytical terms thought up after the end of the event which they describe. They seem to emerge from and shape each writer's work of imagining. They have the feel—to borrow from the title of the well-known book by George Lakoff and Mark Johnson—of metaphors that are being lived by.

In *Metaphors We Live By* (1980), Lakoff and Johnson proposed that 'expressions like *wasting time, attacking positions, going our separate ways*, etc., are reflections of systematic metaphorical concepts that structure our actions and thoughts'. The metaphors we usually call 'dead' are in fact ' "alive" in the most fundamental sense: they are metaphors we live by'.[17] The claim has similarities to that made by Derrida, in 'La mythologie blanche' (1971), about the roots of abstract words used by philosophers: though superseded, the old meanings are never quite left behind, and exert an insidious metaphorical pressure: 'le concept de concept ne peut pas ne pas retenir...le schème du geste de maîtrise, prenant-maintenant, comprenant et saisissant la chose comme un objet' ('the concept of concept cannot not retain the pattern of the gesture of mastery, taking-now-and-maintaining, comprehending and seizing the thing as an object').[18] Derrida's claim is the more fluid and therefore the more persuasive, for Lakoff and Johnson do not offer any argument to support the metaphors ('structure', 'systematic') that structure and systematize their own discussion. Quite what it is for 'war' (one of their examples) to 'structure' a concept of argument, rather than—say—'guiding' or 'influencing' or 'exerting pressure on' it, is never made plain by them. In my own descriptions I will therefore aim for something more like Derrida's apt tentativeness ('retenir...le schème du geste'), while also relying on Lakoff and Johnson's compelling innovation: their attention to groups of metaphors which reveal persistent habits of thought.

The metaphor in the word 'translation' is—as we have seen—rather like 'concept' or 'wasting time': it limits and guides what people say with the word, whether or not they mean it to. But the other metaphors which will be at the heart of this book are not 'dead' (or rather undead), at least not to the same extent. They tend to be (but are not always) deployed more consciously: they rise up out of dissatisfaction with the model of translation rigidly conceived and they embody the design of supplementing or displacing it. And then they are not (as Lakoff and Johnson claim for their 'metaphors we live by')[19] all-but universal in the culture but are particular to individual translators, or sometimes groups of translators, together with some of their readers. Nevertheless, the perception which Derrida and Lakoff and Johnson all, broadly speaking, shared—that a metaphor can be a way, not just of saying something but also of doing and experiencing it—is the basis of my argument about translation. If you say that you are, not translating (or not only translating), but transcribing or transposing or building bridges or Prometheanly unbinding-within-bounds, then you may be, not just using a different word for what is still fundamentally one thing, 'translation', but doing something that asks to be distinguished from translation rigidly conceived. The word 'translation' has been used to name more activities than can be reduced to that model; the metaphors adopted by translators delineate these various kinds of imaginative work.

In pursuing this thought, we must heed James St André's reminder that 'metaphors are not just interpretations; they themselves are also subject to (re-)interpretation'.[20] To notice that translation is being understood in the image of—(say)—'transcription' is therefore only a first step: as we have seen, one needs then to explore what 'transcription' is being understood as and felt to imply. But we can take heart from a state of affairs that Gerard Steen, as a cognitive linguist, seems to lament: the lack of 'a generally accepted procedure for deriving conceptual metaphors from linguistic metaphors', so that inferring pathways in the mind from metaphors in language is 'basically an art'.[21] As we endeavour to practise this art, we will give due recognition to the metaphors of translation that are explicit in prefaces and other critical writings; but we will also be struck by metaphors that may inhere in a translator's practice but never quite reach the surface of expression. Even when metaphors are made explicit, it is rare for them to be wholly under the translator's control: none of them—save perhaps for 'translation as carrying across'—has the clarity and obduracy of a 'system' or 'structure' but rather the diffuse sway of a 'disposition'. And when they are left latent, or are barely hinted at, they need not therefore be the less revealing of the practice that gives rise to them and that they help define.

In their original formulation of the theory, Lakoff and Johnson took it that the metaphors we live by originate in an 'experiential basis' and are then transferred to areas that are less immediate to us. 'War' supplies metaphors for argument, and not the other way around, because war—they thought—is more fundamental to human experience than is argument. Even if this were ever true, it seems unlikely to be so these days when comparatively few people—at least in the West—have encountered war at first hand. In any case, no experience is wholly unmediated, wholly 'basic': more recent research in cognitive science and communication has recognized that the workings of metaphor in the mind must be more fluid. As David Ritchie pointed out in 2003, words like 'defend', 'position', 'manoeuvre', and 'strategy' are shared between war, sport, argument, and games such as chess, all of which can form metaphors with each other, and indeed with other fields. Often the reference is indeterminate. 'Now we are winning', an accountant might say when working on your tax return: is the idea of chess or argument or war or sport more present in the utterance? Neither of you need know, and it need not matter. Equally, that usage, or merely the possibility of it, can leach back into remarks that might at first seem wholly literal. 'Now we're winning', you might say at a football match soon after, or even long after, or even perhaps before; and the memory (or anticipation) of the nightmare of your tax return might surface in your mind. As Derrida has argued, all utterances are prey to this metaphorical slippage, even (for instance) calling the sun 'the sun': 'le soleil est métaphorique déjà, toujours . . . il . . . a toujours été autre, lui-même: le père, la semence, le feu, l'oeil, l'oeuf, etc' ('the sun is metaphorical, always, already .. it has always been other, itself: father, seed, fire, eye, egg, etc.).[22] It is impossible to call a spade a spade.

When Barrett calls her 1833 translation 'a Prometheus *twice* bound' she (obviously) brings in a word from Aeschylus's play; and no doubt the usage owes something also to her personal experience of being bed-bound because of illness, as well as more everyday kinds of binding involving bandages, bits of string and indeed books (a book is 'half-bound' if it has a leather spine and cloth sides—a phrase which must—rebounding—give some impetus to '*twice* bound'). But once binding has been connected to translation, that connection cannot but re-inflect the binding that happens in the play, so that Prometheus, asserting himself despite an imposed fidelity, seems to have something in common with translators, as well as vice-versa. He made the world understandable to humans, they who previously did not know its language, and 'hearing, heard not'. What it is for one word-and-thought to be adopted as a figure of another, though, is not for the two to become identical. We must avoid the Steiner trap of saying '*self-assertion within bounds equals translation*': if we fall into it we lose our grasp on the particular pressure that the idea of Prometheus exerted on Barrett's translation, and vice versa. The challenge for criticism is to map both overlaps and disjunctions between the terms that are layered together, tracing what their interaction illuminates and makes possible, and also what it hobbles and obscures.

7

The Roots of Translatorly Metaphors

The metaphors that form the spine of my discussion—metaphors of interpretation, of friendship, desire and passion, of vision and perspective, and of death, rebirth, and metamorphosis—all emerge, like Barrett's binding and unbinding, from the translators' own work with words. In this, they differ from the scheme of descriptive figures proposed by Douglas Robinson in *The Translator's Turn* (1991). Robinson brings his categories across from classical rhetoric: a translation may be 'metonymical', that is, focus on a single element of the source, or synecdochic (offering part for whole), or metaphorical ('the metaphoric translator seeks to *be* the SL [source language] writer'), or hyperbolic, or ironic, or metaleptic, and so on. Throughout, Robinson is keen to assert the inventiveness of both translators and readers: his 'taxonomy', he says, is offered in this spirit. It is meant to supply 'shifting and I hope interesting but by no means stable . . . perspectives on what translators really do'.[1] Yet it is in the nature of a 'taxonomy' to feel somewhat 'stable' however much you wish it not to. For all his well-grounded unease about the abstractness of much other theorizing about translation, Robinson's own theory cannot but take on something of the same high-handedness. The labelling of Ezra Pound, for instance, as a 'hyperbolic' translator, that is, one who exaggerates or improves the source 'in order to give it its "proper" fullness', seems driven by a desire, not so much to capture the reality of Pound's practice, as to fit him in to the prescribed structure.[2]

The metaphors I explore provide a less tidy summation than Robinson's; but they will I hope map the processes of literary translation more closely. As it happens, they also suggest an explanation of why some of those processes take on the shapes they do. Metaphors of translation can have many origins: I will show in Part II that the image of 'opening' which mattered to Dryden came to him from a long tradition of thinking about how to understand the Bible. Yet often—startlingly often—they turn out to have a root in the work that is being translated: the case of Elizabeth Barrett is by no means exceptional. And when a translation metaphor does have its origin, or part of its origin, elsewhere, it can still interact with similar images—doubles of translation—in the source text. For Dryden, the metaphor of 'opening' took on particular strength and salience when he was translating the *Aeneid*, a text in which doubles of 'translation as opening' abound: the collaboration of translation metaphor and source text does much to explain the distinctive energy of his version. The same is true of Pope, whose idea of translation as 'catching fire' came to him from Longinus but developed a particular inwardness with the *Iliad*; and of Pound, whose idea of translation as 'bringing a dead man to life' derives from Browning but matters especially in his *Homage to Sextus Propertius* because the Propertius poems he translates are much concerned with modes of life after death. It has long been recognized that styles of translation vary according to the kind of text translated. We take it for granted that poetry is likely to require different tactics than prose, and that translation for theatrical performance will be different again. Genre too, exerts an influence. Pope's share of the translation of the *Odyssey* was, he admitted, 'an exacter version than that of the *Iliad*' because the *Odyssey* was in itself a less epic work, and therefore required a less epic effort of translation; Dryden's collaborative translation of Roman satire was, he said, looser than his translation of Virgil: 'it was not possible for us, or any men, to have made it pleasant any other way'.[3] But individual source texts can also exert a particular influence on what is done to them via the metaphors they hold out to translators.

The chapters ahead will explore some major instances from across the history of English literature. But examples of the same propensity abound in the landscape of verse translation today. We have already skimmed over one fleet instance: the Muldoon Montale, in which the eel's journey and return bear a glancing resemblance to the to-ing and fro-ing of the translating imagination between English words and the 'ur-poem'. There is a more solid case in Michael Hofmann's Englishing of selected poems by Durs Grünbein, *Ashes for Breakfast* (2006). In his Preface, Hofmann explains that usually his translations have been 'dutiful' but that occasionally something more 'interesting' has occurred. He gives as example a passage which begins:

> Back in front of the telephone, under the cheese cloche,
>   The cosh, the Alexander Graham Bell jar, ...
>
> Wieder vorm Telephon, in der Vitrine
>   Wie unterm Glassturz, ...[4]

This is from the second section of the sequence 'Variations on no Theme'. The first section has imagined a digression, a heading-off in search of something new, some excitement—only the sought-for

experience turns out to be displaced and commodified: new faces are no
better than clock faces behind a shop window. In this second section, the
same happens, but at home. Standing by the telephone is like being on
display: someone can pick you out and dial your number, obliging you to
perform the routine of a phone call. Conversely, much of the world is
available to you through the phone whose key pad is a 'decimal mandala /
Tempting you by its availability'—though again, the fact of having to reach
out for something, to order it in, will fix it as an object of your desire, and so
establish an insidious glassy separation between you and it.[5] (The Internet
might have suited this pattern of feeling; but it was not yet flourishing when
Grünbein's poem was written in 1994.) In the German here, 'Glassturz' is
an unusual word which means a glass dome or bell jar and has perhaps
within it a linguistic tension, a possibility of shattering: a 'Sturz' can be a fall
or a rushing along (which perhaps spawns Hofmann's 'cosh') while 'Sturz'
can be a surname which perhaps helps licence the pun about Alexander
Graham Bell. Still, it is Hofmann who has invented that pun, brought in
the reference to Plath's *The Bell Jar*, turned the German 'Vitrine' (meaning
display cabinet) into a 'cloche', and introduced the cheese. How come?

In the Preface, he says:

> I don't know why this happened like that to this poem. Perhaps it was the
> single-sentence rush of the thing; perhaps it began with the cheese cloche,
> and turned, as is in the nature of cheese, into a nightmare.[6]

This charmingly reminds us that good translation is not only a matter of
conscious technique but draws on unknowable reaches of the imagination.
Yet it turns out that we can shine some light into those dark places because
the word 'nightmare' appears to have wormed its way into Hofmann's
explanation from the next-but-one section of the poem being translated:

> And in the morning, you turn on the shower
>   And out comes . . . water, what did you think?
> Red and blue stand for hot and cold.
>   The skin wasn't peeled off in strips like wallpaper.
> That's just a nightmare, silly.[7]

Translating this passage here Hofmann makes his words line up pretty
predictably with the German. 'Red and blue' stand for 'Rot und Blau' just
as much as for 'hot and cold'. But the wallpaper is his innovation: it is
helped to happen by appearing in a simile (as we will see in the chapters
that follow, simile is often a site of freedom for translators); and also by the
mention of nightmare. For just as Grünbein, in the preceding sections,
has built his poems out of a dreamwork of neurotic interconnection, so
Hofmann here allows himself a moment of nightmarishly inward

response. And this must also be what happened at the earlier moment of anxiety in front of the telephone. He turned on the tap of translation and what came out was, not the obvious routine 'display case' but the 'nightmare' of 'the cheese cloche, / The cosh', ending up with a pun—'the Alexander Graham Bell jar'—which, even if you do not look across at the German, you know is very unlikely to be in the original.

Within Hofmann's general practice of 'dutiful'—though always poised and responsive—translation, there comes this flicker of something else, not understandable as word-for-word, nor sense-for-sense, nor even as effect-for-effect, not, finally, as 'translation rigidly conceived' at all. Yet it is no less closely hooked in to the source, no less wholly caused by it. It follows on from Grünbein's German with all the inevitability of what we so wrongly call 'free association'. It is a moment of 'translation as nightmare'.

In Ciaran Carson's *Inferno of Dante Alighieri* (2002), the reconfiguring of 'translation' in reaction to the source is less stark but more pervasive. Hofmann has the responsibility of being the first translator to introduce Grünbein into English, and so much of the time holds himself to the figure of 'translation as carrying across'. But Carson has been preceded by hundreds of Englishers of Dante, and so feels the freedom to vary the metaphor by which he (more loosely) translates. 'The deeper I got into the *Inferno*, the more I walked', he says, opening his 'Introduction' with an image that touches into life the etymology of that word, asking us to feel that we are being introduced, or 'led into', the poem behind him as he walks. 'Hunting for a rhyme'—he says—'trying to construe a turn of phrase, I'd leave the desk and take to the road, lines ravelling and unravelling in my mind.'[8] One of Carson's own great subjects is the mingling of landscape and language—as in his poems 'Serial' and 'Belfast Confetti'—and Dante had pre-empted him in this regard. *Inferno* is a re-travelling in verse of a long walk in which voices from across Italy and beyond are encountered and construed. For Carson, translation became 'a way of making the poetry of Dante intelligible to myself. An exercise in comprehension: "Now tell the story in your own words." '[9] The idea has been helped into focus by the many exercises in comprehension that Dante is put through as he hears the damned souls' stories and retells them in his own 'own words'. 'Ridir'—saying again—is one of his definitions of what he is up to, Dante-as-author recalling and writing down what Dante-as-character is supposed to have felt and heard.[10]

Carson's view of what translating Dante should be results in a text that sticks very close to the narrative structure and form of the source (it is almost line for line) but has great independence of tone. The play of voice is richest when Carson endeavours to comprehend moments at which characters in the source are also endeavouring to comprehend something or one another. Here, in Canto I, Dante begins to realize who is speaking to him through the dusk:

> 'Are you then Virgil, that superior fount
>   which spouts so generous a verbal brook?'
> I bashfully replied to his account'[11]

The words in Italian are smoothed by assonance and alliteration into what feels like a tone of achieved reverence:

> 'Or se' tu quel Virgilio e quella fonte
> che spandi di parlar sí largo fiume?'
> rispuos'io lui con vergognoso fronte'.[12]

Carson echoes some of the sounds of the Italian: 'fount' from 'fonte', 'spouts' from 'spandi'. But in the different tonality of his Hiberno-English the harmonies of homage go askew. The inserted word 'superior' has an undertow of sarcasm which continues in 'spouts' (like a gutter?): 'spandi' generally means something closer to 'pours' or 'spreads'. And the warmth of 'generous' is undermined by its application to 'brook' (brought in to rhyme with 'book') since a brook, though it could once be a strong flowing stream, is nowadays by definition a little thing. The reverence which comes easily to Dante turns awkward when it is re-enacted in Carson's 'own words'. We can point, by way of explanation, to general shifts in cultural disposition: people just don't do deference so much these days. But the altered tone of the Carson version also seems to react against the veneration with which Dante has so often been viewed: he 'speaks to the noble, the pure and great', Carlyle intoned; he is 'the most *universal* of poets in the modern languages', decreed T. S. Eliot.[13] In Dante's obeisance to Virgil, Carson must see an image of what his own attitude to Dante might be expected to be. And so he does, instead, his own distinctive thing, voicing in his 'own words' an irreverence which is not incompatible with real admiration, and may well be a precondition for a properly searching translation. For, on reflection, in the light of the Carson version, it may be that there is a tiny counter-surge of bile in Dante's words (perhaps it lurks somewhere in all acts of obeisance), in which case Carson opens a fault line that was already there.

   Translators always leave a mark on their work. Their translations have an origin in their own selves, obviously, as well as in their sources. Often concealed or ignored, their contribution can be made tangible by notes or introductions which, as Theo Hermans has shown, 'make the actual translation into an object of contemplation':[14] the prefatory material in the Hofmann and Carson volumes does exactly this. Where there are previous translations—as Hermans goes on to observe—each new rendering 'exhibits its own reading and, in so doing, marks its difference from other readings, other interpretations':[15] Carson's Dante does this as well. Yet the distinctive ways with language that we have begun to explore can often be noticed without the promptings of commentary, and often with only the haziest awareness of previous interpretations or of the source—though attention to these other texts will always help clarify what is happening. 'Alexander Graham Bell jar' is obviously unlikely to have been in the German; while if you know anything of Dante you can guess that 'superior fount' is not quite in his style as it has generally been represented in English as well as Italian culture. These 'translation effects', to adopt Philip Lewis's phrase,[16] signal that the source has been responded to according to a figure somewhat different from that of translation rigidly conceived. In doing so, they create a textual pregnancy which asks for particular interpretive attention. The 'Bell jar' moment in the Hofmann suggests an unnerving inwardness with the source, or perhaps better a shared recognition of the otherness within both writers, as the nightmare spreads from German into English. The Carson has a feeling of camp about it, almost pastiche, which asks us to see that the translation is not rising to the high dignity the *Commedia* is usually taken to possess, but is instead designedly aiming lower, inserting (or perhaps discovering) tones of everyday humanity.

These deviations from, or within, 'translation' are more common in poetry than in prose, even literary prose. As we saw, Jean Starr Untermeyer felt herself to be a musical interpreter; and she was a translator of prose. But this budding metaphor is kept subjugated to 'translation as carrying across':

> The task was not so much like transposing a composition from one key to another, as of re-orchestrating a composition for another set of instruments, taking utmost care to preserve the structure, the phrasing, and the musical line, and to substitute for the original sonorities others of equal depth.[17]

Prose fiction in general is translated according to the idea of translation rigidly conceived—and rightly so, given the preponderance of elements of reference and narrative structure which are amenable to being 'carried across' (In the first of the two senses I established in Chapter 4) without much loss. But other metaphors can press in. Like any kind of writing, prose can be put through programmes of intervention such as those pursued by Susanne de Lotbinière-Harwood: 'my translation practice is a political activity aimed at making language speak for women. So my signature on a translation means: this translation has used every translation strategy to make the feminine visible in language'.[18] Extraordinary prose texts such as *Finnegans Wake* are liable to release their own figures of rewriting. And it does also occasionally happen that prose translation is nudged by promptings from the source text to take on something of the shape of another metaphor in just the way we have been exploring.

Translating *We* for publication in 2006, Natasha Randall was, she says, fascinated by 'Zamyatin's relationship to the sounds of words', his feeling that 'O is high, deep, sea-like, bosom. I is close, low, pressing', and so on. In response—she continues—'I chose lingual and labial permutations that matched Zamyatin's where I could. I distinctly recall the moment of deciding to render *sverkayuschii* (a very important word in the novel) as "sparkling" rather than "gleaming."' This can certainly be taken as one variety of translation rigidly conceived, the carrying-over, or 'matching'— as Randall puts it—of phonetic values across languages, like Untermeyer's substituting 'for the original sonorities others of equal depth'.[19] Yet *We* is filled with potential doubles of translation; and in the light of them Randall's attention to linguals and labials takes on, even if unconsciously on her part, a different shape. The 'One State', with its structures of 'transparent and eternal glass', imposes a regime of what is taken to be perfect communication between its citizens: 'we are so identical', the protagonist, D-503, remarks, having begun his first-person narrative with words that are not his own: 'I am merely copying out here, word for word, what was printed today in the *State Gazette*'. But the model of mechanical word-for-word reiteration is at once challenged by a different image of transmission, 'honeyed yellow pollen' carried in 'from the wild plains out of sight in the distance' on the wind: 'this sweet pollen dries the lips—you keep running your tongue over them—and every woman you meet (and every man, too, of course) must have those sweet lips'.[20] Running her linguals over her labials, Randall gives at least some allegiance to this more personal, bodily and accidental kind of togetherness: 'translation as the sharing of sensations'.

In translation for the theatre, it is often assumed that what needs most importantly to be 'carried across' is a speech's rhetorical impact. 'Anything, literally anything that can be shouted'—Pound urged, protesting at how Browning had transcribed Clytemnestra's announcement of the fall of Troy; 'anything but a stilted unsayable jargon'. Browning had written 'Troia the Achaioi hold', rendering as always the 'idea' that seemed to him to be carved into the syntactical form of the speech.[21] In some of his own poem-translations (as we will see in Chapter 23) Pound adopted a metaphor of translation that owed much to Browning's 'transcription'; but when faced with a theatrical utterance it was the impact that seemed to him to matter, the surge of Clytemnestra's emotion. Translation for the theatre has its own complexities, of course; but the immediacy of performance militates against the proliferation of metaphors that we have begun to explore. When 'translation as carrying across' is challenged by a different metaphor, is it often one of updating—as for instance in Seamus Heaney's *The Cure at Troy* (1990) and Tom Paulin's *The Riot Act* (1985) which adapted Sophocles's *Philoctetes* and *Antigone*, respectively, to the Ireland of the troubles. 'Paulin isn't taking liberties with Sophocles he's liberating him' as an adapter in a similar vein, Blake Morrison, put it in a lecture in 2007.[22] Establishing relevance to the present is the overriding concern.

Yet it is possible to imagine 'Troia the Achaioi hold' being, if not shouted, at least howled. If it were, it would have a strangeness about it that would interrupt an audience's reaction and perhaps create something like a Brechtian *Verfremdungseffekt*, holding the utterance at a critical remove. Such overlaps of translation effect and theatrical effect help to explain the enduring excitement of Tony Harrison's *Oresteia*, produced at the National Theatre in 1981. His version of Clytemnestra's announcement is:

'The Greek armies have taken the city of Priam.'[23]

It's not unsayable like Browning's line; but it's not obviously shoutable either. Harrison subjugates Clytemnestra's exclamation to the order of his verse, whose often alliterative dactylic and trochaic pulse sounds strongly throughout the play, marking the characters as being under the sway of something beyond them—the fates, perhaps or, finally, the gods. Together with the formalized energy of the choreography and the grotesque—though historically sanctioned—masks worn by the actors, it keeps the drama strange. This overarching air of distance from the audience allows Harrison to deploy wildly varied modes of rewriting, from rendering colloquial and relevant ('I'd sooner die / Than live two seconds under tyranny') to the phonetic knee-jerk of 'kin-killers / child-charnel man shambles' and the baffling, moving inarticulacy of Cassandra's last line: 'That pain's also nothing makes life a heartbreak'.[24] Such styles flourish in the translation of printed poetry: here they are brought into the theatre. Harrison's translation owes much to Browning's *Agamemnon of Aeschylus* which was never meant to be performed. 'The seeds of my principal choices', Harrison says, referring to his alliterations and verbal compounds, 'were lurking there in Browning from the beginning'.[25]

Nevertheless, the metaphors that I will be exploring flower best in the slow quiet of the printed page. They are fostered by the greater licence which we take for granted may be necessary in translating poetry; and they rely on being read with that greater attention to verbal texture which poetry characteristically elicits.

In 'Die Aufgabe des Übersetzers', Benjamin asks whether there can be something about a work that lends itself ('zulasse') to translation, even demands it ('verlange'). Of course, there are many reasons, of cultural importance, fashion, newsworthiness, etc., that may result in texts in general being translated; but Benjamin has in mind those literary translations which are more than mere cribs—'mehr als Vermittlungen sind'—and which, by perpetuating what most matters in the source, allow it to continue its unfolding, 'Entfaltung', in world culture.[26] For Maurice Blanchot, in his commentary on Benjamin's essay, this propensity to be translated derives from a linguistic unsettledness, a text's feeling of being 'foreign to itself'.[27] Maybe so, although it seems likely that any literary text might appear foreign to itself if looked at in the right way. But a more demonstrable factor—as the ensuing chapters will (I hope) show—is that texts offer stimulus to imaginative translation when they hold within themselves portrayals of friendship, interpretation, metamorphosis and so on, in which translators can see reflections or refractions of their own activity, and which can therefore become metaphors of translation.

In novels, one kind of imaginative richness arises when your act of reading finds an echo in something like reading that is being done by a protagonist, whether it be Madam Bovary, or Pip, or Bloom, or Jaques Deza in Javier Marías's *Fiebre y Lanza*. Indeed, an assumption widespread among novels is that to be a 'character' is to be a kind of reader. In poems, as Christopher Ricks has shown, allusions to other writing often spark when something similar to allusion is being described:

> We should notice when the subject-matter of an allusion is at one with the impulse that underlies the making of allusions at all, because it is characteristic of art to find energy and delight in an enacting of that which it is saying, and to be rendered vigilant by a consciousness of metaphors and analogies which relate its literary practices to the great world.[28]

Translators, of course, do not have such liberty to allude as other writers since translation is by definition a sustained allusion to an evident original. But they can find themselves—like readers of a novel—face to face with doubles of themselves, elements in the source which can become metaphors of the imaginative work they are engaged in. Such doubles may supply self-images which translators adopt; or they may harmonize or clash with figures that are already implicit in the translators' own practice. This does not happen always in the translation of poetry: I am aware of many brilliant poetic translations which are not (so far as I can see) amenable to being read in the way I have been proposing and am about to pursue: Gawin Douglas's *The xiii bukes of Eneados of the famose poete Virgill*, for instance; or Dryden's translations of Persius and Juvenal; or those by Ted Hughes and János Csokits of János Pilinszky. This is one more indication that I am not offering a 'theory of translation' (since such a theory must leave so much that is interesting unexplored). Not every poem-translation is a poem *of* translation: as we have seen, 'translation' is a loose term for different kinds of imaginative work, and the poetry of translation is only one of the sorts of writing that are done in its name. Nevertheless, it is an important one, for, as we will see, many of the translations that have established themselves as great poems in English literature have been energized and shaped by metaphors projected by their sources. When translation is doubled in this way, it can turn into a particularly complex and subtle kind of writing about all those relationships and processes—from friendship and desire to death and rebirth—which become metaphors for translation, and which are shaped by the metaphor of translation in their turn. This is the poetry of translation.

PART II

TRANSLATION AS 'INTERPRETATION', AS 'PARAPHRASE', AND AS 'OPENING'

8

Are Translations Interpretations?
Gadamer, Lowell, and Some
Contemporary Poem-Translations

'Translation is a form of interpretation', says Umberto Eco, echoing Roman Jakobson, for whom translation is 'an interpretation of verbal signs by means of some other language'. The philosopher Karl Popper tells us that 'every good translation is an *interpretation* of the original text'. We can read in *The Cambridge Companion to Ovid* that 'every translation, of course, is an interpretation', while a study of the Old Testament goes further: 'it is a truism that any translation is an interpretation'.[1] These different voices swell a chorus that has become all but universal in contemporary translation criticism. But what exactly does it mean?

The Latin *interpretari* could mean, simply, 'to translate', a usage which hovers in the early centuries of the life of the word 'interpret' in English; and today we still speak of oral translation as 'interpreting' and oral translators as 'interpreters'. But the main current of 'interpretation', as applied to writing, has always tended to distinguish itself from translation. As we saw in Chapter 3, translations make a flickering claim to identity with the source; while the value of an interpretation—like that of a paraphrase—lies primarily in how it differs from whatever it is an interpretation of (for instance in being clearer or shorter). As the core definitions of 'to interpret', the *OED* gives: 'to expound the meaning of (something abstruse or mysterious); to render (words, writings, an author, etc.) clear or explicit; to elucidate; to explain'. The statements made by Eco et al. take the difference between translation and interpretation for granted since without it they would be meaningless: 'every translation is, of course, a form of translation'.

Eco's phrase has the shape that is often used to express relationships of inclusion: 'a cuckoo is a form of bird' or 'translation is a form of activity'. But, as we have seen, it is not the case that translation simply belongs to the class of interpretations in the way it simply belongs to the class of activities. To say that translation is a form of interpretation highlights some aspects of translation (for instance the meanings that seem to be ascribed to the source) and obscures others (for instance the translator's self-expression through translating). This shows that Eco's statement includes an unacknowledged strand of metaphor—the sort of thing that is obvious in statements like 'life is a form of journey'. The same is true, and more emphatically, of those rephrasings which ditch the qualifier 'a form of'. What is really meant by 'any translation is an interpretation' is: 'let's think of translation on the model of interpretation'. Interpretation is a metaphor for translation just like those other metaphors—transcription, transposition, bridge-building, unbinding-within-bounds, nightmare, etc. —which we have already encountered.

Yet, as the vehicle of a metaphor, 'interpretation' is unusually problematic. As we saw in Chapters 5 and 6, any metaphor is open to being taken in different ways: its meaning can be pinned down only by exploring the practice from which it has emerged and which it endeavours to define. But the word 'interpretation' is radically ambiguous, perhaps more so even than 'literal' or 'free'. Of all the metaphors we will investigate, therefore, translation-as-interpretation is the most entangled.

Some of the different processes that can count as 'interpretation' have been traced by Axel Bühler: you can 'interpret' by identifying 'communicative intentions', by giving a 'structural description', by 'inferring... thoughts not explicitly stated', and so on.[2] And then there is the use of 'interpret' to describe what actors do to scripts or musicians to music; images which, as we saw in Chapter 6, were adopted by Jean Starr Untermeyer and Gayatri Chakravorty Spivak in their accounts of their translations. This way with the word dates only from the end of the last century and must owe something to an influential argument put forward by Matthew Arnold in 1865. 'The grand power of poetry', he said, 'is its interpretative power':

> by which I mean, not a power of drawing out in black and white an
> explanation of the mystery of the universe, but the power of so dealing
> with things as to awaken in us a wonderfully full, new, and intimate sense of
> them, and of our relations with them.[3]

Arnold closes off interpretation's connections to clarifying and analysing ('not a power of drawing out in black and white') to make space for the new sense he wants to graft in. This might still perhaps be thought of as a kind of 'expounding': poetry's interpretative power, he goes on to say, makes us 'feel ourselves to be in contact with the essential nature of... objects', to 'have their secret'.[4] But the importance given to 'feeling' pulls this usage away from understandings of interpretation as explanation and as making clear.

As we saw in Chapter 6, all metaphors for translation need careful interpretation: the metaphor 'translation is interpretation' needs it more than any. We have to ask: 'which, of the various and at times conflicting kinds of interpretation, do you mean?' But few answers have been offered by devotees of the phrase. It is generally used as a step in that complicated tango of critical rhetoric which we investigated in Chapter 3. It is called in to state the obvious truth that no translation is the same as its source: not a 'substitute' (to deploy that wobbly word for one last time) but a 'parallel text', or a 're-embodiment'—or maybe an 'interpretation'. It can come as a warning: do not trust translations, for 'they are merely interpretations': they are conditioned by the circumstances of their making, loaded with ideological assumptions, and so on. But more often it gives recognition to the element of creativity in the work of translators: 'this is not merely translation, it is interpretation'.

Nevertheless, this metaphor—or bundle of metaphors—has an insidious consequence. For there is something that all varieties of interpretation, even poetry as understood by Arnold, have in common. All achieve their eye-opening effect by introducing a change of medium or genre. Poetry deals with the world in its special way by representing it in language. Literary criticism deals with poetry by representing it in meta-language. It is possible to argue that a poem is really an interpretation of another poem; but, in arguing that, you are saying that it should be read differently, which means you are proposing to change its genre. The shift that distinguishes interpretation is taken to be illuminating; but it is therefore also, inevitably, narrowing. A critical interpretation is—we say—'just one reading' of the source; King Lear as played by Ian Holm is 'just one interpretation'. Poetry, in Arnold's view, may be 'magical' and 'inspired' but even it cannot but be less complex than the world that it interprets. To call something an interpretation is to imply that it does not need to be interpreted in its turn; at least, not as much as the material it itself has interpreted.

As we will see, this inevitable but awkward interplay of translation and interpretation has been probed by some recent translations of poetry; but what is going on in them has tended to elude the critical terms with which this sort of writing is typically reviewed and understood. Both the terms and the practice owe a debt to Dryden, whose work in this area is—frankly—more complex and thought-through than anything in contemporary verse translation. In Dryden's cultural circumstances, translation was more central and more vital than it is today: as I will show, questions left over from the great Reformation enterprise of translating the Bible lingered provocatively in his imagination. He understood the interpretive aspect of translation as 'opening'; but he felt uneasy about this metaphor, to which he was nevertheless committed: the resulting conflict flourishes especially in his translation of Virgil's *Aeneid*. That work will give us our first full instance of this book's twin emphases: that translation is defined by metaphors; but that textual counter-currents, created in part by inter-actions between the metaphor that shapes the translation and similar metaphors that appear in the source, mean that the definition supplied by the guiding metaphor is never complete. Dryden's *Aeneis* is both an 'opening' of Virgil's *Aeneid* and a sustained criticism of the metaphor 'translation is opening'; other translations likewise both obey and attack the metaphor 'translation is interpretation'.

Linguists have a word for the urge that translations should clarify their sources. 'Explicitation' is 'the process of introducing information into the target language which is present only implicitly in the source language';[5] and some researchers have speculated that it may be 'a universal strategy inherent in the process of language mediation'.[6] One need only think of the Zukofskys' Catullus to see that this 'strategy' is not 'universal' among translators, but it is certainly widespread. For texts with a straightforward communicative intention—an instruction manual—this need not matter. In fact, it may even be an advantage: as we saw in Chapter 3, such a text is well translated when the translation allows it to fulfil its function. Even philosophical writing—which is what Popper had in mind when saying a translation has to be 'an interpretation' if it is to be 'good'—might be taken to benefit from being disambiguated. An interpretive translation of Hegel, for instance, might be thought of as continuing the process of trying to get things clear in which Hegel himself was engaged (one could also argue against this view). But for literary texts, whose value is so entwined with their need to be interpreted, the metaphor of translation-as-interpretation creates a difficulty. It entails that a literary translation can never be as literary as its source.

This difficulty erupts in the middle of the argument, in Gadamer's *Wahrheit und Methode* (1960; revised 1985), that has most fuelled the idea that every translation is an interpretation. I quote from the standard English translation, *Truth and Method*, by W. Glen-Doepel, revised by Joel Weinsheimer and Donald G. Marshall (1989):

> Every translation is at the same time an interpretation. ... No one can doubt that what we are dealing with here is interpretation, and not simply repro-duction. A new light falls on the text from the other language, and for the reader of it. ... Translation, like all interpretation, is a highlighting ... Every

translation that takes its task seriously is at once clearer and flatter than the original. Even if it is a masterly re-creation, it must lack some of the overtones that vibrate in the original. (In rare cases of masterly re-creation the loss can be made good or even mean a gain—think, for example, of how Baudelaire's *Les fleurs du mal* seems to acquire an odd new vigour in Stefan George's version.)[7]

For Gadamer, the movement from one language to another will tend to produce an 'interpretation' whatever the intention of the translator. As with overlapping circles in a Venn diagram, the area of intersection between the two languages is narrower than that covered by one: only those elements of the text which can be rendered in the receiving language will be 'highlighted'. Yet, just as the argument seems to be reaching its conclusion, the counter example of literary translation butts in (even if it is kept quarantined inside parentheses). The English translation at this point is—just as Gadamer predicts—at once clearer and flatter than the German, where the thought of this kind of translation (if it is still translation) that for once might *not* be clearer and flatter stirs up much linguistic murk. The word rendered as 're-creation' is in fact 'Schöpfung' which has no feeling of 're-' about it and means something close to 'creation'. It stands in a difficult relation to Gadamer's other word for the kind of translation that does not result in loss, 'Nachdichtung'— version, or after-writing. Writing, or after-writing: just how 'new' is the 'odd new vigour' of the Stefan George Baudelaire? The original vigour seen from a new angle—or a wholly new vigour, as though *Les fleurs du mal* had acquired an odd new hat? Again, reference to the German complicates the question: the word rendered as 'vigour' is 'Gesundheit' which is closer to 'health'. This 'new health' is not merely 'odd' but more like 'peculiar' or 'distinctive' ('eigentümliche'); and it is not 'acquired' but rather 'breathed' ('atmen').[8] When faced with the puzzle of masterly poetic translation, which strikes him as both creation and re-creation, both new and the same, Gadamer makes the common move that we identified in Chapter 6: he reaches for new metaphors. George's 'Schöpfung' prompts him to a 'Schöpfung' of his own.

The same pattern of perplexity, according to which the translation of a poem is required to be a poem in its turn; but being a poem in its turn seems to conflict with its being a translation; appears in Robert Lowell's 'Introduction' to his *Imitations* (1962):

> Boris Pasternak has said that the usual reliable translator gets the literal meaning but misses the tone, and that in poetry tone is of course everything. I have been reckless with literal meaning, and laboured hard to get the tone.

Most often this has been *a* tone, for *the* tone is something that will always more or less escape transference to another language and cultural moment.[9]

This begins with an instance of that shimmy of argument which we encountered in Chapter 4. Translation is eschewed for the sake of something that might be given a different name—in this case 'imitation'—but which is still conceived as translation, though of a special kind: the 'getting' and 'transference' of 'tone'. The work of the 'usual reliable translator' could readily be labelled 'interpretation', as could Lowell's labour in pursuit of 'the tone', though with the proviso that this is in a less 'black and white', more Arnoldian, actorly, or musical vein. So far, both translator and imitator remain focused on the source, aiming to 'expound' it or give us a 'sense' of it. But then something different happens. Just as with Gadamer's word 'Schöpfung', the imitator's text breaks away from its source: 'the tone' becomes '*a* tone' as the original aim of transference is trumped by the need to compose a poem that Lowell can hear in English.

If we look at it from a hermeneutic point of view, that is, asking what a Lowell 'imitation' can show us about its source, the significance of this moment is plain. The imitation turns away from what it set out to imitate: it ceases to be a sure guide to the 'tone' of the original any more than it ever reliably conveyed the 'literal meaning'. But looked at ethically, that is, as a kind of behaviour towards the source and the person who wrote it (insofar as his intentions can be ascertained), Lowell's action becomes more complex. He eschews direct responsibility to his originals; but does so in the name of a higher responsibility, that of writing a poem, for in poetry tone is 'everything'. If the source texts, and their authors, are assumed to share the same commitment, then this higher responsibility is also a responsibility towards them, albeit an indirect one. A similar feeling must underlie many instances of poet-translators saying 'it just isn't working in English: I'll try something different'. Clearly, in the translation of poetry, such a move sometimes, perhaps often, has to be made. But how can this indirect responsibility towards the source be distinguished from mere appropriation of it? The argument needs tying down to particular cases.

When *Imitations* was nearly ready to be published, Lowell sent it to Elizabeth Bishop. 'The atmosphere of the book as a whole', she wrote back, seems 'vivid and personal and *you*.' But then her admiration was overwhelmed by unease:

> You have been careful to call them 'Free translations' and of course that does leave you free to change the line-order, interpolate, point up, call Zeus Jehovah, maybe, put in those 'plebescites'—all for good and obvious reasons.

(In Baudelaire sometimes an up-to-date phrase has a wonderful effect.) But once in a while I think you have made changes that *sound* like *mistakes*, and are open to misinterpretation. Or you have made the poet say the opposite of what he said in the original (a few times). The Rimbaud and Baudelaire poems are all so well known that I don't think you should lay yourself open to charges of carelessness or ignorance or willful perversity...[10]

Bishop recognizes the 'good and obvious reasons' of poetic necessity: of having to reshape, or point up, or update. What drives her to object is in part a suspicion of inaccuracy: of what seems to be ignorance; of what sound like mistakes. But as the protest grows it develops an ethical timbre: not only error but misrepresentation ('you have made the poet say the opposite of what he said'); not only ignorance but 'carelessness' and 'willful perversity'. She gives the example of 'The Malicious Girl', imitated from Rimbaud's 'La Maline'. There is, as she again tactfully puts it, 'what *looks* like a mistake'. In the draft Lowell had rendered 'la cuisine s'ouvrit avec une bouffée' as 'the kitchen gave on a buffet'; in the final version he substituted words offered by Bishop: 'the kitchen opened with a blast'.[11] But in this case, too, she ends up being more worried by something less tangible:

> The poem strikes me as so much more light-hearted than you've made it, and the girl, fussing with plates to make an opening for conversation, is feminine, flirtatious, untidy, by implication young and pretty, 'naughty'— but not sordid or dirty. Although he likes to go in for adolescent shock, a lot of these early poems seem quite gay in spite of formal perfection.[12]

Bishop has a cumulative impression of justice not having been done. Not to the girl imagined in the poem, nor to the particular construction of gender that builds around her, nor therefore to the distinctiveness of the early Rimbaud as Bishop sees him, the challenge he throws out.

Lowell adopted many of Bishop's corrections but did not act on her wider criticism. That he felt the pressure of it, though, is suggested by the defensive rhetoric of the 'Introduction' to *Imitations*. 'My licenses have been many' he announces, in a tone that perhaps oscillates between confession and boast. 'I have been almost as free as the authors themselves', he says, in finding ways to make the poems 'ring right for me'.[13] So keen is Lowell to disclaim fidelity that he overstates his liberty. For *Imitations* very often sticks very close to its sources, so much so that the shift from catching 'the tone' to inventing '*a* tone' can be traced at the level of the phrase. Lowell will seem for a few lines to be labouring hard to get 'the tone', but then will turn away. For instance, at the end of Leopardi's 'l'Infinito':

> E come il vento
> Odo stormir tra queste piante, io quello
> Infinito silenzio a questa voce
> Vo comparando: e mi sovvien l'eterno,
> E le morte stagioni, e la presente
> E viva, e il suon di lei. Così tra questa
> Immensità s'annega il pensier mio:
> E il naufragar m'è dolce in questo mare.

(And as the wind / I hear rustling between these plants, I that / Infinite silence to this voice / go comparing: and the eternal comes over me, / And the dead seasons, and the present / And living, and the sound of it. So among this / Immensity my thought drowns: / And shipwreck is sweet to me in this sea.)

Lowell:

> and when the wind lifts roughing through the trees,
> I set about comparing my silence to those voices,
> and I think about the eternal, the dead seasons,
> things here at hand and alive,
> and all their reasons and choices.
> It's sweet to destroy my mind
> and go down
> and wreck in this sea where I drown.[14]

'Roughing' is good for 'stormir', as is 'I set about comparing' for 'io . . . vo comparando'. The replacement of 'il suon di lei', 'the sound of it', by 'their reasons and choices' is probably one of those changes that Bishop would take to be justified by the need to write sufficiently arresting English verse: it is hard—as other translations have demonstrated—to follow the spiralling movement of the source here without losing imaginative pressure. When he transforms 'quello / Infinito silenzio' into 'my silence', Lowell says the opposite of Leopardi; but then the shiftingness of the comparison between mind and landscape goes some way towards explaining the reversal. Altogether, the movement of the first five lines of this extract is close to the Italian; and the tone is too, at least as it sounds to me.

Then comes the switch: 'it's sweet', much more casual than 'm'è dolce' ('dolce' has high literary associations going back to the 'dolce stil nuovo' practised by Dante, Guinizelli, and others seven centuries ago); 'destroy my mind', with its 1960s' timbre; the suddenly short line; the transformation of Leopardi's soft last noun, 'mare' ('sea'), into an active verb which paradoxically affirms in grammar the identity that is said to be dissolving: 'I drown'.

Similar local hardenings of tone happen throughout *Imitations*: the paradigmatic example is perhaps in 'Dora Markus', where Montale's 'rari uomini, quasi immoti' ('rare men, almost motionless') becomes 'a handful of men, dull as blocks'.[15] Just like Muldoon, in the translation of 'L'anguilla' which we explored in Chapter 4, Lowell brings the impulses of the source into a medium which is in some respects his own: not only American English, and not only American poetry, but American poetry as he can write it. In consequence the volume has, as Bishop said, great vividness, and also great consistency. Nevertheless, it is possible to feel that Lowell—to borrow a phrase from Spivak—might have held his agency a little more at bay; to feel that he too readily slips into a mode of response which Peter Robinson has sharply defined as 'colonizing another person's occasion for a display of incompatible mannerisms'.[16] This is a suspicion that cannot be proved either way, but only—like much else in criticism— held open to a judgement that is inextricably both ethical (insofar as what we are faced with is, at least in part, one person's behaviour towards another) and aesthetic (in that the behaviour is directed also at creating something beautiful). As we saw, Muldoon's 'firebrand' for 'torcia', 'green and pleasant spawning-ground' for 'paradisi di fecondazione', and so on, moved through interpretation and on into something that might better be called collaborative creativity (the echo of Heaney; the hint of Cromwell). Yet this flow of imagination seemed to have been guided by the source, to have been lifted into aesthetic brilliance by the awareness of being answerable to Montale. In contrast, Lowell's 'destroy my mind' and 'dull as blocks' are clichés. They seem not so much to respond to their sources as to shout them down. Wanting to be confident that he has achieved 'tone', Lowell has reached for words that are all too easy to hear.

Robinson himself puts the familiar dilemma like this: 'I prefer translations that stick as close to their originals as possible, but which nevertheless aim to read as poems in their own language'.[17] But what counts as reading as a poem in English? It turns out that Robinson's definition is more ample than Lowell's:

> Your latest blouse, Mercedes
> of mercerized cotton
> has the fresh air of department stores
> where they kit us out for the sea
> with broadest-brimmed white hats
> dear provisioned shade! . . .
>
> La tua camicetta nuova, Mercedes
> di cotone mercerizzato
> ha il respiro dei grandi magazzini

> dove ci equipaggiavamo di bianchi
> larghissimi capelli per il mare
> cara provvista di ombra!...[18]

There is a strangeness to 'dear provisioned shade' and 'the fresh air of department stores' which marks them, not only as sticking close to, but as being palimpsests of the foreign words and sensibility. This verbal fidelity comes at the cost of patterns of sound, for, in Erba's Italian, the precise terms of the description are animated by a swell of alliteration and internal rhyme: 'camicetta...Mercedes...cotone...mercerizzato'; 'grandi magazzini...equipaggiavamo...bianchi / larghissimi...mare / cara'. The translation is flat by comparison: were Lowell to read it, one can imagine him thinking it had no 'tone'. Robinson gives us the precision of 'broadest-brimmed white hats' and leaves it to us to imagine into it, if we can, the note of perhaps slightly comic amplitude which could better have been suggested by a less semantically accurate adjective such as 'enormous'. Yet poetry has the liberty to be puzzling: as we have just seen, the danger of wanting to sound hearably English is that you will come out with the indisputable English of cliché.

Throughout the history of English literature, contact with foreign languages has been a spur to poetic invention. Again and again the clumsy foreignness we call 'translationese' has merged into the prized strangeness of the language of poetry. It happens in Chaucer, in Shakespeare, in Milton, in Dryden, in Byron, in Browning, in Pound: the instances are innumerable, and we shall explore some of them in the pages that follow. Robinson's uncompromising phrases are a small, distinctive instance. The challenge of interpretation they hold out has arisen because English has been kept so close to Italian; but it also has the thought-adjusting power of the literary. If you ask 'how come "fresh air"?' or 'in what sense "provisioned"?' you are led into rewarding areas of imagination (the cool air of indoors? the promise of the summer? 'air' as in look? etc.; 'provisioned' as in 'anticipated'? as suggesting picnics? etc.). Robinson goes hardly any distance along Lowell's slide through interpretation and re-creation to new creation. The result is a text that is perhaps stranger to English readers than the source is to Italians: maybe 'flatter'—to recall Gadamer's terms—but almost certainly not 'clearer'. It leaves readers with nearly all the pleasures of interpretation still before them.

Poetry is 'lost in translation', Robert Frost declared; and he went on to say that poetry is also 'lost in interpretation'.[19] Both ideas, and the link between them, command widespread assent today, for reasons that have roots in the arguments put forward by Gadamer and Lowell. The work of translation, the feeling goes, ends up producing a text that is inevitably 'clearer and flatter' than its source; and this is then taken to be inherently a bad

thing. 'Translation', we read in a column in the *Guardian*, 'entails clarification, and since poetry is a series of assigned ambiguities, such clarification necessarily reduces it.'[20] In consequence, a translation that hopes
to offer readers the complex pleasures of poetry must—it is assumed—at
some point jettison its responsibility to the source; ditch 'the tone' so that
'*a* tone' can be achieved. Poet-translators must finally stop translating and
just compose if they are to produce translations that are also (as the usual
phrase has it) 'poems in their own right'.

Robinson's work and Lowell's practice (rather than his theory), in their
different ways, both disrupt this set of assumptions. Robinson's translations achieve the strangeness and complexity of poetry by interpreting as
little as possible. Lowell, on the other hand, does something more than
interpretation: he imposes his own voice. But this overplus feels like a
falling short of what poetry should be. For no poem is a poem in its
own right. Poetry establishes itself as poetry by relating to other ways
with language: echoing some, for instance earlier poems, and departing
from others, for instance cliché. A poem is an instance of imaginative
behaviour. The way it places itself, its poise in relation to other language
and the people who use it, and, finally, its responsibility towards them, all
this forms part of its value. For the particular range of poems that are
translations-or-imitations-or-versions, a crucial bit of the linguistic sur-
roundings to which they must relate is the source text: how the
translation-or-imitation-or-version behaves towards it cannot but become
part of its meaning. This relationship can be checked up on by comparing
the source. But it also makes itself felt in the texture of the poem-translation.
Muldoon's imagination in 'The Eel' is goaded and honed by the endeavour
to do justice to Montale. Lowell's, in the instances we have explored,
thickens and falters when it turns away from the challenge of the source.
Translating and writing poetry can merge into a single endeavour. Equally, a
carelessness towards the source can result in easy, disappointing verse.

As a metaphor for translation, 'interpretation' is, then, both unavoidable and treacherous. As we saw in Chapter 3, interpretation has a part in
any translation. Even Robinson interprets-and-creates to a small extent as
he turns 'larghissimi' into 'broadest-brimmed' or 'respiro' into 'fresh air'.
If a translation adopts the figure of interpretation more vigorously, this
may be done in the service of poetry: it may be a move away from the
automatism of word-for-wording, an endeavour to imagine what really
matters in the poem, to conjure up the 'ur-poem' that lies within or
behind or beyond it. But this push to grasp the source may also feel
inimical to poetry: it may issue in something uninterestingly flat and clear,
that is simply 'an interpretation'. In that case, the poet-translator's reaction may be to hold back from interpreting, as we have seen Robinson do.

On the other hand, the source may seem to require a more imaginative response: translation as interpretation in the musical or actorly sense; and perhaps something beyond that, interpretation fading into new creation. This can happen in ways that are more responsible towards the source (like the example from Muldoon) or less (like the instances from Lowell). The difference is not so much in the degree of departure from the words of the source, as in the attitude with which it is done. It is possible for texts to be more creatively responsive than those we have explored so far and still not turn their backs on their sources, still not disclaim the responsibility of being at once poems and translations.

Take for instance Jamie McKendrick's version of Catullus 12, 'The Napkin Lifter':

> Marrucinus Asinius, your sinister manoeuvre—
> letting your left hand hover over
> a fellow diner's lap as he leans to hear
> a punchline or pour wine
> from a carafe—respects neither
> the gods of wine nor conversation.
> And what does it mean? It means I'm afraid
> you're at your old trick of stealing napkins
> – an act that isn't that clever, nor even that skilful,
> merely sad and graceless in my book.
>
> Marrucine Asini, manu sinistra
> non belle uteris in ioco atque vino:
> tollis lintea neglegentiorum.
> hoc salsum esse putas? fugit te, inepte:
> quamvis sordida res et invenustast.[21]

Asinius Marrucinus, your left hand / You do not nicely use when we are joking and drinking: / You steal the napkins of the negligent / You think that funny? get away with you, fool / it is the lowest, most graceless thing.

There is much in what McKendrick has written that is not word for word. In fact, this is in the boundary zone of what is likely to be accepted as translation (and much freer than McKendrick's usual practice in translating from Italian). But does it therefore abandon 'the tone' for '*a* tone'? Or ask to be taken as 'a poem in its own right'? In the opening lines, 'your left hand' translates 'manu sinistra'; but so also does 'sinister man-oeuvre'. This must, admittedly, be in part a Lowellian 'licence', a turning away from the source so as to make the English 'ring right'. But it is also simultaneously a delving-in, for 'sinister' brings out an implication that is much stronger in the Latin 'sinistra' than in the English 'left'. The texture of the words helps us to feel that the two languages are being aligned: 'sinister' and 'manoeuvre', etymologically descended from 'manu' and 'sinistra', form a bridge between the frank Latin of the name with which the poem begins and the familiar English of its second line. It is as though Catullus were slowly getting the hang of a prosthetic tongue, or as though we readers were being tuned in to the alien scene and sensibility, leaning in, like the fellow diner, so as to feel our way through the half-rhymes 'manoeuvre' and 'hover' until we 'hear'. To read these lines as poetry 'in English' is to see that English is not only itself but blends into Latin, and to see also that this piece of English writing is a poem, not despite being a translation, but by virtue of how it is behaving towards the poem by Catullus that came before it, and which it has taken on the responsibility of representing here and now.

The phrase 'hover over', which has a place in that pattern of suggestion about the layering of translation and source, again also probes into the Latin, helping us modern readers to visualize the scene. Contrast Josephine Balmer's more straightforward translation:

> Asinius Maruccinus, it's not right
> what your left hand is doing: in wine and laughter
> you're lifting our napkins when we're not looking.
> You think you're clever? You fool, it's impolite,
> just about as cheap and graceless as one gets.[22]

This keeps closer to the words of the original but does not attempt to summon up the world of assumptions in which their meanings can unfurl. We have to work out for ourselves that the scene is a dinner party, that the people are reclining, and just how the 'lifting' of 'napkins' is being done. Of course, all this is left implicit by Catullus too; but it would have been much more quickly inferred by a Roman reader than it is likely to be by a modern. Again, McKendrick delays the mention of 'stealing napkins'; but this allows him to do justice to another meaning that is latent in the Latin. It is not that everyone's napkins are being nicked the same evening; rather, as Kenneth Quinn notes in his edition of Catullus, 'the plural . . . helps to turn Asinius into a habitual thief'.[23] Similar changes throughout the poem can be understood in the same terms. McKendrick reaches through the Latin words to imagine the 'ur-poem' they might represent, and re-represents it, as much as possible, in English words.

One of the most striking characteristics of this version is its conjuring of a voice, one that speaks (it seems to me) with elegant hauteur. Is this 'the tone' or '*a* tone'? Balmer's attempt at chatty vehemence, with its brash clash of 'not right' and 'left hand', might, on first encounter, feel closer to 'hoc salsum esse putas? fugit te, inepte'. But it is hard to imagine anyone actually saying 'you fool, it's impolite'. Searching for a hearable tone in the

Latin, McKendrick must have remembered Catullus's grandeur, his rich family, his life at the heart of the Roman *jeunesse dorée*. Of course, this is not unequivocally 'the tone' of the source: no text has an unequivocal tone. And of course McKendrick's words too might be taken in different ways, for instance with a more fussy, precisian timbre than I have suggested. Nevertheless, the process of creating a tone in English does not end up ditching the source; rather, it is inseparable from trying to discern a tone in the Latin. The endeavour to write poetry and the endeavour to achieve a translation are intertwined.

Where Robinson's translation from Erba does less than is implied by the metaphor 'translation is interpretation', this translation from Catullus does more. Yet, just like the Robinson Erba, this text leaves readers with much interpreting still to do: the English words are poised so as to prompt readers in the direction of McKendrick's imagining of Catullus's imagining, and to wonder also about the relation between the two. Especially so because this is one of those interesting occasions when the source text includes a double of what the translator might be up to, and so is able to stimulate the poetry of translation. Is translation too no better than a 'sinister manoeuvre'? We are prompted to ask this especially at the interpolated question 'and what does it mean?' The poem's speaker, its readers, and its implied translator can all share in putting this question; and it can be directed at the 'it' which is the translation itself as well as at Marrucinus Asinius's behaviour. Is the translator too engaged in stealing under the guise of conviviality, lifting Catullus's poem and making it his own? Yet, by drawing attention to this danger, the translation moves to defuse it. Even the innuendo introduced by the echo of 'shirt-lifter' in the poem's title joins in the play of rejection and recognition, Asinius's unwanted intrusions into people's 'laps' uneasily echoing the closeness of translator to author. The flicker of self-reference acts like a pre-emptive apology, turning this Englished writing into an instance of the kind of behaviour— respectful, skilful—that is valued by the poem's speaker. There is nothing here of the odour of theft, or at least gracelessness, that sometimes clings to poems offered, in Lowell's wake, as 'versions', 'imitations', or 'poems in their own right': McKendrick's poetry emerges from an act of relating to Catullus's; his poem-translation draws attention to that act, and suggests ways of making sense of it. Accepting the invitation held out by the Latin, McKendrick does unto Catullus as he would be done by.

9

Interpretation and 'Opening': Dryden, Chapman, and Early Translations from the Bible

In the introduction to *Imitations* there is no mention of Ezra Pound, Lowell's obvious precursor (as we will see in Chapter 23). It is Dryden whose name pops up, casually, as though it is taken for granted that he is the obvious person to refer to.[1] Dryden supplied the title of Lowell's book; and what goes on within its covers is thoroughly in Dryden's debt as well, for his theory and practice of translation searched the borderlands between interpretation and invention, between catching 'the tone' and creating '*a* tone'. Dryden's sense of the shiftingness of the ground in this area can be seen even in his famous tripartite definition of translation, in the Preface to *Ovid's Epistles* (1680):

> All translation I suppose may be reduced to these three heads.
>
> First, that of metaphrase, or turning an author word by word, and line by line, from one language into another. Thus, or near this manner, was Horace his *Art of Poetry* translated by Ben Jonson. The second way is that of paraphrase, or translation with latitude, where the author is kept in view by the translator, so as never to be lost, but his words are not so strictly followed as his sense, and that too is admitted to be amplified, but not altered. Such is Mr. Waller's translation of Virgils Fourth *Aeneid*. The third way is that of imitation, where the translator (if now he has not lost that name) assumes the liberty not only to vary from the words and sense, but to forsake them both as he sees occasion; and taking only some general hints from the original, to run division on the ground-work as he pleases. Such is Mr. Cowley's practice in turning two Odes of Pindar, and one of Horace, into English.[2]

This explanatory structure underlies Lowell's threefold gradation of 'literal meaning', 'the tone', and '*a* tone', though the nuances are different. For Dryden, even more than for Lowell, the announced categories cannot but blur. Only the tiniest snippet of translation could ever be strictly 'word by word, and line by line', so Jonson's Horace is said to be 'thus, *or near this manner*': it already displays some of that 'latitude' which is then taken to distinguish 'paraphrase'. In Dryden's time, word-for-word translation was commonly contrasted with a second kind, 'sense-for-sense': this binary goes back through St Jerome to Horace and Cicero even though— as Rita Copeland has shown—what it actually meant in practice changed markedly through the centuries.[3] Dryden's 'paraphrase' is a rangier category than the usual 'sense-for-sense'. It overlaps with metaphrase, for to say that the 'words' are 'not so strictly followed' as the 'sense' implies that they are still being followed to some degree. At the other extreme, a concatenation of terms for liberty—from 'amplified' to 'altered' to 'vary' to 'forsake'—leaps the supposed boundary between paraphrase and imitation. By saying that 'imitation' has the liberty '*not only to vary* from the words and sense...' Dryden implies that 'paraphrase' too is able to 'vary'—but is not 'to vary from' a step beyond 'to amplify' and almost the same as 'to alter'?[4]

The tendency of word to morph into sense, and expansion into change, itches unstoppably in Dryden's discussions of translation. Cowley, he says, had no choice but to translate Pindar in the 'way' of 'imitation':

> So wild and ungovernable a poet cannot hope to be translated literally...; a genius so elevated and unconfined as Mr Cowley's was but necessary to make Pindar speak English, and that was to be performed by no other way than imitation.[5]

So this imitation, at least, it seems, does keep the author 'in view'. But almost immediately the opposite feeling bursts into the discussion, and we are informed that imitation is 'the greatest wrong which can be done to the memory and reputation of the dead'.[6] Dryden later said that his own translation of the *Aeneid* (1697) was 'betwixt the two Extreams' of 'Paraphrase' and 'Metaphrase'; and the translations of Juvenal and Persius, done by various people, that he prefaced with his 'Discourse Concerning Satire' (1692) were 'betwixt a paraphrase and imitation'.[7] Back in the Preface to *Ovid's Epistles* he had announced a commitment to paraphrase; but even here, only a few pages later, it is shuffled off: 'I am ready to acknowledge that I have transgressed the rules which I have given, and taken more liberty than a just translation will allow'.[8]

The tentativeness of these definitions shows Dryden's honesty as a critic: unlike some of the modern theorists I mentioned in Part I, he does not squeeze the complexities of actual writing to fit his categories. But it also owes something to earlier discussions by which he was influenced, especially the searching epistle 'To the Reader' with which George Chapman prefaced the 1609 and 1611 editions of his translation from the *Iliad*.

Chapman rejects 'word-for-word traductions' on the usual grounds of ungainliness:

> ... they lose
> The free grace of their naturall Dialect
> And shame their authors with a forced Glose.

And he deprecates no less any translators who would take 'more licence from the words than may expresse / Their full compression and make cleare the Author'. Chapman's own translation, or 'conversion', he says, 'much abates / The licence they take'. And yet Chapman cannot, any more than Dryden, fix a firm distinction between the kind of translation he professes and those he deplores. For he too feels that some freeing-up has to be done by a translator: the 'compression' of words needs 'expressing', just as Dryden's paraphrast is allowed to 'amplify' and perhaps even 'vary' the original's 'sense'. Some 'periphrases', Chapman says, are 'needful'—and 'periphrase', defined by Puttenham (in 1589) as 'circumlocution', implies, if anything, more expansion than 'paraphrase': it is a 'great aid to *Prolixity*', Pope was later to point out in *Peri Bathous* (1727). Chapman is especially exercised by the example of those 'Commentars'—editors and annotators—who have tried to 'showe' Homer, but in the wrong way:

> They fail'd to search his deep and treasurous hart.
> The cause was since they wanted the fit key
> Of Nature, in their down-right strength of Art,
> With Poesie to open Poesie—

Chapman's hostility towards these scholars must have been fuelled by a feeling of indebtedness for, like almost every early-modern translator from Greek, he needed the crutch of parallel text Latin translation and notes: principally the 'traduction' derived from Andreas Divus and the exposition reiterated from the twelfth-century commentator Eustathius which were found in the edition by Spondanus that he mainly used. As Phyllis Bartlett has made plain, explanations from Spondanus are brought into the first, partial printing of Chapman's translation, the *Seaven Bookes of the Iliades* (1598), but then are often excised from it in rewriting, only then occasionally to creep back in. The same happens with some of his own more idiosyncratic 'discoveries' of Homer's meaning. In 1598, Agamemnon warns Achilles not to think

> ... that thy feet into thy breath can transmigrated bee
> To passe me with thy sleightes as well as in outrunning mee

Chapman is trying to bring out fully the etymological layering of παρέρχομαι, to 'pass by' or 'outwit'. In 1609 all this extrapolation must have struck him as extravagant and was replaced by the plain 'outgoe' (other ideas were pressing in around it). But then in 1611 something of the first flowering is allowed to reoccur: 'tis not your swift foot can / Outrun me here...' Scholars have proposed various overarching explanations for Chapman's second and third thoughts. The changes generally show him moving from a more 'ethical' to a more 'Aristotelian' view of the *Iliad* as 'based on emotion and turning on calamity'; they reveal a growing 'discomfort with what his 1598 Agamemnon terms "contumelious wordes"'; they erase the connection between Achilles and the Earl of Essex which had been strong in the 1598 *Seaven Bookes* (Essex was that volume's dedicatee); they 'strip away the familiarizing intermediary of Virgil from the unfamiliar form of Homer'.[9] Yet all these factors can come into play only because of a fundamental malleability in Chapman's theory and practice. He was uncertain as to how much 'opening' his translation ought to do.

Wanting to distinguish translation from the explanation offered by commentary, and yet at the same time including explanation among the translator's aims, Chapman recognizes the conflict that is glossed over by modern critics who equate translation and interpretation. His perplexity has its roots far back in the beginnings of translation into English; especially in translation from the Bible where 'open' had become a charged word. 'Translation it is that openeth the window, to let in the light' wrote the translators of the Authorized Version in 1611.[10] Translation illuminates, obviously, by making the Bible available to people who do not know Latin or Greek or Hebrew; and it joins with the technology of printing to spread the word among a wide readership. A century and a half earlier, Caxton had been inseparably a printer and a translator, for he had had to translate in order to meet the new demand for books.[11] And in 1535, Miles Coverdale, in the Prologue to his own translation of the Bible, gave thanks to God 'that he hath opened vnto his church the gyfte of interpretacyon & of pryntyng'.[12]

By 'interpretacyon', Coverdale means both the interpretation that is part of translation, and the interpretation by lay readers that translation makes possible. Both are implied when he says that, with so many people now endeavouring to interpret scripture, 'every one doth his best to be nyest the marke': it is 'lyke as whan many are shutynge [shooting] together'.[13] So 'opening', in the context of the Bible, has multiple and intermingled denotations: translation, the circulation of books, and the processes of interpretation through which Protestant readers open the text further for themselves, discovering its truths in line with their consciences and bringing them to bear on the conduct of their lives. As the Authorized Version put it, translation 'removeth the cover of the well, that we may come by the water, even as *Jacob* rolled away the stone from the mouth of the well, by which means the flocks of *Laban* were watered'.[14] This application of Genesis 29.10 is itself one of the range of possible 'openings', a perception of relevance. The initial 'openings' of translation and printing enabled further such 'openings' to multiply.

Both Coverdale and the King James translators play down the possibility that, when it comes to interpretation, openness may lead to anarchy. For there is a difference between reading and Coverdale's metaphor of shooting. In shooting, all the competitors can see the same targets; but in Bible interpretation, everyone may end up feeling they have hit their own private bullseye. For opponents of the Reformation this was a disaster. The interconnections of translation, doctrine, and institutional change in the period are of course hugely complex.[15] Nevertheless, it is broadly fair to say that loyalty to the Roman Catholic Church entailed hostility to the spread of 'opening' and a belief that the Bible should be held close in the interpretive embrace of the priesthood.[16] In 1582 the Church sanctioned a translation which was done, paradoxically, in order to resist the 'opening' tendencies that inevitably attach to all translations in some degree. The Rheims-Douai version stuck lovingly to the vocabulary of its source, in the hope that Greekisms such as 'didragmes', 'parasceve', and 'paraclete' could be made to do as English words. But this simply meant that further translation was required, as even the Rheims-Douai's own Preface could not but self-contradictorily show:

> How is it possible to expresse *Evangelizo*, but as we do, *Evangelize*? for *Evangelium* being the Gospel, what is *Evangelizo* or *to Evangelize*, but to shew the glad tydyngs of the Gospel, of the time of grace, of al Christes benefites? Al which signification is lost, by translating as the English bibles do, *I bring you good tydings*.[17]

The word is confidently translated ('what is *Evangelizo*...but to shew the glad tydyngs', etc.) in the course of an argument that asserts its untranslatability.

The linguistic possibility of translation was not all that was at stake. Protestant translators sought, not only to make the Bible comprehensible to a wide audience, but to distinguish its language from that enshrined in the traditions of the Church. Fifty years before Rheims-Douai, Thomas More attacked Tyndale for having translated the Greek ἐκκλησία as 'congregation', not 'church', and πρεσβύτερος as 'senior', not 'priest', among other similar choices. There were precedents in the Latin tradition of Bible translation: 'senior' and 'congregatio' appear in both Erasmus's

Latin New Testament and the Vulgate.[18] Yet, by calquing those Latin words into English, Tyndale disconnects the Bible from the institutional language of Church and priesthood. As Brian Cummings has put it, 'the reader is made to feel' that 'priest' and suchlike words 'were never used or intended in the New Testament but were fabricated by the church'.[19] This is what angered More: 'Tyndale must in his English translation take his English words as they signify in English', he said, meaning that he should use the terms adopted by the Church for its institutions, 'rather than as the words signify in the tongue out of which they were taken into the English'.[20] In reply, Tyndale made a small linguistic concession but did not waver in his Protestant intent. He admitted that 'senior' was 'no very good English' and amended it—not to 'priest', but to 'elder'.[21]

For Protestants, then, translation enabled also an 'opening' of the power structures of the Church. In consequence, the *via media* pursued by the Anglican translators of 1611, as they gathered and adjusted all the work done by Tyndale and his successors, was inseparably linguistic and doctrinal:

> Wee haue on the one side auoided the scrupulositie of the Puritanes, who leaue the olde Ecclesiasticall words, and betake them to other, as when they put *washing* for *Baptisme*, and *Congregation* in stead of *Church:* as also on the other side we haue shunned the obscuritie of the Papists, in their *Azimes, Tunike, Rational, Holocausts, Prœpuce, Pasche*, and a number of such like, whereof their late Translation is full, and that of purpose to darken the sence, that since they must needs translate the Bible, yet by the language thereof, it may bee kept from being vnderstood.[22]

Done 'by his Maiesties speciall Comandement' and 'appointed to be read in Churches'—as the title page announces—the 1611 translation at once 'opens' the Bible and encloses it in an English ecclesiastical tradition.

Throughout the early history of the Englishing of the Bible, doctrinal and political anxieties had pressed in on matters of linguistic detail. During the 1380s and 1390s, probably in Oxford, followers of Wycliffe engaged in intense translatorly work on the Bible, establishing the source text, translating more or less word for word, and then revising their first efforts into a more comprehensible and elegant English.[23] The Prologue to the fully revised translation of the 1390s reflects on this process, and sums it up in what was to become an influential justification of 'opening':

> The beste translating is, out of Latyn into English, to translate aftir the sentence, and not oneli after the wordis, so that the sentence be as opin either openere in English as in Latyn, and go not fer from the lettre; and if the lettre mai not be suid in the translating, let the sentence evere be hool and open, for the wordis owen to serue to the entent and sentence.[24]

The movement of rumination here, with categories being distinguished and then blurred ('not oneli after the wordis . . . go not fer from the lettre'), has similarities to the passage of Dryden we examined earlier. If the letter may not be followed ('suid'), one must turn to the 'sentence', a word which, like 'entent', means 'sense'; although it could also—the *Middle English Dictionary* shows—signify 'a passage of prose or verse', a usage that would soon develop into our modern meaning, 'a series of words in connected speech or writing', which the *OED* first spots in 1447. If you are faced with 'equivok wordis', the Wycliffites recommend that you 'studie wel the sentence bothe bifore and aftir' so as to determine what they say: you establish the 'sentence' in its older meaning by reading through (and beyond) the rest of what we would call the 'sentence' today. Yet what, if we have Dryden in mind, is startling about the Wycliffite Preface is how tiny are the departures from the source that are having to be justified. It transpires that even the rendering of a Latin ablative absolute with 'while' counts as an 'opening': 'as thus *the maistir redinge, I stonde* mai be resolvid thus *while the maistir redith, I stonde*'.[25]

In the case of the Wycliffite Bible, it was not any linguistic detail that led to official condemnation, but rather the further 'opening' caused by the circulation of the translated texts. As David Lawton has put it, 'the question is not what? (An English Bible) but who? (who owns it?)'.[26] With his *Constitutions* of 1409, Archbishop Arundel not only banned unauthorized translation but restricted the preaching and discussion of Christian texts: thereafter, the 'symple men' whom the Wycliffites had in view could be found guilty of heresy for possessing a Bible translation, even though Henry VI himself owned one.[27] Nevertheless, echoes of the Wycliffites' unease about the first stage of 'opening' the 'letter' are discernible in many subsequent Bibles, where little added words like 'while' were marked in parentheses, as by Coverdale, or italics, as in both the Geneva Bible of 1560 and the Authorized Version. And the sensitivities hereabouts were well grounded, for the nub of Luther's attack on the Roman Catholic Church was enclosed in just such a tiny explanatory adjustment: the insertion of 'allein', 'alone', before the word 'Glauben', 'faith', in Romans 3.28, translated in the Authorized Version as 'a man is justified by faith without the deeds of the law'.[28] Luther protested that he had merely opened 'the sense of the text' ('die meinung des text') into the sort of German that is in 'daily use' ('teglichen brauch'):

> If you speak of two things, of which you affirm and deny the other, then you use the word 'solum'—only (allein)—along with the word 'not' or 'no'. As when you say: 'the farmer brings allein grain and no money' (allein korn und

kein geldt); 'no, I really have no money, but only grain' (nicht geldt /
sondern allein korn).[29]

Luther was a startlingly vigorous and confident translator, 'as familiar with
or even as rude to the Bible'—in Diarmaid MacCulloch's view—'as with
the most intimate of old friends'.[30] The typographical conventions
adopted by Coverdale and the others express a more tentative attitude:
they draw attention to the element of interpretation that is inherent
in their translations (and in all translation, as we have seen). By so
doing, they make visible a radical uncertainty as to where the boundary
of translation lies. The words in parentheses or italics were necessary to
'open' the text, and so were in that respect its most crucial elements, the
words that really did the work of translating. And yet, for exactly that
reason, they introduced an unignorable difference from the source, and so
had to be marked out from the words that were felt to be translation
rigidly conceived.

The paradox appears in perhaps its purest form in the Wycliffites'
'major precursor', Richard Rolle's translation of the Psalter (1340):

> In the translacioun .i. folow the lettere as mykyll as .i. may. And thare. i. fynd
> na propire ynglis. i. folow the wit of the worde, swa that thai shall red it
> thaim thare noght dred errynge. In expounynge. i. fologh haly doctours. for
> it may come in som envyous man hand that knawes noght what he sould say,
> that wil say that. i. wist noght what i. sayd, and swa doe harme til hym. and
> til othere.[31]

Rolle's text includes an explanatory commentary: this is what he refers to
when he talks of 'expounynge', in contrast to 'the translacioun'. Yet the
distinction wobbles in just the same way as in all the later texts we have
explored. 'Translacioun' requires Rolle to depart from 'the lettere' and
'folow the wit of the worde'. This cannot but bring in the possibility
of 'errynge'; the need for 'expounynge', with the help of holy doctors, at
once becomes evident. In the text itself, 'translacioun' and 'expounynge'
become even harder to separate. Here, for instance, is the beginning of
Psalm 10:

> In domino confido: quomodo dicitis anime mee, transmigra in montem
> sicut passer. // In lord i. traist: how say ye til my saule, overpasse in til the hill
> as a sparow. // The voice of haly kyrke answers till heretikis and fals brether.
> In my lord i. trayst, that saves all that hopes in him. how then say ye til my
> saule. a blamynge it is. passover in till the hill. that is, come in til oure lyf and
> folow us. that is as a hill heghe in vertu. there ere false brethere that will seme
> goed and ere noght. or that semes bettire than thai ere. and spekis & demys
> all men, bot if thai outher lif at thaire will or folow thaim. bot i will noght

take thaim till my counsaile: for thai haf godis malyson. and if i.doe .i. sall be
like a sparou. that is, unstabile and lyght and withouten charite. as thai ere.[32]

The first English sentence is what is offered up as the 'translacioun': it
sticks as close as possible to the 'lettere' of the Latin. But when the
'translacioun' is repeated in the third section of text, ostensibly so as to
be subjected to 'expounynge', it alters, loosening a little as though to ready
itself for the further opening of commentary. 'In lord' becomes 'In my
lord'; and this tiny interpretive sally is justified by the commentary which
precedes and follows: there is a speaker, 'haly kyrke', who can safely be
thought to call God 'mine' because 'he saves all that hope in him'. The
next phrase too is ever so slightly expanded: 'how say ye til my saule'
becomes 'how then say ye til my saule'. This allows into the translation a
hint of the tone that is identified in the commentary: 'a blamynge it is'.
After this generically unstable passage, the text moves into the frank
'opening' of figurative and ethical interpretation.

Like all the texts we have explored, Rolle's Psalter reveals uncertainty
about the boundaries between translation and 'expounyge' or interpretation. Translation is itself an 'expounynge'. Even the strictest possible
following of 'the wordis' or of 'the lettere' is also translation of the 'wit'
or 'sentence': there are always choices to be made about which of the
possible 'literal' meanings is the most relevant. Yet it is everywhere
recognized that this sort of translation misses something: it is a 'forced
Glose', it is like dancing on ropes with fettered legs. The first step into
'opening' which is a 'word-for-word' translation therefore asks for the
further opening of 'sense-for-sense', that is, a translation which gives more
attention to each word's place in the surrounding texture. And this kind of
translation blurs into the further opening of commentary, and then the yet
further openings of application to people's lives, the spread of both
illumination and dissent. Translation is inextricably part of this avalanche
of 'opening'; and yet, as Coverdale's parentheses and the 1611 italics and
the uncertainties of all the discussions show, it has also to be held separate
from it. For, if it cannot be, it risks losing its status as truly representing
the text which all these other openings are openings of.

10

'Paraphrase' from Erasmus
to '*Venus* T----d'

By the late sixteenth century a new piece of terminology had arrived in English to describe the sort of writing that Rolle had called 'expounynge'. It was 'paraphrase', the word that Dryden was later to adopt for his preferred style, not of 'expounynge', but of translating. Yet this word too, no less than 'open', was dogged by ambiguity.

'Paraphrase' came into English via awareness, and translation, of Erasmus's paraphrases of the New Testament. The paraphrases, in Latin, were written to accompany a Latin translation: when both translation and paraphrase were brought into English (by a group of translators who included Princess Mary Tudor), generic and terminological confusion ensued. The prefatory material to the 1548 *First tome or volume of the Paraphrase of Erasmus vpon the Newe Testamente* at first seems wholly clear:

> A paraphrase is a plain setting forth of a text or sentence more at large, with such circumstaunce of moe and other wordes, as may make the sentence open, cleare, plaine, & familiar, whiche otherwise should perchaunce seme bare, vnfruitful harde, straunge rough, obscure, & derke to be vnderstanded of any that were ... vnlearned.[1]

Just like Rolle's 'expounynge', Erasmus's paraphrase offers an informed and sympathetic reading of the Bible text, 'opening' it by sketching in context, extrapolating feelings and motivations, and clarifying doctrinal consequences. Here, for instance, is a bit of Erasmus's translation (as Englished in 1548):

> But whan the Phariseis had heard that he had stopped the mouth of the Sadduceis, they came together, and one of them being Doctor of lawe, asked him a question, temptyng him.

And here is the corresponding passage of paraphrase:

> The Phariseis were not displeased that the Sadduceis were put to sylence, chiefly in a matter wherin they were cleane contrary one against another.

Therfore whan the Phariseis sawe them put to sylence, and rebuked also for ignoraunce of scripture, they taking harte of grace againe, gather together, and set forwarde a certayne doctor of lawe, which should goe unto Iesus with a clerkly question, that eyther he myght reproue hym of ignoraunce, or els he hymselfe beare away the prayse of learnyng.[2]

On the one hand, translation merges with paraphrase because it begins the process of opening which paraphrase continues; on the other, it has to be kept separate from paraphrase if it is to stand in for the text which the paraphrase is a paraphrase of. The tension here is just the same as in Rolle's Psalter.

Back in the prefatory material, the strain becomes impossible to manage. The word 'paraphrase' balloons to include translation too:

... in this English paraphrase the translatours haue of purpose studied rather to write a plain stile, then to vse their elegancie of speche, partely because there cannot in al pointes be expressed in the English tong the grace that is in the laten ... & partely because there was a special regarde to be had to the rude and vnlettred people, who perchaunce through default of atteigning to the high stile, should also thereby haue been defrauded of the profit and fruict of vnderstanding the sence, which thing that they might doe, was the onely pourpose why it was first translated, and now by the kinges most excellent Maiestie willed to be read.[3]

The translation into English has been done mainly for those who are 'rude and vnlettred' (i.e., cannot read Latin); and English is felt to be in itself a rather unsophisticated language. So the description of translation as something that makes 'plain' and supplies understanding overlaps with the definition of paraphrase that had been given only a page before. When Erasmus's Latin has been 'translated' it becomes 'this English paraphrase'.

As the word 'paraphrase' settled into English usage, it developed a new implication. The 'opening' of a Christian text to believers could include making it readily applicable to their lives in the present. In 1587 Thomas Stockwell translated from Daniel Tossanus *The lamentations and holy mourninges of the prophet Ieremiah with a lamentable paraphrase and exhortation, meete euery way to be applyed vnto these our dayes*. A century later, this idea of 'application' had spread to discovering sharply political relevance. An anonymous pamphlet of 1689 contained *A Poem on the Accession of Their Royal Highnesses the Prince and Princess of Orange to the Imperial Crown of England being a paraphrase on the 45 Psalm*. Via its characteristic processes of verbal dilation, paraphrase enables the text to expand its influence through time: a snippet of close translation in the margin, *'And thy Right Hand shall teach thee terrible Things'*, for instance, yields this bloodthirsty application:

> But since *Kings*, like *God*, must be
> For *Justice*, not for *Mercy* fam'd alone;
>   Since *Wise* as well as *Good*,
>   Is a fit Stile for *Majesty*:
> And since the harden'd *Rebels* Blood
> Still makes the strongest *Cement* for a *Throne*:
>   *Learn*, what thou well dost *Understand*,
>   *Learn*, from thy own dread *Right-hand;*
>   *Learn* from thence to act such *Things*,
> As become offended *Kings*.[4]

Not only biblical texts were liable to be treated in this way. Witness a broadside from the opposite political stance: *Englands sin, and shame: in a paralel between the degenerate estate of old Rome & Great Britain. Or, Hor. Lib. 3. Ode 6. Ad romanos de moribus sui faeculi corruptis. Occasionally paraphrased, and applyed for the 30th. of January 1672. Being the anniversary of the murder of that blessed martyr King Charles I.*

During the same period, 'paraphrase' also came to refer, simply, to translations in verse. Such a 'paraphrase' did not have to boast contemporary relevance, nor expound its sources, nor even expand them any more than was necessitated by metre and rhyme. In 1587, Thomas Watson's *Amyntas* was '*paraphrastically translated out of Latine into English hexameters*' by Abraham Fraunce. The English is not at all 'paraphrastic' in the sense of expansive or elucidative: it is pretty much line for line. But it does have a tic of repetition which it has caught from the source and developed. Watson's 'mentis inops, plenus cura, lachrymosus Amyntas', for instance, becomes 'halfe mad Amyntas, careful Amintas, mournful Amintas'.[5] The 'paraphrastically' in Fraunce's title, then, asks to be taken literally, as 'parallel phrasing': this is the principle not only of the translation's line-for-line connection to its source but of its internal organization. It is a paraphrase both of Watson's poem and of itself. The lesser repetition in the Latin is a figure of lament: it catches the way grief circlingly elaborates its object, expanding on it but not managing to escape it. The doubling, nay quadrupling, of repetition in the English translation creates a remarkable thwarted plangency; as here, where the reiteration of the name is Fraunce's innovation:

> But since Phillis, alas, did leave most cursed Amyntas,
> Pains have plagued, alas, both flesh and bones of Amintas,
> No day riseth, alas, but it heares these grones of Amintas,
> No night commeth, alas, that brings any rest to Amintas,
> Night and day thus, alas, stil Phillis troubleth Amintas.[6]

No change cometh, alas, to give us relief from 'Amintas'.

The 'paraphrase' that was verse translation could also stretch to include something like the expository paraphrase found in Erasmus. For instance, Thomas Middleton's first published work, *The Wisdome of Solomon Paraphrased* (1597), is a translation-cum-exposition in rhyme. The beginning of chapter 1, verse 3, 'for froward thoughts separate from God' in the Authorized Version, launches Middleton into this:

> Temptation rather seperates from God,
> Conuerting goodnes from the thing it was,
> Heaping the indignation of his rod,
> To bruse our bodies like a brittle glasse:
>   For wicked thoughts haue still a wicked end,
>   In making God our foe, which was our frend.[7]

The pattern continues, each whole verse of the source prompting two of these six-line stanzas. Some of the expansions—such as 'For wicked thoughts haue still a wicked end'—seem designed, like a prose paraphrase, 'to make the sentence open, cleare, plaine, & familiar'. But there are also figurative elaborations—'To bruse our bodies like a brittle glasse'. You might find this kind of thing in a sermon, but it is especially provoked by that complex pressure to double—to rephrase, to compare, to rhyme— which is typical of verse. George Sandys's *A Paraphrase upon the Divine Poems* (1638) keeps closer to its source, but still has the same mixed motives for expansion. It clarifies: Job's country of Uz, or 'Hus' as Sandys spells it, is pinpointed as 'a Land which neare the Suns uprise, / And Northern confines of Sabaea lies'. And it poeticizes, as when Job's 'seven sons and three daughters' flower into 'three beauteous Daughters, and seven hopefull Boyes' who 'renew'd his youth, and crown'd his Nuptiall Ioyes'.[8]

These adventures of the word 'paraphrase' extend the ambiguities that we traced in the word 'open'. Translation is inevitably an 'opening' in that it makes the original easier to understand. But for Bible texts, especially, this is a cause of anxiety: if a text is opened it is changed. Translators could quiet this worry to some extent by sticking as close as possible to their sources. But, in that case, their translations were felt to be incomplete unless they were further opened by 'expounynge' or 'paraphrase'. These kinds of writing were felt to be different from translation; but it also seemed that they were what really did the work of translation: they, after all, were what fully brought the meaning across. The ambivalence shows in the marking of explanatory words as not fully part of the text of the Bible translations to which they are nevertheless vital; and in the slippage of the word 'paraphrase' between meaning 'translation' and 'not-translation'.

An extreme manifestation of the widespread anxiety is Obadiah Walker's *Paraphrase and Annotations upon all the Epistles of St Paul* (1684). Here is his rendition of Romans 1.21:

> Because that when- [*as*] they knew God, [*yet*] they glorified [*and honored*] him not as God; neither were thankful [*to their maker, and Author of all that good;*[18]] but became vain [*and silly*] in their imaginations;[19] and their foolish heart [d] was darkned;[20]　　　 d Eph.4.17.

> 18 Or, for this light of knowledg, they had received.
> 19 And disquisitions about the creatures
> 20 With arrogance[9]

The words given the paradoxical status of necessary additions (here doubly cordoned off with parentheses and italics) are more numerous and more elaborative than in the Authorized Version: they are what justify the title 'paraphrase'. Yet, in line with an urge we have noticed before, they are felt to be not enough: more alternatives and elucidations spill out into the still more distanced category of 'Annotations'. The distinction seems arbitrary: there is little difference between attaching 'and silly' to 'vain' and 'with arrogance' to 'darkned'. The boundaries of 'paraphrase' are no firmer than those of 'translation': they too are asserted only to be breached.

As we saw in Chapter 4, the thing grasped in a translation, the whatever-it-is that can be thought of as being 'carried across', only exists in the collaboration between text and reader-translator. It only comes into being as the result of an 'opening'. If that is the case, how can you be sure that it is right? You cannot, any more than with any text: there is no 'rightness', finally, to be had. And so it is that the metaphor of translation-as-opening leads to more openings, more paraphrases. Sometimes these are done by the same person, as, remarkably, in Richard Baker's *Cato Variegatus or Catoes Morall Distichs: Translated and Paraphras'd, with variations of Expressing, in English verse* of 1636. Baker offers as many as twenty alternative versions of each distich. He comments:

> This kinde of writing, seemes not onely a way of meditation, but a Fruit: Not only an Exercise, but a Dilating of Invention; and if there were nothing else, but the Variety; we see, how much the Eye, is delighted with varietie of colours, in the same obiect.[10]

This begins by admitting the question it ends up shutting out: how do you distinguish between 'meditation' and 'Invention' or between 'colours' and 'obiect'? If all its words are different, can an 'obiect' still really be the same? An alternative way in which 'opening' spills over into more 'opening' is for the further paraphrases to be done by other people; for many, as Coverdale said, to shoot together. Sir John Denham expressed the same thought in the Preface to *The Destruction of Troy* (1656), though he called this translation from Virgil, not a 'paraphrase' but an 'essay' (meaning 'attempt'). He hoped, he said, to do Virgil 'more right... by opening this new way of translating this Author, to those whom youth, leisure, and better fortune makes fitter for such undertakings'.[11]

Once the 'opening' of 'paraphrase' has started, why should it ever stop? In theory, Baker could go on stretching the border of 'imitation' and 'invention' indefinitely: only convention (and no doubt some weariness) prevents him. But the possibility that 'paraphrase' might license pretty much anything was vigorously exploited in burlesque writing. For instance, *Ovid's Epistles*, the book that came prefaced with Dryden's advocacy of 'paraphrase' as a mode of translation, attracted a sharp anonymous rejoinder from the cavalier 'wit' Matthew Stevenson: *The Wits Paraphras'd, or, Paraphrase upon Paraphrase in a Burlesque on the Several Late Translations of Ovids Epistles*. Some despairing lines of Dido's, first paraphrased by Dryden like this:

> I rave: nor canst thou Venus' offspring be—
> Love's mother could not bear a son like thee.[12]

were paraphrased upon paraphrase to give this:

> I'm raging mad to think that *Venus*
> With such a Scoundrel shou'd bestein us;
> Such an unlucky Harlots Bird,
> Thou *Venus* Son? thou *Venus* T----d.[13]

In the Preface to *Ovid's Epistles*, Dryden had tried to discipline paraphrase's drift towards liberty by giving it a stipulative definition. He had distinguished it from 'imitation', and from 'metaphrase'—itself in fact just as blurry a term, although a less common one. He had asserted that 'the author is kept in view by the translator, so as never to be lost, but his words are not so strictly followed as his sense, and that too is admitted to be amplified, but not altered'. But, as we have seen, the confidence of these distinctions wobbles even in Dryden's critical prose. In his practice of translation (or is it paraphrase?—or is it something else...?), the ambiguities we have explored nourish some of his most searching verse.

11

Dryden, Behn, and what is 'secretly in the poet'

The anxieties attaching to Bible translation leave traces in the words with which Dryden frames his wobbly tripod of a definition. To translate 'too faithfully', he says in the Preface to *Ovid's Epistles*, 'is indeed pedantically; 'tis a faith like that which proceeds from superstition, blind and zealous'.[1] On the other hand—as Paul Davis has pointed out—the 'latitude' allowed to 'paraphrase' echoes 'the "Latitude-men" who rose to prominence within the Church of England a decade or so earlier offering liberty of opinion on a limited range of peripheral questions of doctrine'.[2] And terms from this discussion of translation in the Preface recur tellingly in the advice on interpretation of the Bible which Dryden was to include in *Religio Laici* a couple of years later: there, the 'honest layman', faced with a text that has been opened in different ways, should ask:

> Which exposition flows from genuine sense,
> And which is forced by wit and eloquence.[3]

Here too, 'sense' is allowed to be 'amplified, but not altered'.

Yet Dryden's definition was attached not to any religious text but to *Ovid's Epistles*—and his discussion of Ovid in particular, rather than translation in general, reveals a contrasting group of concerns. For Ovid was already more 'amplified' than he really needed to be. His genius, Dryden said, was in 'the description of the passions', but 'the copiousness of his wit was such that he often writ too pointedly for his subject, and made his person speak more eloquently than the violence of their passion would admit'. He needed a good editor; or to have edited himself in the wisdom of maturity: 'many things ought to have been retrenched, which I suppose would have been the business of his age if his misfortunes had not come too fast upon him'.[4]

This analysis opens the way for translation to supply the refinement that Ovid was not able to impose upon himself. Ovid's verse has come down to us, Dryden thinks, 'uncorrected': the translator might finish off the interrupted process of composition. Two decades later, in *Fables Ancient and Modern*, he was to do exactly this in his translation of Chaucer, a poet who, he said, 'resembled' Ovid 'in many things'. What struck Dryden as indiscipline in Chaucer's verse was owing not to any personal youthfulness but to his having 'lived in the infancy of our poetry': translating it into 'our language, as it is now refined', Dryden felt licensed to omit what he 'judged unnecessary or not of dignity enough'. Developments in the English language, in ways with verse, and in intellectual culture all contribute to the work of composition. The imaginative impulse, given a first provisional embodiment by Chaucer, can only reach perfect realization—Dryden feels—in the hands of a mature poet in fully modern circumstances.[5]

Ovid, of course, was not writing in the infancy of a language: his 'boyisms'—as Dryden called them—were his own. So when the thought of amending them pushes into the Preface to *Ovid's Epistles* it is at once repulsed: 'if the fancy of Ovid be luxuriant, 'tis his character to be so, and if I retrench it, he is no longer Ovid'.[6] That word 'character' suggests the complexity of Dryden's thinking here, for it spans the boundary between 'words' and 'sense' which he had only just erected. Twenty years later, again in the Preface to *Fables*, Ovid would be said to be distinguished by a particular 'turn of words'.[7] But here in the Preface to *Ovid's Epistles*, it is a 'particular turn of thoughts, and of expression' to which the translator must adapt himself; they 'are the characters that distinguish, and as it were individuate' the source poet. Translators must try 'to give his thought either the same turn if our tongue will bear it, or if not, to vary but the dress, not to alter or destroy the substance'. Rhetoricians had long distinguished figures of thought (or 'substance'), such as simile, from verbal figures (or figures of 'dress'), such as alliteration: but even in the taxonomies of Puttenham or Cicero the categories had been unstable. In Dryden's more fluid process of argument they are even more so: the 'turns' that manifest 'character' are said to be a matter both of 'substance' and of 'dress'. A few lines later the same ambiguity recurs in a different formulation: Ovid has 'superfluous branches' which look as though they might reasonably be lopped off; but then it turns out that, although 'superfluous', they still count as 'sense'—and 'the sense of an author, generally speaking, is to be sacred and inviolable'.[8]

These bulges in Dryden's critical self-presentation stretch to breaking point, or beyond, in his translations. Take, for instance, a notable 'boyism' in Ovid's 'Dido to Aeneas', one of the three epistles he translated for the 1680 volume. 'Will the same winds carry away both your sails and your fidelity?' Dido cries ('iidem venti vela fidemque ferent'); and again, 'are

you resolved, Aeneas, to unmoor both your commitment and your ships?'
('certus es, Aenea, cum foedere solvere naves').[9] Here is Dryden:

> 'Tis then resolved poor Dido must be left
> Of life, of honour, and of love bereft!
> While you, with loosened sails and vows, prepare
> To seek a land that flies the searcher's care.[10]

One of Ovid's turns is mimicked but the other is loosened into a statelier
kind of zeugma: the three indirect objects hooked to 'bereft'. The change
is not a technical accommodation to what 'our tongue will bear'. An earlier
translator, John Sherburne, had rendered the passage like this:

> Shall one winde hence thy sayles and promise beare?
> And wilt thou with thy ships unloose thy vow?[11]

Dryden reacts against the overmuch of Ovid's shrill double turn. He
carries out in practice just such a 'retrenchment' of 'luxuriance' as he
had denied himself in theory.[12]

There are other ways in which Dryden's practice as a translator bears
out his confession 'that I have transgressed the rules which I have given'.
There are frank updatings, as when Dido, envisaging Aeneas's reception if
he were ever to reach his longed-for Italy, makes an intervention in the
political hot topic of 1680, the exclusion crisis (a dispute as to whether
Charles II's heir, the Roman Catholic James, Duke of York, should be
kept out of the succession):

> What people is so void of common sense
> To vote succession from a native prince?[13]

And there are moments of ideological reformatting, especially in the
construction of gender identity. Ovid's Dido makes clear that Aeneas
will be able to go on soldiering if he stays with her: 'there is room for
the laws of peace here; and also for arms' ('hic pacis leges, hic locus arma
capit'). 'If your mind is avid for war' ('si tibi mens avida est belli'), she says,
and if Iulus needs blooding, we will provide an enemy ('praebebimus
hostem').[14] Dryden's Dido presents a more cloying, feminizing temptation after the manner of Homer's Calypso: the two of them will live
together 'secure in soft repose' while the youngster goes off fighting by
himself.[15]

Dryden's translations were written in the awareness that they might
find all sorts of readers, from expert scholars to people unversed in
the classics: Stuart Gillespie and Penelope Wilson have emphasized that
'non-classically trained women were certainly a significant segment of the
potential market for translations' at this time.[16] Readers who knew the

sources could gauge the closenesses and departures of Dryden's writing: as Paul Hammond has shown, they could listen in on the 'dialogue between the Latin and the English'—the two languages and the two worlds.[17] Sensitive if unscholarly readers could get something of the same feeling: it would not have been hard to guess that the jibe about voting succession from a native prince is unlikely to be an exact transcription of the source. Dryden's poem-translations then, were, and were understood to be, complex texts which braided together different kinds of translation and what might be thought to be supplementary writing. In this, they are like Obadiah Walker's *Paraphrase and Annotations*; only the shifts of mode—which are of course more varied and imaginative—are not marked out with brackets and italics. Like Walker, and like many of the translators of the Bible whose work we have explored, Dryden, or part of him, was committed to the idea that translation could capture something called 'the sense' which was 'inviolable'. But, again like many of the Bible translators, he saw that this category was impossible to sustain. Actual writing will always spill over its boundaries, bringing in something more, or something other: 'I am ready to acknowledge that I have transgressed the rules which I have given, and taken more liberty than a just translation will allow'.

Translation entails transgression; and transgression—as is its wont—carries a charge in Dryden's writing of both pleasure and fear. In *Ovid's Epistles*, these tangled feelings emerge creatively in 'Canace to Macareus'. The eponymous pair are son and daughter to Aeolus, and have themselves transgressed. Ovid's poem represents Canace's letter to Macareus, in which she tells him that their newborn baby has been discovered by their father and handed over to the dogs and the birds: she has been sent a dagger with which she must kill herself. The story involves a good deal of concealment; and this is what interests Dryden.

At the beginning of her feelings, Canace sensed she knows not what god in her glowing heart ('nescio quem sensi corde tepente Deum'). She could not come up with any reason why she lost her appetite and was unable to sleep and kept on breaking into groans: 'nec cur haec facerem, poteram mihi reddere caussam [sic]'.[18] Dryden catches all these details; and then gives Canace another secret to reveal: 'I...found', she says, 'a secret pleasure in thy kisses'.[19] In Ovid, her nurse diagnoses the problem, Canace blushes and, the next thing we know, she is pregnant:

> Prima mihi nutrix, Aeoli, dixit, amas.
> Erubui, gremioque pudor dejecit ocellos.
> Haec satis in tacita signa fatentis erant.
> Jamque tumescebant vitiati pondera ventris,
> AEgraque furtivum membra gravabat onus.[20]

My nurse was the one who said to me: 'Daughter of Aeolus, you are in love!"
I blushed, and shame bent my eyes down into my lap; these silent signs were
enough of a confession. And already the weight of my corrupted womb was
swelling and the secret burden was weighing down my sick limbs.

Dryden cannot agree that Canace's 'tacita signa' ('silent signes'—as an
earlier translator, Wye Saltonstall, had called them)[21] are enough ('satis').
Here, as throughout his work with the classics, he will have been given the
tiniest nudge towards 'opening' by the editorial clarifications which ac-
companied the text he used—in this case: '[*Signa fatentis.*] id est, con-
fitentis me amare' ('[*Signs of confession.*] that is, revealing that she loved').[22]
But he goes much further. Not for him the discretion that Ovid has
relishingly, half-pruriently given Canace: all the consequences of her blush
must be revealed:

> 'Tis love', said she; and then my downcast eyes
> And guilty dumbness witnessed my surprise.
> Forced at the last, my shameful pain I tell,
> And, O, what followed we both know too well!
> When half denying, more than half content,
> Embraces warmed me to a full consent:
> Then with tumultuous joys my heart did beat,
> And guilt that made them anxious, made them great.
>   But now my swelling womb heaved up my breast,
> And rising weight my sinking limbs oppressed.[23]

In fact it is Dryden's masculine imagination in drag which 'forces' her to
tell all; his translatory 'embrace' that secures her 'consent' to open the
scandal so thoroughly; his man-of-the-world's presumption—'we . . .
know too well'—that constructs the story she is made to accept as her
own.
   In 'Canace to Macareus' the transgression of the 'rules' of translation is
intertwined with the transgression of social convention in the story that is
told. The results are paradoxical and charged with unease. Dryden's
quandary is a bit like that which dogs tabloid journalism today. He
wants the transgressions committed by the lovers to be fully brought to
light; but in so doing he cannot but reveal a kinship between their desires
and his. Ovid's text leaves him having to imagine the details that he
pretends to find. The boundary between 'amplifying' and 'altering' has
to be crossed. Half frustrated, half excited, he commits a transgression of
his own.
   A bit further on, Canace has had the baby in secret and her nurse is
trying to smuggle it away through her father's court:

> Jam prope limen erat: patrias vagitus ad aures
>   Venit, & indicio proditur ille suo.
> Eripit infantem, metitaque sacra revelat
>   Aeolus. insana regia voce sonat.[24]

> Already the threshold was near—a wail comes to my father's ears and the
> babe is betrayed by his own evidence! Aeolus catches up the child and reveals
> the pretended sacrifice; the palace resounds with his mad cry.

Just like Canace's 'tacita signa' earlier, the baby's inarticulate cry prompts a
transgression in Dryden's Englishing:

> Just at the door th'unhappy infant cried:
> The grandsire heard him, and the theft he spied.
> Swift as a whirlwind to the nurse he flies,
> And deafs his stormy subjects with his cries.
> With one fierce puff he blows the leaves away:
> Exposed the self-discovered infant lay.
> The noise reached me, and my presaging mind
> Too soon its own approaching woes divined.[25]

Aeolus's 'fierce puff' is also the translator's, for the infant is more thoroughly discovered here than in Ovid's Latin—or in the earlier seventeenth-
century translations by Sherburne and Saltonstall (though again there is a
tiny prompt in the Heinsius and Cnipping edition: '[*Revelat.*] Detegit,
remotis frondis').[26] The interpretive sally creates a need for justification:
how can Canace have known about the puff and the leaves if she was
prostrate, as Ovid said, exhausted and petrified on a couch in the next
room? So Dryden creates the couplet about the noise reaching her and the
divination done by her 'presaging mind'. Her mind is also his: for it is he
who has done the presaging, and created the scene which he attributes to
her terrified imagining.

A few lines later, the translator's own interpretive innovation is again
credited to the speaking character. In Ovid, Aeolus sends one of his guards
('patrius . . . satelles'); in Dryden he becomes 'the messenger of death'.
What this guard or messenger hands over is not wholly, and not only, a
message: he gives Canace a sword, saying that her father bids her understand, on the basis of her own merit, what it means ('ex merito scire, quid
iste velit'). In the Latin, Canace quickly sees through the irony and passes
on to accepting its consequences: 'I do know, and shall bravely use the
violent blade' ('scimus; & utemur violento fortiter ense'); she then hits
back rhetorically—which is the only way available to her—with some
irony of her own: 'I will bury my father's gift in my breast' ('pectoribus
condam dona paterna meis'). Saltonstall and Sherburne had both brought
'merito' into English as 'merit'; but Dryden puffs away the irony by

substituting 'crimes'. And he has his Canace linger in the moment of interpretation: 'too well I know the sense those words impart'.[27] Here again it is Dryden who too well knows, that is, he has too well imagined the aura attaching to the messenger, and too thoroughly opened up the sense of 'merito'.

In Dryden, as in Ovid, Canace presents herself as an ingénue. At key moments in her story, she says, she simply did not know what was happening to her. She was caught unawares by love; and ambushed, too, by childbirth: 'Nescia quae faceret subitos mihi causa dolores'; 'not knowing 'twas my labour, I complain / Of sudden shootings', as Dryden puts it.[28] After so much incomprehension, her father at last gives her something she can 'know': what she is meant to do with the sword. Grasping and obeying that meaning is a kind of self-affirmation. 'I myself' will act, she says in the Latin, where the emphatic 'ipsa' is repeated in her closing peroration.[29] But of course the act she performs is one of utter self-destruction, not only killing herself but doing so in obedience to her father's will: not 'acting' but 'acting out'. A scholar of the *Heroides*, Howard Jacobson, has remarked that 'Canace is so dominated by thoughts of her father that she can scarcely see herself as more than an extension of him'.[30] 'Obsequar' ('I will perform it') she declares self-defeatingly at the end, echoing the similarly passive though vigorous resolution she has made regarding her dead baby a few lines earlier: 'I will follow' ('prosequar').[31]

Yet her suicide is also the occasion of her vivid rhetorical self-assertion. She writes with the pen in one hand and the sword in the other, as though it is her father's injunction to know ('scire') that at last enables her to understand and express herself. She inflicts on herself her own sentence. But then again, the Latin emphasizes the mystery of how she has been overwhelmed by her heart and body. The confident explanatory surge of her writing butts up against the moments of unknowing in the story it puts forth: the blushing, the being lost for words. Dryden's translation pulls Canace's experience a bit more fully into the realm of the known. We might say that, as he infiltrates her femininity, he makes her subjugate herself more thoroughly to the Law of the Father—were it not that his additions to her speech are 'transgressions' of his own 'rules', and are flagged as such by the justifications that he feels the need to insert. Being Dryden he does it skilfully, of course; but 'we . . . know too well' and 'my presaging mind' nevertheless have a bit of a sheepish air.

In Ovid, the writing done by the poet merges with the writing that is imagined as being done by the protagonists. Canace, like all the heroines, tells her own story. Even when, as often, the narratives derive from familiar sources, the protagonists remake them for themselves. But Dryden's

Canace is no longer a character in a poem that reworks its origins. She is a character in a poem of translation; and she has been altered accordingly. She has become more of an interpreter. What saves Dryden's work from being a mere interpretation, from being 'clearer and flatter than the original', is that the impulse to interpret is caught up into the action of the poem and attributed to the central character. It becomes part of her predicament. As translated by Dryden, Ovid's drama of ambivalent self-assertion becomes a drama of ambivalent self-interpretation.

To be Dryden was to be imbued with the classics: they helped form the texture of his mind. The translations, then, were not separate exercises but strands of his imaginative enterprise. Paul Hammond has shown how they join with other poems in investigating transience and loss: 'Dryden repeatedly selected... poems or passages which dramatize the precariousness of selfhood and individuation'.[32] And Paul Davis has traced subtle refractions of Dryden's self-image in the translations, for instance how the 'labour' of producing *The Works of Virgil in English* sensitized him to 'pessimistic undertones in the Virgilian ethic of "labor"'.[33]

The pattern of involvement that we have begun to map is no less through-woven in Dryden's imagination; but it arises from the nature of translation itself when that is understood as the 'opening' of a source text that cannot be opened without violation. As we have seen, this paradox lies in wait for any translation; but some poems more than others enable it to be played out exploratively when they are translated. 'Canace to Macareus' is a vivid, complex instance; but all the *Heroides* have an air of incompletion which can stimulate something of the same reaction. As Duncan F. Kennedy has suggested, they embody 'a poetics of "writing in isolation"' and cry out for a 'response'.[34]

Neither Sherburne in 1639 nor Salstonstall in 1636 had heeded this cry put out by their source texts. But in 1680 Dryden was not alone. Throughout the collaborative volume, *Ovid's Epistles*, various translators supply 'openings' which are, broadly speaking, similar to his. This approach was encouraged by the circumstances of the book's publication. As Stuart Gillespie has shown, *Ovid's Epistles* was an 'experiment' on the part of the publisher Jacob Tonson; and it succeeded. Like his several later ventures in translation involving Dryden (including the *Works of Virgil*) it both aimed at and found a wide readership: 'helped by these publications'—Barbara M. Benedict goes so far as to assert—'Dryden became a poet with a popular draw unlike any previously seen in literature.'[35] Even though Dryden and Tonson also had learned readers in view, the wish to reach a new, non-scholarly audience must have nurtured the practice of 'opening' in their case no less than in Reformation Englishings of the Bible. It also mattered that most of the contributors to *Ovid's Epistles* were—like Dryden himself—either playwrights or theatre people.[36] Translation and adaptation for the stage were characteristically very loose modes of rewriting: a trace of the same liberty, together with the need to create a hearable voice, spreads across into these translations of Ovid's verse. Hermetic moments in the Latin needed to be made performable in the theatre of a reader's imagination. Nahum Tate, for instance, faced with the fact that Leander could not escape his parents to visit Hero as he had done before ('non poteram celare meos, velut ante, parentes'), pitches in with a dramatic explanation: 'my stealth is to my jealous Parents told'.[37]

The most freely elaborative translation is by the only woman participant, Aphra Behn, whose contribution is titled 'A Paraphrase on Oenone to Paris', but which is more accurately described in Dryden's Preface as being 'in Mr Cowley's way of imitation only' (this is a neat illustration of the slippages we have been tracing).[38] Throughout her career Behn did much translation, of both verse and prose, and her practice is generally expansive. But here in the paraphrase or imitation of Ovid it is remarkably so, for she invents tens of lines. She reinforces Oenone's bombshell status:

> Me all the Village Herdsmen strove to gain,
> For me the Shepherds sigh'd and su'd in vain.[39]

And she introduces a startling picture of Paris's transformation once he has been recognized as Priam's son and has got together with Helen:

> Wou'd God, when first I saw thee, thou hadst been.
> This Great, this Cruel, Celebrated thing.
> That without hope I might have gaz'd & bow'd,
> And mixt my Adoration with the Crowd;[40]

This brilliant sketch of the sadomasochism of celebrity culture owes much to Behn and her cultural circumstances; and very little to Ovid.

In his Preface, Dryden excuses the liberty of Behn's 'Paraphrase': 'I was desired to say that the author, who is of the fair sex, understood not Latin'.[41] But this gesture reiterates the paradox frequent in the *Heroides* where a speaker's disempowerment releases great rhetorical verve. Behn exploits the liberty of not understanding—or pretending she does not—in order not just to breach but to abandon the 'rules' of translation: she extends, updates, and intellectualizes Oenone's complaint so that it becomes a critique of the abuse of power. 'No sooner you / Became a Prince, but you were Perjur'd too', she points out, before generalizing: 'must they all be faithless who are Kings?'[42] As things look to Behn's Oenone, Paris's new vaunted faith in Helen, his country, and his social status is hypocritical because built on faithlessness to her. 'Faith' and 'faithless' recur throughout the text: in a translation, these are inevitably charged words. We are being nudged to see that Behn's infidelity to Ovid is a way of keeping faith with Oenone. It allows her to join her own rhetorical heft to Oenone's, the more comprehensively to denounce the faithlessnesses of Paris, his gender, and his class.

Dryden's response to Ovid's writing was no less intense than Behn's, but it led him into a more complex process of translatorly interaction. Not willing to allow himself Behn's liberty in expanding the women's voices he adopts,[43] while also being more alert than Tate to the paradoxes of translation-as-opening, he saw the *Heroides* as a drama of secrets and their revelation in which he, as interpreter and translator, could not but play a part. Of the three epistles he translated, 'Helen to Paris' is the comedy version, as Helen responds to her would-be lover's double entendres with innuendos of her own. Dryden sticks close to his source when he has her write 'these are your words, but I can guess your sense'.[44] But he makes more blatant the implicit invitation of her final lines. Saltonstall had stayed fairly near to the Latin, as had Sherburne, who closes the epistle like this:

> What rests we will by *Clymene* confer,
> And *Aethra*, each my Muse, and Counseller.

> (Caetera per socias Clymenen AEthramque loquamur, / Quae mihi sunt comites consiliumque duae.)[45]

Now here is Dryden:

> My woman knows the secret of my heart,
> And may hereafter better news impart.[46]

The innuendo is so fully brought out as to be all but an open confession.

Heroides 7, addressed by Dido to Aeneas, may well have struck Dryden as being already in itself an 'opening' of Book 4 of the *Aeneid*. As Richard Tarrant has said, Ovid's Dido is made 'more loving' than Virgil's, and also 'more scathing', and is given a brisk new 'epigrammatic mode': 'the resulting loss of nuance is deliberate, since from the standpoint adopted by Ovid complexity is just a way of excusing Aeneas'.[47] This more forthright Dido adopts the same paradoxical stance as Canace:

> Adspicias utinam, quae sit scribentis imago!
> Scribimus; & gremio Troicus ensis adest:

Oh! that my writing posture thou couldst spy: / Upon my lap the *Dardan* sword doth lye. (Sherburne)[48]

She takes for granted that her writing is less effective than her presence would be. And her freedom of expression comes at the price of being about to cease all utterance forever. Nevertheless, being the one who writes ('scribentis'), being able to say 'I write' ('scribimus') is a position of power at least in that it allows her to contest the Virgilian account of her which was already canonical by Ovid's time.

In his translation, Dryden flattens Dido's vaunt:

> My life's too loathsome, and my love too strong.
> Death holds my pen, and dictates what I say.[49]

His Dido, shown to be in the grip of forces beyond her control, is more like Virgil's than Ovid's. Dryden has translated *Heroides* 7 so as to re-subject Dido to Virgil's account of her. By doing that, he makes Ovid's poem seem more like a free translation from the *Aeneid* and less like a contestatory response. Years later, Dryden was to echo this passage when he looked back on his 'Dido to Aeneas' in the 'Dedication to the *Aeneis*'. Ovid, he said, 'Dictates a Letter' for Dido; and it is then suggested that Ovid has done no more than taken dictation in his turn: he 'has nothing of his own, he borrows all from a greater Master in his own profession; and, which is worse, improves nothing which he finds'.[50] Dryden's translation of *Heroides* 7 closes down Ovid's aggressive 'opening' of Virgil. It makes Ovid himself seem more like a translator than a poet. It shows Dido, correspondingly, as being no longer her own author but a scribe, taking dictation from Death, that is, from Virgil.

The interplay of secrets and 'opening' in *Ovid's Epistles* helps to explain why, in Dryden's next theoretical account of translation, the Preface to the miscellany *Sylvae* (1685), the secrecy of the source text has become a central idea. 'I have', he says, 'sometimes very boldly made such expositions of my authors as no Dutch commentator will forgive me. Perhaps, in such particular passages, I have thought that I discovered some beauty yet undiscovered by those pedants, which none but a poet could have found.' Where he has 'enlarged' his sources, he says,

> I desire the false critics would not always think that those thoughts are wholly mine, but that either they are secretly in the poet, or may fairly be deduced from him; or at least, if both those considerations should fail, that my own is of a piece with his, and that if he were living, and an Englishman, they are such as he would probably have written.[51]

Dryden's rhetoric here has the same expansive movement as in the Preface to *Ovid's Epistles*, where—as we saw—the discussion swelled from 'words' to 'sense' to 'enlarge' to 'alter' to 'vary' to 'forsake'. But now he accepts that his style of translation includes moments of what might well be thought imitation; and he struggles to justify himself. Back in the Preface to *Ovid's Epistles* it was the practitioner of 'imitation' who aimed to write as he supposes the author 'would have done, had he lived in our age and in our country'.[52] Now it is Dryden who does so, in what is offered as a work of 'translation'. In this, he takes issue not only with his own earlier account of 'imitation', for in a famous passage of *La Deffence, et illustration de la langue françoyse* (1549), Joachim Du Bellay had advocated imitation in preference to translation, the difference being that imitation aimed 'to penetrate to the most hidden and inward parts of the author' ('penetrer aux plus cachées, et interieures parties de l'Aucteur').[53] Just like Dryden's developing style of translation.

Dryden had been goaded to defend himself by a friend of his, Lord Roscommon, whose *Essay on Translated Verse* had been published the year before. It includes this pronouncement:

> *Excursions* are *inexpiably Bad.*
> And 'tis much safer to leave out than *Add.*[54]

No wonder Roscommon's *Essay* made Dryden 'uneasy', as he admits in the Preface, 'till I tried whether or no I was capable of following his rules'.[55] Roscommon had said that 'good *Translation* is no *easie* Art' and Dryden's attention must have snagged on the word '*easie*'.[56] He catches it up and toys with it in the Preface to *Sylvae*, not only by saying that he was feeling 'uneasy', but in the metaphor with which he chooses to begin: 'For this last half year I have been troubled with the disease (as I may call it) of translation'—that little parenthesis is itself a symptom of the trouble, for part of the disease of translation is the uneasiness of not being quite sure what to call it. He had suffered, he says, from 'cold prose fits', having had to translate Louis Maimbourg's *Histoire de la Ligue* at the behest of Charles II; and had hoped for 'a kind of ease' when the 'paroxysm' changed to 'hot . . . in this volume of verse miscellanies'. There had certainly been new enjoyment, for he had found something 'more pleasing' in his translation of pastorals by Theocritus and odes by Horace than in his 'ordinary productions'. The feeling of self-indulgence continues as he speaks of following his 'natural impulses' in translating those parts of Lucretius and Virgil 'which had most affected me in the reading'. Yet all this pleasure does not lead to ease, for Roscommon's *Essay* is nagging in the background. Here again, just as in the Preface to *Ovid's Epistles*, there are 'rules' of translation which the affective, imaginative, involving process of actually translating inevitably transgresses: 'I many times exceeded my commission', Dryden confesses, 'for I have both added and omitted'.[57] Worse, but perhaps also better, than 'no *easie* art', translation is 'uneasy', a quality that seems to depress Dryden, but also to allure him.

It turns out that his unease has a particular object: Virgil, who is 'the plague of translators' because, 'being so very sparing of his words, and leaving so much to be imagined by the reader', he 'can never be translated as he ought in any modern tongue'. In the *Heroides*, secrets had belonged to the dramatic situation conjured in each poem. When he 'opened' them, Dryden joined in the play of discretion and interpretation which Ovid had started, and whose continuation his texts seemed to encourage: each epistle, after all, hopes for an answer. But Virgil's secrecy is felt simply to be inherent in his style; not only that, but to be its great, inimitable virtue. The conflicting desires, to open and not to open, therefore provoke more anxiety now than they had done in the Preface to *Ovid's Epistles*. In *Sylvae*, Dryden says, he has translated the 'Nisus and Euryalus' episode 'too literally'. On the other hand, 'Mezentius and Lausus' has been given 'more scope', with the result that it 'has more of the majesty of Virgil' but 'less of his conciseness'. All in all, he says, 'methinks I come like a malefactor to make a speech upon the gallows, and to warn all other poets by my sad example from the sacrilege of translating Virgil'.[58]

Dryden did not heed his own warning: he went on to translate all Virgil's works. But his unease at doing so never left him. 'I have done great Wrong to *Virgil* in the whole Translation', he announces in the 'Dedication' to the *Aeneis* (1697).[59] In this poem of translation, the concerns that we have explored in 'Canace and Macereus', and which are latent in all Dryden's work as a translator, take on a particular timbre of unease.

12

Dryden's *Aeneis*: 'a thousand secret beauties'

'Leaving so much to be imagined by the reader,' Virgil lured Dryden in. His imagination roused, he was quick to see gleams of his own world in Virgil's writing and to sense echoes of his own feelings. Signs of his inwardness with Virgil's oeuvre are scattered everywhere in his original poems; and hooks to the present—like the reference to the exclusion crisis inserted into Ovid—can be found throughout his work as a translator. But when Dryden brought these two modes of response together by subjecting Virgil to translation, the writing took on a newly personal inflection. Of the passages published in *Sylvae*, 'Nisus and Euryalus' and 'Mezentius and Lausus' murmur (as Paul Hammond has shown) with Dryden's grief at the death of his friend John Oldham.[1] 'The Ninth Eclogue' had a similar though less intimate aspect as it was made to air his financial difficulties. 'The Fourth Eclogue' did the more usual, public thing of discreetly alluding to the pregnancy of Princess Mary.[2]

One aspect of what was 'secretly in' Virgil's texts, then, was the ability to become relevant to personal and public events long after his death. They were therefore especially amenable to that aspect of paraphrase as establishing contemporary significance which we noted in Chapter 10. As Dryden was to put it in a note on the closing peroration of *Georgics* 1:

> The present Wars, in which all *Europe*, and part of *Asia* are ingag'd at present; are wag'd in the same places here describ'd: *Atque hinc* Euphrates, *illinc* Germania *Bellum*, &c. As if *Virgil* had Prophecy'd of this Age.[3]

The medieval tradition of taking Virgil as a prophet, not only of the birth of Christ in the fourth Eclogue, but of all sorts of contemporary events via the *sortes Virgilianae*—the practice of opening the book at random and acting on what you read—had not wholly disappeared by Dryden's time; at least, not from cultural memory. Charles I was supposed to have had recourse to Virgil in the early years of the Civil War and to have asked

Abraham Cowley to translate the passage he lit upon. Lo and behold, it was Dido's cursing of Aeneas:

> Let him to base, unequal terms submit
> In hopes to save his crown, yet lose both it
> And life at once; untimely let him die,
> And on an open stage unburied lie.[4]

There were some strands of superstition in Dryden: he had horoscopes cast on the births of his children.[5] But he cannot quite have believed that Virgil's writing was prophetic in the full sense: his phrasing—'as if *Virgil* had Prophecy'd of this Age'—suggests a healthy leavening of metaphor. Still, the idea haunts him: it reappears when he writes in the 'Dedication of the *Aeneis*' that Virgil's account of the Sibyl's prophecies 'may be as properly apply'd to every word of his: They must be read, in order as they lie; the least breath discomposes them; and somewhat of their Divinity is lost'.[6] As Sir John Harington had noticed a century before, people's reaction to prophecies is often not a matter of outright belief or disbelief, but of something cloudier: 'I find they give a presage and leave an impression in their minds that seem most to scorn them' ('presage' means, roughly, 'foreboding').[7] Literary texts by definition speak to different people in later times: they are all, in a very loose and general sense, prophetic. But Virgil made on Dryden an impression that was more than usually defined and compelling. The conviction that Virgil's situation under Augustus had similarities to his own under William III leaves marks everywhere in the translation: they have been mapped with ever-increasing subtlety by Steven Zwicker, William Frost, Paul Hammond, and John Barnard.[8] For Dryden, the political impact of *The Works of Virgil in English* clearly mattered intensely: this was a public 'cultural project', 'the first example of a major literary work by a *living* writer to be published by subscription', whose subscribers represented 'overlapping and competing groups' from Whig grandees to notorious Jacobites, and which therefore clearly 'spoke to and for a wide variety of constituencies in terms of age, politics, social and professional standing, and gender'.[9] Yet Virgil's texts held other secrets too.

To judge from Dryden's 'Dedication' of his *Aeneis*, it was, of all Virgil's works, Book IV of the *Aeneid*, the episode of Dido and Aeneas, that struck him as being the most freighted with presage. 'Let us consider the secret Reasons which *Virgil* had, for thus framing this Noble Episode,' he says:

> Possession having cool'd his Love, as it increas'd hers, she soon perceiv'd the change, or at least grew suspicious of a change; this suspicion soon turn'd to Jealousie, and Jealouise to Rage; then she disdains and threatens, and again is humble, and intreats; and nothing availing, despairs, curses, and at last

becomes her own Executioner. See here the whole process of that passion, to which nothing can be added. I dare go no farther, lest I shou'd lose the connection of my Discourse.[10]

The writing follows Dryden's characteristic movement of interpretation: he is first drawn into exposition, then ambushed by a feeling of having transgressed; at which he breaks off, re-establishing the 'rule' of his 'discourse'. What so tempts him in the episode of Dido and Aeneas is the thought that within it lies, not any political foretelling, but the secret blueprint of all desire: the 'process' of their 'passion' will be worked out (barring, usually, Dido's suicide), not only in their story but by all lovers through all time. It is a universal prophecy.

Others among the 'thousand secret Beauties'[11] that Dryden discerned in the *Aeneid* were allusions to Virgil's own historical circumstances. For instance, names from 'the great *Roman* Families' are adopted, flatteringly, for 'Captains of Ships, or Leaders in the War': it is an early variant of product placement. 'Your Lordship knows with what Address he makes mention of them,' Dryden writes, addressing a compliment of his own to the member of a great English family to whom his translation was dedicated.[12] This style of interpretation was, as his phrasing implies, uncontroversial: it goes back at least to Servius in the fifth century and indeed continues in modern criticism.[13] What is more personal to Dryden in this line of argument is, again, his focus on Dido and Aeneas. He devotes a long passage to defending the episode from charges of anachronism, before arriving at the vexed question of whether the lovers can be said to have got married. He gives weight to the goad directed against Aeneas by Mercury when he is sent by Jupiter to break off the relationship: 'he calls *Aeneas* not only a Husband, but upbraids him for being a fond husband, as the word *Uxorius* implies'. The interpretation has a secret reason at its root:

> *Virgil* is so much concern'd to make this Marriage ... to make way for the Divorce which he intended afterwards ... : I more than conjecture that he had in his eye the Divorce which not long before had pass'd betwixt the Emperour and *Scribonia*.[14]

Here again, Dryden feels that his interpretive digression (which is, incidentally, wholly implausible to the modern Virgil scholar)[15] has led him to transgress: 'I have detained your Lordship longer than I intended on this Objection'.[16] The impulses of Dryden's criticism are developing a strange synergy with the narrative movement of the *Aeneid*. For him, just as much as for Aeneas, Carthage becomes a place of temptation and delay.[17]

The word 'address' with which Dryden praises Virgil's allusions to his powerful contemporaries is inseparably aesthetic and ethical: it is like 'tact' for us today. It is to be found also in the *Aeneid*'s connections, not to the world beyond, but within itself, between its different parts. For instance, Aeneas's narration of how, 'having secur'd his Father and his Son, he repeated all his former Dangers to have found his Wife':

> And here your Lordship may observe the Address of *Virgil*; it was not for nothing, that this Passage was related with all these tender Circumstances. *Aeneas* told it; *Dido* heard it: That he had been so affectionate a Husband, was no ill Argument to the coming Dowager, that he might prove as kind to her. *Virgil* has a thousand secret Beauties tho' I have not leisure to remark them.[18]

To observe Virgil's 'Address', then, is to open the secrets of the words by paying attention to their poise and movement, to their position in the narrative, and their relation to the world into which they were released.

Dryden's translation nudges its readers towards appreciating Virgil's 'Address'. In Book X, Aeneas, at war in Italy, is brutalized by the death of his beloved Pallas. He is pulled close to the model of Achilles's fury after the death of Patroclus in the *Iliad*, as here when he rejects his enemy Magus's appeal for mercy:[19]

> belli commercia Turnus
> Sustulit ista prior, jam tum Pallante perempto.
> Hoc patris Anchisae manes, hoc sentit Iulus.
> Sic fatus galeam laeva tenet, atque reflexâ
> Cervice orantis capulo tenus abdidit ensem.

'Such trafficking in war Turnus first put away, even in the hour when Pallas was slain. Thus judges my father Anchises' spirit, thus Iülus'. So speaking, he grasps the helmet with his left hand, and bending back the suppliant's neck, sheathes the sword up to the hilt.

> Thy *Turnus* broke
> All Rules of War, by one relentless Stroke
> When *Pallas* fell: So deems, nor deems alone,
> My Father's Shadow, but my living Son.
> Thus having said, of kind Remorse bereft,
> He seiz'd his Helm, and drag'd him with his left:
> Then with his right Hand, while his Neck he wreath'd,
> Up to the hilts his shining Fauchion sheath'd.[20]

We could relish the skill with which Dryden has found a tone in Virgil's verse and Englished it—for instance the shape of the reference to Anchises and Iulus, Aeneas's 'Father' and 'Son'. Or we might notice the slight echo of the pattern of rule and transgression from Dryden's critical writing when he hardens 'belli commercia' into 'Rules of War'. But, when it comes to 'Address', the crucial 'secret' attaching to these lines is hinted at by the word 'orantis' (suppliant), and by the fact that Virgil's narrative allows no space for any representation of Aeneas's thought between his speech and his cruel act. Virgil leaves us to infer for ourselves that Aeneas's characteristic dutifulness and circumspection have suddenly been cast away. Dryden gives us the point explicitly in his main 'enlargement' of the passage: Aeneas is 'of kind Remorse bereft'.

The same happens a few hundred lines later when Aeneas, hitherto the epitome of 'pietas', sees that quality in someone else. Lausus is defending his wounded father; and Aeneas, who had once been so devoted to his own father, mocks him for it. The youth spits back and 'with insulting Scorn / Provokes the ling'ring Prince':

> . . . Whose Patience tyr'd,
> Gave Place, and all his Breast with Fury fir'd.
> For now the Fates prepar'd their sharpen'd Sheers;
> And lifted high the flaming Sword appears:
> Which full descending, with a frightful sway,   }
> Thro Shield and Corslet forc'd th'impetuous Way,   }
> And bury'd deep in his fair Bosom lay.   }[21]

Various touches suggest Dryden's shocked involvement: 'flaming' is his insertion, as is 'fair Bosom'. But the 'enlargements' that most bring out the 'Address' of Virgil's writing are 'ling'ring' and 'Whose Patience tyr'd, / Gave Place'. Virgil makes the patient, remorseful Aeneas of the earlier books simply disappear from this part of the text, though he is no doubt meant to remain troublingly in a reader's memory. Dryden writes the recollection back in, keeping 'Patience' and 'Remorse' in proximity to Aeneas even though syntactically they are denied him. 'I thought fit'— Dryden was to write of the translatorly mode of the *Aeneis*—'to steer betwixt the two Extreams, of Paraphrase, and literal Translation.'[22] In the texture of the work, this 'steering betwixt' becomes a style of narrative. The pull of metaphrase gives us what happens and what is said in Virgil; the swerve to paraphrase adduces an extra little bit of what Virgil leaves his readers to imagine. In passages like these from Book 10, that means a touch more revelation of mental processes.

This is a searching, tactful practice of interpretation. Yet it undeniably creates a text that is a shade easier, a shade more 'open', than Virgil's. Just as Lausus is dying at his hand, Aeneas is hit by remorse, at last recognizing in the youth a likeness to his own filial devotedness. All of a sudden he can again call himself 'pius Aeneas'.[23] In Virgil, this is the startling return of a feeling that had seemed to have been annihilated by the rage of battle. In Dryden, war is made less utterly dehumanizing because Aeneas's *pietas* is kept explicitly present, though in abeyance, all along. The moment of its reappearance is in consequence less sudden and less strange.

These 'openings' are smaller and more subtly woven into the text than those in 'Canace to Macareus' two decades before. They do not seem uneasy. But signs of trouble do surface elsewhere in the *Aeneis*, at moments when Virgil's text itself has to do with secrecy and interpretation. Take for instance the most famous secret of all, concealed within the wooden horse. As Aeneas recounts the events to Dido and her court, the horse, left behind when the Greeks appear to have abandoned their siege, presents the Trojans with a problem of interpretation. Should it be brought within the ramparts, or consigned to flames, or searched for 'hidden Frauds'? Laocoön is certain it has a nefarious purpose: perhaps there are Greeks hidden inside ('hoc inclusi ligno occultantur Achivi'), or, as Dryden puts it, it may 'inclose, / Within its blind Recess, our secret Foes':[24] wording which signals his inwardness with Laocoön's activity of mind, since the phrase 'blind Recess' is itself an extrapolation from the secret places of Virgil's verse. Laocoön's probing of the Greeks' mysterious work continues, and continues to be shadowed by Dryden's probing of Virgil's mysterious work (I have underlined the 'enlargements', insofar as they can be isolated; the prose that follows the quotation from Virgil is Ruaeus's paraphrase in the edition Dryden used):

> Thus having said, against the Steed he threw
> His forceful Spear, which, <u>hissing as it flew</u>
> <u>Pierc'd through the yielding Planks of jointed Wood</u>,
> And trembling in the hollow Belly stood.
> The sides <u>transpierc'd</u>, return a ratling Sound,
> And Groans <u>of *Greeks* inclos'd</u> come issuing <u>through the Wound</u>.

> Sic fatus, validis ingentem viribus hastam
> In latus, inque ferui curvam compagibus alvum
> Contorsit: stetit illa tremens, uteroque recusso
> Insonuere cavae gemitumque dedere cavernae.

Cum haec dixisset, immisit totis viribus magnam hastam in latus, & in uterum equi curvatum iuncturis: hasit illa tremens, & repercusso utero cava spatia sonuerunt & emiserunt gemitum.[25]

'Hissing as it flew' is an enlargement that can safely be made since all spears hiss when flying: it is also a nice example of how the need to write couplets fuels the tendency to 'open' the source. But thereafter something stranger and more transformative begins to happen. In the Latin, the great energy of Laocoön's throw cannot break through the horse's carapace: the verb of hurling, 'contorsit', butts up expressively against the verb of sticking, 'stetit'. Dryden has the planks yield, the spear pierce through, and the sides, again, be 'transpierc'd'. The horse suffers a 'wound' and what emerges from it is not just groans, as in the Latin, but groans that are interpreted: 'of *Greeks* inclos'd'. Virgil's Aeneas is here re-creating in his narrative the Trojans' ignorance: they hear something, but are not sure what—and are then at once distracted by the arrival of Sinon, with his story of the horse's beneficence. Dryden's alteration keeps Aeneas at more of a critical distance: he is made to interpret the scene with hindsight, rather than living it again.

Yet the yielding, the piercing, and the wound all still feel unexplained—as though they might be motivated by a secret of Dryden's own. Something must have conspired to give that extra force to Laocoön's interpretive probe—something, perhaps, to do with Dryden's feelings about secrets and how best to try to open them. Redescribing his aims as a translator in the 'Dedication to the *Aeneis*', he now expresses a hope that 'the Additions' will seem 'easily deduc'd from *Virgil*'s Sense ... not stuck into him, but growing out of him'.[26] Events at the wooden horse make this scenario almost comically literal; and also weirdly dysfunctional. Something is stuck into the horse; there are 'Groans' instead of 'growing'; the easy deduction is not made; and the effort of interpretation leaves a wound. The scene sends out filaments of suggestion towards Dryden's unease at his own work of transpiercing by translating.

The *Aeneid* is itself a narrative of opening. Events are driven, the poem announces at its start, by fate, and by the rage that curdles deep in Juno's being. 'Secret Seeds of Envy lay behind', as Dryden translates:

> Deep graven in her Heart, the Doom remain'd
> Of partial *Paris*, and her Form disdain'd.[27]

In Virgil, Paris's words are 'stored up' ('repostum').[28] In Dryden, the word 'graven' makes them seem inscribed in the flesh of Juno's heart: the seeds of Envy are planted in written furrows. Fate too is commonly thought of as being written down—as when, a bit further on, Jupiter reveals the 'secrets' ('arcana') of fate's scrolls: 'Know, I have search'd the Mystick Rolls of Fate', Dryden translates, allowing a hint of camp into the king of gods' declamation.[29] Aeneas's success is assured and, beyond that, the rise of the Romans:

> To them, no Bounds of Empire I assign;
> No term of Years to their immortal Line.

> His ego nec metas rerum, nec tempora pono:
> Imperium sine fine dedi.[30]

For Virgil, it was an ardent and plausible hope that the Roman Empire might have no bounds; but for Dryden the Empire had reached its term centuries before. This is one of the moments in the poem when the perspectives of author and of translator are most sharply pulled apart. Yet Dryden might nevertheless have taken Jupiter's words as giving a true presage, for Rome still asserted its Empire culturally over Europe, through the immortal lines of the *Aeneid* and other works. His choice of words here prompts us to see that, by translating, he is helping to extend that empire's bounds, continuing the unrolling of its writing.

As the secrets written in the rolls of fate and the hearts of the gods begin to bud into the open, Dryden starts to use of them the word 'design'. 'Second my Design', says Juno, pleading with Aeolus to whip up a storm against Aeneas and his fleet. 'Somewhat is sure design'd', proclaims the suspicious Laocoön of the wooden horse; and the Trojans would have believed him, 'had not Heav'n the fall of *Troy* design'd'—as Aeneas, looking back, laments. A 'design' is a plan, but also a representation. The Carthaginians are building houses which they have 'first design'd'; but when Aeneas comes across the wall-paintings of the fall of Troy he devours 'what he saw so well design'd'.[31] Design, then, exists before the events it designs, and then passes through them, shaping them, so that it can be apprehended afterwards: it is both intention and interpretation.

Reading with a view to translating, Dryden sought out his original's design. Before beginning his *Aeneis* he had, he said, long 'studied *Virgil*'s Design'—just as, two decades earlier, he had traced Ovid's 'beautiful design, which he first establishes, and then contrives the means which will naturally conduct it to his end'.[32] In the *Aeneis*, characters likewise ponder the designs that are unfolding through them, and conducting them towards an end, via the hints that emerge in prophecies and omens. During the catastrophe of the fall of Troy, for instance, Anchises at first refuses to leave: but then a flame, gentle and harmless ('tactu... innoxia'), appears at his grandson Iulus's forehead—or his 'Temples', as Dryden translates, taking the gift supplied by the English language to highlight the contrast between this flame and those which are simultaneously devouring the temples of Troy. Anchises, 'vers'd in Omens' (Dryden's comment), thinks some meaning might be secretly in the phenomenon, and asks Jove to 'confirm the glad Presage'. At which, 'there shot a streaming Lamp along the Sky', which 'swept a path in Heav'n, and shone a Guide': Anchises 'implor'd / The Gods protection and their Star adored' ('sanctum sidus adorat').[33] Dryden did not need to do any enlarging to make a further presage peep out through the line. As R. G. Austin put it in his commentary on *Aeneid* II, 'it is hard not to suppose that these words may have brought to the mind of many a medieval Christian reader the thought of another Star'.[34] The same thought might well strike later readers too.

Confronted with the shape of things to come, and understanding what he can of it, Anchises changes his mind. He tells Aeneas that he gives in, and does not refuse to go with him: 'cedo equidem nec, nate, tibi comes ire recuso'—a line which Dryden opens like this:

> At least accomplish what your Signs foreshow:
> I stand resign'd, and am prepar'd to go.[35]

The word 'resign'd' feels the pressure of 'Signs' in the line before, which urges it to adopt the connotation 're-sign'd'—re-signified or rewritten. As he is brought into being in Dryden's translation, itself a work of re-signing, Anchises is nudged towards recognizing that he exists in a world of signs. Just as with Canace, though more subtly and profoundly, his sense of himself is inflected by Dryden's sense of him as being a character in a poem of translation. He knows that a design is passing through him; and also that its secrets are not fully in his grasp.

13

Dryden's Dido: 'Somewhat I find within'

Dido is the character who suffers most from the opening of a secret design. It all starts when Venus prepares 'new Designs' to have Cupid take on the form of Aeneas's son and infuse his 'Venom' in Dido's 'Veins'.[1] In Virgil, Cupid begins, little by little, to wipe her dead husband Sychaeus from her mind ('paulatim abolere Sychaeum / Incipit') and tries to surprise her with a living love ('vivo tentat praevertere amore').[2] Dryden has him operate more vigorously, and also more like an artist. He:

> Works in the pliant Bosom of the Fair;
> And moulds her Heart anew, and blots her former Care.
> The dead is to the living Love resign'd.
> And all *Aeneas* enters in her Mind.[3]

'Pliant' and 'mould' suggest sculpture, though they also reach figuratively towards verse: we 'mould our thoughts into easie and significant words', as Dryden had put it in 'An Essay of Dramatick Poesie'.[4] 'Blots' certainly is an image from writing, and it tugs 'resign'd' a little towards the meaning we have seen it assume for Anchises. Reimagining what is going on inside Dido, Dryden reaches for the language of artistic representation. He does so again the next time her feelings are described, at the start of Book IV. She has, he says, a 'secret Fire' which is increased when Aeneas's looks are 'imprinted in her Heart' (the Latin is 'caeco . . . igni' and 'haerent infixi').[5] These details of vocabulary imply a feeling of kinship in Dryden between what he is doing and what is happening to her. For he too is moulding something anew, replacing a dead with a living language—though in the hope that this will not produce such infidelity to Virgil as Dido's to the memory of Sychaeus.

As her secret pushes to be revealed, Dryden's Dido becomes her own interpreter. In Virgil she expresses herself to her sister with clear conviction, in the ringing, famous phrase 'agnosco veteris vestigia flammae'.[6] In Dryden, her diagnosis is more hesitant:

> Somewhat I find within, if not the same,
> Too like the Sparkles of my former Flame.[7]

But Dryden's narrator is less circumspect. In Virgil, Dido shows off to Aeneas her 'Sidonian wealth and the built city; she begins to speak but stops in the middle of a word':

> Sidoniasque ostentat opes urbemque paratam:
> Incipit effari, mediaque in voce resistit.[8]

The Latin shares her discretion by not making explicit what it is that she is trying to say. Dryden translates these two lines accurately; but also enlarges them in order to open what he takes to be their meaning. 'This pomp she shows to tempt her wand'ring Guest', he explains, for Dido is displaying to Aeneas what 'Love, without his Labour, makes his own'.[9] It is the same speaking-on-behalf of a character that we have traced in 'Canace to Macareus' and elsewhere in Dryden's poetry of translation; which is to say, it is an instance of that same transgression-through-translation which was a source of 'unease'. Here in Book 4, uneasy counter-currents soon appear.

Juno designs events so that Dido and Aeneas are lured together into a place of secrecy, are hidden by 'one common Cavern in her Bosom', as Dryden puts it: 'Bosom' is his innovation and allows in just a hint of a fancy that this Bosom is an expanded version of Dido's own, the place of 'living love' where 'all *Aeneas*' had entered a little while before.[10] Now that her secret has been penetrated, Dido feels no need for any more concealment. I give Dryden's version, with his significant 'enlargements' under-lined:

> The Queen whom sense of Honour cou'd not move
> No longer made a Secret of her Love;
> But call'd it Marriage, by that specious Name,
> To veil the Crime <u>and sanctifie the Shame</u>.
> The loud Report through *Lybian* Cities goes;
> Fame, <u>the great Ill</u>, from small beginnings grows:
> Swift from the first; and ev'ry Moment brings
> New Vigour to her flights, <u>new Pinions to her wings</u>.
> Soon grows <u>the Pygmee to Gygantic size</u>;
> Her Feet on Earth, her Forehead in the Skies.[11]

Dido opens her secret out into language; but the narrator—in Virgil no less than in Dryden—immediately rejects the name she chooses for it, defining it as something deceitful, a veil, rather than a true expression (the Latin says this with a verb, 'praetexit').[12] Fame carries on the dispute and, in Dryden, snatches Dido's rhymes, 'Name' and 'Shame', using them to name and shame her:

> She fills the Peoples Ears with *Dido*'s Name;
> Who, lost to Honour, and the sense of Shame,
> Admits into her Throne and Nuptial Bed
> A wandring Guest...[13]

The gossip swells pruriently for several more lines, moulding Dido anew into someone 'Dissolv'd in Ease' and 'abandon'd to her Lust'.[14] This is all done a notch more vigorously in Dryden than in Virgil, and so tallies with those 'enlargements' he made to the description of Fame. He too, like Fame, adds new Pinions to Virgil's lines and swells them, if not from Pygmee to Gygantic size, at least to something plumper than they were before. But the wording also points in the other direction, suggesting, via its echo of the famous tag from Lucan about pygmies standing on the shoulders of giants, that it is Dryden who is the pygmy, lifted high on Virgil's shoulders, puffing himself up by taking the great man's words and altering them and filling the people's ears with his name. Dryden's 'Fame' translates the Latin 'Fama', a word which a few lines before has popped up, not as the name of the evil goddess, but as a common noun with the positive sense rendered by Dryden as 'Honour'. The different English words split open the Latin's ambiguity, the more so when 'Fame' is at once blackened by being called 'the great Ill'. Yet this innovation creates a new ripple of uncertainty. Not all fame is bad, surely? The emphasis lets in something of the self-inculpatory feeling that Dryden vents in the introduction, regarding his own contribution to the spread of Virgil's fame: 'I have done great wrong to Virgil in the whole translation'.

The episode of the spread of Fame through the Lybian cities is one of a string of scenes of 'opening' in the first half of the *Aeneid*. Mingling 'Truth with Lyes' ('pariter facta atque infecta'), filling 'the peaceful Universe with Cries' ('nocte volat coeli medio, terraeque per umbram, / Stridens') through her 'millions of opening Mouths' ('totidem ora'), Fame resembles the Sybil whose voice in Book 6 is a 'rushing Whirlwind' (Dryden's image) that 'roars' through the 'hundred Doors' ('ostia...centum') of her cave, and who is likewise unreliable, for she too 'some Truths reveal'd, in Terms involv'd the rest' ('obscuris vera involvens').[15] As Paul Davis has shown, this passage itself resounds with echoes of Roscommon's 'Essay on Translated Verse', suggesting that Dryden associated the Sybil 'not just with the inspired poet in general but with the instrumental figure of the translator in particular'.[16] Dryden also increases the similarity between the Sybil's chaotic utterance and the winds which, in Book 1, had been released by Aeolus to raise a storm against Aeneas's fleet: 'The raging

Winds rush through the hollow Wound' ('venti...Quà data porta, ruunt') and 'with mix'd Confusion roar' ('ruunt, creberque procellis'). Dryden's word 'wound' sends out a filament of connection towards the wound made by Laocoön in the side of the wooden horse; the more so as Aeolus has inflicted it in the same way: 'He...hurled against the Mountain side, / His quiv'ring Spear' ('cavum conversa cuspide montem / Impulit in latus').[17] This concatenation of misleading or frankly destructive instances of 'opening' is interlinked more strongly in Dryden than in Virgil, and presented by him in terms that imply an uneasy recognition of likeness to his own practice of 'opening' through translation. The suggestion is clinched by an extraordinary change he makes to the effectiveness of 'Fame'. In Virgil, Fame's tales reach Dido's rejected lover Iarbas, who protests to Jupiter, who then looks down and sees that Dido and Aeneas are being forgetful of their better fame ('oblitos famae melioris'). This corresponds to what we have been told by the narrator before Fame set out on her career of exaggeration: Dido is no longer bothered by honour or decorum ('neque enim specie famâve movetur').[18] But in Dryden, what Jupiter sees is not this truth of the matter but the more heated version that Fame has put about:

> The lustful Pair, in lawless pleasure drown'd:
> Lost in their Loves, insensible of Shame;[19]

Dryden's 'Fame' has the power to create the truth which she pretends only to report. She is a nightmare double of the translator.

In the company of these warning, self-critical episodes, Dryden's own practice of 'opening' becomes especially pointed. When Aeneas has been ordered by Jupiter to leave Dido and seek out Italy for the sake of glory and his heirs, it is now he who is in the position of having a secret, put inside him by a god, which he must find a way of bringing into the open. After much wavering, which Dryden tracks carefully, slightly enlarging as he goes, Aeneas calls three commanders and has them get the fleet ready discreetly ('classem aptent taciti'), keeping the cause of the change hidden ('quae sit rebus causa novandis / Dissimulent').[20] Dryden's rephrasing connects this moment to the pattern of secret designs that we have been exploring:

> Some plausible Pretence he bids them find,
> To colour what in secret he design'd.[21]

As Aeneas wonders how on earth to open the design to Dido, Dryden does some opening of his own (additions and alterations are underlined):

> Himself, mean time, the softest Hours wou'd chuse,
> Before the <u>Love-sick Lady</u> heard the News;
> <u>And move her tender Mind, by slow degrees</u>,
> To suffer <u>what the Sov'raign Pow'r decrees</u>:
> <u>*Jove* will inspire him, when, and what to say</u>:
> They hear with Pleasure, and with haste obey.

sese interea, quando optima Dido / Nesciat & tantos rumpi non speret amores, / Tentaturum aditus, & quae mollissima fandi / Tempora, quis rebus dexter modus. Ocyus omnes / Imperio laeti parent ac jussa facessunt.[22]

It is uncertain, in the Latin no less than in the English, how many of the words attributed to Aeneas are actually spoken by him and how many are looser representations of his thoughts. His commanders are present throughout. In the Latin, the command they set off to obey at the end has been given in indirect speech at the beginning: he told them to prepare the fleet, etc. 'Sese interea' ('Himself, mean time') then sounds as though it might be continuing, still in indirect speech, the outline of the plan. But the emotiveness of some of the phrases ('optima Dido', 'tantos . . . amores') makes them unlikely to have been said out loud. Austin describes this well in his commentary: 'the words represent Aeneas' thought', and 'optima', especially, 'is heart-breaking in its context', for it means that 'Dido was all the world to him'.[23] It is one of the little touches, often adjectival, which let us glimpse the passion Aeneas is having to suppress in order to fulfil the duty laid on him by Jupiter. In the Latin, then, the language seems to drift inwards, no longer reporting speech but getting drawn into sympathetic representation of Aeneas's thoughts and feelings.

There is something of this in the Dryden too. 'And move her tender mind, by slow degrees' itself slows the progress of Aeneas's thoughts, making him linger tenderly on the problem. But the other alterations pull in the opposite direction. 'Love-sick Lady' has an air of romantic comedy: Dryden had used the phrase before in an epistle to George Etherege, the dramatist and libertine.[24] As a rendering of 'tantos . . . amores' it is startlingly trivial. Then 'what the Sov'raign Pow'r decrees' is more grandiose and certain than its little, rather baffled counterpart in the Latin, 'rebus', from 'res', meaning 'the thing'. And the line about Jove's inspiration has an air of blokeish bluster: 'don't worry lads, something will crop up'. Dryden's opening of Aeneas's plan to open his secret to Dido pulls it more into the public world of chat. The secrets within his Aeneas are fewer and less mysterious.

But Dryden's Dido has an affinity for secrets:

> She was the first to find the secret Fraud
> Before the fatal News was blaz'd abroad.[25]

In Virgil, her presentiment mingles with the hearing of gossip, nicely catching the way a suspicious mind can leap to the right conclusion. As Austin puts it, 'Virgil is careful not to make it plain whether her knowledge came from *Fama* alone'[26]—and the ambiguity is preserved in other English translations, such as those by Sir Robert Howard and by Waller and Godolphin which Dryden knew well. But Dryden makes it plain that the workings of her discovery were not at all plain: it was not at all due to *Fama*. Something interpretive but non-linguistic sparked between her and Aeneas: 'Love, the first Motions of the Lover hears, / Quick to presage'.[27]

Both in Virgil and in Dryden, Dido accuses Aeneas of breaking a binding agreement which he denies he had ever entered into. But Dryden's translation makes the agreement more specifically verbal than it is in the Latin. The tragedy, for his Dido, is that the secret of her heart, the secret she had thought she shared with Aeneas, cannot survive once it is opened out into the public world of speech. In Virgil, she says he has forgotten the 'data dextera', the pledged right hand which was a gesture in the Roman wedding ceremony. He has abandoned 'connubia nostra', 'our marriage'. Dryden gives 'plighted Vows' and, again, 'holy Vows'.[28] The Latin Dido calls Aeneas 'perfide', false one. Dryden enlarges the accusation: 'False as thou art, and more than false, forsworn'. For Aeneas too, the nub of the matter is more completely a verbal contract in the English than in the Latin. He never pretended, he says, 'to the Lawful Claim / Of Sacred Nuptials, or, a Husband's Name'.[29] What is drawing him away is also felt to be a verbal power. Not just the fates—'fata'—but 'Fate's Decree'.[30] In Virgil, his love of Dido competes with another love, for Italy: 'hic amor, haec patria est'. In Dryden he is compelled towards Italy by a verbal contract: 'all my Vows are terminated there'.[31] Granted, some of these adjustments owe something to the difference between Roman and English wedding customs, and some are helped to happen by rhyme. But cumulatively they bring into being an Aeneas for whom the experiences and commitments that matter are those that have been fixed in unambiguous words; and a Dido who, for all the rhetorical energy of her speeches, cannot establish what matters to her in the open language of statement and verbal contract.

Dryden's Aeneas conforms himself to the text that has been written for him by 'sacred Pow'r'. He adopts a turn of phrase with which we have become familiar:

> To thy bless'd Orders I resign my heart:
> Lead thou the way; protect thy *Trojan* Bands
> And prosper the Design thy Will Commands.[32]

He knows his place in a hierarchy of signification which is both divinely and publicly sanctioned, both 'bless'd' and shared with the '*Trojan* bands'. But Dido is left alone. In consequence, her knowledge of the world begins to wobble. Dryden translates tentatively, only half opening the lines:

> Oft, when she visited this lonely Dome,
> Strange voices issu'd from her Husband's Tomb:
> She thought she heard him summon her away;
> Invite her to his Grave; and chide her stay.
> Hourly 'tis heard, when with a bodeing Note
> The solitary Screech-Owl strains her Throat:
> And on a Chimney's top, or Turret's hight,
> With songs obscene, disturbs the Silence of the Night.

> Hinc exaudiri voces & verba vocantis
> Visa viri, nox cum terras obscura teneret;
> Solaque culminibus ferali carmine bubo
> Saepe queri & longas in fletum ducere voces.[33]

In Virgil, it seems that she hears cries, 'words from her husband calling'. Dryden makes explicit her activity of interpretation ('she thought'), and then draws out her thoughts about what the strange voices might mean, blending them with his. In Virgil, the owl's cries are blurred together with the sounds from the tomb because they are given the same word, 'voces'. Dryden does something similar, linking the two noises with 'when': she thinks she hears her husband's summons 'when with a bodeing Note / The solitary Screech-Owl strains her Throat'. Both texts create an ambiguous soundscape which resounds also in their own echoic phonemes. Dryden, as always, pushes further towards an interpretation, using a character as the vessel of his own enquiries. But here, crucially, his openings are left uncertain: they are just as likely to represent Dido's own foreboding as the bodeings of oracles. Contrast the no-nonsense 'opening' of the lines by Edmund Waller, in the translation which, two decades before, Dryden had adduced as an exemplary paraphrase:

> Hence every night proceeds a dreadful sound;
> Her husband's voice invites her to his tomb,
> And dismal owls presage the ills to come.[34]

Here, the translator's determination to interpret destroys the uncertainty of interpretation which is the great achievement of Virgil's lines.

For Dido is withdrawing from the communal realm in which the meaning of things is agreed and secured. Her nearest confidante is her sister; and she deceives even her. She is 'alone'; she designs a 'secret Fun'ral' in 'the secret Court'; she talks to herself 'within her secret

Mind'. Dryden's tolling word signals that Dido is being pulled into herself towards the condition of secrecy where all her love and pain began. On the hidden pyre, in Dryden just as in Virgil, she places 'the Nuptial Bed' with, upon it, 'the Man's Image' which had once been printed in her heart.[35] Bursting out all around her will come the fire that she had once held secret within. But Dryden's clarificatory nudges have made Dido's backwards progress seem more clearly to be enjoined by forces which all her spouts of rhetoric, her talk of vengeance and glory, cannot quite grasp. Translating, Dryden is subjected to Virgil's design. And so Dido strikes him all the more forcefully as being destroyed by a design that has its origin and its destination beyond her ken, and which she can only partly comprehend.

Looking back at Dido's fire across the sea from his ship, at the start of Book V, Aeneas has a breezier view:

> The Cause unknown; yet his presaging Mind,   }
> The Fate of *Dido* from the Fire divin'd: }
> He knew the stormy Souls of Woman-kind: }
> What secret Springs their eager Passions move,
> How capable of Death for injur'd Love.

quae tantum accenderit ignem / Causa latet; duri magno sed amore dolores / Polluto, notumque, furens quid foemina possit, / Triste per augurium Teucrorum pectora ducunt.[36]

Virgil makes Aeneas seem cruel by losing him in the crowd, implying that he felt no more concern for Dido than did the rest of the Trojans ('Teucrorum'). Dryden takes a different line, singling him out, and giving salience to his heuristic confidence ('He knew') against the mystery of the fire ('the cause unknown'). This echoes the clash of knowing and un-knowing in Dryden's early foray in translation, 'Canace to Macareus': here, as there, it suggests connections between political rule, masculine cruelty, and the drive to interpret which is inseparable from the impulse to translate.

But here, more than there, the boast of knowing is held up to criticism. In a simple sense, of course, Aeneas has worked out the reason for what he sees. Yet the deeper motives he attributes to Dido are no more than blunt received ideas, a reasonable shorthand for the Trojans as a group to have recourse to, but shameful when attributed to him as the sum total of his understanding of what has happened: it is of a piece with Dryden's own flattening of 'tantos ... amores' into 'the Love-sick Lady'. The element of self-loathing which shadows Dryden's enjoyment of translation, his un-ease that 'opening' entails simplification, and that he has done Virgil a 'great wrong' comes through strongly here; for in Aeneas's drive to interpret and make use of Dido he must see a double of his own drive to interpret and make use of Virgil. And it is this self-critical layering that saves Dryden's work from being what he fears it might be; that lifts it into being a poem of translation. For Dryden's text does not support Aeneas's bright confidence. It has shown us that the motives of Dido's drift towards death are other than these; and that she is more than he here, on his mission, surrounded by his comrades, can allow himself to know of her. Opening Dido's secrets into such a trite translation, Aeneas is shown to be doing her one last great wrong.

As translated by Dryden, the episode of Dido and Aeneas plays out a struggle that occurs in every word of his translation: of interpreting and getting wrong; of 'opening' and the element of misrepresentation which it inevitably creates. This text is a refutation of the idea that translation 'is' interpretation; and a brilliant and heartfelt exploration of the ways in which translation and interpretation are nevertheless inseparably and agonistically intertwined.

PART III

TRANSLATION AS 'FRIENDSHIP', AS 'DESIRE', AND AS 'PASSION'

14

Translating an Author

Dryden translated from printed books. They offered him the 'letter' and the 'words' which he 'opened' to reveal the 'sentence' and the 'sense'. But there was something more that he extrapolated from the pages. It was 'Virgil' whose secrets he thought he could uncover, 'Virgil' whom he hoped to enable to 'speak...English', 'Virgil' to whom he feared he had done a great wrong. What Dryden felt himself to be translating into English was, finally, not 'letter', nor 'words', nor 'sentence', nor 'sense', nor even a 'poem'. It was an 'Author'.[1]

This metaphor seems first to have been given firm shape by Sir John Denham a couple of decades earlier. In *The Destruction of Troy*, his translation from Book II of the *Aeneid* published in 1656, Denham hoped, he said, to 'do *Virgil* less injury than others have done' and to allow him to 'speak not onely as a man of this Nation, but as a man of this age'.[2] There had been hazy precursors to these turns of thought and phrase. Back in 1561, Sir Thomas Hoby described himself as having made Castiglione's *The Courtyer* 'an Englishman...and welwilling to dwell in the Court of Englande'. But Hoby personifies the book instead of conjuring its author; and the image did not extend to his practice of translation which he describes in the then usual terms of following the 'very meaning & woordes'.[3] In 1579, Sir Thomas North, in the preamble to his translation of a French translation of Plutarch, repeated this from his intermediary Jacques Amyot:

> the office of a fit translater, consisteth not onely in the faithfull expressing of his authors meaning, but also in a certaine resembling and shadowing out of the forme of his style and the manner of his speaking.[4]

This is closer to Denham. But North does not go on to imagine the author fully into being as an individual. Denham gathered these threads of precedent into a coherent pattern of metaphor. The result was that translation could be understood as a form of social behaviour. You could cause 'injury' to Virgil just as you might to a living person.

As Lawrence Venuti and Paul Davis have shown, Denham's theory and practice of translation had marked socio-political affiliations.[5] Produced by a royalist who spent time under house arrest and in exile, *The Destruction of Troy* recounts the beheading of a king and is written with courtly *sprezzatura*: in 1656 the currents—hardly undercurrents—of suggestiveness were strong. This barbed relevance must have been what Denham had most in mind when he boasted of having launched a 'new way of translating', even though he tactfully pretends to set it up in opposition to 'Verbal' (i.e. word-for-word) translation: *The Destruction of Troy* is not in fact especially unliteral, and many earlier translators had taken greater liberties.[6] As we have seen, Dryden (and others) followed Denham in relating their translations carefully to the politics and culture of the present.

The idea that he was translating an 'author' freed Denham to be contemporary. *If Virgil were alive and in the present*—it allowed him to think—*these are the attitudes he would have adopted.* And the metaphor soon caught on. It pops up in a letter by the poet Katherine Philips (known as 'Orinda') about her version of Corneille's *La mort de Pompée* (1662).[7] It reappears in the *Traduction de l'Eneide de Virgile* by Jean Regnault de Segrais (1668).[8] And it mattered a great deal to Dryden who, just like Denham, was confident he could extrapolate from his idea of Virgil to body him forth speaking 'such *English*, as he wou'd himself have spoken, if he had been born in *England*, and in this present Age'. Dryden worried more than Denham about the 'injury' he might inflict by doing so, as we saw in Chapters 12 and 13: 'I have done great Wrong to *Virgil* in the whole Translation'.[9] 'The maintaining the character of an author which distinguishes him from all others', Dryden said, was the translator's hardest and implicitly most important task.[10]

This metaphor partly underwrites and partly limits the metaphor of 'opening' which we explored in Chapters 11 to 13. For Dryden, what is 'in' Virgil—his historical relevancies, his illocutionary suggestions—needs to be brought to light: it is part of what makes him him. But his air of secrecy is another aspect of his 'character' and so needs to be maintained as well—though, as we saw, Dryden tends in practice always to diminish 'secrecy' for the sake of 'opening', however regretful he may have felt about doing so. The idea of the author emerges from his texts and then floats half free, reflecting back on them and prescribing how they are seen. The translator has an epistemological duty of truthfulness towards this imagined authorial figure:

> If the fancy of Ovid be luxuriant, 'tis his character to be so, and if I retrench it, he is no longer Ovid.[11]

And also a social duty of courtesy with which truthfulness must be balanced: 'a translator is to make his author appear as charming as he possibly can,' Dryden says, 'provided he maintain his character'.[12]

The metaphor of translating an author flourished for decades after Dryden. But it began to falter in the second half of the eighteenth century when—as Louis Kelly tells us—'translation theory and practice generally moved towards greater literalism'.[13] As translators change their behaviour, so the metaphors that inform it alter. In the Preface to his *Iliad and Odyssey of Homer* (1791), for instance, William Cowper's principal targets were Pope's Homer and the tradition of translating epic into rhyming couplets. But he also kicked against the opinion, which still seemed to him 'commonly received', that 'a translator should imagine to himself the style which his author would probably have used, had the Language into which he is rendered been his own'. This 'direction', he goes on, 'wants nothing but practicability to recommend it'. If you ask six people to write like 'the same Antient', all of them will do it differently. Hence, 'by probable inference', not one of them can be 'right'. As Cowper sees it, the endeavour to conjure an author out of his work requires too much invention: a translator who thinks of himself as being faithful to an 'author' risks binding himself, Narcissus-like, to nothing more than his own image. Cowper does still use the word 'author'; but he holds it closer to the letter of the source than Dryden did. He aims, he says, to be 'true to the original author's style and manner', while also making sure to 'let slip nothing of the text'. But he admits that he has found the 'balance . . . nearly impossible' to maintain. In practice, verbal fidelity has had the greater weight: 'my chief boast is that I have adhered closely to my original'.[14]

Take, for instance, the very beginning of his *Iliad*:

> Achilles sing, O Goddess! Peleus' son;
> His wrath pernicious, who ten thousand woes
> Caused to Achaia's host, sent many a soul
> Illustrious into Ades premature,
> And Heroes gave (so stood the will of Jove)
> To dogs and to all rav'ning fowls a prey,
> When fierce dispute had separated once
> The noble Chief Achilles from the son
> Of Atreus, Agamemnon, King of men.[15]

Several phrases here bear out his claim of 'close adherence'. 'O Goddess!' stands for 'θέα', adhering to it more closely than the usual 'Muse'. A bit further on, 'into Ades' sticks similarly close to '"Άϊδι', while 'fierce dispute had separated' painstakingly renders both elements of 'διαστήτην ἐρίσαντε'· Now here is Dryden's rendering of the same lines in *Fables Ancient and Modern* (1700):

> The wrath of Peleus' son, O Muse, resound,
> Whose dire effects the Grecian army found,
> And many a hero, king, and hardy knight,
> Were sent, in early youth, to shades of night:
> Their limbs a prey to dogs and vultures made;
> So was the sovereign will of Jove obeyed:
> From that ill-omened hour when strife begun,
> Betwixt Atrides great, and Thetis' godlike son.[16]

'Muse', 'shades of night', and the absence of anything corresponding to 'separated' are so many departures from the wording of the Greek. But Dryden holds on to the fact that the poem begins with the Greek word for 'wrath', placed in balance with 'the will of Jove' which appears towards the other end of the sentence's proliferating spans of syntax. Cowper, in startling contrast, has bumped 'wrath' out of the epic's first line, presumably thinking the sacrifice worth making since it leaves him room for all of 'Achilles . . . Peleus' son', word for word with his 'original'. Again, Dryden leaves out Agamemnon's epithet, 'King of men' ('ἄναξ ἀνδρῶν'); but this allows him to set up 'Atrides' head to head with 'Thetis' godlike son'— Achilles—in a single line just as Homer does. Dryden, then, sees shapes in the Greek and is ready to cut individual words in order to preserve them. For all Cowper's boast of close adherence, it would be hard to say whether he or Dryden is in fact closer to the entity we call the *Iliad*, which is, after all, not the same as its vocabulary. Cowper offers English counterparts for more of Homer's words; but Dryden gives a more powerful representation of the shape of the verse, that is, the traits of Homer's style.[17]

Of course, the difference owes much, simply, to Dryden's greater vim as a writer. But it also owes something to the different permeating metaphors according to which the translations are being composed. Translating an 'author', Dryden feels able to infer what Homer would have done if he were writing in English pentameter couplets: he would have ditched Agamemnon's epithet and preserved the head-to-head with Achilles. To Cowper, that judgement seems a mere liberty on the part of the translator, a violation of the gluey metaphor of 'close adherence'. This metaphor also puts couplets out of the question, for rhyme—Cowper says—necessitates too much rewriting, making 'a just translation of any antient poet . . . impossible'.[18] (Some rewriting is required also by his preferred form of blank verse, and is of course inherent in the act of translation per se, but Cowper's metaphor helps him not to see this.) Dryden's confidence that he can discern an 'author' gives him the freedom necessary to write in rhyme. Equally, his commitment to rhyme requires him to adopt that metaphor, or something like it, because it makes word-for-word equivalence very obviously impossible. There is a symbiosis between metaphor and medium.

As we saw in Chapter 4, to read verse (indeed, to read anything) is to collaborate with the words on the page so as to bring into being an imagining which they point to but do not encapsulate. No doubt Cowper is right that six different people will imagine six slightly different poems. But to hold back for that reason from the work of imagining is to decline the invitation the verse extends to its readers: it is to refuse to help conjure a poem into being. And of course the element of collaboration cannot be avoided entirely because it is intrinsic to the act of reading. Because Cowper will not admit this, his departures from the wording of the source are unmotivated: they feel like failures rather than interpretive choices. But since Dryden's alterations are made designedly, they signal interpretive discoveries, asking to be interpreted in their turn. This is true of his way with Virgil's 'secrets' and 'address', as we saw in Chapters 12 and 13; and it is true also of his attention to the movement of Homer's verse. The idea that what is being translated is 'the author' both stimulates and guides this process of reading-imagining-translating.

Nevertheless, Cowper's *Iliad and Odyssey of Homer* signals a wider loss of confidence in the metaphor of translating an 'author'. Shelley's 'Defence of Poetry' (written in 1821 but not published until 1840) defended poetry by asserting that it is all but impossible to translate:

> It were as wise to cast a violet into a crucible that you might discover the formal principle of its colour and odour, as to seek to transfuse from one language to another the creations of a poet. The plant must spring again from its seed, or it will bear no flower—and this is the burthen of the curse of Babel.[19]

This seems mainly to urge the necessity of utter reimaginings such as those of Aeschylus in *Prometheus Unbound* and of Dante in 'The Triumph of Life'; though it must also somehow leave room for the harmonious but actually quite close translations that Shelley made from the Homeric Hymns. Whatever the scope of its recommendation, the focus of this argument is not the 'poet' but his 'creations': 'the plant' that 'must spring again from its seed, or it will bear no flower' appears to be independent of its author.

Shelley's combative rhetoric suggests that he sensed the swelling of a trend in the opposite direction: in reviews at the time, 'literal fidelity' was on its way to becoming the major criterion of praise. Take this, from an article by the translator George Moir which appeared in the *Edinburgh Review* in 1835:

> In translation . . . we have of late been acquiring some new ideas; and it seems now to be pretty generally felt that the main object of a translator should be to exhibit his author and not himself. If a work is worth translating at all it is worth translating *literally*.[20]

Moir holds on to the word 'author' but moulds it to fit Cowper's notion of 'adherence': Dryden and Pope must be in his mind when he mentions the sort of translator who wishes to 'exhibit . . . himself'. For Moir, to translate an 'author' means to translate his 'work'; and to translate his work means to translate '*literally*'.

Over the preceding decades of romanticism it had become harder to think of poetry in the way Pope had done: as the best expression of 'what oft was *Thought*'.[21] For the young Tennyson, in 1830, a poet's 'mind' was secret, as it had been for Dryden; but it also asked to be left that way: 'Vex not thou the poet's mind; / For thou canst not fathom it'.[22] In the company of such views, a mode of translation that relied on not only fathoming but reimagining the intentions of an author could hardly flourish. So Dryden's middle 'way' of paraphrase was largely blocked; and the extremes of 'verbal version' and of 'imitation' took its place. Literalism came to dominate what was thought of as 'translation'—with the proviso that no literalism is wholly literal, as we saw in Chapter 5. Translations in this vein were taken to supply knowledge about the source text—to 'furnish . . . the very turn of each phrase in as Greek a fashion as the English will bear', as Browning said of his *Agamemnon of Aeschylus*, the sublime example of this mode.[23] On the other hand, poets fled the bounds of translation and took to freer forms of response, as we will see in Chapters 16 and 21. Even those comparatively few translations that still operated along lines quite similar to Dryden's 'paraphrase' were not presented as translations of an 'author'. Elizabeth Barrett's sense of herself as being true to Aeschylus' 'genius' in her second version of *Prometheus Bound* meant something rather different from being faithful to him as an author, as we saw in Chapter 6. And while Edward FitzGerald did at times think of himself as translating 'Omar Khayyam', as well as his *Rubáiyát*, this metaphor was much complicated by others, as we will see in Chapter 24. In general, for most translators, fidelity to an 'author' had lost its charm.

15

The Author as Intimate

Still, for a century and a half, roughly between Denham and Cowper, the idea of the author was at the heart of translatorly imagining. It was vividly conjured and elaborated by Lord Roscommon in a poem that mattered to Dryden, as we saw in Chapter 12: the 'Essay on Translated Verse' (1684):

> Examine how your *Humour* is inclin'd,
> And which the *Ruling Passion* of your Mind;
> Then, seek a *Poet* who *your* way do's bend,
> And chuse an *Author* as you chuse a *Friend*.
> United by this *Sympathetick Bond*,
> You grow *Familiar*, *Intimate* and *Fond*;
> Your *Thoughts*, your *Words*, your *Stiles*, your *Souls* agree,
> No Longer his *Interpreter*, but *He*.[1]

Roscommon's notion is rooted in famous discussions of friendship by Aristotle, Cicero, and Montaigne; but it also draws on the poetry of Katherine Philips, herself both a friend of Roscommon's and a translator before her early death in 1664. Philips had presided over a 'society of friendship' and, in her verse, had elaborated distinctive notions of what it meant to be a friend. She protested against the tendency of 'men t'exclude / Women from friendship's vast capacity' and valued emotional communion over what had been the main feature of friendship in the classical tradition, the pursuit of virtue. 'The chiefest thing in Friends', she said, 'is Sympathy . . . Which made two souls before they know agree.'[2]

Roscommon sticks close to Cicero when he emphasizes the care that should be taken in choosing an author to be friends with. And Cicero does say that the souls of friends may mingle with one another so as to become almost one ('cuius animum ita cum suo misceat, ut efficiat paene unum ex duobus').[3] Only 'almost', though ('paene'): strict limits are imposed on the unanimity to which friends should aspire. It should not conflict with honour and, when one friend is dejected, the other should not sink into sympathetic melancholy but rather strive to cheer him up. The surge towards utter oneness in Roscommon's lines owes more to Philips. Take, for a final instance, her 'L'amitié: To Mrs M Awbrey':

> Soule of my soule! my Joy, my crown, my friend!
> A name which all the rest doth comprehend;
> How happy are we now, whose souls are grown,
> By an incomparable mixture, One.[4]

With their gathering of energy towards a final, unifying monosyllable, these lines lay down the rhetorical pattern followed by Roscommon.

In the early 1680s Roscommon founded an informal 'academy' with the aim of improving English language and literature via translation from the classics. Dryden was associated with it; the other members were of varying literary distinction but uniformly grand social standing, such as the Marquess of Halifax, the Earl of Dorset, and Lord Maitland, the future Earl of Lauderdale, whose manuscript translation of the *Aeneid* Dryden later borrowed to help with his work on the poem.[5] So the 'Essay on Translated Verse' had a cultural prominence that matched its rhetorical ambition. We have seen how intently Dryden responded to it; and its influence continued through the ensuing decades. It appears to have given Pope the phrase 'the ruling Passion' which became central to his 'Moral Essays' (and greatly irritated Dr Johnson).[6] Thomas Francklin's 'Translation: A Poem' of 1753 takes issue with it, and Alexander Tytler's *Essay on the Principles of Translation* (1791) is greatly in its debt. And yet Roscommon's idea of friendship via translation had only a hesitant and fragmentary afterlife, even though it seems an obvious extension of the popular idea that translation should happen to an 'author'.

Friendship is mentioned in the prefatory material to Pope's *Iliad of Homer* (1715):

> There is something in the Mind of Man, which goes beyond bare Curiosity, and even carries us on to a Shadow of Friendship, with those great Genius's whom we have known to excell in former Ages. ... a Tendency to be farther acquainted with them, by gathering every Circumstance of their Lives; a kind of Complacency in their Company, when we retire to enjoy what they have left; an Union with them in those Sentiments they approve; and an Endeavour to defend them when we think they are injuriously attack'd, or even sometimes with too partial an Affection.[7]

The account of readerly affection is fleshed out with traditional details from Cicero and Montaigne. But the writing is itself shadowed by the awareness that what is being described is only friendship's 'Shadow'. If we wish to become acquainted with dead great geniuses, the best we can do is to gather 'Circumstances' of their lives; and all they can offer by way of

'Company' is for us to enjoy 'what they have left'. This is more circumspect than Roscommon's bond of sympathetic union; and it is kept at a
remove from the activity of translating by the fact that it is the opening,
not of Pope's own discussion of translation, but of the separate 'Essay on
the Life, Writings, and Learning of Homer' written for him by Thomas
Parnell. In the translation itself, Pope does seem especially alert, as Hester
Jones has argued, to 'moments of response, recognition, and exchange
between two people or two characters, moments which'—she says—
'frequently approach the "shadow of friendship"'.[8] But here again, friendship itself is not at the heart of Pope's imagining. Jones's delicate phrase,
'approach the "shadow"', is just right, for his way with such moments in
fact expresses a more general concern with the spread of passion, as we will
see in Chapter 19. Pope never describes translation as an act of friendship.

Dryden's connection with the idea was similarly tentative. He did
profess to have 'a soul congenial' to Chaucer's. But this was in the course
of justifying a group of translations that were unusually free: 'I durst not
make so bold with Ovid', he went on; and he did not make so bold with
Virgil or Homer either.[9] In the Preface to *Ovid's Epistles* (1680) he talks, as
Roscommon was to do four years later, of the steps by which a translator
and author become close:

> ... nor must we understand the language only of the poet, but his particular
> turn of thoughts, and of expression, which are the characters that distinguish,
> and as it were individuate him from all other writers. When we are come thus
> far, 'tis time to look into ourselves, to conform our genius to his, to give his
> thought either the same turn if our tongue will bear it, or if not, to vary but
> the dress, not to alter or destroy the substance.[10]

Just as in Roscommon, the translator gauges the author's personality and
measures it against his own; and then there is a movement into togetherness. Yet Dryden employs none of Roscommon's vocabulary of amity and
his syntax does not have the same affective impetus: there is no sympathetic bonding, no fondness, no finally becoming one. And in fact he was
quite ready to translate poets whose humours did not naturally bend his
way, and with whose thoughts—let alone souls—he did not fully agree.
Lucretius, for instance, whose 'fiery temper', his 'scorn and indignation',
are dispassionately weighed by Dryden before he assumes the burden of
translating him, laying by his 'natural diffidence and scepticism for a
while, to take up that dogmatical way of his...which is so much his
character as to make him that individual poet'. Even then, Lucretius's
'opinions concerning the mortality of the soul' continue to strike him
as 'absurd'.[11]

Dryden did not, any more than Pope, ever quite adopt friendship as a metaphor of translation. Yet, just as with Pope, it does lurk in the margins. Dryden's early efforts as a translator were part of a sociable enterprise, not only because of his connection with Roscommon's academy, but because the volumes in which they were published—*Ovid's Epistles*, the *Miscellany Poems* of 1684, *Sylvae*—were all collaborative ventures.[12] Here was a community of imaginative endeavour into which the source poets might well have been welcomed as friendly associates: only they never quite were. Among Dryden's poem-translations at this time is one made by extracting, from *Aeneid* Books 5 and 9, the story of Nisus and Euryalus, an older and a younger warrior who are linked 'by the sacred bonds of amity'.[13] As Paul Hammond has pointed out, Dryden made a 'series of additions' which 'emphasises the bond between the friends': he was especially sensitized to the episode because he had recently lost a young friend of his own, John Oldham, and had mourned him in lines that recollect the Nisus and Euryalus episode.[14] Nevertheless, the subject and manner of translation do not interact as we saw them being prompted to do by episodes of 'opening': Dryden's text does not ask to be read as an act of friendship towards Virgil. The particular energies of the poetry of translation do not quite flow. There is the same tantalizing non-start in his 'Palamon and Arcite', his translation of Chaucer's *Knight's Tale* published in *Fables Ancient and Modern* (1700). His feeling of being 'congenial' to Chaucer allows him to take liberties:

> I have presumed farther in some places, and added somewhat of my own where I thought my author was deficient, and had not given his thoughts their true lustre.[15]

He adopts and perhaps extends that principle of courtesy towards his author—to make him 'appear as charming as he possibly can'—which he had announced in the Preface to *Sylvae*.[16] But this presumption on his part is presented as an act, not of friendship, but of historical repair: Chaucer is a 'rough diamond', held back from shining by the 'want of words in the beginning of our language'.[17] The translation itself does not behave in ways that are amenable to being understood as distinctively friendly. Dryden elaborates the discussion of 'fate and fortune' and increases 'the Homeric participation of the gods'. He alters the divisions of the poem so as to create a 'clearer narrative line', and he introduces 'a clearer logic' in comparisons.[18] Stylistically, the work of polishing exacerbates what was already a strange automatism, part-satirical, part-melancholic, in Chaucer's descriptions of feeling (lovers are 'now vp, now doune, as boket in a well'): the translation extends the clockwork structure of parallelism and contrast.[19]

Even in the passage from Roscommon's 'Essay on Translated Verse', friendship is not all that is being suggested. As Alan Bray has shown, the rhetoric of friendship had, in the Renaissance, been structured so as to 'divert attention' from undercurrents of sexual desire: the steps taken to avoid revealing them revealed that their presence was felt.[20] Katherine Philips had raised expressions of amity into a more openly amorous vein: recent critics have in consequence been exercised over the degree to which she should be considered a lesbian writer.[21] And Roscommon is a degree more heated still. 'You grow *Familiar, Intimate* and *Fond*', he says—phrasing which the *OED* shows to have been more at home in talk of love than of friendship. His crescendo of agreement culminating in an impossible union of identities—'No longer his *Interpreter*, but *He*'—is a pattern that could be shared by physical seduction and consummation. This thought certainly occurred to the clergyman, dramatist and translator Thomas Francklin when he rewrote the passage in his 'Translation: A Poem' in 1753:

> Unless an author like a mistress warms,
> How shall we hide his faults, or taste his charms,
> How all his modest, latent beauties find,
> How trace each lovelier feature of the mind,
> Soften each blemish, and each grace improve,
> And treat him with the dignity of love?[22]

It may be that a smiling awareness of this strand in his writing was what led Roscommon, in the next line of his 'Essay on Translated Verse', to escalate his metaphor towards explicit seduction, though of the translator, not the translatee: 'with how much ease is a *young Muse Betray'd*, / How *nice* the *Reputation* of the *Maid*!'[23]

When Roscommon goes on to describe interpretation, hints of eroticism flower once more:

> Take pains the *genuine* Meaning to explore,
> There *Sweat*, there *Strain*, tug the laborious *Oar*:
> Search *ev'ry Comment*, that your Care can find,
> Some here, some there, may hit the Poets *Mind*;[24]

One can imagine the leer with which Lord Rochester might have read these lines: in his notorious satire 'On King Charles', the courtesan Nelly, though she does not quite 'tug' at an 'oar', is cost 'pain', and is 'laborious', as she struggles to 'raise the member she enjoys'.[25] Or compare Dryden's translation from Lucretius, 'Concerning the Nature of Love', published in *Sylvae* the year after Roscommon's essay, where echoes of this passage—the word 'strain', the idea of searching—briefly sound:

> Our hands pull nothing from the parts they strain,
> But wander o'er the lovely limbs in vain:
> Nor when the youthful pair more closely join,
> When hands in hands they lock, and thighs in thighs they twine,
> Just in the raging foam of full desire,
> When both press on, both murmur, both expire,
> They gripe, they squeeze, their humid tongues they dart,
> As each would force their way to t'other's heart—
> In vain; they only cruise about the coast,
> For bodies cannot pierce, nor be in bodies lost:
> As sure they strive to be, when both engage
> In that tumultuous momentany rage;[26]

In the Preface to *Sylvae*, Dryden gave a justification for translating this salacious extract:

> I am not yet so secure from that passion but that I want my author's antidotes against it. He has given the truest and most philosophical account both of the disease and remedy which I ever found in any author, for which reasons I translated him.[27]

'Disease.' As we saw in Chapter 11, Dryden had begun this Preface by calling translation, too, a 'disease'. What the two ailments, translation and desire, have in common is the impossibility of achieving the perfect union they cause to be craved. We lose the author's 'spirit', as Dryden put it, 'when we think to take his body'; concentration on the spirit brings compromises too.[28] Texts, no more than bodies, cannot pierce, nor lose themselves in one another. What follows is the sense of failure by which Dryden was so haunted; and also the resolve to repeat the attempt. As he puts it in his Lucretius:

> A pause ensues; and nature nods a while,
> Till with recruited rage new spirits boil;
> And then the same vain violence returns,
> With flames renewed th'erected furnace burns.
> Again they in each other would be lost,
> But still by adamantine bars are crossed;
> All ways they try, successless all they prove,
> To cure the secret sore of lingering love.[29]

The history of translation, too, is a history of repeated attempts at union, though usually by different writers. As we saw in Chapter 10, John Denham had imagined himself giving way to 'those whom youth, leisure, and better fortune makes fitter for such undertakings'.

No doubt Dryden's involvement with Lucretius is mainly driven by his own sexual interests and experiences. But the encounter is energized by the latent metaphor of translation as desire. Dryden will have been helped to feel this way about his work because the conceptual ground had been prepared by the metaphor of 'translating an author'; and also by a crucial peculiarity of publishing history. David Foxon has shown that in Dryden's time it was via translation that much pornographic and erotic writing appeared in English—for instance, Nicolas Chorier's *Aloisiae Sigeae Tole-tanae Satyra Sotadica de arcanis Amoris et Veneris*, written in Latin and printed probably in Lyons round about 1660; translated into English—but only in manuscript—in 1676; and finally appearing in English print in 1688, as a *Dialogue Between a Married Lady and a Maid*, when it was subject to prosecution. Dryden's publisher Jacob Tonson did not deal in this sort of material; but he was well aware of it, as is shown by a cheeky attempt to exploit the pulling-power of Chorier's text. In 1681, Tonson published *Aloisia, or the amours of Octavia Englished, to which is adjoyned the history of Madame du Tillait, both displaying the Subtilties of the fair sex*. This book, though satirical, was not salacious: it was designed, Foxon says, to be a 'sucker trap' since its characters have been given the same names as Chorier's.[30] So the bibliographical environment quickened the connection between translation and desire.

This connection crystallizes into a guiding metaphor for Dryden's translation of Lucretius. For the passage is itself full of vain violence. In his attempt to grasp his source's 'fiery temper', Dryden has made his own spirits boil.[31] It is he who contributes the 'flames renewed', 'th'erected furnace', and the idea of being 'each in other . . . lost'. In the abstract, these additions might be thought of as 'openings' like those we explored in Chapters 9–13; but, in their context, where the ideal of utter union is so prominent, they figure also, and more strongly, as barriers to the body-into-body, text-into-text dissolution that is longed for. Both varieties of desire 'still by adamantine bars are crossed'—another line contributed by Dryden, as though to illustrate the point. Translation, here, is made to seem a 'vain violence' too.

At any time, and in any cultural circumstances, friendship is likely to be a tempting metaphor for translation because it expresses the affection translators tend to feel for texts with which they are imaginatively involved. In Dryden's moment, several factors made it even more attractive than usual: the work of Katherine Philips; Roscommon's advocacy; the fact that it tallied with the prevailing broader metaphor of 'translating an author'; the sociability of Tonson's miscellanies. Why, then, did it never quite catch on? Why did it never get drawn into the processes of translation, energizing and shaping them in the manner of the metaphors of 'interpretation' and 'opening' that we explored in Part II, and of the other metaphors which we are still to encounter?

Restoration libertinism no doubt had something to do with it: any rhetoric of intimacy was perhaps, in those decades, especially prone to be ambushed by a rhetoric of desire—just as the word 'tug' was especially liable to create an innuendo. But more powerful reasons lie in the texts that were being translated, and in the practice of translation itself. As I am arguing throughout this book, the metaphors with which the translation of poetry is conceived take on strength and energy when they interact with or derive from metaphors in the text that is being translated. Dryden's imagination was especially exercised in 'opening' the *Aeneid* because in the *Aeneid* itself—as he saw it—much 'opening' occurs. But friendship was not so pervasive in the poems that were being translated; and it is simply not so fundamental a topic of Western poetry as the other sources of metaphor that we will go on to investigate—desire and passion; perspective; death and rebirth.

Still, friendship does sometimes figure importantly in a source text—as in the Nisus and Euryalus episode, and *The Knight's Tale*, and the scenes involving Achilles and Patroclus in the *Iliad* (a problematic instance which I will explore further in Chapters 19, 20, and 22). But even here, it does not rise up off the page and become a metaphor for translation. The explanation lies, not so much in particular cultural circumstances, as in feelings that have attached to the act of translation (to varying degrees in different translators) throughout the centuries covered by this book.

Authors of source texts can seem too distant to be quite friends with, especially when the texts are in Latin or Greek. Dryden was able to feel 'congenial' to Chaucer because both were English, and so belonged to a native family of poets in which 'Milton was the poetical son of Spenser, and Mr Waller of Fairfax' and so on.[32] 'Congenial' in the sense of 'friendly' is layered with 'congenial' in the sense of 'kin'. But even when an author is not so intimidatingly classic as Homer or Virgil, the metaphor of friendship tends to founder: Dryden and Chaucer are not the only case. As we have seen, Edward FitzGerald was one of the few Victorian translators who gave serious credence to the idea of translating an author. He wrote of Omar Khayyam with warmth: the imaginative connection was, according to a recent editor, 'his most important literary friendship'.[33] Yet in FitzGerald's letters, talk of friendship with Omar veers into something more patronizing. Omar is 'this remarkable little Fellow'; he is 'my property'; 'it is an amusement to me', FitzGerald says, 'to take what Liberties I like with these Persians'.[34] Cultural distance combines with an imperialistic assumption of superiority to turn Omar into someone less respected than a friend, someone like a familiar servant who can be toyed with. Written texts, after all, cannot answer back.

Though in some ways distant, written texts are in other ways very intimate. You hold them, finger them, gaze at them long and searchingly; they penetrate into your mind. Their double character puts pressure on the metaphor of translation as friendship even when the translator and author are contemporaries and not only that but actual friends. Jean Starr Untermeyer and Hermann Broch knew each other well; but when describing her first go at translating him she reaches for other terms:

> With the constant help of the dictionary, and with frequent recourse to the author, I began to dig out the meaning of these rather abstruse lines. But before the whole intent became clear, I experienced a tingling, a vibration of accord. ... With no thought of presumption I claimed kinship.[35]

The idea of 'kinship' comes in to regulate a feeling that starts out more inward and amorous: 'a tingling, a vibration of accord'. Georges Poulet has described 'the falling away of the barriers' between a reader and a book: 'you are inside it, it is inside you; there is no longer either outside or inside'.[36] But that is only half the story. You can put a book down—indeed, you have to. Bits of it may seem to remain inside you but the whole of it is never grasped. This mixture of distance and interanimation is especially visible to translators, for it gives rise both to the feeling that a translation should achieve utter oneness with the source and to the impossibility of its ever doing so. The paradox pushes translation away from the metaphor of friendship into the arms of metaphors of desire.

16

Erotic Translation

Desire (which presses towards fulfilment) is intertwined with fantasy (in which fulfilment is dreamed). Each nourishes the other. If desire is blocked, fantasy may flower. In Dryden's 'Lucretius: Concerning the Nature of Love', translation took on the lineaments of an endlessly repeatable struggle for physical union. But the inevitable failure of that struggle could also spark an explosion of fantasy. Sometimes, unable to lose himself in the source text and make it utterly his own, Dryden invents a dream of it instead.

As we are learning to expect, this mode of translation is released especially at moments when thwarted desire is being described in the source. In Theocritus's third Idyll, which Dryden Englished in 1684, a shepherd serenades Amaryllis who neither answers nor emerges from her cave: throughout the poem she appears only in the speaker's longing recollection. Here is the Greek:

> Ὦ χαρίεσσ' Ἀμαρυλλὶ, τί μ' οὐκέτι τοῦτο κατ' ἄντρον
> Παρκύπτοισα καλεῖς, τόν ἐρωτύλον;

Charming Amaryllis, why no more dost thou peep out of this thy cave and call me in—me, thy sweetheart? [1]

And here is what it grows into in Dryden's translation:

> Ah, beauteous nymph, can you forget your love,
> The conscious grottoes, and the shady grove,
> Where stretched at ease your tender limbs were laid,
> Your nameless beauties nakedly displayed?
> Then I was called your darling, your desire,
> With kisses such as set my soul on fire. [2]

This is a bit like some of the 'openings' of *Ovid's Epistles* which we explored in Chapter 11. The interpretations of the 'tacita signa' in 'Canace to Macareus', for instance, were similarly prurient. But whereas they could be justified as filling in gaps in the story, this addition to Theocritus swells and coarsens a moment of nostalgia. And whereas they were more or less in tune with the confessional impetus of the Ovid, this all-but hardcore passage has little in common with the sweet pain of the Theocritus: on the contrary, it contributes to what Stuart Gillespie has called the translation's 'highly problematic instability of tone'.[3] This is a moment of translatorly fantasy. Goaded by the mention of the now-forbidden cave, Dryden's imagination rushes into it and indulges in a heated dream of what might have happened there.

In this mode of translation, the author is held less in mind than when his works are being interpreted, or his 'address' admired, or when he is being (however sporadically and ambivalently) viewed as a friend. His imagined control over his texts weakens as they become the occasion for self-indulgence on the part of the translator. But the idea of the author does not disappear completely: it is kept in view so it can be given the blame. 'I am only the translator, not the inventor, so that the heaviest part of the censure falls upon Lucretius before it reaches me', announced Dryden gaily, by way of excuse for the fruitiness of 'Concerning the Nature of Love'.[4] Two decades later he was still rolling out the same excuse: 'let their authors be answerable for them', he proclaimed, of any 'irreverent expression' or 'thought too wanton' that might have popped up in *Fables Ancient and Modern*, his collection of translations from Boccaccio, Chaucer, Ovid, and Homer. Any immoralities, he says, are 'nothing but imported merchandise and not of my manufacture': 'they are crept into my verses through my inadvertency'.[5]

The argument would hardly be unassailable even if, in all these translations, it were not Dryden himself who had invented many of the rudest lines. Yet it does suggest the degree to which a translator's imagination may run away with him in the act of translating when—more truly than a public figure caught in a moment of madness—he is 'not himself'. Certainly, the idea that translation was an occasion for fantasy flourished in the homosocial, rather libertine context of the collaborative volumes where Dryden's early translations appeared. Turn over the pages of *Miscellany Poems* (1684) and you come across a translation of Ovid, *Amores* I. 5. The Latin is this:

> Aestus erat, mediamque dies exegerat horam:
>   Apposui medio membra levanda toro.
> Pars adaperta fuit, pars altera clausa fenestrae
>   Quale fere silvae lumen habere solent.[6]

Our modern-day, reliable Loeb Classical Library proposes this as a translation:

'Twas sultry, and the day had passed its mid hour; I laid my members to rest them on the middle of my couch. One shutter of my window was open, the other shutter was closed; the light was such as oft in a woodland.[7]

But in 1684 Dryden's associate Richard Duke came up with this:

> 'Twas Noon, when I scorch'd with the double fire
> Of the hot Sun, and my more hot desire,
> Stretcht on my downey Couch at ease was laid,
> Bigg with Expectance of the lovely Maid.[8]

This is the same sort of reading-in and working-up as in Dryden's 'Amaryllis', though done in a more frankly laddish tone. Excited by the source—and perhaps also by the thought of the women readers who were being initiated into the classics via translation[9]—the translator uses it to indulge his own reverie. As Duke hints, the English text burns with 'double fire'. Translation as desire here narrows into something more like translation as self-pleasuring.

In other cultural circumstances, and with other source texts, desire and translation interact in different ways. In 1600, the puritan gentleman Edward Fairfax published *Godfrey of Bulloigne*, his Englishing of Tasso's *Gerusalemme Liberata*. As Colin Burrow has shown, Fairfax manipulates Tasso so as to express a 'very English' concern with 'distributive justice', 'to suggest that the ideal commonwealth is one in which high places are justly apportioned by a monarch who recognizes and rewards virtue'.[10] But Fairfax also has a countervailing susceptibility to the mingled textual and sexual desire which the *Gerusalemme*, like all romances, is designed to provoke—even if Tasso is uniquely vigorous in trying to subject the genre to a Christian frame. 'Romance' (in Patricia Parker's definition) 'is characterized primarily as a form which simultaneously quests for and postpones a particular end.'[11] This tantalizing behaviour occurs in the narrative, where knights glimpse and then lose the objects of their affections, or set out on missions only to be led astray; and it affects the syntax too, where impetus gathers and fades as sentences cross the expanse of the eight-line stanzas. Fairfax's translation of Tasso has been described by Charles G. Bell:

> Beginning with a strict base of literalness (especially at the opening of each stanza), then aureately transfiguring his original as metrical exigencies and the promptings of imagination led him.[12]

Albeit unwittingly, this account makes clear the kinship between Fairfax's tactics in translating and those of the romance text which was his object. 'In the major part of his work', Bell goes on, 'Fairfax follows his text with the greatest care'—unlike Sir John Harington who had vigorously truncated Ariosto's *Orlando Furioso* in a translation published in 1591, impatient with its romance commitment to 'wandering' ('errare').[13] Nevertheless, the more Fairfax is drawn into each of Tasso's stanzas the more he veers away from it, so that the wandering phrases of the Italian wander a little further as they come into English. A favourite tactic is to exploit the greater compactness of English vocabulary to extend Tasso's lists. In Book IV, for instance, the 'hideous formes and shapes' in hell are said by Tasso to provoke 'terrore, e morte'; in Fairfax they do that and more: they 'fear, death, terror and amasement bring'. In Book II, Olindo loves Sophronia but is ignored: 'Ò non visto, ò mal noto, ò mal gradito'; neglect which in Fairfax becomes more comprehensive: 'not regarded, / Unseene, unmarkt, unpitied, unrewarded'.[14] The reiterations seem determined to pin down the sense of the Italian; but at the same time each new word brings new nuances, so that meaning is dissipated the more it is pursued. Fairfax's predecessor as a translator of Tasso was Richard Carew who published the first five cantos in 1594: Carew boasted of the 'strict...course' with which 'the translator hath tyed himselfe in the whole work, vsurping as little liberty as any whatsoeuer'.[15] This resolve brings a feeling of constraint to the resulting text which clashes with the capaciousness deriving from the source. Fairfax's romance style of Englishing was more in harmony with the style of the *Gerusalemme Liberata*. It made for a poem-translation that was long admired for its mellifluousness, its air of 'ease', as Charles Lamb was to put it, praising *Godfrey of Bulloigne* in conversation with Coleridge, Hazlitt, and Wordsworth.[16]

But there are moments when Fairfax is more assertive. Bell notices that 'whenever he comes to a description of night or day, sunrise or sunset, he grows inspired and soars off on his own wings'.[17] Alluring damsels have something of the same effect, tending to focus and intensify the general habit of elaboration. Take, for instance, the temptress Armida as she appears in Book IV. In Tasso her breasts are fresh and untouched ('acerbe, e crude'), half-covered by an irritating piece of clothing which blocks the eye but is no obstacle to amorous thought ('l'amoroso pensier già non arresta'). There follows a charmingly abstract and scientific description of that exploratory thought: it is said to be like a ray of sunlight that penetrates through water and gets to contemplate the truth of so many wonders bit by bit ('contempla il vero / di tante maraviglie à parte, à parte'). Fairfax repeats this description and, just like Tasso, says that Armida's clothes are a barrier to sight, 'her envious vesture greedie sight repelling'. Yet he also, and self-contradictorily, pushes through the vesture that obstructs desire, satisfying his own 'greedie sight' with prosthetic English breasts that are lingeringly, palpably brought into being:

> Sweet, smooth and supple, soft and gently swelling,
> Betweene them lies a milken dale below,
> Where love, youth, gladnes, whitenes make their dwelling.[18]

Typically for Fairfax, the list in that last line drifts away from what might at first appear to be its aim. There is none of the goal-driven bawdy of Dryden's response to Theocritus or Duke's to Ovid. But there is a surge of eagerness in this sudden overplus of listing: it is very unusual for Fairfax to indulge his propensity in alternate lines.[19]

Fairfax's heat appears again when the Christian knight Tancredi seeks rest in the shade of a pleasant wood:

> A Pagan damsell there unwares he met,
> In shining steele, all save her visage faire,
> Her haire unbound she made a wanton net
> To catch sweete breathing, from the cooling aire.
> On her at gaze his longing lookes he set,
> Sight, wonder; wonder, love; love bred his caire,
>   O love, O wonder; love new borne, new bred,
>   Now growne, now arm'd, this champion captive led.[20]

Fairfax introduces the third and fourth lines describing the 'haire unbound': thereafter it is as though he has himself got caught in the 'wanton net' of his own invention. His translation seems to share Tancredi's 'longing lookes', swelling the chorus of response to the seductive figure of the damsel. Here is the Tasso:

> Egli mirolla, & ammirò la bella
> Sembianza, e d'essa si compiacque, e n'arse,
> O meraviglia; Amor, ch'à pena è nato,
> Già grande vola, e già trionfa armato.[21]

The sequence of verbs—he gazed at her (mirolla), admired (ammirò), liked (si compiacque), and burned (arse)—rises in crescendo, its movement speeded by the slide of 'la bella / Sembianza' (the beautiful look of her) across two lines. Fairfax does not break the bounds of his stanza; but he more than matches the surging effect of the Italian with his domino-like concatenation of responses: 'Sight, wonder; wonder, love; love...'. It seems that the translator is himself wonderingly entering into and expanding what he reads, having a new feeling born and bred in him just as he says it is in Tancredi.

So the metaphor of 'translation as desire' is not peculiar to Dryden and his libertine contemporaries, though it flourished among them with a particular blunt vigour. Some mild dose of desire (if only to arrive at a translation) is likely to inhere in any act of translating; this connection has the potential to grow into a metaphor whenever amorousness is present in the source. One further, small example, from as long after Dryden as Fairfax was before him. Charlotte Smith's very popular first book, *Elegiac Sonnets* (1784), included some translations from Petrarch. In the sonnet numbered 90 in modern editions, 'Erano i capei d'oro', the speaker remembers a time when Laura's hair blew loose in a thousand sweet knots: this is one of the origins of the 'wanton net' that Fairfax adds to Tasso. In Petrarch, it seems that Laura's face took on the colours of pity (''l viso di pietosi color farsi')—or, as Smith puts it:

> Ah! surely, nymph divine,
> That fine suffusion on thy cheek was love;
> What wonder then those lovely tints should move,
> Should fire this heart, this tender heart of mine!
> Thy soft melodious voice, thy air, thy shape,
> Were of a goddess, not a mortal maid;[22]

Smith translates the poem across genres as well as languages: 'suffusion', with its mingling of body and emotion, and 'nymph divine', with its languorous tautologousness, were already staples of eighteenth-century English sentimental writing. Petrarch's sharp-edged, bleeding lines are softened to suit the elegiac mood announced by the title of Smith's volume. But desire is at work here, too. In Petrarch, the speaker catches fire with one verb, 'arsi', rather than Smith's two 'should move, should fire'. There is just one breast ('petto'), not 'this Heart, this tender heart'; Laura just has a way of walking ('l'andar suo') not an 'air' and also a 'shape'; her voice is not 'soft' and 'melodious' but just a voice.[23] Here, as with Fairfax, it is the comparative brevity of English words that allows Smith to make these additions. But the way she makes them suggests a translator feelingly entering into Petrarch's writing and expanding it echoically. The desire expressed in the poem grows as it is shared.

Smith's poem of translation does not have the masculine, penetrative drive of the examples from Dryden, Duke, and—in his milder way—Fairfax. It sympathizes fulsomely with the desire that comes to it from the source, rather than pushing it towards a fantasized fulfilment. But what it has in common with those other instances of 'translation as desire' is a tendency to expand which derives more from the translator's emotional response than from the source's need to be 'opened' or explained. This distinction is not watertight. A source does not in itself have a need to be 'opened'; rather, a translator—in harmony or otherwise with varying cultural circumstances—may perceive that it does. The perception will often come with a feeling attached, if only of curiosity. As we saw throughout Part II, other feelings may be drawn into the process.

Fraunce's 'paraphrase' of Watson's *Amyntas* swells with grief via structural elaboration; Dryden's 'opening' of 'Canace to Macareus' includes more than a hint of prurience. Nevertheless, there must be a tipping point at which the translation starts to serve the feelings of the translator more than the perceived needs of the source. Again, emotions other than desire can make this happen. In the chapters to come we will encounter examples of rage doing so; and further instances of grief. But desire is the most common and most powerful driver, not only because it is such a domineering emotion in itself but because it is so central to European poetry.

As we have seen, 'opening', interpretation, and paraphrase are all modes of increase. They expand on the source when they expound it; not only that, but they encourage further, competing translations because each 'opening' or interpretation or paraphrase is obviously partial. In all these kinds of writing, the tendency to expansion is restrained by the need to represent the source, to be understood, not as adding to it, but as revealing something that is latent in it. This is a rather stretched manifestation of the paradox by which, as we saw in Chapter 3, translation is defined: 'this text is different from the source and yet it is also somehow the same'. There was of course room for endless debate as to where the boundary between opening and adding lay. When translation was ambushed by desire, and desire took on the form of fantasy, this unstable criterion was put further under pressure. Smith inserts a 'tender heart' into the protagonist of Petrarch's sonnet, and Dryden finds 'nameless beauties nakedly displayed' in Amaryllis's cave, less because they are implicit in their originals than because the translators want to write them in.

When a text is allowed to be represented by the feelings and the dreams that it provokes in its rewriter, the limits of translation can be stretched towards and, finally, beyond their breaking point. That loss of confidence in 'translating an author' which spread among translators during the late eighteenth and nineteenth centuries did not only result in a new literalness. It also released a new mode of fantasy response: poems like Leigh Hunt's *The Story of Rimini* (1816), which spun 108 pages out of the brief episode of Paolo and Francesca in Canto 5 of Dante's *Inferno*, or Felicia Hemans's 'La Pia' (1820), which multiplies Dante's even briefer mention of its eponymous heroine by forty-one times, or Swinburne's 'Anactoria' (1866), a similarly expansive reimagining from the exiguous fragments of Sappho. All these poems fill in scenic and narrative possibilities left undeveloped by their sources. But they are also brimmingly emotive and so ask to be read as expressions of the feelings and fantasies that reading has aroused. Defending 'Anactoria' from accusations of indecency, Swinburne resorted to the hallowed notion of translation of the spirit: 'I tried to reproduce in a diluted and dilated form the spirit of a poem which could not be reproduced in the body'.[24] But his poem is in fact intensely physical: it has been well characterized by Yopie Prins as a desire-driven 'fragmentation of the Sapphic body enacted rhetorically'. As Prins points out, elements of the beginning of Swinburne's poem derive from Sappho's fragment 31, where 'eyes are blinded, ears are suffused with sound, fire burns under the skin, and the entire body trembles on the verge of death':[25]

> My life is bitter with thy love; thine eyes
> Blind me, thy tresses burn me, thy sharp sighs
> Divide my flesh and spirit with soft sound,
> And my blood strengthens, and my veins abound.
> I pray thee sigh not, speak not, draw not breath . . . [26]

The movement of expansion via reiteration ('and . . . and . . . and') suggests, rather like Fairfax's Tasso, a reader-and-rewriter being drawn into the source but at the same time inevitably diverging from it as his imagination responds. Only here the response continues much further as Swinburne elaborates his fantasy of Sappho for a further 299 lines. Just as with the Smith Petrarch, but more comprehensively, the pronouns of the source and the pronouns of the scene of translation merge. 'My blood' is also—in fact primarily—Swinburne's; and the imagined quietening of Sappho's lover is also his silencing of her. This poem cannot be taken as a translation: it makes no plausible claim to be in any way 'the same' as Sappho's text. And yet it has its origin in a translatory impulse, 'to reproduce . . . the spirit'. In this case, the desire sparked by translation issues in writing that not only transgresses but far overflows translation's bounds.

17

Love Again

Writers respond so elaborately to Dante because his poetry is so economical. The cultural turn towards the rough, the Gothic, and the sublime no doubt does much to explain the surge of Dante's stock in English culture during the late eighteenth and early nineteenth centuries (the first full translation of *Inferno* appeared in 1782; translations and responses have flowed unabated since). But another reason must have been his suitability for the sort of free response that began to flourish as confidence in 'translating an author' waned. The *Commedia* gives extracts from lives, with much narrative and historical circumstance left to be filled in by the assiduity of commentators or the imagination of other poets: Robert Browning combined both modes in his *Sordello* (1840). And this provocation was especially effective when the desire provoked by Dante's snippet-view storytelling was combined with desire in the story told. It was Paolo and Francesca, rather than Ugolino or Farinata or Brunetto Latini, who gave rise not only to *The Story of Rimini*, but to Richard Le Gallienne's 'Paolo and Francesca' (1892), Stephen Phillips's stage adaptation (1900), and to many other such expansions, including at least twenty operas written between 1825 and 1914.[1]

In the case of Sappho, a similar conjunction of text and theme was produced by the ravages of manuscript transmission. The longing represented in the fragments was doubled by a longing felt by readers for the fragments themselves to be made whole. As Joseph Addison put it in an influential pair of articles in his *Spectator* in 1711, Sappho is one of those ancient authors who have been wrecked in the sea of time, 'very much shattered and damaged' and 'quite dis-jointed and broken into pieces'. The recognition that something is missing prompts speculation as to what it might have been:

> One may see, by what is left . . . that she followed nature in all her thoughts, without descending to those little points, conceits, and turns of wit with which many of our modern Lyrics are so miserably infected. Her soul seems to have been made up of love and poetry: She felt the passion in all its warmth, and described it in all its symptoms.[2]

When Dryden revealed what he thought likely to be missed by readers of Virgil—what was 'secretly in' the poet—he had masses of textual and circumstantial detail to nourish his imagining. His translatorly work was therefore shaped by the metaphor of 'opening', that is, interpretation. But about Sappho hardly anything was—and is—known, and of her poetry very little survives. So Addison, filled with desire to possess her for Augustan culture, is free to project his own vision of her into the space where she is not, just as Fairfax satisfied his 'greedie sight' by imagining a body beneath the veil of Armida's clothing. There is no more conventional ideal than a love poetry that is free from convention.

This despite the fact that the two chunks of Sappho's verse showcased in the *Spectator* are substantial enough to be both peculiar and complicated—qualities that are not wholly erased in the translations by Ambrose Philips which Addison quotes. They present desire as permeated by representations of itself, as repeated, and as competitive: 'natural' perhaps in the sense of commonly experienced; but certainly not in the senses of unmediated or pure. In the first, sometimes called the 'Hymn to Aphrodite', a speaker asks the goddess to visit her on the grounds that she has done so before—or, as Philips puts it, 'if ever thou hast kindly heard / A Song in soft Distress preferr'd'. In Sappho the word 'δηὖτε' ('this time') is repeated thrice in four lines as Aphrodite asks—I quote Anne Carson's recent translation—'what (now again) I have suffered and why / (now again) I am calling out' and 'whom should I persuade (now again) to lead you back into her love'.[3] The tone might be anything from exasperated to fond; but what is certain is that love has already taken on the air of a routine, not that that makes it any the less sharply felt. Philips neglects the repetition; but he goes on to give quite a good impression of the automatic quality of Aphrodite's answer, even though he changes the gender of the recalcitrant beloved:

> Tho' now he shuns thy longing arms,
> He soon shall court thy slighted charms;
> Tho' now thy offerings he despise,
> He soon to thee shall sacrifice;
> Tho' now he freeze, he soon shall burn,
> And be thy victim in his turn.[4]

It feels like a wish-fulfilment fantasy, with Aphrodite's response being ventriloquized by the poem's main speaker: in this respect, it prefigures, and pre-emptively criticizes, Addison's wish-fulfilment fantasy of Sappho. The markers of love and of not-love are already conventionally established. Aphrodite's alternating syntax offers a change from one set of signs to the other, a switch from stop to go.

Addison's other exhibit was the text now known as 'Fragment 31', which was later to give Swinburne the opening of 'Anactoria', and which had been preserved in that hugely influential work of literary criticism, *On the Sublime*, then attributed to Longinus. In these verses, the speaker sees a woman, referred to as 'you', in conversation with a man, and at once experiences a rush of bodily symptoms. Philips:

> My breath was gone, my voice was lost:
>
> III.
>
> My bosom glow'd; the subtle flame
> Ran quick through all my vital frame;
> O'er my dim eyes a darkness hung;
> My ears with hollow murmurs rung.[5]

And so on through a startling image which Philips does not manage to translate (Carson: 'greener than grass / I am') until the speaker seems to herself dead, or almost dead—or, as Philips rewrites it in his sentimental idiom 'I fainted, sunk, and dy'd away'. Addison comments: '*Longinus* has observed, that this Description of Love in *Sappho* is an exact Copy of Nature' and he goes on to tell the story of a doctor who used Sappho's poem as a medical guide, diagnosing love in a patient who was pretending to be physically ill.[6] But Sappho nowhere says that 'love' is the emotion whose 'nature' her poem is meant to represent; and the poem's distinctive dramatic set-up allows for other possibilities. Is it not envy of the man, more than love of the woman, that sets off the speaker's reaction? Many readers have thought the poem to be 'about jealousy'; equally many have disagreed.[7] What the poem describes, then, is uncertain: by decreeing that the topic is 'love', Longinus has created the 'nature' that the poem is said to 'copy'— and Addison then copies this attribution.

In the 'Hymn to Aphrodite', love is reiterative. In 'Fragment 31', love (if that is the right word) piggy-backs on another relationship, and is interwoven with competitiveness. In neither is it a simple emanation of 'nature'. And yet that is how Addison presses for the poems to be seen, as originary representations of love which anchor a tradition of poetry that has come after them: 'several of our countrymen, and Mr Dryden in particular, seem very often to have copied after it in their dramatic writings, and in their poems upon love'.[8] This English work is derivative, and its derivativeness is signalled by those 'conceits and turns of wit' which distinguish 'so many of our modern Lyrics' from Sappho. Yet the same derivativeness also, paradoxically, functions as a guarantee of authenticity, for it connects these poems to the original poetry which Sappho derived from 'nature'—and which was itself not wholly pure of conceits and turns of wit, as we have seen. The modern English poems are certified copies of a certified copy of nature.

Addison may well have been thinking of a scene in Dryden's successful comedy *Sir Martin Mar-All* (1667). The eponymous unhero has to serenade his beloved Millicent, but he cannot sing. So his servant voices the words for him while Sir Martin mimes:

> My soul's all on fire,
> So that I have the pleasure to dote and desire,
> Such a pretty soft pain
> That it tickles each vein;
> 'Tis the dream of a smart
> Which makes me breathe short when it beats at my heart.[9]

The source of the utterance is not only doubled but trebled: Sappho sings (more or less) through the servant who sings through his master. But Sir Martin then gets so carried away by his fake performance that he keeps on mouthing after the music has ceased. He makes comically actual the loss of voice—or, more literally, 'broken tongue'—imagined by Sappho. The scene, then, is not only imitative: it is a drama of imitation. And, like all good comedy, it is funny because it hooks into something serious, in this case an anxiety which, by Dryden's time, had long dogged the representation of love in the European lyric tradition. If it is really love, your love must be in some way unique and inimitable: it must derive from and devote itself to the particularity of the person loved; and it must traverse your own innermost being. But, at the same time, how can it really be *love* unless it is the same as the love felt by other people, and especially the same as the love described by great authorities such as Sappho or Petrarch. To be original in the expression of love therefore seemed both imperative and impossible. At the start of the sonnet sequence *Astrophil and Stella* (written 1581–2; published 1591), Sir Philip Sidney had written that he was 'loving in truth' and wanted 'to show' his love in verse. He reads other love poems for inspiration; but 'others' feet still seemed but strangers in my way'. So he opts for pure self-expression. ' "Fool," said my muse to me, "look in thy heart, and write" '—only the trouble is that his muse, too, has been reading the same old books: 'such professions of sincerity', Sidney's editor drily remarks, are 'in themselves conventional'.[10] A century later, Sir Martin is placed in a comic version of the same quandary. He is ridiculous because he cannot speak his own particular love in his own words. And yet nobody speaks their own particular love in their own words, not even Sappho who, in her 'Hymn', shows her feeling to be a copy of a feeling she has had before, and not only that but an example of the familiar predicament that is Aphrodite's professional concern. How, then, can the uniqueness of each love be represented? Sir Martin's silent, fish-like mouthing is a fair representation of the difficulty.

As we saw in Chapter 3, translation has the strange capacity to function as a quotation in different words. In the latest twist of what is turning out to be the complicatedly interactive metaphor of 'translation as desire', the derivative novelty of translated language is brought into play as writers find ways of handling the paradox of self-expression via unavoidable convention. This witty tactic flickers in and out of life in medieval and early modern verse; during the eighteenth century it was largely stifled by sentimental views like those of Addison and Charlotte Smith; but it flamed up again strongly in the work of Byron, as we will see in Chapter 18.

Translation has been at the heart of love poetry in English at least since Chaucer, in *Troilus and Criseyde* (*c*.1385), made Troilus describe his new emotion—' "O god, what fele I so" ', etc.—with verses translated from Petrarch.[11] The tone of this decision is now—and perhaps always was— hard to grasp. Medieval literature was largely made up of varieties of rewriting, so that 'translation and original composition were not habitually opposed'.[12] Chaucer himself, having taken the 'pioneering' decision to write his court poetry in English rather than French, turned himself into a channel for the importation of foreign texts: he translated Boethius and the *Roman de la Rose*; rewrote Boccaccio to create 'The Knight's Tale' and *Troilus and Criseyde*; and patched together other works—for instance 'The Parson's Tale'—from different sources.[13] Nevertheless, there is something distinctive about the embedding of that lyric nugget of Petrarch into a narrative texture that is in general more freely reworked from Boccaccio. The lines from Petrarch, which become Troilus's first sustained attempt to grasp his feelings, are marked out in the manuscripts as a song, 'Canticus Troili'; and there is the same conjunction of song, reflection on love, and momentary change of source-text later in the poem where the second 'Canticus Troili' is pasted in from Boethius. Petrarch's sonnet is stretched to fill three stanzas of seven-line rhyme royal; nevertheless, the work of translation here is noticeably more constrained than in the surrounding narrative. All except one of the Italian lines are translated pretty much word for word; the greater length of Chaucer's version is caused, not by general expansiveness, but by the insertion of discrete lines of extrapolation and commentary. One effect of these changes is to make Troilus exclaim at the strangeness of what is happening to him: 'Allas, what is this wondre maladie?' Another—as Robin Kirkpatrick has pointed out—is to reduce 'the complex Petrarchan oxymora to a series of highly predictable oppositions'—'ffor ay thurst I the more that ich it drinke' and so on. The translation, then, moves in two contrary directions: it asserts its own strangeness while also making itself less strange than it might have been.

For Kirkpatrick, the second shift—of simplification and rigidification—shows Troilus to be 'in the grip of a malady', overcome by 'intoxicating phrases'.[14] We need to bear in mind here that the 'Canticus Troili' is the first known translation of a Petrarch sonnet into English, so for Chaucer's audience the Petrarchan oppositions would not have been predictable at all. But Chaucer was not averse to lacing his writing with connections that only he and perhaps a few initiates could spot. His rewritings of Dante's *Commedia*, for instance, are full of what—given English ignorance of Dante at that time—must have been private jokes, as when the gates of hell (in *The Parliament of Fowls*) are relocated so as to lead straight into the earthly paradise, or when Virgil and Beatrice, Dante's earnest guides to the afterlife, are metamorphically combined into the impetuous, hectoring Eagle of *The House of Fame*.[15] It has to be conceivable that so brilliantly self-aware a poet might, when it came to the 'Canticus Troili', have savoured a paradox in the fact that the paradoxes with which Troilus is made to express his newly vivid inwardness are so markedly second-hand. To Barry Windeatt, Troilus' 'first experience of love' seems 'sincere, uncalculated'; to John V. Fleming, it is 'distinctly literary . . . controlled by specific and identifiable literary texts'.[16] These opposite perceptions are both true, and they are compacted most impossibly together in the 'Canticus', which is at once a spontaneous, feeling utterance and an especially calculated act of translation. 'Ffrom whennes cometh my waillynge and my pleynte?', Troilus asks; the obvious answer is: from Petrarch, whose words—'onde 'l pianto e lamento'—he is saying again in English.[17]

As Paul Strohm has shown, the 'Canticus' was, after not many decades, being copied out separately from the rest of *Troilus and Criseyde* and understood as a precursor of that 'remarkable expansion of Petrarchan influence in the fifteenth and, especially, sixteenth centuries'. In this retrospect, it dislodges itself from the narrative that surrounds it, and figures as 'a predictive kernel, an intimation of the "not-yet"'.[18] What it intimated was not only Petrarchanism, but an interplay of Petrarchanism and translatedness which develops further in the work of Thomas Wyatt. Between his visit to Italy in 1527 and his death in 1542, Wyatt translated or responded to thirty lyrics by Petrarch (and a few others by writers in the same tradition such Serafino d'Aquilano, Dragonetto Bonifacio, and Clément and Jean Marot) in among his production of two hundred-odd poems. In Wyatt's cultural moment, with the spread of humanist scholarship, and the existence of printed books to facilitate comparison of translations and their sources, translation was beginning to be more sharply distinguished from original composition than it had been for Chaucer. (Print had not yet become a medium for newly composed lyric poetry, but Wyatt's prose translation from Plutarch, *The Quiet of Mind*, was print-published in 1528, and he knew Petrarch through printed editions.)[19] Nevertheless, 'originality' was not a 'prime concern' for Wyatt.[20] The translations were not identified as such in early manuscripts—including his own—nor when some were published in *Tottel's Miscellany* (1557) a decade and a half after his death.

Like Chaucer, Wyatt seems to have encountered Petrarch's writing via his travels as a diplomat; but he was employed at a higher level than Chaucer, and in more fraught circumstances. As Stephen Greenblatt first argued, this experience leaves its mark in his poetry, and especially in the poem-translations, which 'are all a kind of elaborate masking', a vehicle for what Karla Taylor—summing up this approach more recently—has called the 'double voice of the diplomat negotiating the perilous straits of the absolutist Henrician court'.[21] One such strait arose in 1527 when Wyatt was asked by Queen Katherine, herself in not very happy fortune at the time, to translate Petrarch's *Remedy for Ill Fortune*. Wyatt substituted the Plutarch *Quiet of Mind*: he must have wanted—Greg Walker suggests—to avoid any risk of being seen to make 'a tacit acknowledgement that she was indeed facing undeserved adversity in a hostile environment, pressed by the King's supporters to agree to a one-sided "investigation" of the validity of their marriage'. By offering instead 'a text that focused on the need for the virtuous soul to reconcile him or herself to fortune and adversity', Wyatt signalled 'his willingness to meet the Queen's wishes, while simultaneously refusing to compromise his loyalty to the King on the most important issue of the moment'.[22]

Greenblatt discerned similar prudence in 'Whoso list to hunt', the poem-translation which has traditionally been read as alluding to an attachment of Wyatt's to Anne Boleyn. The text includes only three lines translated from Petrarch, but, on Greenblatt's account, it is crucial that Wyatt found there the idea of referring to a woman as a 'hind': 'it would have been suicidal folly to write directly about the loss of Anne Boleyn to Henry'.[23] Whether or not Wyatt had in fact been dangerously involved with the future queen, the reflexes of intrigue spread into many of his poem-translations about love which, in consequence, have much to say about power, fear, and reputation. 'Caesar, when that the traitor of Egypt' (closely Englished from Petrarch's 'Cesare, poi che'l traditor d'Egitto') compares the discretion of the lover and the political leader. Just as Caesar concealed his joy at the death of Pompey, and just as Hannibal hid his sorrow when defeated, so Petrarch covers his amorous misery by laughing and singing ('rido, o canto'); and Wyatt does likewise, cloaking his care 'but under sport and play'. And just as Petrarch's 'canto' must include the song of his poetry, so Wyatt's 'cloak' must hint at the 'feigned visage' created by translation.[24]

Yet this sonnet undoes the feigning by describing it, and therefore opens the way to a reading of the poem-translations as asking to be seen through. They are not so much masks in themselves as explorations of the need to mask, and so of the motives that may lead one writer about love to adopt the words of another by translating them. There is something at work here other than the imposed need for 'prudence'. It is striking that, in 'Whoso list to hunt', the lines in which Wyatt departs from Petrarch are also those in which his speaker abandons—or at least tries to—his subjugation to the discipline of love (here figured as the hunt). Petrarch's poem is a dream vision of a doe, with golden horns and a 'sweet proud' visage, which the speaker sets out to follow as a miser follows gold: the dream ends with him falling into water and the creature vanishing. Wyatt, in stark contrast, substitutes a chatty, drab scenario, starting out as though he is cannily sharing a tip ('I know where is an hind') and going on to present himself as a lagging, weary hunter, giving up the chase 'sithens in a net I seek to hold the wind'.[25] But the lines in which he does translate the Petrarch describe something being successfully held close—the hind (I quote the Petrarch from an edition that includes the commentary by Vellutello which he used):

> And graven with diamonds in letters plain
> There is written her fair neck round about:
> '*Noli me tangere* for Caesar's I am,
> And wild for to hold though I seem tame.'

> Nessun mi tocchi al bel collo d'intorno
> Scritto havea di diamanti et di topati;
> Libera farmi al mio Cesare parve:

Et a similitudine di quelle cerve che da Cesare erano con uno monile al collo lassate in liberta, nel quale erano impresse queste parole Nolli me tangere quia Cesaris sum, e cosi da nessuno erano mai toccate ne offese.[26]

(And like those does that by Caesar were with a collar on the neck left in liberty, in which were printed these words Do not touch me because Caesar's I am, and so by nobody were they ever touched or hurt).

Wyatt's '*Noli me tangere*' is not only translated word for word from Italian but transcribed from the commentary which identifies the source Petrarch must have had in mind. Like Browning in his *Agamemnon of Aeschylus* (1877)—which I discussed in Chapter 5—Wyatt's version is here more literal than his original.

Is there anything to be made of this veering-in of imaginative response, from standoffish disenchantment to tight adherence? If there is a connection between the translator's behaviour and his speaker's it is not straightforward. The lines in which Wyatt is most distinct as a writer are also those in which the speaker most expresses his individual stance: 'I know', 'I may', 'I am', and so on. But that stance is the opposite of self-assertive: 'I may no more'. And though Wyatt, translating, holds to the words that hold the hind, those same words are what put the hind beyond the speaker's grasp. What is more, the translation is in spirit almost opposite to the source here, where in letter it is so close. Petrarch's doe is 'libera' in ethical and religious senses, free in will and free of sin: 'Cesare' stands for God; and 'nessun mi tocchi' most echoes Christ's words in John 20.17. But in Wyatt, 'wild for to hold' has a wholly secular tone, charged with aesthetic amazement and physical longing (this distinctive Wyatt note sounds again in 'They flee from me that sometime did me seek': 'When her loose gown from her shoulders did fall / And she caught me in her arms long and small'—it is the wondering conjunction of 'fall' and 'caught' that echoes 'wild for to hold'). Wyatt's *'Noli me tangere'* and 'Caesar' correspondingly have little to do with Christianity and much to do with courtly powerplay.[27] There is a complex interaction, then, between what happens in the poem and what Wyatt does in translating. His move away from and then into closeness with the source releases and then interacts with a meditation on the value of liberty (self-discovery? giving up?) and of constraint (oppression? frisson?).

Elsewhere among Wyatt's poem-translations similar interplays occur. A poem begins:

> Was I never yet of your love grieved
> Nor never shall while that my life doth last.[28]

The resolution to stay faithful is itself faithful to Petrarch's 'Io non fu' d'amar voi lassato unquanco'. The implications are complex. Perhaps the self-limiting commitment of translation harmonizes with the lifelong romantic attachment, suggesting a thoroughly settled mind. Or perhaps the speaker's resolve is doubtful, or at least in need of buttressing, if it is having to be reiterated from the prompt-card Petrarch has supplied. In another sonnet, 'The long love that in my thought doth harbour', the speaker again declares his amorous fidelity in words that are no less faithful to Wyatt's source. This time, the consonance registers in a choice of word. 'Good is the life, ending faithfully', the speaker concludes: as this act of translation has ended faithfully, so will his loving life.[29] Here, though, the connotations seem not at all vexed. The emotional fulfilment that is being imagined makes it seem that Petrarch's model has been adopted with wholehearted gratitude.

It is not only in 'Whoso list to hunt' that a deviation from the source is interestingly in harmony with a deviation from the love imagined in the poem-translation. In 'My heart I gave thee, not to do it pain', a sonnet made from two strambotti (eight-line poems) by Serafino, Wyatt takes a hint from the Italian, 'Non ti spiaccia s'io torno in libertate' and elaborates it:

> Displease thee not if that I do refrain
> . . .
> . . . since it please thee to feign a default,
> Farewell I say, parting from the fire.[30]

As the speaker parts from the fire, so Wyatt parts from Serafino. And, when he writes sonnets that are not at all translations, Wyatt is correspondingly free to make his speakers proclaim their freedom: 'my doting days be past'; 'me think it good reason / To change purpose like after the season';

> Farewell, Love, and all thy laws forever.
> Thy baited hooks shall tangle me no more.[31]

Of course there is not a straightforward equation (how dull the poems would be if there were). In his songs and ballades, Wyatt writes much in his own voice about the constraints of love. Nevertheless, among the 28 sonnets, about 18 of which are more or less translations, there does seem to be a loose but significant correlation between not-translating and asserting liberty from love.

And among the sonnet-translations of constraint, it is not only the word 'faithfully' that winks with plausible self-reference. In 'My galley charged with forgetfulness', Englished from 'Passa la nave mia colma d'oblio', the lover is powerless in a galley, propelled by an 'endless wind' and steered 'with cruelness' by 'mine enemy, alas, / That is my lord'. The image is of course not wholly applicable to the relation between translator and source; but it does have a latent partial consonance with Wyatt's position as writer here, abandoning himself utterly to Petrarch's gust and form. The thought peeps through in Wyatt's one marked alteration. Petrarch ends: 'incomincio a desperar del porto' (I begin to despair of the port).[32] Wyatt ends: 'And I remain despairing of the port'. What Petrarch has begun, Wyatt's speaker feels himself to be continuing. Again, in 'I find no peace and all my war is done', closely translated from 'Pace non trovo, e non ho da far guerra', Wyatt repeats after Petrarch that love is an ambivalent jailor:

> That looseth nor locketh, holdeth me in prison
> And holdeth me not, yet can I scape no wise;
> Nor letteth me live nor die at my device.

'At my device' (i.e., 'as I might choose') is Wyatt's small particular addition, accentuating the question of desire's relation to free will, and itself done at his own 'device'—though of course that, too, is not unequivocally free since it has arisen from, and is constrained by, the chain of rhyme. Translation joins with metre and rhyme to create a 'prison', one that the writer-translator cannot exist without, any more than the speaker-lover can exist without his love.

Probably some time after the composition of this poem, Wyatt was actually imprisoned in the Tower of London, in 1536 and again in 1541. And it was almost certainly during one of those confinements that he was delivered of a new act of translation: his *Paraphrase of the Seven Penitential Psalms*.[33] Here, once more, translation is associated with a prison, for the *Paraphrase* was in part a work of spiritual self-discipline (a common use of those Psalms), a devotional counterpart to his physical subjugation. But it was also—Walker has shown—an enterprise of political self-assertion, in which Wyatt developed an analogy between King David and King Henry, thereby settling old scores, albeit only in imagination. In the versions from Petrarch too, translation figures as a medium of constraint which Wyatt by turns relishes, chafes against, and breaks away from. In this early, complex instance of the poetry of translation, fidelity to the source is at once a gift, a duty, and a burden. It doubles and appraises the analogous impositions of desire.

When many of them were published in *Tottel's Miscellany* (1557), Wyatt's approximations to Petrarch's idiom and form helped start a fad for Petrarchan sonneteering in English.[34] This wave of writing substitutes, for the subtle calibrations of translation and not-translation, the blunter pressure of a 'tradition'. John Kerrigan points out that the first sonnet sequence published in English, Thomas Watson's *Hekatompathia* (1582), 'directs its resources quite frankly, almost vauntingly, towards conventional encomium'. The work rolls out what had by then become well established Petrarchan images—the mistress praised is given the name Laura—and Watson also credits later Italian writers indebted to Petrarch such as Ariosto and Aeneas Silvius Piccolomini (who became Pope Pius II).[35] The explicit comparisons of lips to coral, of 'yellow locks' to 'beaten gold' and so on are therefore shadowed by latent comparisons of these comparisons to those in the verse of Watson's precursors.

Later sonnets try out ways of escaping from the tradition while not also (as in Wyatt's) abandoning love. The conventional pursuit of sincerity in Sidney's *Astrophil and Stella* leads the speaker to disparage his predecessors who had complained 'Of living deaths, dear wounds, fair storms and freezing fires'. He feels, he says, 'as much as they'; but his emotion is sufficiently displayed 'when trembling voice brings forth, that I do Stella love'.[36] But this utterance arrives only in his last line: the rest of the poem is filled with the images he professes to reject; and his plain words have force only in comparison with them. They give his statement imaginable content even though he rejects them rhetorically. Likewise with Shakespeare's Sonnet 130, the one that begins 'My mistress' eyes are nothing like the sun' and goes on to say that coral is far more red than her lips, that there are no roses in her cheeks and so on. The poem ends:

> And yet, by heaven, I think my love as rare
> As any she belied with false compare.[37]

('She' here functions as a noun: 'as any woman'.) Kerrigan observes that the sonnet 'refuses to submit the mistress to a convention'[38]—yet this refusal still requires the convention to be in place if it is to have significance. The mistress may not be 'submitted' to 'false compare'; but she is still compared to it. Like Sir Martin Mar-All, Sidney and Shakespeare here very obviously reiterate the words of others; but they are more adept than he at re-angling the familiar material.

All writing is of course entrammelled in intertextuality. But the debt to Petrarch in Renaissance love poetry was especially intense; and this affected the translation of other poems where Petrarchan traits appeared. Italian romance is by its nature a profligately derivative genre; and Petrarch was one of its major sources, along with classical epic, Dante, and the Bible. Charles Bell has pointed out that Fairfax, in *Godrey of Bulloigne*, tends to make explicit the classical and biblical references that Tasso had left undeclared.[39] Fairfax, then, realizes that the *Gerusalemme Liberata* melds different traditions together and he makes this hybridity the more evident in his translation. He is guided, less by an idea of the text's author—which promotes consistency across a work—than by an interest in the variety of genres that are brought together in its weave.

When he spots a strand of Petrarchanism in the *Gerusalemme*, Fairfax feels licensed to extend it, not so much according to the Drydenian principle of what Tasso might have written had he been alive in England and in the present day, but in line with his own knowledge of the Petrarchan mode. For instance, in Book III, Tancredi is attacked by the warrior maid Clorinda, whom he loves: the scene is an arabesque on the martial imagery often deployed in love poetry—Cupid's arrows, love's wounds, the cruelty of the mistress, and so on. Here, as often, Tasso gentles down his rhetoric towards the end of each stanza so as to lead readers' imaginings on into the next. But Fairfax gives his stanzas more of a final clinch, so that each one takes on something of the conclusiveness of a sonnet; and the resources of the Petrarchan tradition help him do this. When Clorinda's helmet is knocked off in the Tasso, her hair flies in the wind and she simply appears, a young lady: 'e le chiome dorate al vento sparse, / Giovane donna in mezzo'l campo apparse'—this comes as no surprise to readers since we have known all along that that was what she was.[40] Fairfax substitutes a sparky Petrarchan comparison:

> About her shoulders shone her golden locks,
> Like sunnie beames, on Alablaster rocks.

The same happens in the next stanza: Tasso's narrator reminds Tancredi that he has seen Clorinda before, cooling her forehead at a solitary fountain. But Fairfax spots an opportunity for paradox:

> The same that left thee by the cooling streame,
> Safe from sunnes heat, but scorcht with beauties beame.

As he does again when a 'soldier wilde' injures Clorinda and so enrages Tancredi: 'The smart was his, though she receiv'd the wound'.[41] Aware that Tasso is writing in collaboration with an idiom, Fairfax joins in the enterprise, intensifying the Petrarchanism of the scene by a process of sympathetic elaboration.

Sir John Harington, in his translation of Ariosto, had been no less alert to the many modes of romance writing. But the *Orlando Furioso* has a different character from the *Gerusalemme Liberata*: it is more sardonic about the patterns of feeling and strands of narrative which it nevertheless pursues. As Colin Burrow has argued, Harington will have been sensitized to this aspect of the source by his concern—widely shared among humanistic writers—to inculcate moral and martial virtue in the hereditary aristocracy; and his own 'rambunctious energy' and 'roughness' must have contributed too.[42] The result is that Harington takes Petrarchanism as a prompt, not to enrichment, but to irony.

In Book I, a character called Sacripante—Sacrapant in the English—is near the bottom of a long list of knights who are in love with Angelica. He is introduced to us as suffering from a touch of Petrarch:

> – Pensier (dicea) che'l cor m'agghiacci & ardi,
> E causi'l duol, che sempre il rode e lima,
> Che debbo far, poi che son giunto tardi,
> E ch'altri à corre il frutto è andato prima?
> A pena havuto io n'ho parole e sguardi,
> Et altri n'ha tutta la spoglia opima.[43]

Oh thought (he said) that freeze and burn my heart, and cause the pain that continually gnaws it and wears it away, what should I do since I have arrived too late, and another has been to gather the fruit first? I have barely had words and glances from her, and another has all her richest booty.

Harington makes the Petrarchanism more emphatic:

> Alas (said he) what meanes this diverse passion?
> I burne as fire, and yet as frost I freese.
> I still lament, and yet I move compassion.
> I come too late and all my labour leese.
> I had but words and looks for shew and fashion,
> But others get the game and gainful fees.[44]

The opening question is a distant echo of the *Canticus Troili*, and the comparatively fluid movement of the Italian is shackled into a structure of parallelism and opposition rather like Chaucer's, or indeed like that which Ambrose Philips was later to impose on the stanza from Sappho's 'Hymn to Aphrodite'. Looked at in isolation, this stanza might seem to share in Fairfax's endeavour of warmly intensifying the Petrarchan elements in Tasso. But, in context, the overplus contributed by Harington includes a vein of irony: the sensitivity to translatedness which lay all but dormant in the 'Canticus', and which was so suggestively if quietly alive in Wyatt, here sharpens and acidifies. In the previous stanza, Sacripante has been shown to suffer from the usual paradoxical symptoms:

> Sospirando piangea, tal ch'un ruscello
> parean le guancie, e'l petto un Mongibello.[45]

Sighing, he wept, his cheeks seemed like a stream, and his breast a Mount Etna.

There is already no doubt something of an authorial smile in the mention of 'Mongibello' (Mount Etna). Harington expands on the hint:

> His heart did seeme a mountaine full of flame,
> His cheekes a streame of tears to quench the same.[46]

'To quench' is the sarcastic touch, a geographical impossibility (a stream flowing up a volcano?) that guys the Petrarchan contraries by suggesting what would result if they were brought together: a lot of steam and hot air.

In what follows, Sacripant tries to quieten his desire by reiterating an argument taken (as Harington notes in his margin) from Catullus 62: a 'virgine pure' is like a rose, delighting many until it has been plucked. In Ariosto, Sacripante at once refuses to apply the advice to his own case: 'Dunque esser può, che non mi sia più grata; / dunque poss'io lasciar mia vita propia' (so could it be that I no more desire her? / so could I abandon my own life). But Harington turns this protest into an admonition: 'Then leave to love this ladie so ungrate'. Even when, in the next line, Harington's Sacrapant changes his mind, he is made to offer himself up to be disapproved of: 'Nay, live to love (behold I soon recant)'. And when

Ariosto, now again apparently straight-faced, explains that love is the source of all Sacripante's pain ('di sua pena ria / sia prima, e sola causa essere amante'), Harington inserts his own definition and expostulation: 'That trickling wound, that flattering cruell foe; / Most happy they that know and have it least'.[47]

In such moments in Harington's Ariosto, translation becomes a means for reflecting on the element of convention which dogs the representation of love, and which was agonistically at the heart of Renaissance verse. It is the weariest variant of 'translation as desire'. Though later exploited to some extent by Dryden, the ironies that can attach to this metaphor were then largely quashed by sentimental convictions like those we have encountered in Addison and Charlotte Smith. But in the second decade of the nineteenth century, Lord Byron, in revolt against the dominant literary currents of his culture, turned his attention to Ariosto and other writers in the same tradition, such as Boiardo and, above all, Pulci. He admired their freedom with social and sexual taboos, and recognized that it was inseparable from their mobility of tone. As he put it in the 'Advertisement' to his translation from Pulci's *Morgante Maggiore*: 'it has never yet been decided entirely, whether Pulci's intention was or was not to deride the religion, which is one of his favourite topics'.[48] *Don Juan*, he made clear, was a poem in the same vein. Just like the *Gerusalemme Liberata* and the *Orlando Furioso*, it includes varieties of writing which are recognized to be conventional. Like Fairfax, Byron sometimes exaggerates these modes; like Harington, he sometimes turns on them sardonically. As here:

> There was the Donna Julia, whom to call
>   Pretty were but to give a feeble notion
> Of many charms in her as natural
>   As sweetness to the flower, or salt to ocean,
> Her zone to Venus, or his bow to Cupid,
> (But this last simile is trite and stupid.)[49]

The comparisons figure as washed out remnants of the tradition of writing that we have been exploring. They seem to sprout inverted commas as one reads through them, until they are jettisoned from serious consideration by the parenthetical last line. They figure as being, not necessarily translated, but certainly imported into Byron's poem from a world of ways of language all around it. This cultivation of linguistic second-handness is, metaphorically speaking, a translatory sensibility. As we will see, translation between languages is at the centre of its play.

18

Byron's Adulterous Fidelity

In Venice, in November 1819, Byron was correcting the printed text of Book I of *Don Juan*, with its story of lovers caught in adultery, at a time when the husband of his mistress, Countess Teresa Guiccioli, was trying to put an end to their liaison. As he wrote to his publisher John Murray:

> Tonight as Countess G observed me poring over 'Don Juan' she stumbled by mere chance on the 138th Stanza of the first Canto—and asked me what it meant —I told her—nothing but 'your husband is coming' as I said this in Italian with some emphasis—she started up in a fright—and said '*Oh My God* ——is he *coming?*' thinking it was *her own* who either was or ought to have been at the theatre.—You may suppose we laughed when she found out the mistake.[1]

Their relationship was permeated by fictional texts in several languages: this misunderstanding over *Don Juan* is only the starkest (and most droll) example. There was an Italian translation of Mme de Staël's *Corinne*, adored by Guiccioli and read by Byron in her garden one day when she was not there:

> —my Love—you were absent—or I could not have read it.—It is a favourite book of yours—and the writer was a friend of mine.—You will not understand these English words—and *others* will not understand them—which is the reason I have not scribbled them in Italian—but you will recognize the handwriting of him who passionately loved you—and you will divine that over a book which was yours—he could only think of love.[2]

The book, a favourite of hers written by a friend of his, is a link between them. But it is also a marker of separation, not only because he has read it—and says he could only read it—in her absence, but because *Corinne* tells of a love between an Italian woman and an English 'milord' which ends unhappily. Byron goes on to imagine the same happening to him and Guiccioli: 'think of me sometimes when the Alps and the Ocean divide us

—— but they never will —— unless you wish it'.[3] By writing in the book, Byron reaches out towards her, fending off the possibility of their separation; but, since writing implies its own endurance through time, as well as the absence of its addressee, he slips into thinking of their love as being in the past: 'him who passionately loved you'. That he writes in English rather than Italian, their shared language, layers the gesture with further complexities. These are words which—rather like an inscription on a tombstone—will never be read by the person whom they most concern. Relying on this obstruction, Byron expresses a strand of his feelings that it might have been hard for him to communicate to Guiccioli: that he wishes she had stayed in her convent, or at least that he had never met her in her married state. Her presence as a focus of his thoughts prompts him to write things to her that he trusts she will not read. But equally he trusts that she will understand the countervailing implication of his handwriting, the record of his touch in pages that have also been touched by her.

The book, then, as medium and as barrier. There was also the book as illustration. In a letter written in the early weeks of the affair, when he was in Venice and Guiccioli had returned to her home town of Ravenna with her husband, Byron quotes some lines from the Renaissance playwright Giovanni Battista Guarini's pastoral tragi-comedy *Il Pastor Fido*:

> 'Che giova a te, cor mio, l'esser amato?
> Che giova a me l'aver si cara amante?
> Perchè crudo destino—
> Ne disunisci tu, s'Amor ne stringe?'[4]

What use is it to you, my heart, being loved? / What use to me having so dear a lover? / Why, cruel destiny, / do you separate those whom Love holds tight?

In the context of Byron's letter, the quotation releases an innuendo: what use is our loving each other if we cannot make love? Perhaps it is also meant, half-smilingly, to offer reassurance: the predicament of Amarilli, the speaker of these lines in the play, is far worse than Byron's or Guiccioli's since the survival of the entire realm of Arcadia requires her to give up her lover—and still she is allowed to find happiness in the end. But overarching these particular implications is the fact that simply reaching for a parallel opens imaginative space and so offers some respite from the narrow channel of one-to-one communication, however prized that communication may be. The quotation allows the lovers to feel that they have company, that others have felt the same way. Yet it also reinforces their sense of their own uniqueness since the act of quoting maintains a distance between the writer and the quoted words: it implies comparison rather than identity. Here are the familiar conflicted feelings that we have been exploring: love is common; our love is unique. Byron says as much in his previous letter to Guiccioli: 'è un caso commune il quale abbiamo di soffrire con' [*sic*] tanti altri poiche [*sic*] l'Amor non è mai felice, ma noi altri l'abbiamo di soffrire di più...'[5] ('it is a common circumstance which we have to suffer along with so many others since love is never happy, but the two of us have to suffer it more... ').

The feeling of self-definition established by quotation is not easy to maintain. Just before the lines from Guarini, Byron wrote the following: 'Ti bacio mille volte'[6] ('I kiss you a thousand times'). His own expression? Or an echo of words in a famous poem by Catullus, 'da mi basia mille' ('give me a thousand kisses'), which he had once imitated in verse?[7] But then the phrase is hardly unusual, and might first have been said to him by any of the many women who so generously deepened his knowledge of Italian words and habits. The fact that Byron was writing in his second language increases the likelihood that he was taking grateful refuge in a conventional phrase: he faced, as he said, 'la doppia difficoltà di esprimere un' [*sic*] dolor' insopportabile in una lingua per me straniera'[8] ('the double difficulty of expressing unbearable pain in a language that is foreign to me'). On the other hand, the same fact increases the likelihood that the phrase will have had for him some savour of novelty. Laboriously in his second language, Byron negotiates the familiar predicament for writers about love: much of what he says has been said before in roughly or even exactly the same words (the same, of course, may happen to any writing about anything: but, as we have seen, it figures as a particular problem with love because of the intense conventionality and intense individuality which love, paradoxically, combines). His self-expression shifts from quotation to reiteration to would-be original assertion; as with Wyatt, the meaning of the different steps is fluid too. The inevitable 'ti amo', uttered so many millions of times before—and not a few by him—might come as a regretful acquiescence in cliché, or as an ecstatic gesture of linguistic as well as personal self-abandonment.[9]

The text that most permeated Byron's relationship with Guiccioli was the one in which, of all European literature, the permeation of desire by a text is most provocatively staged: the Paolo and Francesca episode from Canto 5 of Dante's *Inferno*. Their first flirtation included a discussion of it, prompted by the fact that Guiccioli was born, like Francesca, in Ravenna.[10] The connection was soon being elaborated in Byron's letters. To heaven without Guiccioli, he wrote in the early days of their affair, he would prefer Hell 'basta che tu fosti meco come Francesca col'suo Amante' ('so long as you were with me like Francesca with her Lover'). A couple of weeks later he was telling her that 'quella storia di amor funesto, che sempre m'interessava, adesso m'interessa doppiamente, dopo che Ravenna rinchiude il mio cuore' ('that story of fatal love, which always interested me, now interests me doubly, since Ravenna holds my heart'). When she reached the point of separation from her husband, with consequent scandal, he felt there had been 'nothing like it since the days of Guido di [*sic*] Polenta's family, in these parts'—that is, since the murder of Paolo and Francesca by the cuckolded husband.[11]

When Dante enters the circle of the carnal sinners in Canto 5, he understands just from looking at it that he is faced with those who subjugate reason to instinct or desire ('la ragion sommettono al talento').[12] What he sees are souls flying through the air like starlings or cranes, being driven hither and thither by the wind. Desire, then, is figured as a natural force: giving way to it sweeps you off into the natural world, makes you into a creature like a bird: responsive, graceful—and less than human. Each soul is alone save for one couple whom Dante invites to talk to him. Only the woman speaks: the man weeps beside her. Soon Dante recognizes her and, calling her only by her Christian name, Francesca, asks her how 'love allowed her and her lover to know the doubtful desires' ('concedette amore / che conosceste i dubbiosi desiri'). She explains:

> 'Noi leggiavamo un giorno per diletto
> di Lancialotto come amor lo strinse;
> soli eravamo e sanza alcun sospetto.
>   Per più fiate li occhi ci sospinse
> quella lettura, e scolorocci il viso;
> ma solo un punto fu quel che ci vinse.
>   Quando leggemmo il disïato riso
> esser basciato da cotanto amante,
> questi, che mai da me non fia diviso,
>   la bocca mi basciò tutto tremante.
> Galeotto fu 'l libro e chi lo scrisse:
> quel giorno più non vi leggemmo avante.'[13]

('One day we were reading for pleasure about Lancelot and how love squeezed him; we were alone with no suspicions. Many times, that reading pushed our eyes together and discoloured our faces; but only one point was what defeated us. When we read the longed-for laugh being kissed by such a lover, this man, who will never be divided from me, all trembling kissed my mouth. Galeotto [a Pandar] was the book and whoever wrote it: that day we read no further on.')

The loss of agency figured by the birds in the wind is here brought down to the act of reading. The push of the repeated words for reading, 'leggiavamo', 'lettura', 'leggemmo', 'leggemmo', is dissipated via a mesmerizing play of sound among the words around—'diletto', 'Lancialotto', 'lo strinse', 'soli', 'scolorocci', and so on up to 'Galeotto' (the word for bed, 'letto', almost seems itching to be mentioned). Francesca recreates in her speech the sensual excitement of her reading which ends up with the passive verb of what is happening on the printed page, 'esser basciato' ('being kissed'), leaping up like a picture in a pop-up book and becoming active through their bodies: 'mi basciò' ('he kissed me'). The book becomes a person, a 'Galeotto'—and it is all his fault. Her argument is especially troubling for Dante as he imagines himself listening to her, for among the first words she spoke in self-justification were some that sounded much like a line of verse he had written in his youth: 'Amor, ch'al gentil cor ratto s'apprende' ('Love which quickly catches in a noble heart'), she says, echoing a lyric that began 'Amor e'l gentil cor sono una cosa' ('Love and the noble heart are a single thing').[14] In Francesca and her punishment, Dante sees embodied the moral consequences not only of Arthurian romance but of his own love lyrics. The episode offers justification for the different kind of poem he is now embarked on writing—a moral and theological epic. But the cost of the transformation is made clear when Francesca finishes speaking. As she gave way to the words she read, so he gives way to the words she speaks: '... di pietade / io venni men così com'io morisse. / E caddi come corpo morto cade'[15] ('... from pity / I fainted away as though I were dying. / And I fell as a dead body falls'). 'Pietade' here seems to stand for a complex of feelings: sympathy, horror, and probably some self-inculpation.

This is the epitome of the sort of scene we explored in Chapter 16, where desire described in the narrative coalesces with the provocation of desire in readers. As Teodolinda Barolini has said, it is 'a *mise en abyme* where our passions are engaged as we read of passionate readers reading about passion'.[16] Yet this characterization betrays Barolini's own passionate involvement as she skips a layer of complication: in fact we read of a passionate protagonist—Dante—hearing of passionate readers reading about passion. His response poses a question about ours: is falling for Francesca's story the right way to respond? Many readers and translators, in many places and times, have thought that it definitely is; and the trend was strong in Britain in the early years of the nineteenth century. H. F. Cary's translation (1805), which became canonical after Coleridge praised it in 1818, holds mainly to a principle of all-but-literal closeness. Yet when he translates Francesca's speech, Cary finds room for little intensifying touches which reveal the presence of desire in the translation, rather as with Fairfax's Tasso or Smith's Petrarch. Guinevere's laugh or smile is doubled—'that smile ... the wishèd smile'. It is not just kissed but kissed 'so rapturously'—and then that swooning 'so' is swooningly repeated in the rendering of 'cotanto amante' as 'one so deep in love'.[17] In the much freer circumstances of Leigh Hunt's *The Story of Rimini*, desire elaborates the moment more extensively.[18] As they read, Paulo, 'by degrees, gently embraced / With one permitted arm' Francesca's 'lovely waist', while their 'cheeks, like peaches on a tree, / Leaned with a touch together, thrillingly'. Then they arrive at Lancelot and Guinevere's kiss:

> That touch, at last, through every fibre slid;
> And Paolo turned, scarce knowing what he did,
> Only he felt he could no more dissemble,
> And kissed her, mouth to mouth, all in a tremble.
> Sad were those hearts, and sweet was that long kiss:
> Sacred be love from sight, whate'er it is.
> The world was all forgot, the struggle o'er,
> Desperate the joy.—That day they read no more.[19]

In a genteel redemption of the fall of Eve (with peaches as upmarket apples), the lovers' kiss is presented as both natural, a matter of touches sliding along nerve-fibres, and virtuous, an escape from dissimulation. The four lines that follow the kiss are the narratorial equivalent of Dante-the-character's swoon, though they replace the *Inferno*'s ambivalent 'pietade' with a gush of approving sentiment.

As we have seen from his letters, Byron felt the affective pull of Francesca's speech; and he is *The Story of Rimini*'s dedicatee. But his own elaboration of the episode, which is scattered through Book I of *Don Juan*, is also sensitive to the contrary tendencies in the Dante, the prompts to thought which interfere with the tugs on the heart strings. His imagination is hooked by Francesca's remark that she and Paolo suspected nothing, were 'sanz'alcun sospetto'—which might mean both that they had no idea of what they were about to do and that they had no fear of being interrupted. When the sixteen-year-old Juan is first tantalized by the lovely Donna Julia, he had—we are told—'no idea / Of his own case, and never hit the true one'. Instead, his feelings launch him into a 'glowing reverie'. He thinks 'about himself, and the whole earth, / Of man the wonderful, and of the stars', and much, much else; pretty much everything, in fact, except—the narrator tells us—what he really wanted: 'A bosom whereon he his head might lay ... With – several other things, which I forget, / Or which, at least, I need not mention yet'. Juan's shy adolescent inability to admit his own desires finds a sardonic echo in the narrator's knowing self-interruption. This nudges readers towards seeing that Juan is (just like Paolo and Francesca) under the control of a narrative without realizing it. The narrative does not have to appear on paper in Byron's poem because we all know it already: we all know the Paolo and Francesca episode or tales like it. Readers can write the denouement for themselves: this is a comically obvious, and so partly defused, version of that textual reticence-cum-suggestiveness which provoked such desire in Dryden and Duke.

Donna Julia is unsuspecting too, or rather 'unsuspecting' in inverted commas: not ignorant but self-deceiving. Virtuous married woman that she is, she recognizes the danger she is in and takes appropriate precautions: 'she vow'd she never would see Juan more, / And next day paid a visit to his mother'. Frustratingly, Juan fails to drop in on his mum that day so she decides 'to face and overcome temptation', fortified by the idea that 'there are such things as love divine: / Platonic, perfect, "just such love as mine"'. When, before long, she and Juan are alone together, she gives his hand 'a pure Platonic squeeze'. There is no need for them to read a book together: the texts that are leading them on are all around them.

Giovanni Boccaccio, at once deferring to and arguing with Dante, subtitled his *Decameron* (1349–51) 'Prince Galeotto'. Half a millenium later, *The Story of Rimini* and Cary's translation both in their different ways adopt the same role: they draw their readers into emotional communion with the lovers. Byron's innovation is that, while allowing his text to hold out the same lure, he simultaneously obstructs it—as when, not long after the Platonic squeeze, Julia finds herself in a pose reminiscent of *The Story of Rimini*: 'half embraced / And half retiring' from Juan's 'glowing arm':

> Yet still she must have thought there was no harm,
> Or else 'twere easy to withdraw her waist;
>   But then the situation had its charm,
> And then—God knows what next—I can't go on;
> I'm almost sorry that I e'er begun.

This echoes 'Quel giorno più non vi leggemmo avante' ('that day we read no further on') with the startling difference that here it is the narrator who stops—or rather pretends to stop—narrating, not the readers who stop reading. The interruption makes a joke out of what might otherwise be the narrator's sensual involvement in his story, and draws attention—by thwarting them—to readers' expectations of being imaginatively seduced. The moment presents *Don Juan* as the latest twist in the tradition to which the Lancelot romance belonged: in that respect the poem is itself a Galeotto. But, at the same time, the complexity of this great comic moment protests against Dante's valuation of the romance mode as a mere pander to feeling over reason. It is, rather, a philosopher who should be blamed. Julia's Galeotto is 'Plato! Plato!' His 'confounded fantasies' lead to 'immoral conduct' because they make people believe there is a 'system' through which the 'controlless core' of their hearts can be subdued. He is:

> a bore,
> A charlatan, a coxcomb—and have been,
> At best, no better than a go-between.
>   117
> And Julia's voice was lost, except in sighs

The word 'system', together with the baggy, cacophonous verbality of those last lines of stanza 16, associate Plato with the contemporary practitioners of 'cant'—Southey, Wordsworth, Coleridge, Castlereagh—whom Byron attacks in the dedication of *Don Juan*, and against whose ponderous and hypocritical ways with language (as he saw it) his own brilliant chatty nimbleness was aimed. Wordsworth, in *The Excursion*, has given the world 'a sample from the vasty version / Of his new system to perplex the sages'; Castlereagh's oratory is a 'set trash of phrase, / Ineffably, legitimately vile'.[20] Yet the phrasing with which Byron's narrator attacks the charlatan Plato is itself not unvasty, nor untrashy. Byron recognizes here—and this is a large part of the tough brilliance of *Don Juan*—that his own mouthy and (in its own way) moralizing work has something in common with his enemies. What separates it from them is his recognition of its likeness to them. Flowing from that recognition come two further qualities: the ironical self-underminings of his verse, and a concomitant awareness of what lies beyond its powers of representation. The mention of Julia's lost voice points to a passion that is beyond expression: both the act of love—which could not be described without offence—and the 'controlless core' of human hearts which cannot finally be grasped.

Throughout *Don Juan*, therefore, Byron lets his words grow implicit inverted commas, shadowing them with irony and so keeping them at one remove from what might really be going on: so many possible ways of representing it; none of them authoritatively right. The digressions and interruptions that crowd Book I collaborate with this imaginative enterprise: they repeatedly stage the turning away from something that is thereby made to seem unrepresentable. Even when Julia at last gives vent to her feelings, after the affair has been discovered and she has been confined to a nunnery, her utterance seems to float away from her, taking its place among the other descriptions of what has happened but not trumping them. The speech powerfully reiterates a series of commonplaces about passion: 'I had not lived till now, could sorrow kill', etc. The statements about women—that love is 'woman's whole existence' and that the 'feminine' brain cannot 'forget'—are pure concentrates of ideology, seeming both to revel in this construction of gender and, because of their blatancy, implicitly to protest against it. Old favourites about love are replayed. Othello's 'One / Who loved not wisely but too well' pops up in

Julia's "Tis wise—'tis well . . . To love too much has been the only art / I used'. And there are four lines that recall and argue with Francesca: the distinctive mode of translated allusion suggests here, as in the instances we explored in Chapter 17, the conventional quality of the passion which nevertheless has become everything to her. 'I loved, I love you, for that love have lost / State, station, heaven, mankind's, my own esteem', she laments, echoing Francesca's triple bell-peal around 'love', 'Amor, ch'a null'amato amar perdona' ('love which allows no loved one not to love back'), and which led her and Paolo to a single death ('ad una morte'). Julia goes on to say that she 'can not regret' what her love 'hath cost, / so dear is still the memory of that dream'—reversing Francesca's view that there is 'nessun maggior dolore / che ricordarsi del tempo felice / nella miseria' ('no greater pain than to remember happy times in misery'). In the *Inferno*, this dictum suggests that the ability to remember is an aggravation of Francesca's punishment. Perhaps the presence of the shade of her beloved is too: a continual reminder of what once had been, but with no physical body left for her to touch in comfort. For Francesca, 'nella miseria' has a specific application: 'in Hell'. But in *Don Juan*, since Julia has not suffered quite such a dire fate, her no less passionate declaration is left more vulnerable to irony. Byron's narrator, of course, does not miss the chance. At the end of her heartfelt letter he sums up the whole business: 'this was Don Juan's earliest scrape'. The shocking remark sets up an endless oscillation of judgements: on the one hand, 'Donna Julia is giving way to "cant"'; on the other, 'the narrator is blind to human feeling'. Here again is that brilliance of *Don Juan* which allows nothing to be taken for granted. Yet even this characteristically Byronic switchback has a root in Dante's Canto 5, for Francesca's speech too is offered up for a double reading. On the one hand, a noble tale of tragic love. On the other, a symptomatic account of the sin of lust.

Byron's relationship with Guiccioli started half a year after he had finished Canto I of *Don Juan*: following the ironies that we have explored, the earnestness of his references to Francesca in his letters is striking. Only in letters to male friends does he (occasionally) adopt a different tone, as here, to John Cam Hobhouse, in the early days of the affair:

> . . . the die is cast—and I must (not figuratively—but *literally*) 'pass the *Rubicon*'—you know I believe that is in my way,—The Adventure is so far past preventing that —— that we had consummated our unlawful union with all the proper rites four days and daily—previously to *her* leaving Venice.

There is a salacious quip in '*Rubicon*', 'con' being the French for 'cunt': this is the language of the 'scrape'. But when he writes to Guiccioli herself, Byron draws on the established language of romantic love, quoting and echoing some of its famous texts—just as he had made Donna Julia do—and adopting its conventions: 'Tu sei il mio unico ed ultimo Amor' ('you are my only and last love'). Just as in *Don Juan*, this assortment of descriptive modes is held a little away from a core of emotion that is felt to be inexpressible and impossible to control. Imagining that she might fall in love with another, he reflects that 'Il Sentimento'—a word which here seems to stand for the panoply of love, desire, and passion—'non dipende da noi—ma . . . è la cosa più bella e fragile della nostra esistenza' ('does not depend on us—but . . . it is the most beautiful and fragile thing in our existence'). 'Tu mi giurasti la tua costanza' ('You swore to me your constancy'), he says, 'ed io non ti giuro nulla, vedremmo [*sic*] chi di noi sara [*sic*] più fedele' ('and I swear nothing to you, let us see which of us will be the more faithful').

One way in which he lived out this explicitly unspoken promise of fidelity was by undertaking writing connected with her. 'The Prophecy of Dante' (1810; published 1821), a poem of political exhortation, was done at her request; and his translation of the first canto of Pulci's *Morgante Maggiore* (1819–20; published 1823) involved the sustained interpenetration of her language and his. In a letter to his publisher John Murray, Byron asked that the translation be printed 'side by side with the original Italian because I wish the reader to judge of the fidelity—it is stanza for stanza—and often line for line if not word for word'. Stylistically, too, Byron's *Morgante* flaunts its fidelity—like a jousting knight wearing his lady's token—in lines of obvious translationese:

> And thus at length they separated were
> E così il me' che seppe gli divise
>
> 'When hither to inhabit first we came
>   These mountains . . .'
> Quando ci venni al principio abitare
>   Queste montagne . . .
>
> 'I to the friars have for peace to sue.'
> Co' monaci la pace si vuol fare.[21]

Not long after his mention of translatorly fidelity in that letter to Murray, Byron jumps to discussing the behaviour of women in Venetian and Ravennese society: 'they marry for their parents and love for themselves.—they exact fidelity from a lover as a debt of honour—while they pay the husband as a tradesman—that is not at all'. As we would by now expect, the hint of a connection between fidelity in love and in translation strengthens when he turns to translating a text that has to do with love: the episode of Paolo and Francesca. According to Guiccioli's memoir, she and Byron read the passage together and she asked him if it had been translated into English. 'Non tradotto, ma tradito,' he replied ('not translated, but betrayed'), echoing the Italian commonplace for the difficulty of translation, 'traduttore traditore' ('translator traitor'). So he set about translating it himself, working his way through several versions. In the headnote to the final text, he wrote: 'I have sacrificed all ornament to fidelity'. He wanted to print his 'Francesca of Rimini' in one volume with either the Pulci translation or 'The Prophecy of Dante', in what might have taken on the aspect of a tribute volume to Guiccioli; but in the event the 'Francesca' was published only posthumously.[22]

Fidelity to what or whom? 'To the letter' or 'to the spirit' are the usual answers. As we saw in Chapter 14, 'to the author' is an alternative that would have made sense to Dryden or Pope: it would imply subjugating local translatorly decisions to the intention which is felt to transpire through the work as a whole. Byron does not translate the whole *Commedia*, nor all of *Inferno*, nor even all of Canto 5. He begins with words of Francesca's. There is no description of her circumstances and no indication, crucially, that she is speaking to anyone. In the Italian, she begins with an address to Dante-the-character; in Byron's English it has been cut, so that she starts off speaking in what seems almost to be the decontextualized voice of a lyric poem.

Releasing her from her place in the *Commedia*, and in hell, Byron adopts a gallant principle of fidelity to the character. And this continues in his verbal choices. In the Italian, Dante exclaims 'quanto disio' ('how much desire') led the lovers to their fate. Byron increases the compulsion: 'what strong ecstasies'. He does the same when Francesca is asked 'come concedette amore / che conosceste i dubbiosi disiri' ('how love allowed you to know the doubtful desires'). To Byron's Francesca, the question is put in more dignified terms:

> . . . how thy love to passion rose
> So as his dim desires to recognize?

In the Italian, Francesca, so trenchant in her speech, asserts that she was passive in the events that provoked her death and damnation: love led her; the book lifted her eyes; Paolo kissed her. It is another instance of that layering of rhetorical power and actual impotence which is frequent in Ovid's *Heroides*, as we saw in Chapter 11. Byron strengthens this claim of Francesca's for mitigation, making Dante speak of her 'sad destinies' and 'evil fortune', concepts which, in the *Commedia*—as you would expect for such an avowedly Christian work—are treated gingerly and never accepted as justification for a person's deeds.

Here is Byron's version of the familiar scene:

> 'We read one day for pastime, seated nigh,
>   Of Lancelot, how love enchain'd him too;
>   We were alone, quite unsuspiciously.
> But oft our eyes met, and our cheeks in hue
>   All o'er discolour'd by that reading were;
>   But one point only wholly us o'erthrew.
> When we read the long-sighed-for smile of her
>   To be thus kissed by such a fervent lover,
>   He, who from me can be divided ne'er,
> Kiss'd my mouth, trembling in the act all over—
>   Accursed was the book, and he who wrote;
>   That day no further leaf we did uncover'.
> While thus one spirit told us of their lot
>   The other wept so, that, with pity's thralls,
>   I swoon'd, as if by death I had been smote,
> And fell down even as a dead body falls.

Byron introduces a lovely formal innovation for the moment of the kiss which leaps from book to lip: the rhymes for what should be two separate interlocking tercets become almost identical, as though attempting not only to mingle but to merge: 'were'—'of her'—'lover'—'all over'—'uncover'. He also works up a suggestion of military compulsion which is just hinted at by Dante in the image of the dead body falling and in the verb for what the reading did to the lovers—'ci vinse' ('us o'erthrew', as Byron puts it). In Byron, love not only squeezed or embraced or confined Lancelot ('lo strinse'), but 'enchain'd him', and the insertion of 'too' extends the chain to Paolo and Francesca. 'Thralls' is also Byron's touch, and connects to the increased confinement of Lancelot in that it is here being taken (unusually) to mean something similar to 'chains'. And there are more connections. In the first draft, it was Dante who swooned 'to see the misery which both enthralls'; in Cary's translation it had been Lancelot who was 'thralled' by love. Byron translates so as to increase the rigidity of the compulsion which ricochets from Lancelot to Paolo to Francesca to Dante and then implicitly on to translator and to reader.

After Canto I of *Don Juan*, the wholesale straight emotiveness of this seems odd, a throwback to the dark romantic heroism of 'Lara' or 'The Corsair' (both published 1814): 'The Corsair' takes its epigraphs from *Inferno* 5, and in both poems a good deal of passionate rising up goes on. Since then, Byron had come under the influence of Ariosto, Tasso, Berni, and Pulci, and had accomplished his decisive shift towards the mock-heroic: with *Don Juan*, he set himself against the wrong 'system' of romanticism to which he had previously in part subscribed. Yet this revolution in his creative being did not mean that the impulses of his earlier writing were abandoned. Instead, they are staged in such a way as to be opened to criticism—not therefore necessarily to collapse beneath it, but to be braced against its pressure. Juan's affair with Julia can be called a 'scrape'—but Julia has something to say against that valuation. In 'Francesca of Rimini', the heartfelt expression of feeling is challenged by the underlying fact that this text is also an exercise in translation. Like the 'Canticus Troili', the 'Francesca' makes a claim to sincerity while also, paradoxically, asserting its own translatedness. Here, as so often before, translation becomes a medium for exploring the constraints and liberties of desire. But the configuration has shifted. Desire is now conceived as 'passion': the source text has become, not an object to be possessed, nor a script to be parroted and departed from, but the origin of an overwhelming impulse. In the adulterous fidelity of Byron's translation, his paradoxical understanding of passion is crystallized: it is something nebulous and glorious to which you 'rise'; but it is equally a chain. At once rising in his sympathy with Francesca, and subjugating himself to the chains that felled her, Byron enthralls himself to the metaphor of 'translation as passion'.

19

Pope's *Iliad*: the 'Hurry of Passion'

In his hostility to 'cant', Byron was buttressed not only by the Italian comic romancers but also by an English poet: Alexander Pope. It was the Pope of *The Rape of the Lock* and *The Dunciad* who most nourished *Don Juan*; but Pope's translation of Homer mattered to Byron too, and provided him with the archetype of the sort of response he was later to have to Francesca: 'as a Child I first read Pope's Homer with a rapture which no subsequent work could ever afford'.[1] Byron's way of reading Pope's Homer is in tune with Pope's way of reading Homer—at least, the Homer of the *Iliad*: 'no man of true Poetical Spirit is Master of himself while he reads him,' Pope wrote in the Preface to his translation, so 'forcible' is the poet's 'Fire and Rapture'. There is a sensuous, rather feminizing drift to this description which Pope immediately stamps on: his reaction to Homer turns out to be more disciplined and vigorous than the passionate readings we have encountered so far. 'The Reader is hurry'd out of himself' (not seduced) 'by the Force' (not suggestiveness) 'of the Poet's Imagination' and takes on body and presence in an imagined public world: he turns 'in one place to a Hearer, in another to a Spectator'.[2] For Paolo and Francesca, the impulse that came from the book they were reading prompted them to stop reading and take action—but the action they took was conceived as a private giving-way. Reading issued in a passive sort of activity. But when Pope is swept away by Homer all he does is keep on reading, though in a more alert manner—one which will eventually develop into the especially active reading that is translation, though Pope does not say so here. Reading becomes an active sort of passivity. Two somewhat distinct models, then; yet they have a crucial element in common. In neither of them does the text figure in the ways we explored throughout Part II and in Chapter 16: as an object for the reader or translator to go to work on, whether to interpret its ambiguities or open its secrets or fill its alluring lacunae. Instead, it is the origin of an impulse. To read is to respond; and to translate is, above all, to transmit that impulse so that others can respond in their turn. The major example in English of the metaphor of 'translation as passion' is not an amorous work but an epic. 'The Endeavour of any one who translates *Homer*', Pope says, 'is above all things to keep alive that Spirit and Fire.'[3]

There are traces here, in the Preface to Pope's *Iliad* (1715–20), of the language adopted by Dryden and his predecessors. Pope talks of 'following' Homer's 'footsteps', of 'transfusing the Spirit of the Original', and of endeavouring to 'give his Author entire and unmaim'd'.[4] But this familiar phraseology is surrounded and overwhelmed by a fresh vocabulary of emotive response. The source for much of the new way of putting things was the same writer who guided Addison's characterization of Sappho: 'bold *Longinus*', Pope called him in his *Essay on Criticism*[5]—or rather, Longinus as translated by the hugely influential French critic Boileau in 1674. Boileau titled his version *Traité du Sublime*, launching a concept— the sublime—which at once caught on in France and spread to Britain over the next two or three decades.[6] Homer was the great exemplar of the sublime; and its effects, according to Boileau's Longinus, were these:

> Il ravit, il transporte, & produit en nous une certaine admiration meslée d'estonnement & de surprise...il donne au Discours une certaine vigueur noble, une force invincible qui enleve l'ame de quiconque nous écoute...il renverse tout comme un foudre.[7]

> It ravishes, it transports, & produces in us a distinctive admiration mixed with astonishment and surprise...it gives the discourse a distinctive noble vigour, an invincible force which carries off the soul of whoever is listening to us...it scatters everything like a thunderbolt.

Here is a precedent for Pope's talk of the loss of readerly self-possession caused by Homer's 'Fire and Rapture'. And here, too, a counter-current stops the sublime from being simply overwhelming. After the first reaction of yielding to an invincible force, readers find that something more assertive builds within them. Boileau catches the shift in emphasis with the switch of a single letter, from 'enleve' ('carries off') to 'esleve' ('lifts'):

> Il esleve l'ame, & lui fait concevoir une plus haute opinion d'elle mesme, la remplissant de joie & de je ne sçay quel noble orgeuil, comme si c'estoit elle qui eust produit les choses qu'elle vient simplement d'entendre.[8]

> It lifts the soul, and makes it conceive a more exalted opinion of itself, filling it with joy and with I know not what noble pride, as if it were the soul itself that had produced the things that it had simply heard.

Loss of identity makes way for growth of identity. The genius of the author echoes in the reader who is like a cave that thinks the voice that sounds within it is its own. For most, this borrowed exaltation is a temporary illusion; but for some readers who are also writers it can last. An encounter with the sublime enables them, in their turn, to produce sublime works which, although done by them, are in origin not wholly theirs. These writers, we are told, are like the priestess of Apollo, swept into prophecy by the divinity who inspires her (in Boileau as in Longinus, the language of exaltation here blends back into that of dissolution): 'ils sont comme ravis & emportez de l'enthousiasme d'autrui' ('they are as though ravished and carried away by the enthusiasm of another').[9] Herodotus, Stesichoros, and Archilocus strike Longinus as having been bumped into sublimity by Homer. And Longinus himself struck Boileau in the same way: 'en parlant du Sublime, il est lui mesme tres sublime'.[10] Pope copied faithfully: Longinus, he says in '*An Essay on Criticism*', '*Is himself* that great *Sublime* he draws'.[11]

Reading Boileau's Longinus, Pope found an account of reading. But the reading he read about—the reading of sublime poetry—was different from the reading he gave the critical text, however '*Sublime*' he courteously credited Longinus with being. For the sublimity of Homer could not be grasped and reproduced in the way Pope grasped and reproduced Boileau's Longinus. And neither could it be 'understood', nor 'interpreted', nor 'opened'. It has to be felt; and feeling it initiates a process that moves through the impression towards (sometimes) the reality of new creation. Startlingly, this domino effect of the sublime occurs also within works for which only one author is responsible. Boileau's view of Longinus, as being sublime in his description of the sublime, echoes Longinus's view of Homer which, in Boileau's translation, is sharpened into a similar soundbite: 'Homere est heroïque lui-mesme; en peignant le caractere d'un Heros' ('Homer is himself heroic when painting the character of a hero'). As example, Longinus quotes the moment from Book 17 of the *Iliad* when Zeus has covered the battlefield in darkness to advantage the Trojans. Ajax, struggling, calls out, not for his life to be saved—this is what impresses Longinus—but for the darkness to be lifted so that he can at least die by the light of day. What is sublime in Ajax is his determination to suffer 'une fin digne de son grand coeur, quand il devroit avoir à combattre Jupiter mesme' ('an end worthy of his great heart, even if he had to fight against Jupiter himself').[12] Exactly what is sublime about Homer's account of Ajax's sublimity (insofar as the two are separable) is not made entirely clear; but contributing factors must include the imaginative sympathy and precision with which the poet has crystallized this moment of self-revelation out of the given reality of battle; and perhaps also the grand plainness of the words he has written for Ajax to utter: 'ποίησον δ' αἴθρην, δὸς δ' ὀφθαλμοῖσιν 'ιδέσθαι' ('make clear sky, so that we can see with our eyes').[13] That is the sort of phrasing which anchored the traditional comparisons of Homer to the Old Testament: as Pope put it, 'his style must...bear a greater resemblance to the sacred

Books than that of any other Writer'.[14] Longinus sees Homer as being so
involved in his own description of the battle at this point that he is himself
best described with lines he wrote of another one of the warriors, Hector,
when, in Book 15, he is said to be raging like Ares or like a fire consuming
the thickets of a deep forest. This first simile stretches and splits Hector's
identity and so opens the way for a further simile to be grafted onto it: as
Boileau translates, Homer 'ne se remuë pas avec moins de violence, que s'il
estoit épris aussi de fureur'[15] ('acts with no less violence than if he too were in
the grip of fury'). Hector's fury is expressed by the comparison to Ares and to
the forest fire; and Homer's fury—in a new manifestation of the domino
effect of the sublime—is expressed by the comparison to Hector.

There is a circularity to this account of Homer's being inspired by
something that he has himself imagined. The idea may have been influenced by the way in which Homer was thought to have worked. As the
prefatory material to Pope's *Iliad* points out, it had long been realized (and
is indeed clear from the poem itself) that Homer lived some time after the
historical siege of Troy and must have drawn on hearsay about it.[16] Parts
of his work were, then, more invented by him, and parts less. Yet this
consequence of the materiality of composition does not bring us quite to
the point of Longinus's argument. It must often, perhaps always, be the
case that the imagination takes something that feels as though it has to
happen—whether for historical reasons or, if it has been made up, for
reasons of narrative structure or argument or rhyme—and develops out of
it details which can in their turn delight or move the mind that has
imagined them, prompting more creation. However historically rooted
or otherwise a work may be—Longinus thinks—its author and the text,
though everywhere interpermeable, can also pull apart. This model of
creative to-ing and fro-ing allows for some parts of an author's writing to
feel more 'him' or more 'her' than others, and so justifies Longinus's tactic
of describing Homer with a line Homer had written about one of his
characters. This, he must think, is the really Homeric bit of Homer. And
Pope again follows his critical master. Here is a fuller quotation from a
passage I have referred to before:

> What he writes is of the most animated Nature imaginable; every thing
> moves, every thing lives, and is put in Action. If a Council be call'd, or a
> Battle fought, you are not coldly informed of what was said and done as from
> a third Person; the Reader is hurry'd out of himself by the Force of the Poet's
> Imagination, and turns in one place to a Hearer, in another to a Spectator.
> The Course of his verses resembles that of the Army he describes,
>   Οἱ δ' ἄρ' ἴσαν, ὡς εἴ τε πυρὶ Χθὼν πᾶσα νέμοιτο.<II.780>
>   *They pour along like a Fire that sweeps the whole Earth before it.*

Verbal echoes show that Longinus is here partly being mediated by Madame Dacier, the French translator whose prose *L'Iliade d'Homere* (1711) was to Pope both a great help and a great provocation: 'Il ... anime les choses les plus insensibles,' she had written, 'tout vit dans ses vers'.[17] But Pope is also responding directly to Longinus's text, in a way that reveals a striking conceptual debt. For he too picks out a line of Homer's and turns it back on itself, making it function as a description of the work of which it is a part. And here, again, a simile in that line helps it to be used in a further simile. The army's sublimity is expressed by the comparison to the fire; and Homer's sublimity is expressed by the comparison to the army.

Where Longinus, writing in Greek, was able simply to quote Homer, Pope, writing in English, quotes and then translates. And the translation he offers is itself not unforceful, as we can see if we compare translations that preceded him and which he knew:

> ... as if a fire fed on the trembling grass (Chapman, 1611)

> But th'Army march'd as th'Earth had been on fire (Ogilby, 1660)

> Swiftly as when a fire runs ore a Plain
> Which *Phoebus* had with a long Summer parch'd (Hobbes, 1676)

> ... veluti si igni terra tota depasceretur (Barnes, 1711)

> L'Armée s'avançoit donc en ordre de bataille. A l'esclat de ses armes on l'auroit prise pour un embrasement qui ravageoit la plaine (Madame Dacier, 1711)[18]

All except Barnes alter the passive construction 'ὡς εἴ ... Χθὼν πᾶσα νέμοιτο' ('as if the whole earth were grazed upon');[19] and all except Barnes and Chapman neglect the verb's counter-current of pastoral. But only Pope sees the fire, not as sweeping over the earth, but as sweeping the whole earth before it; and only he jumps the action into the present tense. Hurried out of himself by the force of the line, he reads his own rapture back into it: the army seems to sweep the earth before it because Pope is swept before Homer's verse. Translating, he turns the line into an image of what the line does to him. 'To keep alive that Spirit and Fire' means writing into the translation the spirited and fiery response that has been provoked in the translator.

This line of prose parallel-text translation in the Preface is tepid in comparison with the fully fired-up counterpart in the verse version:

> Now, like a Deluge, cov'ring all around,
> The shining Armies swept along the Ground;
> Swift as a Flood of Fire, when Storms arise,
> Floats the wide Field, and blazes to the Skies.[20]

'They pour'—in the Preface—has expanded into something even more overwhelming and taken on the more explicit form of a simile: 'like a Deluge, cov'ring all around'. This morphs confusedly into the image of the fire via the compacted expressiveness of the third line: storms do not usually cause floods of fire, so the words must mean that this flood of fire that is being imagined is as swift as the flash floods that can occur during storms. And then the fire itself is more vividly described. Maynard Mack has noticed that Shakespeare's *Henry V* is a presence in Pope's translation:[21] here the phrase 'swift as a Flood of Fire' includes a hint of that play's rhythmically identical opening exclamation, 'O for a Muse of Fire'. And aptly so, for here fire is Pope's muse. Longinus would have recognized the tumble and mix of images as a sign that the writer himself was both enflamed and swept away: as he says of metaphors, in Boileau's translation: 'il y a des occasions où l'on en peut emploier plusieurs à la fois; quand les Passions, comme un torrent rapide, les entraînent avec elles necessairement, & en foule'[22] ('there are occasions when you can employ many at a time; when the Passions, like a rapid torrent, drag them along with them by necessity and in a crowd').

Homer's *Iliad* at this point moves on directly from the image of the grazing fire to another: the earth groans as when Zeus (or Jove in Pope's translation) hurls a thunderbolt. As Pope remarks in a note:

> The Comparison preceding…of a Fire which runs thro' the Corn and blazes to Heaven, had exprest at once the dazling of their Arms and the Swiftness of their March. After which *Homer* having mention'd the Sound of their Feet, superadds another Simile, which comprehends both the Ideas of the Brightness and the Noise: for here (says *Eustathius*) the Earth appears to *burn* and *groan* at the same time.[23]

This shows the similarity between Pope's practice in translating and what he takes to be Homer's in composing. Pope too superadds another simile in which two ideas—the flood and the fire—are comprehended. As Longinus would see it, Homer's expansiveness here shows him being lifted into sublime expression by the sublimity of what he is describing. Pope's expansiveness shows him being lifted into a sublime act of translation by the sublimity of the words before him.

The description of the army which is like a fire which is like a flood epitomizes an overplus which characterizes Pope's translation throughout. As Maynard Mack has put it, the Greek is subjected to 'almost continual aggrandizement' as Pope searches for what he calls '"the Majesty of Epic Poetry, where every thing ought to be great and magnificent." Homer's "nine or ten thousand" multiplies to "shouting millions;" his simple house-fly to a "vengeful Hornet"'—and so on.[24] The trend collaborates with the greater 'pictorialism' and greater 'sententiousness' which Mack also notes, and with other kinds of elaboration such as the 'heightening' and 'refinement' that have been chronicled by Robin Sowerby.[25] As we have seen, this style of translation was inward with Pope's own individual experience of reading. But it also clearly answered a cultural need, not only because the version was immediately popular, but because contemporaries could understand it in the same Longinian terms that Pope had used. Here, for instance, is the young man of letters, and future translator, William Melmoth, in a letter dated 1719 and published in 1748:

> Mr. Pope seems in most places to have been inspired with the same sublime spirit that animates his original; as he often takes fire from a single hint in his author, and blazes out even with a stronger and brighter flame of poetry.[26]

But to later readers Pope's very determined enterprise of rewriting has often looked like a rhetorical exercise, an almost automated makeover of the *Iliad* to fit a particular canon of taste: the Augustan. Certainly, parts of the translation leave it vulnerable to being thought, as Coleridge thought it, an 'astonishing product of matchless talent and ingenuity' rather than of the *echt* imagination—something that might be admired as craft but could not really be felt as poetry. For Coleridge, the work's artificiality was evident throughout in its language. Pope's *Iliad* was, he said, 'the main source' of what he called 'our pseudo-poetic diction'. As we saw in Chapter 1, that means diction which seems to express, not 'poetic thoughts', but 'thoughts translated into the language of poetry'.[27]

Yet—as I hope this book has begun to show—it is possible to be more sympathetic to language that asks us to bear in mind that it has come into being through translation. If, like Melmoth, we follow the hints in Pope's Preface and take his *Iliad*, not as an attempt to reproduce Homer's text nor, primarily, to 'open' or 'interpret' or 'penetrate' it, but as a poem of translation which endeavours to 'keep alive that Spirit and Fire' by including a passionate reaction on the part of the translator, then even some of the most egregious moments of pseudo-poetic diction start to look more interesting. In Book 1, Achilles is forced to give up his slave mistress Briseïs, for whom he appears to have developed a *tendresse*. Homer has him burst into tears ('δακρύσας'), go away from his comrades, and sit down on the shore of the pale sea ('θῖν' ἐφ' ἁλὸς πολιῆς').[28] Pope works the scene up into this:

> ... sad retiring to the sounding Shore,
> O'er the wild Margin of the Deep he hung,
> That kindred Deep, from whence his Mother sprung.
> There, bath'd in Tears of Anger and Disdain, ... [29]

It is not out of the question for Pope to allow a hero to 'weep'. Achilles will do just that in Book 24 when he 'takes his sad Couch' to grieve for Patroclus.[30] Nevertheless, here in Book 1, an idea of decorum, of what seems fitting for an epic hero, does impose itself on the translation for, as he admits in a note, it is Pope who has 'ventur'd' to say that the tears are 'of Anger and Disdain... of which a great and fiery Temper is more susceptible than any other'—rather than their being, say, tears of childish petulance or sexual longing.[31] But a stronger motive for expansion is sympathy with what Pope takes to be Homer's sympathy with Achilles's grief. We can watch given words—words translated pretty straightforwardly from the Greek—being translated again within English, as Coleridge said, into 'the language of poetry'. The 'Shore' is mentioned, and then reiterated more grandly as 'the wild Margin of the Deep'; and 'the Deep' is reiterated in its turn as 'that kindred Deep'. This pattern of wave-upon-wave suggests a swelling of emotion as Homer's scene of grief is transformed into a scene of sympathy. Pope's responsive imagination takes the idea of Achilles's mother Thetis being out there listening somewhere in the sea and makes her responsiveness spread to the sea itself, 'that kindred Deep', and to the shore, 'the sounding Shore'. The lines layer the *Iliad* with a passionate response.

The same metaphor of passionate translation is at work in Pope's version of the 'Nightpiece' at the end of Book 8, widely (though not universally) admired by his contemporaries and later famously derided by Coleridge.[32] Darkness has put a stop to the fighting, and the Greeks, who have been gaining ground, camp on the battlefield and keep watch. Their fires shone, Homer says, 'just as stars in the sky around the shining moon shine very brightly when the air is still' ('ὡς δ' ὅτ' ἐν οὐρανῷ ἄστρα φαεινὴν ἀμφὶ σελήνην / φαίνετ' ἀριπρεπέα, ὅτε τ' ἔπλετο νήνεμος αἰθήρ').[33] Pope translates:

> The Troops exulting sate in order round,
> And beaming Fires illumin'd all the Ground.
> As when the Moon, refulgent Lamp of Night!
> O'er Heav'ns clear Azure spreads her sacred Light,
> When not a Breath disturbs the deep Serene;
> And not a Cloud o'ercasts the solemn Scene;
> Around her Throne the vivid Planets roll,
> And Stars unnumber'd gild the glowing Pole.[34]

The tactics are familiar: the given 'Moon' is retranslated within English to produce 'refulgent Lamp of Night'; Homer's simile comparing the fires to the stars is capped with further imagining of Pope's own which turns the moon into a 'Throne' and then switches across to (presumably) the pole star, gilded and glowing. Here the emotion that swells and spreads through Pope's response is reverence. 'It is the most beautiful Nightpiece that can be found in Poetry', he remarks in a note;[35] and furthermore it must suggest to him a famous later scene involving one bright significant star. Hence the adjective 'sacred' tacked on to the light, and the 'conscious Swains' who pop up a few lines later, multiplied from a single 'shepherd' in Homer. But this time there is none of the focused energy of the army which is 'Swift as a Flood of Fire', none of the effective (if now unfashionable) sentimentality of the 'wild Margin of the Deep'. Given planets that roll around a throne and a glowing pole gilded by stars there is really no way of rebutting Coleridge's protest that 'it is difficult to determine whether...the sense, or the diction, be the more absurd'.[36]

Pope himself may well have felt some undercurrent of unease about these lines, for they are not so very different from the sort of writing he was later to satirise in *Peri Bathous* (1727):

> When a true genius looks upon the Sky, he immediately catches the idea of a piece of blue lutestring, or a child's mantle.
>> *The skies, whose spreading volumes scarce have room,*
>> *Spun thin, and wove in nature's finest loom.*[37]

(The target here is Sir Richard Blackmore's epic poem *Prince Arthur* [1695], where Raphael wears 'the purest piece of Heav'n's Etherial Blue' for a mantle, and a robe of 'Celestial Linnen, finely Spun and Wove'.)[38] It is hardly less likely that when 'a true genius' looks upon the moon he will catch the idea of a refulgent lamp. This trace of potential self-criticism points to a difficulty with the metaphor of 'translation as passion', especially when it attaches itself to a work as enormous as the *Iliad*. An impulse is, by definition, sporadic and unpredictable; but the work of translation is long, and a style, once established, asks to be sustained. The formal gestures of passionate response are, then, likely to recur even when there is no felt passion for them to embody.

This is what links 'translation as passion' to its variously ironized siblings which we explored in Chapter 17; and this is what enables the double mode of response which—as we saw in Chapter 18—was so virtuosically performed by Byron. Conventionalized writing, which has the look of poetry but not its substance, is what Pope most attacks throughout *Peri Bathous*, a work whose title ('Of Depth') announces it to be a satirical inversion of *Peri Hypsous* ('Of Height'). The bathetic is an attempt at the sublime which fails because it is not suited to its occasion, or because it is in itself grotesque or absurd, or else, simply, because it is a cliché. Pope was adept at criticizing this sort of writing because he was adept at producing it. It is likely that he himself penned several of the anonymous examples he attacks in *Peri Bathous*; even more strikingly, his work in translating Homer overlaps (at its beginning) with the composition of *The Rape of the Lock* and (at its end) with the writing of *The Dunciad*—both masterpieces in the vein of mock-epic, which is to say in the purposeful deployment of bathos. The resulting interplay between epic and its ticklish underbelly has been much discussed by scholars as revealing the seriousness with which Pope approached his social satire.[39] It also points to the stylistic vulnerability of parts of the translated *Iliad*. Not much more than a year before he was penning 'as when the Moon, refulgent Lamp of Night!', Pope had written the following lines describing a tea party in a genteel drawing room:

> For lo! the Board with Cups and Spoons is crown'd,
> The Berries crackle, and the Mill turns round.
> On shining Altars of *Japan* they raise
> The silver Lamp; the fiery Spirits blaze.
> From silver Spouts the grateful Liquors glide,
> While *China*'s Earth receives the smoking Tyde.[40]

Here are not only a 'lamp', but fire, and the word 'round' in rhyme; and a view that ranges from high ('raise') to low ('Earth') like the span from 'Ground' to 'Heav'n' in the 'Nightpiece'. In *The Rape of the Lock*, the incongruity of style and occasion is set up to be enjoyed. But in the *Iliad* translation the failure to achieve sublimity is a threat, not a joke; and it is not always fended off. Several lines from the 'Nightpiece' are candidates for inclusion in *Peri Bathous*.

Yet the passage also includes that current of self-reflectiveness which typifies the poetry of translation. In a letter to Lady Mary Wortley Montagu, then living in Constantinople, Pope imagines her looking across the Hellespont so as to 'contemplate the Fields of Asia, in such a dim and remote prospect, as you have of Homer in my Translation'.[41] As translated by Pope, the 'Nightpiece', with its 'shady Lustre' shooting 'o'er the Field', its 'Rocks' that rise 'in Prospect', itself becomes a scene of dim and remote prospects. By an undertow of feeling, all the fire, which at other points in the poem seems to leap from Homer into Pope, is here felt to stay back in an inimitable distance. 'The long Reflections of the distant Fires'—a line invented by Pope—includes a hint of its own status as a long, lesser reflection of Homer's distant fire.[42] The same melancholy recognition is at work throughout the passage, with its determined elaborateness, its air of trying too hard.

The passages where Pope's translation responds most intently to
Homer's Greek, and which therefore ask for the most intent response
from readers in their turn, tend to be those where Homer's fire, as Pope
feels it, burns most fiercely: where it is not mediated via sympathy or
beauty but leaps with Longinian vigour from scene to poet to reader and
translator. As we have come to expect, the presence of this metaphor in his
translatorly imagining leads Pope to give special attention to doubles of it
in the work he is translating. Of which there are many, for the *Iliad* is full
not only of fire but also of the metaphorical or implied sparks which leap
from person to person via inspirational utterances—when warriors argue
with one another in councils or goad their enemies, or shout encourage-
ment to their friends. Words, in the *Iliad*, repeatedly morph into action:
war is the continuation of speech by other means. When Pope sees this
happening he typically narrows and strengthens the flow of energy. In
Book V, for instance, one of the Trojan allies, Sarpedon, rebukes Hector
for not taking more of a lead. The speech is forceful but is framed in
decorous terms: G. S. Kirk, in his commentary, hears the tone as 'emotional' and 'earnest'.[43] This aspect of the source had been drawn out in
Chapman's characteristically verbose rendition:

> '. . . That deserves in thee so hote a care
> As should consume thy dayes and nights to hearten and prepare
> Th'assistant Princes, pray their minds to beare their far-brought toiles
> To give them worth with worthy fight; in victories and foiles
> Still to be equall; and thy selfe (exampling them in all)
> Need no reproofes nor spurs. All this in thy free choice should fall.'[44]

Now here is Pope:

> 'Rowze all thy *Trojans*, urge thy *Aids* to fight;
> These claim thy Thoughts by Day, thy Watch by Night:
> With Force incessant the brave *Greeks* oppose;
> Such Cares thy Friends deserve, and such thy Foes.'

The repeated sharp commands, the tick-tock of structurally parallel but
semantically opposite phrases ('Thoughts by Day' / 'Watch by Night'; 'thy
Friends' / 'thy Foes') sets going a pulse of energy which keeps resounding
as Sarpedon's words rouse Hector to action. He 'impetuous springs' from
his chariot to the ground, and then:

> . . . animates his drooping Bands,
> Revives their Ardor, turns their Steps from Flight,
> And wakes anew the dying Flames of Fight.
> They turn, they stand: . . .[45]

This repeats not only Sarpedon's rhyme but also the rhythm and shape of his speech, as the ardour of ' "Rowze all thy *Trojans*, urge thy *Aids* to fight" ' emerges into an almost identical pattern of activity: 'Revives their Ardor, turns their Steps from Flight'. What Hector urges, his soldiers do: 'They turn, they stand'—that word 'stand' seeming to condense the phonetic energy of words that have led up to it: 'Steps', 'Bands', 'And'. Pope's own awakened flames here catch from some stylistic sparks in the Greek. Sarpedon's goad has its effect on Hector via an alliterative flurry:

Ὣς φάτο Σαρπηδών, δάκε δὲ φρένας Ἕκτορι μῦθος

The verb 'δάκε' means 'bit' or 'stung': 'so spoke Sarpedon and his speech bit Hector in the heart'. Both the balance and the energy of the line are prompts for Pope. But he has much expanded on them, writing into his English the passionate response that Homer's lines have provoked in him.

It is the same everywhere in the translation. When one character calls out to another, Pope too responds. Homer's Hector 'shouts out' when he charges at the Greeks (κεκλήγων); Pope's 'fires his Host with animating Cries'.[46] When Agamemnon urges on his men, Pope adds reinforcements in the form of two lines of his own:

> Let glorious Acts more glorious Acts inspire,
> And catch from Breast to Breast the noble Fire.[47]

This emphasizes the merging of individualities which already happens in the Greek when one fighter adopts the will of another or suffers a reflex reaction to an enemy's taunt. But Pope's choice of words here also suggests another merging of identities—his and Homer's—which happens throughout the translation and especially at moments such as this. He too is inspired by glorious acts; fire catches also to his breast.

Perhaps the most startling instance of inspiration in Homer, and also of Pope by Homer, occurs in Book 15 where Zeus decides to reanimate Hector who had been smitten in the chest by Ajax with a stone. Hector had been left gasping for breath and vomiting blood, his 'Senses wandring', as Pope puts it, 'to the Verge of Death'.[48] Zeus sends Apollo down to speak to him:

> There *Hector* seated by the Stream he sees,
> His Sense returning with the coming Breeze;
> Again his Pulses beat, his Spirits rise;
> Again his lov'd Companions meet his Eyes;
> *Jove* thinking of his Pains, they past away.[49]

'Pulses' and 'Spirits' are decorous substitutions for Homer's 'gasping' ('ἆσθμα') and 'sweat' ('ἱδρὼς')[50] and the insertion of 'lov'd' before 'Companions' is a characteristically emotive touch. Pope remarks in a note—adopted, as often, from the influential twelfth-century commentator Eustathius—that 'this is a very sublime Representation of the Power of *Jupiter*, to make *Hector*'s Pains cease from the Moment wherein *Jupiter* first turn'd his Thoughts towards him'.[51] His translation brings out the sublimity by altering Homer's straightforward past tense construction 'ἐπεί μιν ἔγειρε Διὸς νόος' ('for the will of Zeus roused him') to the more mysterious '*Jove* thinking of his pains . . .'.[52] Pope feels his way into how Jove's thoughts feel their way into Hector. He writes intensely tactile verse whose words themselves seem to sense and respond to each other in the beat of its pulses: 'returning' met by 'coming'; 'seated' and 'beat' joining in internal rhyme with 'meet'; the phonemes of 'Pains' dissipating in 'past away'. The 'coming Breeze' is his invention and it seems, image of poetic inspiration that it is, to suggest Pope's own sense of himself as joining with Homer and with Zeus in the work of thinking Hector back to life.

Boundaries in general are more hazy in Book 15 than anywhere else in the *Iliad*. It is night; Hector rises from the all-but dead; the gods join the battle, breathing 'immortal Ardour from above'; the Trojans breach the Greeks' defences and fight in among their ships; fire leaps from heated speech to fiery act to actual flame. Pope too, here more than anywhere, gives himself up to Homer, being swept away by the passion of the source and channelling his response into his translation. For instance when Hector, reanimated, charges into battle (I have underlined Pope's significant additions):

> And o'er the Slaughter stalks gigantic Death.
> On rush'd bold *Hector*, gloomy as the Night,
> Forbids to plunder, animates the Fight,
> Points to the Fleet: For by the Gods, who flies,
> Who dares but linger, by this Hand he dies:
> No weeping Sister his cold Eye shall close,
> No friendly Hand his fun'ral Pyre compose.
> Who stops to plunder, in this signal Hour,
> The Birds shall tear him, and the Dogs devour.
>   Furious he said; the smarting Scourge resounds;
> The Coursers fly; the smoaking Chariot bounds:
> The Hosts rush on; loud Clamours shake the Shore;
> The Horses thunder, Earth and Ocean roar![53]

To the fourth of these lines, Pope attaches an appreciative note:

It sometimes happens (says *Longinus*) that a Writer in speaking of some Person, all on a sudden puts himself in that other's Place, and acts his part; a Figure which marks the Impetuosity and Hurry of Passion. It is this which *Homer* practises in these Verses; the Poet stops his Narration, forgets his own Person, and instantly, without any Notice, puts this precipitate Menace into the Mouth of his furious and transported Hero.[54]

The idea is that Hector bursts into utterance at 'For by the gods' without there being any marker of direct speech: Pope follows Longinus in taking this to show Homer's impetuosity in making Hector impetuous. But in fact, as Richard Janko explains in his commentary, there is an ambiguity in the Greek at this point: it may be that the direct speech has in fact been signalled a couple of lines earlier, in which case the 'Figure which marks the Impetuosity and Hurry of Passion' would disappear.[55] Among translations Pope knew, Madame Dacier's French and Joshua Barnes's Latin were both influenced by Boileau's Longinus and parse the construction in the way he suggests. But Chapman in 1611, Ogilby in 1660, and Hobbes in 1676 had all taken it the other way: the ambiguity would have been visible to Pope. So he proves himself a willing follower of Longinus when he reads into the text the animation that the text has prompted in him, precipitately putting into Homer's mouth the precipitateness he thinks Homer has put into Hector's.

There are other ways in which Pope's translation here fans the flames. There is the Miltonic frisson of the first lines of the passage, the super-imposition of similes and adjectives, the emotive contrast of the weeping eye of the sister and the cold eye of the corpse. The threat to deny an actual 'Pyre' only emphasizes the figurative fire that is all around, in the rushing, the animation, the smoking of the chariots, the thunder, the fury. Syntax splits under the pressure. In Homer, in the last four lines of this passage, Hector whips his horse, and shouts again to the Trojans who are organized in ranks ('στίχας'—a word that can also mean lines of verse); and they answer back, and they all go forward. But in Pope this human agency is dissipated: the lines of soldiers are not mentioned and the lines of verse, fractured by repeated strong ceasurae, threaten to fragment: 'the smarting Scourge resounds; / The Coursers fly; the smoking Chariot bounds...'. Here, just as in the description of Homer's 'Fire' in the Preface, 'every *thing* moves, every *thing* lives, and is put in action'. But what, there, had been an admirable characteristic of the sublime imagination is layered, here, with a vision of lost control in the heat of fight. A bit further on in the battle, Pope's translation follows the Greek closely when it says that the warriors are fighting 'with Faulchions, Axes, Swords, and shorten'd Darts'; but then it spawns some weird life of its own:

> The Faulchions ring, Shields rattle, Axes sound,
> Swords flash in Air, or glitter on the Ground;
> With streaming Blood the slipp'ry Shores are dy'd,
> And slaughter'd Heroes swell the dreadful Tyde.[56]

(Only the ideas of the swords falling to the ground and of the earth flowing with blood are in the Greek.) Objects come to life; and people die.

Throughout the fighting, in Pope as in Homer, hero after hero appears, only to be extinguished. Their names are mentioned as a sign that they themselves are lost, and capsule biographies at once register and dismiss the lives that are no more: '*Mycenian Periphes*', who was 'in Wisdom great, in Arms well known to Fame'; or 'unhappy *Lycophron*' who was 'an Exile long, sustain'd at *Ajax*' Board'.[57] Gearing up to translate, Pope wrote to a friend: 'the Lord preserve me in the Day of Battle which is just approaching!'[58] It was only half a joke. His feeling of being swept away by Homer darkens in this part of the poem. His verse becomes more gestural, more frankly and powerfully impressionistic, as the inspiration he is channelling from Homer flares almost out of control. Pope glimpses in his own self-abandonment a miniature reflection of the warriors' self-sacrifice: they too have been inspired by someone else's words. A translator who thinks of himself as 'opening' or 'interpreting' his source will retain a large degree of analytical detachment. But one who, like Pope, thinks of himself as being swept away by his source, inspired by it, as catching fire from it, must feel that his own identity is put at risk. And especially so when what he catches fire from is the *Iliad*. For the mixture of inspiration and destruction which Pope lives out imaginatively as he translates is also at the heart of the poem he is translating. The *Iliad* is a great work of imaginative creation that recounts the uncreation of a great many lives.

PART IV

TRANSLATION AND THE LANDSCAPE OF THE PAST

20

Pope's *Iliad*: a 'comprehensive View'

Homer's 'Invention', which transmits the fire of passion to his readers, also conjures up a world before their eyes, a 'wild Paradise'—Pope calls it in his Preface—which enables them 'to comprehend the vast and various Extent of Nature'. In the *Iliad*, we can see 'the full Prospects of Things', as well as 'several unexpected Peculiarities and Side-Views' which are 'un-observ'd by any Painter but *Homer*'. As we discovered in Chapter 19, a reader affected by 'Rapture' is 'Hurry'd out of himself' by a 'Fire' which 'can over-power Criticism'. But the *Iliad* asks also for a different response: comparatively dispassionate investigation by someone who takes 'a view' of the poem rather than being overwhelmed by it.

> There is a Pleasure in taking a view of that Simplicity in Opposition to the Luxury of succeeding Ages; in beholding Monarchs without their Guards, Princes tending their Flocks, and Princesses drawing Water from the Springs. When we read *Homer* we ought to reflect that we are reading the most ancient Author in the Heathern World; and those who consider him in this Light, will double their Pleasure in the Perusal of him. Let them think they are … stepping almost three thousand Years back into the remotest Antiquity, and entertaining themselves with a clear and surprizing Vision of Things no where else to be found, the only true mirror of that ancient World.[1]

The fierce emotional reaction of 'Rapture' and 'Hurry' must coexist with this gentler response in which 'Pleasure' arises from 'Perusal'.

Pope's descriptions of both 'Rapture' and 'Pleasure' are organized by the latent pattern of 'metaphors we live by' which, in everyday speaking and thinking, connect space and time: a time can be long or short, can pass, stretch out before us, and so on. This way of arranging experience is so fundamental as to be coterminous with western culture: 'sing from the time when first …' Homer asks his muse at the start of the *Iliad*, and the preposition translated as 'from', 'ἐκ', is inseparably a descriptor of space and time.[2] It follows that translation from the past can readily be thought of 'as looking or travelling across space'.

Pope's particular variant of this broad metaphor, 'translation as taking a view', develops with unusual persistency and detail. It owes something to cultural trends, and something else to Pope's distinctiveness as a participant within them. During the decades in which he was translating Homer, the 'contemplation of landscape'—as John Barrell has shown—was starting to become 'an important pursuit for the cultivated'.[3] James Thomson's commanding landscape poem, *The Seasons*, appeared later in the 1720s; but Pope himself had already written in a similar vein in *Windsor Forest* (1713). Before he finished work on his *Iliad* he had bought a stretch of land in Twickenham and was building his famous garden and villa there with the help of his friend Lord Burlington, the pioneer of Palladian architecture in England, to whom he had been close since 1715.[4] '*Nature* and *Homer*' are 'the *same*', Pope had written in *Essay on Criticism* (1711), giving snappy utterance to a view that was not at all unusual.[5] More characteristically Popeian was what grew from this belief: that translating Homer was therefore in part like viewing a landscape garden.[6]

As we would by now expect, the metaphor 'translation as taking a view' also has a root in the text that was being translated. As well as being full of fire and rapture, the *Iliad* contains much vividly imagined and organized landscape; and distant views are often taken across it. Still, the metaphor has of course not always been adopted by translators of the poem, any more than every translator of the *Aeneid* has followed Dryden's tack of 'opening' it. As we will see in the next chapter, Cowper in the late eighteenth century did not think of himself as 'taking a view' of Homer; and neither did F. W. Newman and Matthew Arnold in their energetic dispute about how to translate him in the mid-nineteenth. The same pressures that blocked the idea of 'translating an author' seem to have obstructed this metaphor too. Just like the mode of 'translation as desire' which we explored in Chapter 16, 'taking a view' was pushed sideways into freer kinds of response during the Victorian period; and it mingled with metaphors of 'travel' and 'encounter' which arose from the *Odyssey*. Ezra Pound then reclaimed this bundle of metaphors for translation as part of his proliferating translatorly enterprise which I will discuss further in Chapter 23. But it took a different writer, in different circumstances, fully to adopt, re-energize and therefore redefine the metaphor of 'taking a view': Christopher Logue, whose tactic of 'translation as zoom' in his versions from the *Iliad* owes much to late twentieth-century film. I discuss his work at the end of this Part of the book, in Chapter 22.

For Pope, then, to read Homer is to open up a landscape of the past. When you are in the grip of 'Rapture' you simply materialize in the midst of that landscape—'in one place . . . a Hearer, in another . . . a Spectator'—

with no sense of distance between you and what you are experiencing.[7] But when you are engaged in 'Perusal' you calmly and purposefully 'step back' into the landscape, knowing that that is what you are having to do, and carrying your critical faculties with you so that you can 'reflect' and 'consider'. When you 'take a view' there is no need to stay 'at a distance' (to adopt a metaphor from the same field) in the sense of not looking at things closely. On the contrary, you are expected to be struck by details: by 'Peculiarities and Side-Views'.[8] In this respect, you might feel that you are getting as 'close' to Homer when you 'view' him as when you feel his 'Fire'. Nevertheless, the larger picture—of Homer's world, and of your distance from it—maintains a presence in your mind. You will remember your usual place on the landscape of history, and his, and the space between them. Whatever the precision of your intellectual focus, a degree of emotional detachment will be maintained.

This notion of 'taking a view' of Homer comes into Pope's Preface at the point where he touches on the so-called *'querelle des anciens et des modernes'*, a long-running French debate about the relationship between the classics and contemporary culture. English echoes of one side of the controversy had sounded in *A Discourse of Free-Thinking* (1713), by the landowner and philosopher Anthony Collins, who presented the *Iliad* as a poem 'design'd for Eternity' which displayed 'universal Knowledge of things'. Echoes of the other side resounded in the retort by Richard Bentley, the Cambridge classicist who is later supposed to have called Pope's version 'a pretty poem' but not 'Homer': 'poor *Homer* in those Circumstances and early times had never such aspiring thoughts. He wrote a sequence of Songs and Rhapsodies, to be sung by himself for small earnings and good cheer.'[9] Among the French precursors of Collins's view was the satirist Jean de la Bruyère who had argued in 1688 that the classics had as much to do with the present as with the time when they were written because human nature, at its core, was unchanged: 'les hommes n'ont point changé selon le coeur et selon les passions, ils sont encore tels qu'ils étaient alors' ('people have not at all changed in their hearts and in their passions, they are still the same as they were then'). And among Bentley's antecedents was Saint-Évremond, a gentleman of letters domiciled in Britain, who had claimed in 1685 that absolutely everything had changed since Homer's time: 'tout est changé: les Dieux, la nature, la politique, les moeurs, le goût, les manières' ('the Gods, nature, politics, morals, taste, manners').[10] Madame Dacier, the French translator of Homer to whom Pope's own version and notes were much indebted, agreed that much (at least) had changed; but she thought that Homer was therefore all the more to be admired: 'those Times and Manners', Pope quotes her as saying, 'are so much the more excellent as they are more contrary to ours'.[11]

Pope did not agree with Dacier. 'Who'—he objects—'can be so prejudiced in their Favour as to magnify the Felicity of those Ages, when a Spirit of Revenge and Cruelty, join'd with the practice of Rapine and Robbery, reign'd through the World?' Yet he was no more in sympathy with her opponent Houdart de la Motte who had, Pope says, been 'shock'd at the *servile Offices* and *mean Employments* in which we sometimes see the Heroes of *Homer* engag'd'. Pope's sidestep into the metaphor of 'taking a view' is angled against the oversimple trenchancies of both sides. The world Homer represents, and the values implicit in the way he represents it, are indeed in many ways different from Pope's own. But some of what is different is a pleasure to behold: for instance those traits which accord with an ideal of pastoral 'Simplicity'. Even customs which, by the eighteenth century, had come to seem reprehensible can be a source of enjoyment once you 'take a view of them' and reflect that you are reading the 'most ancient Author in the Heathen World'. Cruelties and desecrations are anaesthetized as they cool into objects of knowledge, so that 'what usually creates . . . Dislike, will become a Satisfaction'.[12]

Nevertheless, what remains most remarkable about Homer is his sublimity; and sublimity (as we saw in Chapter 19) abolishes all sense of distance, whether cultural or critical, in a rapturous response. The two metaphors to which Pope most gives his allegiance as a translator—that of 'passion' and that of 'taking a view'—are almost opposites. But not completely. It is, for instance, nearly true to say that 'passion' reacts to Homer's genius whereas 'taking a view' reacts to the culturally conditioned material he had to work with and the culturally conditioned way in which he presented it. But 'genius' is not wholly separable from its subject matter and circumstances: much of what fires Pope in the *Iliad* depends on exactly them—the vigorous spear-throwing, the divinely inspired acts of heroism. Again, it is broadly fair to say that 'passion' is fundamentally an emotional response whereas 'taking a view' is basically an operation of reasoning and judging—so long as you remember that 'taking a view' can cause 'satisfaction', 'surprise', and 'pleasure'. The two metaphors both vie and intermingle as guides to the translation's tactics. In consequence, they hold out interestingly entangled cues for readers to respond to.

Like Dryden's *Works of Virgil*, Pope's *Iliad* was published by subscription, with the difference that the work came out serially in instalments over five years, rather than in one big volume. Another novelty was the marked distinction between the books that went to the subscribers—quartos, embellished with numerous engravings—and those on general sale—larger folios, which were all but bare of images. The opening pages of both publications are designed to help readers 'take a view' of Homer. But the subscribers got the better view, for they had pictures to help them.[13]

When you open the first of the luxurious subscription volumes, published in 1715, signals of Pope's present and Homer's past take turns to flicker. After an initial statement of the title, 'HOMER'S ILIAD', comes a print of a stone bust of Homer, looking blind but rapt, marked as being '*Ex marmore antiquo in Aedibus Farnesianis, Romae*' (this engraving survived into the folios).[14] Marble image and Latin caption anchor the book in antiquity, advertising the pastness of the past as a picture of Homer living would not have done. Dryden's Virgil, in contrast, had been shown in vigorous good health, and as being crowned by the muscly immortal god Apollo—an assertion of the continued vivacity of his writing. But the print at the start of Pope's *Iliad* murmurs a question as to how far this book in English in your hands can still be said to be 'Homer's', to belong to him whose image has so all but vanished into archaeology. Turn over and, on the title page, the work's name is slightly adjusted as though in answer: 'THE ILIAD OF HOMER, Translated by MR. POPE'. 'Mr' was Pope's usual style on his title pages, but it is given salience here by the fact that Homer is not called 'Mr', and, indeed, that it is inconceivable he should be, any more than Dryden would have talked of 'Mr Virgil' or 'Mr Ovid'. 'Mr', in this context, signals Englishness and comparatively lowly status. Pope, like 'Mr Dryden' before him, is marked by that title as being not in himself a classic but the enterprising modern, in perhaps slightly upstart italics, through whom the classic is purveyed to us. Further down, after a quotation from Lucretius, is another claim to possession of the work: 'Printed by W. BOWYER, for BERNARD LINTOTT between the *Temple-Gates*. 1715'. This, again, is a standard formulation but it, too, is unusually reinforced: a royal licence, reproduced on the next page, announces that 'GEORGE R' grants Lintott 'Royal Privilege and Licence for the sole printing and publishing' of Pope's translation and notes for 'the Term of fourteen Years'. The licence is of course dated precisely: 'the sixth Day of *May* 1715'. On the following several pages are more names of people who have a stake in this *Iliad* of Homer as made available by Pope in 1715: 'THE SUBSCRIBERS' who have stumped up money (or the promise of it) in advance, enabling the work to be done, and securing for themselves a volume a year until 1720.

So many modern signatures; so many claims to ownership of what is being made of Homer in England for a few years before and after 1715: the translation done by Pope; the edition put out by Lintott under royal protection; the particular sets of it bought by the subscribers. After all

these hooks into the present come a series of texts designed to ease readers'
minds back in the direction of the ancient poem which is the origin of the
eighteenth-century publication but which is not exactly present within it.
There is Pope's 'PREFACE', and then an 'ESSAY ON THE LIFE, WRIT-
INGS AND LEARNING OF HOMER', composed by Thomas Parnell, which
surveys, in order to discount them, 'fabulous Traditions' of biography
before locating Homer on the landscape of the past, 'about three hundred
Years after the taking of *Troy*, and near a thousand before the *Christian
AEra*': it also offers '*A View of the Learning*' of his '*Time*'.[15] The impression
that we are being guided 'almost three thousand Years back' so as to gain 'a
clear and surprizing Vision of Things' is sharpened by the image that
surmounts the title of each section, as well as by little illustrated initial
capital letters which allow us to glimpse scenes implied by the writing.
Above the beginning of Pope's Preface is a view of an ancient temple being
cut down by a scythe-sweeping figure of Time, though one statue—
presumably of Homer—is guarded by an angel who points offstage left
towards what must be meant to be the future. Above the opening of the
'Essay' are images of medals on which Homer is represented; successive
sections have other illustrations: of a bas-relief of the poet surrounded by
his works and hailed by the Muses, and of the temple to him in Smyrna.
Finally, at the start of the first book of the poem-translation itself, there is
an image, not of a stone or metal relic of Homer, but of an animated scene
imagined by him, the quarrel between Agamemnon and Achilles. In
previous translations, such as the one by Ogilby that had entranced
Pope as a child, illustrations had typically been located on facing pages;
if there were headpieces at the start of each book they were merely
ornamental.[16] Pope's innovation was to place an illustration in each
headpiece, bringing image and text unusually close together so that the
pictures signpost the layers of time through which the verbal text is
guiding us as it passes over introductory exposition and on into translation. As we move back towards the historical figure of Homer, and then
beyond it into the partly fictional and partly factual world of his imagining, time is arranged before our eyes in rather the same way as spatial
perspective was constructed in paintings by Claude and his followers: not
'a gradual diminution in the size of things', as John Barrell has put it, but
'a series of horizontal bands' enabling the eye to take successive 'leaps into
the distance'.[17]

   Their visual senses alerted, readers are brought face to face with the
poem-translation, ready, certainly, to be entertained by a 'Vision of
Things no where else to be found' and perhaps also to be 'hurry'd out'
of themselves and to turn 'in one place to a Hearer, in another to a
Spectator'. With its invocation to the 'heav'nly Goddess' to 'sing' of

'Achilles' Wrath', of 'the Souls of mighty Chiefs untimely slain', and of 'fierce Strife' and 'Sov'reign Doom', the poem begins with a blast of sublimity.[18] One can imagine readers responding to its call in the way Agamemnon expected of his warriors: 'catch from Breast to Breast the noble Fire'.[19] And yet, as the poem goes on, the possibility of adopting the more detached attitude of 'Perusal' is repeatedly held out by the textual apparatus which frames the poem-translation itself. After the 'Catalogue of Ships' in Book 2, for instance, a section of 'Observations on the Catalogue' encourages us to 'look upon this Piece with an Eye to ancient Learning'.[20] Further help is supplied by maps of Greece and the Aegean Islands, together with an explanatory 'Geographical Table'. Whatever our emotional response to the crowds of warriors (and this is one part of the poem where a trace of ennui may be among a reader's feelings), we are asked, now, to extract ourselves from it. We are to look down on the army from the height of encyclopaedic knowledge and to pinpoint its origins across the expanse of Homer's world. Something similar happens before the start of Book V where, just as the fighting is getting under way, a panoramic illustration gives us a bird's-eye—or god's-eye—view of the battlefield, together with more 'Observations' on the battles 'in general'. Throughout the translation, each book is prefaced by an 'Argument' which supplies a verbal overview of the action, together with a statement of its 'Scene' and of the time it takes up. And each book is followed by ample notes, again called 'Observations', which are keyed to particular lines. You might plunge into a Book, allow yourself to be swept away by it, and only peruse the 'Observations' when you emerge. Or you might check them as you go along, stepping in and out of involvement, experiencing 'rapture' and 'reflection' by turns.

Pope says that the 'principal Design' of these regular 'Observations' is not scholarly comment or elucidation. Instead, they are 'to illustrate the Poetical Beauties of the Author'.[21] As we have seen, poetical beauties can leap like fire from antiquity to the present, abolishing any feeling of difference in the experience of rapture. But they can also emerge more slowly as the result of a spiral process in which response prompts reflection which guides further response. When Chryses sues for the release of his daughter Chruseïs in Book 1, Pope writes in the translation that, 'lowly bending down', he 'extends the Sceptre and the Laurel Crown'. The beauty here needs clarifying with some considerations taken from Eustathius:

> There is something exceedingly venerable in this Appearance of the Priest. He comes with the Ensigns of the God he belong'd to; the Laurel Crown, now carry'd in his Hand to show he was a Suppliant; and a golden Sceptre

which the Ancients gave in particular to *Apollo*, as they did a silver one to the
Moon, and other sorts to the Planets.[22]

The 'illustration' provided in the 'Observation' enables details in the
narrative to become significant. It gives us the information we need to
interpret them. 'Viewing', in the sense of 'seeing', merges with 'viewing' in
the sense of 'understanding'. Repeatedly, Pope's 'Observations' guide
readers to a point from which they can, in this composite sense, 'view'
the poem-translation more fully. Though they are inevitably detached
from the verse while they peruse the notes, the perspective gained there is
not inimical to emotional response, even including the fierce involvement
of 'Rapture'. This observation from Book 1 helps us to see, and therefore
to feel, that Chryses is 'exceedingly venerable'; and elsewhere, as we saw in
Chapter 19, even the fieriest parts of the poem-translation are accompan-
ied by 'Observations' which point attention towards the super-adding of
similes or the figures that express the 'Impetuosity and Hurry of Passion'.
Rightly informed, you can return to the poetry and be rightly moved.

From the viewpoint of the 'Observations', Pope sometimes allows
himself to voice and ponder criticisms reminiscent of Houdart de la
Motte. In Book 24, Thetis advises Achilles to seek respite from his grief
over the death of Patroclus by making love to a woman ('γυναικί περ ἐν
φιλότητι / μίσγεσθ'), especially as he has not long to live. Pope resorts to
some mild euphemism in his translation:

> O snatch the Moments yet within thy Pow'r,
> Nor long to live, indulge the am'rous Hour![23]

But disapproval bursts out in his note: 'In short, I am of Opinion that this
Passage outrages Decency.' Yet the splutter has no sooner left him than the
calmer attitude, typical of the 'Observations', reasserts itself and he con-
siders the matter more at length:

> Indeed the whole Passage is capable of a serious Construction, and of such a
> Sense as a Mother might express to a Son with Decency: And then it will run
> thus; ' ... Short is thy Date of Life, spend it not all in weeping, but allow
> some part of it to Love and Pleasure!' But still the Indecency lies in the
> manner of the Expression, which must be allow'd to be almost obscene, (for
> such is the Word μίσγεσθ' *misceri*) all that can be said in Defence of it is, that
> as we are not competent Judges of what Ideas Words might carry in *Homer*'s
> Time, so we ought not entirely to condemn him, because it is possible the
> Expression might not sound so indecently in ancient as in modern Ears.[24]

First, Pope sets about building his remedial 'Construction' (interpretation); but then the shock of direct contact with the indecent Greek
reasserts itself—only for a new calmative perspective to open up between

us and it: 'as we are not competent judges . . . it is possible'. This tentative
discussion reveals what is always implicit in the stance of taking a view:
that the gathering of relevant knowledge and the forming of critical
judgements blend into ethical considerations of 'Decency' and of possible
moral condemnation. As Peter J. Connelly has shown, the visual evoca-
tiveness of Pope's translation results from the application of principles that
are more 'moral' than 'pictorial'. Not the prettiest, but the most ethically
significant features of a scene are selected for emphasis: in the description
of Chryses, for instance, the primarily visual adjective 'golden' ('χρυσέῳ')
has been dropped, even though it is given salience in the Greek by its
phonetic interplay with the name 'Chryses', and primarily evaluative
terms such as 'awful' have been brought in. Pope's aim here and—
Connelly says—throughout the translation, is to achieve a 'morally intelligible unity'.[25]

In the case of Thetis, too, the long view of the 'Observations' spreads
across into the texture of the translation, where Pope's phrase 'indulge the
am'rous Hour' is designed to pull the Greek in the direction of his note, to
make it seem amenable to being understood in that way. Elsewhere, the
critical and ethical perspective of the 'view' is written into the translation
much more fully; for instance, in another shocking moment, in Book 6,
where Agamemnon rebukes Menelaus for wanting to spare the youthful
Trojan Adrastus. 'Let no-one escape,' he cries, 'not even a child in the
womb' ('μηδ᾽ ὅν τινα γαστέρι μήτηρ / κοῦρον ἐόντα φέροι'). Worse,
Homer's narrator appears to condone the sentiment, for he says that
Agamemnon's urging was right (αἴσιμα παρειπών).[26] Before Pope,
Ogilby and Hobbes had registered unease by dropping the narratorial
remark; but they, and Chapman, had all faced the basic horror squarely.
Chapman:

> . . . even th'infant in the wombe
> Shall tast of what they merited . . . . . .

Ogilby (1660):

> . . . No not the Infant in the Mothers Womb
> Must be exempted . . . . . .

Hobbes (1676):

> . . . Nor spare the Child yet in his Mothers womb[27]

The same interpretation appears in the Latin parallel text of the edition
of Homer by Joshua Barnes which Pope used.[28] But Madame Dacier
had taken a different tack. In his 'Observation', Pope explains why he
has chosen to see things like her:

I think Madame *Dacier* in the right, in her Affirmation that the *Greeks* were not arrived at that Pitch of Cruelty to rip up the Wombs of Women with Child. ... Besides, he would never have represented one of his first Heroes capable of so barbarous a Crime, or at least would not have commended him (as he does just after) for such a wicked Exhortation.[29]

This considered view spreads into the translation:

> ... not Sex, nor Age,
> Shall save a *Trojan* from our boundless Rage:
> *Ilion* shall perish whole, and bury All;
> Her Babes, her Infants at the Breast, shall fall.
> A dreadful Lesson of exampled Fate,
> To warn the Nations, and to curb the Great!
>   The Monarch spoke: the Words with Warmth address
> To rigid Justice steel'd his Brother's Breast.[30]

It is not only the 'Infants at the Breast' that have come into being via a process of reflective perusal. Agamemnon's couplet about the 'dreadful Lesson of exampled Fate' is Pope's invention, as is the spin that is put on 'Justice' by the words 'rigid', 'steel'd', and 'with Warmth'. Just as he did with Thetis, Pope has given a 'serious Construction' to Agamemnon's words: he endeavours to justify them from the perspective of the succeeding ages and the 'Nations' and the 'Great' who will inhabit them. But this time the long view, as it spreads from the 'Observations' into the poem-translation, is attributed to the character who needs the benefit of its calmative reflection. Agamemnon is made to predict the interpretation that Pope has given him, and to understand his actions in its light. He takes a view of himself, and concludes that he is being cruel to Troy so as to be kind to future times. Pope's narrator seconds this opinion. Saying that Agamemnon speaks 'with Warmth', rather than, say, 'Heat', 'Fury', or 'Rage', he implies that this 'rigid' policy towards the Trojan babies is, in a long perspective, not only a just but a sympathetic course.

Throughout Pope's *Iliad*, 'Homer's individual and unique persons, acts, speeches'—as Maynard Mack has put it—are 'studiedly urged ... in the direction of types, roles, emblems, aphorisms'.[31] And throughout, just as we have seen with Agamemnon, this happens not only in the way characters are presented by the narrator but in their understanding of themselves and one another. In Book 2, for involved and not wholly perspicuous reasons, Homer's Agamemnon tests the Greek army by trying to persuade it to give up the siege. 'Our wives and children must be missing us,' he says, prompting Pope to insert two lines of extrapolation:

> 'Love, Duty, Safety, summon us away,
> 'Tis Nature's Voice, and Nature we obey.'[32]

The wives and children dissolve into the abstract principle they are taken to represent. The same happens in Book 10, when wise Nestor sees troubles ahead for Hector, and Pope has him utter this:

> 'How ill agree the Views of vain Mankind,
> And the wise Counsels of th'eternal Mind?'[33]

Instances can be found on virtually every page. This practice of translation is different from Dryden's 'openings' of mental states and dramatic implications; and different again from the desiring and passionate expansions we explored in Part III, even those performed by Pope himself. When he translates in this way, Pope takes a view of what goes on in Homer's poem, and makes its characters too take a view of themselves and what they are involved in, so as to draw general ethical conclusions which, though they may not wholly agree with the wise counsels of th'eternal mind, are nevertheless worth handing down through the long tracts of time to come. This practice of translation has been said—rightly—to embody the 'generalizing habit' of Pope's imagination, and to fulfil contemporary expectations that epic should be morally improving.[34] But these very broad considerations are caught up into, and given definition by, the permeating metaphor of 'taking a view', in which, as we have been discovering, the visual, the epistemological, and the ethical all come together.

Pope's creation, in his *Iliad* volumes, of the awareness of a distance crossed, allows his Homer translation to assume a peculiar abstract relevance to (and from) its immediate social and political circumstances. As Howard Erskine-Hill has shown, Pope's early verse—including his debut extract from Homer, 'The Episode of Sarpedon', published in a Tonson *Miscellany* of 1709—is tinged with Jacobite sympathy.[35] When he began work on the whole *Iliad* the political tensions around him strengthened. The decline and death of Queen Anne in 1714, and the accession of George I, brought a surge in Whig power and increased the likelihood that new measures would be taken against Roman Catholics such as Pope. In his letters, his awareness of these possibilities mingles jokily but still uneasily with his thoughts of Homer. In August 1714, he wrote to his friend Edward Blount about the possibility that revived anti-Catholic legislation would force him to get rid of his horse:

> To disarm me indeed may be but prudential, considering what armies I have at present on foot, and in my service: a hundred thousand *Grecians* are no contemptible body; for all that I can tell, they may be as formidable as four thousand *Priests*.[36]

The following year came not only the publication of the first volume of his *Iliad* but also the Jacobite rebellion. Here is part of a composite letter written after dinner by John Gay, Charles Jervas, John Arbuthnot, and Pope to a fellow member of the Scriblerus Club, Thomas Parnell (these particular words seem to have been penned by Arbuthnot):

> Mr pope [*sic*] delays his Second Volume of his Homer till the Martial Spirit of the Rebells is quite quelld it being judgd that his first part did some harm that way.[37]

This time the tone is more straightforwardly jovial: as the editor of the *Correspondence* remarks, 'the writing is strongly redolent of wine'.[38]

Pope's ambition of translating the *Iliad* had at first been nourished by Joseph Addison and the other Whig writers and politicos gathered around him at Button's, his preferred coffee house. But over this same couple of years, Pope's views and connections had shifted: the Scriblerus Club was a markedly Tory grouping. In consequence, the Buttonians tried to spoil Pope's moment by putting out, in the same week as his, a rival version of Book I of the *Iliad* by Thomas Tickell, an Oxford don and protégé of Addison's. The political suggestiveness of Tickell's version is clear. It is dedicated to 'the Late Earl of Halifax', a Whig grandee committed, Tickell says, to 'the Cause of Liberty'.[39] After this dedication, the *Iliad* begins at once. There is no introduction whatsoever, let alone the careful calibration of perspective done by Pope. When, therefore, one discovers, on page two of the translation, Chryses referring to the Greeks' 'Cause', an echo of what was said of Halifax is quick to sound. Next, we are told of an Agamemnon who wields 'arbitrary sway', in contrast to an Achilles who has dutifully 'Summon'd a Council, by the Queen's Command' (albeit a queen 'who wields Heav'n's Sceptre in her Snowy Hand', as the next line reminds us—in case the thought of any other queen might have flickered across our minds). Homer's terms are being overwritten wholesale with the categories of eighteenth-century high politics.

Pope's *Iliad*, by contrast, does not have a dedicatee. The many sub-scribers have varied political complexions, as do the great men whom Pope thanks at the end of his Preface, from Halifax to Bolingbroke. Nowhere in the prefatory material is there an allusion to contemporary politics, not even the sort of measured implicit comparison that (in Chapter 12) we noticed in Dryden's 'Dedication' of his *Aeneis*. And in the translation itself—as we have begun to see—Pope is assiduous in endeavouring to grasp the strangeness of the poem that faces him, while also imagining ways of leading his readers across into that distance. In Chapter 19 we touched on the overlap between the *Iliad* translation and *The Rape of the Lock*: and it is no doubt true, as Steven Shankman has argued, that Pope's later, even greater strength as a satirist was nourished by thoughts of kinship with Achilles.[40] But the connection between Pope's *Iliad* and his satirical writing is crucially a connection across distance. This is why he and his associates could not help smiling at any suggested link between the translation and anti-Catholic legislation or the 1715 rebellion. From the vantage point that translating the *Iliad* opened up for him, Pope could take a backward 'view' of his own 'Age', and strengthen his own 'clear and surprizing Vision' of it.

Just like 'translation as passion', and just like Dryden's 'translation as opening', this metaphor of 'translation as taking a view' responds to cues held out by the text that is being translated: the *Iliad* opens many perspectives on the events that are at its core. There are the frequent epic similes by which what happens in battle is compared to processes in the natural world and ordinary human culture: storms, avalanches, floods, lions hunting; craftsmen and women stretching hides or staining ivory; a child playing in the sand. These similes, it has often been remarked, divert attention from the violence as much as they describe it. In Book 4, for instance, Athena saves Menelaus by warding off an arrow 'as a mother sweeps a fly from her child when he lies in sweet sleep'.[41] The image suggests Athena's tenderness towards Menelaus as well as the astonishing grace and strength of the gods, that they are to mortals as mortals are to flies (a similar thought was to strike Shakespeare's Lear rather more painfully); but it also partially obscures the fighting with a gentle domestic scene. In offering such moments of respite from the mêlée all around, the similes inevitably disrupt the chronology of the scene represented. They are imaginative timeouts which, as Richard Buxton has put it, connect the action to 'a world alongside, a world which will exist when all the bloodied dust has settled'.[42] The uniqueness of what happens at Troy makes similes necessary to try to do it justice: it calls out for comparison because it is incomparable. But that uniqueness is also inevitably dissipated when it is compared. Placed in a landscape of ongoing time and the rest of life, the heroic deeds stand out for a moment; then fade into the distance.

Another kind of perspective is opened by the capsule biographies which, as we saw in Chapter 19, typically accompany a death, like unusually vivid gravestone inscriptions—that of Iphidamus, for instance, slain by Agamemnon in Book 11: he dies far from his wife who was so newly wed that he had not known any happiness with her ('οὔ τι χάριν ἴδε') even though he had paid an enormous bride-price.[43] These vignettes give the impression of many, many diverse lives, from across the Aegean, being sucked into the war and ending there. And then there is the fact that the gods too take part, so that not only individuals fight, but the principles of Love, Wisdom, Earth, Light. As Pope put it in one of his 'Observations': 'Heaven and Hell, all Things mortal and immortal, the whole Creation in short was engag'd in this Battel, and all the Extent of Nature in Danger.'[44] Overseeing it all (except when he has been seduced by Hera in Book 14) is Zeus on the top of Mount Ida. Pope translates so as to make his gaze even more comprehensive than it is in the original: 'Thence his broad Eye the subject World surveys', Pope writes, where Homer has him merely looking down on Troy and the Greek ships; 'Round the wide Fields he cast a careful view' is Pope's insertion when, at the start of Book 15, the king of gods awakes from his post-coital snooze.[45]

Pope stretches Zeus's gaze in this way because he too, as he reads and translates, is observing events at Troy from a distant viewpoint; and he sees their ramifications extending even further than they do for Homer. Just as his sense of himself as being impassioned by Homer leads him—as we saw in Chapter 19—to be inspired especially when characters are inspiring one another, so also his sense of himself as 'taking a view' leads him to elaborate on moments of seeing. In Book 3, for instance, Menelaus and Paris agree to fight a duel and the Trojans gather on the Scaean gate to observe them and the Greek army. 'This View of the *Grecian* Leaders from the Walls of *Troy*, is justly look'd upon as an Episode of great Beauty,' Pope comments in his 'Observation' of their observation.[46] He is not explicit about the causes of the beauty, but they must include the vividness with which the Greeks are described, the dramatic tension in the fact that it is Helen who points them out, and the feeling that a landscape is opening up within the landscape of the poem; that we are taking a view of a view. Already in Homer, the distance surrounding the episode is not only that of space: Menelaus prays that he will get revenge and be a warning to people in the future ('ὀψιγόνων ἀνθρώπων') not to break the laws of hospitality: 'Let this Example future Times reclaim', in Pope's translation.[47] But Pope gives similar breadth to other characters too. In Homer, the Trojan elders are good speakers ('ἀγορηταὶ / ἐσθλοί'); in Pope they are 'Wise thro' Time, and Narrative with Age'.[48] In Homer, Helen mentions Odysseus's tricksiness and cunning; but Pope's Helen views Pope's Ulysses with the generalizing solemnity of a longer view: 'His Fame for Wisdom fills the spacious Earth'.[49] Throughout the poem-translation, Pope's warriors become spectators of the war in which they are also involved: he makes the stadium view of Book 3 always available for them to take up. In Book 15, as the Greeks are beaten back by the revivified Hector, Patroclus sees what is happening and goes to tell Achilles: Pope turns him into 'a mournful Witness of this Scene of Woe'.[50] A moment later, Hector sees his cousin Caletor killed by Tela-monian Aias; but for Pope mere seeing is not enough: 'Great *Hector* view'd him with a sad Survey'.[51] When Athene clears the dark mist that Zeus had laid across the field, Pope brightens Homer's brightness: 'the Scene wide-opening to the Blaze of Light'.[52] Sounds, too, carry further in the translation than in the original. When, in Book 16, Patroclus appears dressed up in Achilles's armour, Homer says that the ships resounded frighteningly under the shouting of the Greeks ('ἀμφὶ δὲ νῆες / σμερδαλέον κονάβησαν ἀϋσάντων ὑπ' Ἀχαιῶν'). Pope makes the resounding resound again:

> From Shore to Shore the doubling Shouts resound,
> The hollow Ships return a deeper Sound.[53]

When Patroclus and Hector are fighting like two lions, Pope adds a reverb that is all his own: 'And echoing Roars rebellow through the Shades'.[54] The form of the rhyming couplet, itself a miniature echo chamber, doubtless encourages this tic in Pope's translation (similar additions occur throughout). But it is also the case that all these noises come more echoically to Pope than to Homer, since they have travelled through so much time and space to reach him.

In Homer's *Iliad*, some characters take a broader view of things than others: Calchas, for instance, the Greek prophet who in Book 1 rightly blames Agamemnon for the plague that is ravaging the Greek army. Homer says he has knowledge of what is, what is to be, and what has been ('ὃς ᾔδη τά τ'ἐόντα τά τ' ἐσσόμενα πρό τ'ἐόντα'); and Pope translates closely:

> That sacred Seer whose comprehensive View
> The past, the present, and the future knew.[55]

'View' in rhyme with 'knew' aptly catches the complexity of the Greek verb εἴδω, 'I see', which, in the perfect tense, means 'know' and in the pluperfect, as here, 'knew'. But so much does Pope admire the faculty of comprehensive view that he develops any hint of it in the original. In Homer, the Trojan Polydamas, who advises Hector in Book 13, claims to have a good mind ('νόον...ἐσθλόν'). Pope credits him with something vaster: 'A wise, extensive, all-consid'ring Mind'.[56] During the ceasefire in Book 3, Homer's Menelaus praises the wisdom of age as embodied in Priam: an old man sees both before and after ('ἅμα πρόσσω καὶ ὀπίσσω'). Pope expands the thought:

> Cool Age advances venerably wise,
> Turns on all hands its deep-discerning Eyes;
> Sees what befell, and what may yet befall.[57]

The sagest of all these figures is Nestor who throughout promotes order and calm. In Book 23, he instructs his son Antilochus in the art of chariot-driving; Pope translates so as to extend filaments of comparison towards his own art as poet-translator. In Homer, Nestor 'spoke' for Antilochus's 'good' ('μυθεῖτ εἰς ἀγαθὰ'); in Pope, he 'directs his Judgment, and his Heat restrains'. In Homer, Antilochus is skilled even though he is 'young' ('νέον'); in Pope, he is so 'tho' youthful Ardor fire thy Breast'. In Homer, the race is won by 'skill' or 'cunning' ('μήτι'); in Pope, ''tis the Artist wins the glorious Course'.[58] Pope clearly feels a flicker of identification with this other young artist, and so gifts him with that 'fire' which, as we saw in Chapter 19, is so crucial an element of his own response to Homer. Only here the fire is to be greeted not with 'Rapture' but with discipline. The same emphasis is present in Pope's translation of a passage in Book 4 where Nestor is organizing his troops:

> He gives Command to curb the fiery Steed,
> Nor cause Confusion, nor the Ranks exceed.[59]

'Fiery' and 'nor the Ranks exceed' are both Pope's insertions. Nestor justifies his advice with an appeal to history:

> Our great Fore-fathers held this prudent Course,
> Thus rul'd their Ardour, thus preserv'd their Force,
> By Laws like these Immortal Conquests made,
> And Earth's proud Tyrants low in Ashes laid.[60]

The middle two of the four lines are Pope's innovation. He renders the passage so as to make it chime with those elements of his Preface to the *Iliad* which express unease about the proliferation of Homer's fiery, animating invention: its luxuriance and wildness; the problematic exuberance of the similes; the need for 'Art' to 'reduce the beauties of Nature to more regularity' so that it is possible to 'see' them more 'distinctly'.[61] When Pope is guided by the metaphor of 'passion', poetic excellence abolishes time in the experience of 'Rapture'. But here, in line with the metaphor of 'taking a view', immortality is thought of as passing through time, not leaping across it; and it is achieved not by genius but by the application of judgement and restraint.

Nestor, then, is a partial double of the translator. But only partial because what Pope finally most admired in Homer was the 'Fire' which Nestor is always determined to curb. Elsewhere in Pope's *Iliad*, as we saw in Chapter 19, that 'Fire' is given very free rein. In general, the two contradictory metaphors come and go as guides for his translation in response to the cues that are put out by its source.

But Achilles brings them together. In Homer, he is already the fieriest of warriors; in Pope, he is even more so. 'My Soul's on flame', Pope makes him say; and has Patroclus remark to Nestor: 'Thou know'st the fiery Temper of my Friend'.[62] And yet Achilles is also, for the first three-quarters of the poem, a detached observer of the action: 'Calm he looks on, and every Death enjoys', as Nestor replies to Patroclus, in a line Pope has invented. It reads like a bitter parody of his phrase in the Preface: 'there is a Pleasure in taking a view'.[63] Achilles has other affinities with those who hold the comprehensive view. He knows at least one aspect of the future: he knows he is doomed to die young. Waiting for Patroclus to return from battle in Book 18, he is full of foreboding: 'all that Fate design'd, / Rose in sad Prospect to his boding Mind', as Pope puts it.[64] Achilles's sense of himself as overlooked by a known timescape harmonizes with the way Homer makes him inhabit the landscape. As we saw in the last chapter, in Book 1 he runs to the shore, calls out, and is heard by his mother in the depths of the sea. In Book 18 his mourning for Patroclus similarly resounds across miles and leagues, until it arrives 'Far in the deep Abysses of the Main' (as Pope translates), at which Thetis and her nymphs travel all the way back to Troy to comfort him.[65] His first move towards revenging Patroclus is to go up onto the 'Rampart' of the Greek fortification, and to command the battlefield by simply allowing himself to be seen and heard: 'Hosts dropp'd their Arms' at the sound of his shout; they 'turn their Eye-balls' from the sight of him.[66] Once he throws himself into the fray he whizzes everywhere unstoppably: 'he blazing shot across the field'; he 'burst like Light'ning thro' the Ranks'. In a grim reprise of the stadium moment in Book 3, Priam 'views' him with 'careful Eyes' from the distance of the Trojan walls.[67]

The great shield that Thetis has made for Achilles in Book 18 is forged by Vulcan 'the Father of the Fires'—it belongs then, on the one hand, in the company of 'Rapture'. On the other hand, it is decorated with a vision of all time and all space: Pope prints an engraving of his own vision of this vision, and reflects, in his 'Observations', that it demonstrates Homer's mastery of 'Aerial *Perspective*'.[68] Achilles likewise epitomizes both passion and perspective; both the figures that were so important to Pope as a translator. For him, as for many readers before and since, Achilles is the most inspiring of characters, the one most likely to cause the amoral excitement of rapture, to sweep you away. And he is also, with his obduracy towards Agamemnon, and his defilement of Hector's corpse, the character most in need of being held at a critical distance and subjected to ethical judgement. As Pope translates Achilles's bloody quest for vengeance, the two modes of response intensify and clash. In a fearsome passage at the end of Book 20, Achilles, hacking his way through Trojans, is compared to a fire burning its way through the deep valleys ('βαθέ' ἄγκεα'); and his horses trampling the dead are compared to bulls threshing white barley. The word for 'deep' is repeated in the Greek; but on its second appearance Pope reverses the emphasis:

> Then o'er the Stubble up the Mountain flies,
> Fires the high Woods, and blazes to the Skies[69]

Homer's particular 'barley' becomes something very general, 'Autumnal Harvests'; and a line is inserted to spread the effects of Achilles's progress: 'Around him wide, immense Destruction pours'. The translation doubles and exaggerates the Greek, in the way which, as we saw in Chapter 19, characterizes 'translation as passion'. But it also generalizes and (implicitly) moralizes, in the style of 'translation as taking a view'. Achilles's greatness is a source both of rapture and of unease. The feelings combine to produce a powerfully ambivalent poetry of translation, for instance in the extraordinary lines with which the book ends. Homer has Achilles pressing on to win glory ('κῦδος ἀρέσθαι'), his invincible hands spattered (like his chariot wheels) with gore. Pope has this:

> High o'er the Scene of Death *Achilles* stood,
> All grim with Dust, all horrible in Blood:
> Yet still insatiate, still with Rage on flame;
> Such is the Lust of never-dying Fame!

With their repetitions, their visual intensity, their exclamation, these much-elaborated lines are fired by Achilles's example (Pope himself was no stranger to the lust for fame). But they are also pushed away by it: 'grim', and 'horrible', Achilles provokes disgust which was wholly absent from that earlier, excited description of the Greek army as 'swift as a Flood of Fire' which I discussed in Chapter 19. This passage could be pronounced as convincingly with repelled detachment as with passionate admiration: the one calls out the other; and the two combine in the stunned response that makes Achilles hold 'still', achieving never-dying fame while provoking never-ending horror. He stands 'High', not only over the battlefield at Troy, but over all the intervening space and time, and all the killing that has happened in it. He is so much the more grim here than in Homer, and yet also so much the more admirable, because he still commands attention after so many centuries, compelling such as Pope to translate him.

21

Some Perspectives after Pope: Keats, Tennyson, Browning, Pound, Michael Longley

Like all the metaphors we are exploring, Pope's 'passion' and 'taking a view' admit and make sense of the difference between his translation and its source. Fire grows when it spreads; the translation of sublimity likewise requires intensification and expansion. 'Taking a view' of something entails generalizing from it, broadening its field of relevance. As we have seen, Pope's cultural circumstances and his own disposition both helped shape his conflicted response to Homer. But crucially he was also reacting to prompts he discerned in his material. We established in Chapter 4 that such prompts are not simply uttered by a text: discerning them is a matter, not of mere reception on the part of the reader-and-translator, but of imaginative collaboration. And in Chapter 19 I discussed a clear instance of Pope's mind cooperating with a line of the *Iliad* in order to build into it the meaning that Pope could then think of himself as reading off from it. Homer's verse was said to be like his own description of his army; but his own description of his army was silently adjusted by Pope to look more like a description of Homer: '*They pour along like a Fire that sweeps the whole Earth before it*'. Nevertheless, for all that Pope's response to the *Iliad* was active, it was still a response to something. Over the last two chapters, we have explored some of the many instances of 'passion' and of 'taking a view' that are latent in the *Iliad*, lying ready to be lifted up by a reading imagination and made into metaphors of translation. The *Iliad* invited the sort of translation Pope gave it.

For two centuries after Pope, the invitation he accepted was barely, if ever, taken up by other translators. One reason was, simply, his success: there seemed to be nothing left for a translation in a similar vein to do. Another was the hardening of assumptions about translation which I discussed in Chapter 14. As we saw, William Cowper, in his *Iliad and Odyssey of Homer* (1791), abandoned the resources of interpretive imagining that were implied by Dryden's word 'paraphrase', and which gave rise to what he called Pope's 'deviations'. He could see nothing except infidelity in the fact that Pope 'has sometimes altogether suppressed the sense of his author, and has not seldom intermingled his own ideas with it'. And so he gave his allegiance to the illusory metaphor of 'adherence', a variant of 'translation rigidly conceived': 'my chief boast is that I have adhered closely to the original'; 'I have omitted nothing; I have invented nothing'.[1] Yet, as we saw in Chapters 3 and 4, nothing can be carried over unchanged in translation from any text, let alone from a poem. When translators of poetry persuade themselves that that is what they are doing the consequence is a narrowing and flattening of what they can allow themselves to notice in the source. By the end of the eighteenth century this tendency had become strong, and especially so with classical epic which demanded particular respect. 'Translators of Virgil' too, Colin Burrow has noted, 'were presenting themselves as accurate copyists'.[2]

The same commitment to 'translation rigidly conceived' dominates the next major episode in the history of the translation of Homer's epics into English: F. W. Newman's *Iliad* of 1856 and its denunciation by Matthew Arnold in his lectures as Oxford Professor of Poetry in 1860–1. Neither man advocated word-for-word translation, and both emphasize more than Cowper had done the need for a translation to pay attention not only to the source text's 'sense' but to its style. This they characterize by the effect they think it would have had on a Greek of the fifth century BC (there is a shared tacit comparison of Victorian England to Periclean Athens). Once apprehended, Homer's style must be reproduced via 'translation rigidly conceived'. As Newman put it, echoing Cowper's gluey metaphor, a translator's 'first duty' is 'to adhere closely' to his source's 'manner and habit of thought', that is, in Homer's case, to be 'direct, popular, forcible, quaint, flowing, garrulous'.[3] Of this list of qualities, only the quaintness and the garrulousness are readily apparent in Newman's translation itself; but this is the result rather of his shortcomings as a writer than of the metaphor he has adopted. What enraged Arnold was not Newman's aim of close adherence but his characterization of what was being adhered to. As Arnold apprehends it, Homer's style is not 'garrulous' but 'rapid'; it *is* 'direct', but in a 'plain' sort of way. It is not 'popular', but 'noble'. And there is absolutely nothing 'quaint' about it.[4] Arnold's attack twitches with cultural anxiety. F. W. Newman (brother to Cardinal Newman) had started his career as a brilliant Oxford scholar. But he became a vigorous opponent of established Christianity, and a strong supporter of women's rights. He taught, not at Oxford, but at the newly established University of London, and he hoped his translation would be read by 'working men'.[5] This, rather than a difference over what translation should do (i.e. over what metaphor should define it) is what drives the disagreement.

Newman's words, Arnold says, 'do not correspond in their effect upon us with Homer's words in their effect upon Sophocles'.[6]

There were of course exceptions to the dominion of 'translation rigidly conceived'. We have touched on some in previous chapters and will touch on others in chapters to come. But the metaphor of adherence was dominant throughout the nineteenth century, and particularly so in translations of classical epic. Styles varied from very archaic, as in William Morris's *Odyssey* (1887), through pretty archaic (Newman), to mildly archaizing (as in Arnold's own sample versions). But the idea that what these different kinds of words were doing was 'sticking close' to their source was persistent. Here, for instance, is the Preface to an *Iliad* published by Lord Derby in 1864, in one of the lengthy intervals between his brief stints as Tory prime minister:

> It has been my aim throughout to produce ... such a translation ... as would fairly and honestly give the sense and spirit of every passage, and of every line; omitting nothing, and expanding nothing; and adhering, as closely as our language will allow, even to every epithet which is capable of being translated.[7]

Derby's assumption is clear. If you cannot think of yourself as 'adhering' to something it is not 'capable of being translated'. Other practices of translation, with their associated metaphors, have been shut out.

In Chapter 16 I showed that loss of confidence in the metaphor of translating an 'author' in the late eighteenth and early nineteenth centuries helped create the conditions not only for a new interest in literalism but for a new surge of fantasy response. There, I was discussing texts that had to do with desire; but all poems were affected by this change. When the middle way of 'paraphrase' was blocked, the translatorly energies it had channelled were diverted to both extremes. Translation became restricted by the metaphor of 'translation rigidly conceived'; and the sort of imaginative work that Pope had done via the metaphors of 'passion' and 'taking a view' was left to freer kinds of response. In the case of Homer, an early, powerful instance is Keats's sonnet 'On First Looking into Chapman's Homer' (1816). Keats had, he says, often been told of the 'wide expanse' that Homer ruled, but had never breathed 'its pure serene / Till I heard Chapman speak out loud and bold':

> Then felt I like some watcher of the skies
>   When a new planet swims into his ken;
> Or like stout Cortez when with eagle eyes
>   He stared at the Pacific, and all his men
> Looked at each other with a wild surmise—
>   Silent, upon a peak in Darien.[8]

Like Pope, Keats takes a view of Homer, and in a way which responds to the views that Homer himself creates: with its juxtaposition of terrestrial and celestial panoramas, the sonnet echoes the 'Nightpiece' which I discussed in Chapter 19. But the echo is faint and is all but overwhelmed by the residue of other texts—of John Bonnycastle's *Introduction to Astronomy* (1807 edition) in which Keats had read of F. W. Herschel's discovery of the planet Uranus in 1781, and of William Robertson's *History of America* (1777) which described how Vasco Núñez de Balboa (not in fact Cortez) became the first European to see the Pacific.[9] Both Uranus and the Pacific are beyond the reach of the person who stares at them: whereas Pope, the translator, felt he could step into Homer's landscape, Keats, the Greekless reader of a translation, feels held back from it. With its displacements from Homer to Herschel to Balboa to Cortez, from being a 'watcher of the skies' to staring 'at the Pacific' to looking 'at each other' to the implicit imaginative gaze which pinpoints Cortez erroneously in the Isthmus of Darien, the sonnet speaks less of imaginative contact being brokered by translation than of differences creeping in and distances opening up. And the sonnet's own identity, an Italianate form, written in English, imagining a central American location, is a long, long way from the Mediterranean, epic ancient Greek texts by which it is inspired.

When Tennyson, in the 1830s, began writing poems that derived from Homer and related classical texts, he brought into the texture of his writing a similar awareness of change and distance. These poems do not ask to be taken as translations. But, just like Pope's *Iliad*, or Dryden's *Aeneis*, they admit and make sense of their departures from their origins by establishing a metaphorical connection between what they describe and how they have come to be the way they are. 'Tithonus' is a monologue spoken by the unfortunate man who (as it is told in the Homeric *Hymn to Aphrodite*) was loved by Aurora and was granted eternal life by her, but not eternal youth. 'I wither slowly', as Tennyson makes Tithonus say, 'a white-haired shadow, roaming like a dream'.[10] There is a correspondence between what is happening to the character and what has happened to the myth of him as it has wandered through time, withering (on the whole) as the culture that created it has sunk into the past. By writing his poem, Tennyson prolongs Tithonus's life in the imagination but does not rejuvenate him. The printed words in which Tithonus's speech is embodied share his bodily predicament: like him, they will endure through time (verse being, traditionally, a deathless monument); like him they will fade as their nuances, then their meanings, then their forms disappear through language change—until, as happened to Chaucer's words courtesy of

Dryden, they will need to be transformed via translation (Tithonus himself, in the legend, was transformed into a grasshopper).[11]

Similar flickers of self-reference recur in Tennyson's other classical poems. 'Tiresias' is spoken by a prophet whose voice, solidified into literature, has become as far-reaching and perhaps as 'vain' as his own power of foresight: Tiresias was doomed to 'speak the truth that no man may believe', and Tennyson, in his gloomier moments, had a similar view of the truth-telling capacity of poets. In 'The Lotos-Eaters', the melodies of the verse beckon readers to lose themselves in its alluring, slow-motion texture, in rather the same way as Ulysses's men, in the story reiterated by the poem, lost themselves in the repetitive pleasure of lotus-eating. Here again the stretched timescales of literary transmission find an echo in the slow temporality of the scene that is described. Ulysses himself, in the monologue that bears his name, is made to reflect on the dissemination of his fame to which the poem itself contributes. 'I am become a name,' he says; 'I am a part of all that I have met.'[12] All these texts adopt the self-referential tactics of the poems of translation that we have been exploring. But the processes of transmission which they describe and embody are something other than translation: too much is lost, changed, or invented. Poems of thwarted continuation, then; penned at a time when poems of translation had become all but impossible to write (FitzGerald's *Rubáiyát of Omar Khayyám* is a complicated exception, as we will see in Chapter 24).

Browning's verse, too, was animated by the narrowing of translation to 'translation rigidly conceived'. His painter monologues, 'Fra Lippo Lippi' and 'Andrea del Sarto' (1855), are very free extrapolations from Vasari and other foreign texts. The thought that he is doing something securely different from what translation had now become frees him to conjure these vivid characters from his sources. His long poems, *Sordello* (1840) and *The Ring and the Book* (1867–8), are massive expansions of, respectively, a bit of Dante and a bundle of Latin and Italian court records. *The Ring and the Book* is animated by an idea, not of translation, but of reimagining the past as 'looking or travelling across space'. 'The life in me abolished the death of things', as Browning puts it towards the beginning of *The Ring and the Book*, at the point where, having first translated its title page 'word for word', his narratorial persona lays aside his source text, steps 'out on to the narrow terrace' of his apartment in Florence, and imagines his way across the Italian landscape, past 'the Apennine', Arezzo, Castelnuovo, to 'Rome itself', where he finds that he can see, with his 'eyes', the events of the story acting themselves out before him.[13] Here, the flight through space represents the escape from word-for-word translation into a more freely imaginative mode of response.

In works of the ensuing decade, Browning worried at the boundary between this reanimating ambition of his imagination and 'translation rigidly conceived'. The differing modes of response are all plotted in geographical space. Both *Balaustion's Adventure* (1871) and *Aristophanes' Apology; including a Transcript from Euripides* (1875) incorporate translations. Both are set in the fifth century BC, and both include sea voyages to suggest the process of cultural transmission in which they are themselves engaged. In *Balaustion's Adventure*, the eponymous heroine has fled from Rhodes to Athens where, in the countryside, she recites an abridged version of Euripides's 'Alcestis' with interpolated commentary, thereby re-enacting a recitation she had done before, on board ship, in order to win over the crew of a hostile Spartan galley. The layered utterances and location register the changes through which the translated text has come into being. In *Aristophanes' Apology*, Balaustion is again at sea, and this time recalls an evening when she and her husband, quietly 'in the house', hear of the death of Euripides. There comes 'suddenly, torch-light! knocking at the door' and in bursts Aristophanes, drunk and ebullient.[14] He is conjured up as a character in the way Browning was used to doing in his monologues; only this time the speaker is anchored to his origins by profligate quotation from Aristophanes's plays, some of it in transliterated Greek. Here is an embodiment of the spirit of Aristophanic comedy, bulging with all the creative energy that would be lost if subjected to 'translation rigidly conceived'. Balaustion gets him to quieten down and listen to a recitation of Euripides's *Herakles* which Browning renders in absolutely the opposite way, transcribing it into pretty much the standard, flat idiom of Victorian literal translation. The contrasting modes of response harmonize with the genres and locations to which they are attached: the free spirit of comedy meets the marmoreal significance of tragedy; the cacophonic energy of a street festival comes up against the quiet concentration of a domestic interior. Arriving, as it does, after all this, *The Agamemnon of Aeschylus, Transcribed by Robert Browning* (1877), which I discussed in Chapter 5, is one last experiment in the interaction of translation and poetic imagining. Offered to the reader with no imaginative frame, it is a wilful overdoing of 'translation rigidly conceived', a doomed endeavour to make the English 'adhere' more closely to the Greek than the Greek does to itself.[15]

When Ezra Pound chose to begin his *Draft of XVI Cantos* (1925) with a passage of translation from the *Odyssey*, these nineteenth-century precursors nourished his sense of what translation could be. He pays explicit homage to Browning (even more so in the *Three Cantos* (1917) at whose end the passage originally appeared).[16] Browning nurtured that interest in the material stuff of cultural transmission which makes Pound translate, and announce that he has translated, not from Homer direct but from the Latin translation by 'Andreas Divus, / In officina Wecheli, 1538' (also used by Chapman).[17] The frank oddity of some of the diction is Browningesque too. But Tennyson's shadow also falls here, for his 'Ulysses' had come via an intermediary, the reimagining of Homer in Dante's *Inferno*. And the part of the *Odyssey* that Tennyson drew on—Book 11. 100–37—overlaps with the passage translated by Pound.

At the start of the *Cantos*, translation figures as a threshold sort of writing: itself the product of textual transmission, it eases a reader's transition into the work. And, in just the way we would expect in the poetry of translation, this imaginative work that the text itself does finds a double in what it describes. Where the *Iliad* switches between long views across space and fierce combat at close quarters, the *Odyssey* is a poem of journeying—of transition and tentative encounter. In the passage selected by Pound, Ulysses and his companions come to the shore, get into their ship and set out. They arrive at the edge of the known world and breach the boundary of the afterlife: dead souls flock around them and the veil of the future is rent by the soothsaying of another character who interested Tennyson: Tiresias. All Tennyson's poems of thwarted transmission happen in liminal spaces: the shore, the edge of the world, the brink of suicide. And in Browning's the sea voyages, landscapes, cityscapes, and domestic interiors shadow the kinds of imagining and transporting that are going on in the poetry. Like Pope's 'taking a view', these spatial metaphors offer ways of understanding the linguistic, cultural, chronological, and geographical distances that are crossed by the poems in which they appear. The difference is that, in the nineteenth century, they did not become part of the act of translation, but appeared in its environs, or as escapes from it, or as markers of a different kind of writing. Pound brought the shaping power of metaphors back into the heart of poetic translation. This is why his practice matters so much to what has come after it: every twentieth-century poet-translator owes something to him. As one instance, let us consider the Belfast poet Michael Longley, whose poems of translation done from Homer in the early 1990s develop the metaphors of travelling and looking across space which we have been exploring.

'Inside epics such as the *Iliad*', Longley has said, 'there are lots of little works of art waiting to be set free'. What he does is 'to wade in against the narrative flow and freeze-frame telling moments to make what I hope are self-contained lyric poems'.[18] Self-contained save for the fact that—as we established in Chapter 8—poem-translations cannot shrug off their connection to their sources. In his freeze-frames from the *Odyssey*, published in *Gorse Fires* (1991), the presiding doubles of translation are—as they were at the start of Pound's *Cantos*—journeying, arrival, and recognition.

Peter McDonald has suggested that Longley seeks out 'moments of reconciliation' in the *Odyssey*, 'cutting away as much as possible of the broader narrative context' so as to make them into 'points of lyric intensity'.[19] Yet, though recognition is frequent in these lyric-translations, it does not always flower into reconciliation: encounter is always cross-hatched with loss. There is Odysseus's dog Argos, in a summary of Book 17. 300–27, 'struggling to get nearer to the voice he recognises / And dying in the attempt'.[20] And there is his nurse Eurycleia, in a close translation from 19. 468–72:

> ... recognising him she let go of his leg
> Which clattered into the basin—water everywhere,
> Such pain and happiness, her eyes filling with tears,
> Her old voice cracking...[21]

There is Laertes, at 24. 345–8, recognizing his son, 'great Odysseus':

> Who drew the old man fainting to his breast and held him there
> And cradled like driftwood the bones of his dwindling father.[22]

And there is Odysseus recognizing the soul of his mother, Anticleia, in the passage from Book 11 that also interested Tennyson and Pound:

> You lunge forward three times to hug her and three times
> Like a shadow or idea she vanishes through your arms.[23]

In all these poems, Longley's own encounter with Homer echoes and intermingles with the encounters he describes.[24] Passages of summary and invention lead up to, and also sometimes follow, the moments of close translation. These moments might be taken to 'give us Homer'—to recall the phraseology we encountered in Chapter 3—especially as Longley's long verse-line is so in harmony with Homer's, echoing its dactylic and spondaic pulse. But they are shadowed by awareness of the imposition that inevitably accompanies the endeavour to grasp something in translation, as we saw in Chapter 4. 'Cradled like driftwood' is Longley's invention: the image pushes to make Homer more tangible; but, because it is written over him, it cannot but simultaneously make him dwindle, just like Odysseus's 'dwindling father' who faints when he is embraced.[25] 'Idea', likewise, in the lines about Odysseus's encounter with Anticleia, is Longley's idea of what to do with the Greek word 'ὄνειρος' whose meaning is usually closer to 'dream'.[26] Ideas are more likely than dreams to occur as the result of an act of volition: they are more under our control. The step from 'shadow' to 'idea', then, suggests a shift from something cast, or received, to something at least partially invented. A shadow begins to vanish when you think of it as being an 'idea'. Anticleia turns out to be too insubstantial to be hugged: likewise, the thought that what we are holding in our hands to read may not be Homer's shadow, but Longley's idea of him, makes the *Iliad*, too, seem to vanish from our grasp.

In the last of these poems from the *Odyssey*, also the last poem in *Gorse Fires*, Longley brings over some of the violence that the other 'freeze-frames' might seem to have dodged. 'The Butchers' is from the scene in Book 22 when Odysseus puts nooses around the necks of the women of his household who had been having sex with Penelope's suitors ('the disloyal housemaids', as Longley decorously calls them), and hangs them, 'their heads bobbing in a row, their feet twitching but not for long'. The mass murder is observed unflinchingly; but then Longley introduces a movement towards possible redemption, cutting straight to the magical moment when, at the start of Book 24, Hermes gathers the souls of the dead suitors (also massacred by Odysseus) and leads them to the underworld. In a gesture of restorative gender equality, Longley allows the souls of the women to join the procession:

> Along the clammy sheughs, then past the oceanic streams
> And the white rock, the sun's gatepost in that dreamy region,
> Until they came to a bog-meadow full of bog-asphodels
> Where the residents are ghosts or images of the dead.[27]

'Clammy sheughs' is a close translation of εὑρώεντα κέλευθα but not a translation into the standard dialect of English: 'sheugh' is a markedly Ulster and Scots word (it means furrow, trench, or ditch).[28] As often in literary writing when a regional word pops up among otherwise standard vocabulary, 'sheugh' brings with it a distinctive feeling of place; and the feeling continues in what follows. There are no bogs in the Elysian fields (nor in Homer at this point) but many in Ireland. The scene might appear to be set for an assertion of fulsome continuity between the here and now and the there and then, via the earth to which everyone is connected—the sort of uplift that is so dear to Seamus Heaney, 'bog' being a favourite Heaney word in such a context. But Longley ends the poem questioningly. 'Residents' is a modern, flat, official term that pulls away from the mystico-pastoral imagining that has preceded it: you can—say for tax purposes—be a 'resident' of Northern Ireland but not, usually, of a 'dreamy region'. 'Ghosts or images' accurately tracks the Greek at this point ('ψυχαί, εἴδωλα'),[29] but coming where it does, after the disturbance introduced by 'residents', in the last line of this poem of translation, it brings with it the same tonality as 'shadow or idea': a flicker of self-doubt as to how the 'images' in Longley's poem are related to the 'ghosts' in Homer's. The same oscillation of connection and schism reappears throughout Longley's poems from the *Odyssey*, in the embrace that fails or causes fainting; in the death that interrupts the attempt to get near, in Eurycleia's reaction to Odysseus: 'recognising him she let go'. That is why these poems of translation are at the heart of *Gorse Fires*, a volume in which 'moments of poignant healing', as Fran Brearton has said, are throughout 'counterbalanced by acts of butchery': 'the poems traverse the distance between the two as they also acknowledge their mutual dependence'.[30] The book offers a subtle, complex imagining of human contact shadowed by human loss; and it is nurtured by the loss that is inseparable from gain in the activity of translation.

The presiding doubles of translation in these poems—journeying, arrival, recognition—are all dominant elements in their source, the *Odyssey*. They are less so in the *Iliad*; but still, in two of the four poems he drew from that other Homeric epic in his next volume, *The Ghost Orchid* (1995), Longley developed his own encounter with the Greek out of encounters between characters in the narrative. Here again, an ambivalence already present in the source is drawn out and given a new flicker of self-reference in translation:

> Put in mind of his own father and moved to tears
> Achilles took him by the hand and pushed the old king
> Gently away, ...[31]

That is the beginning of 'Ceasefire', freeze-framed from the meeting of Achilles and Priam in Book 24. And here is the beginning of 'The Helmet', from the scene usually thought of as 'Hector and Andromache' towards the end of Book 6:

> When shiny Hector reached out for his son, the wean
> Squirmed and buried his head between his nurse's breasts
> And howled, terrorised by his father, ...[32]

A taking by the hand followed by a push; a reaching out that is met with terror: these counter-currents continue those in the poems from the *Odyssey*.

But now Longley also responds to the stimulus of another kind of scene that is more typical of the *Iliad*, and whose importance for Pope we have already explored: a view across a landscape, 'The Campfires':

> All night crackling campfires boosted their morale
> As they dozed in no man's land and the killing fields.
> (There are balmy nights—not a breath, constellations
> Resplendent in the sky around a dazzling moon—
> When a clearance high in the atmosphere unveils
> The boundlessness of space, and all the stars are out
> Lighting up hilltops, glens, headlands, vantage

> Points like Tonakeera and Allaran where the tide
> Turns into Killary, where salmon run from the sea, . . .[33]

The first seven lines are closely translated from Book 8. 553–65. But distinctly modern phraseology introduces an element of disruption, rather like the word 'residents' in 'The Butchers'. 'Boosted their morale' is a contemporary military cliché, while 'no man's land' and 'the killing fields', which expand on Homer's πτολέμοιο γεφύρας ('lines of battle'), are similarly familiar modern phrases, hooked, respectively, to the First World War and to the Khmer Rouge in Cambodia.[34] The effect is complex. On the one hand, Longley's choice of diction stretches Homer's scene through time and across the world and therefore brings it, as we tend to say, 'close' to his readers. Fighting was much the same, the words imply, at Troy in the mists of time BC, in western Europe in 1914–18, in Cambodia in the 1970s and, implicitly, in Northern Ireland in the 1990s. On the other hand, familiar phrases, as Victor Shklovsky pointed out, in general make experience seem routine: they lose touch with sensation.[35] So the situation of Homer's warriors is updated but at the same time made less immediate. War is, to adopt the common word, 'universalized'; but its universality is made to seem wearying. But then again, the fact that one can become inured to such horrors is (by a final counter flow of suggestion) all the more horrific.

Then comes a new drift of feeling. 'Balmy nights' brings a hint of travel brochure schmaltz as the writing turns away from the battlefield to the pure calm of the moon, the stars, the boundless sky. As Homer extends his view, Longley extends his, for the lines about vantage points like Tona-keera and Allaran, the tide turning into Killary, and the salmon running from the sea are his invention. Composed from his vantage point, they extend the *Iliad*'s scope to the landscape of West Mayo where he lives part of the time. Homer is brought home. Except that this is not, any more than in the poems from the *Odyssey*, an unequivocal connection. In the English, as in the Greek, the hinge that links the skyey scenery to the battlefield is a simile between the number of fires and the number of stars: 'when . . . all the stars are out . . . That many campfires sparkled in front of Ilium'. The landscape beneath the stars is not essential to the comparison: it is brought in by that wild luxuriance of Homer's imagina-tion which so fascinated and troubled Pope. And its relation to the scene of battle is ambivalent: it might suggest the pause and comparative calm in the men's spirits as they doze; or it might contrast with their focused tenseness. The ambivalence extends into Longley's extension of Homer. Are Tonakeera and Allaran and Killary mentioned because Ireland is like Ilium? Or because it is different? At the end of this poem of translation,

Longley returns, as Homer does at the end of his simile, to the field
outside Troy:

> Shuffling next to the chariots, munching shiny oats
> And barley, their horses waited for the sunrise.[36]

At sunrise, in Troy, the killing will recommence. And in Mayo?

For in Longley's poems from the *Iliad* there is an insistent possibility of
local political relevance. 'At that time we were praying for an IRA ceasefire,' Longley says; and so he called the freeze-frame of Achilles and Priam
'Ceasefire', and, 'hoping to make my own minute contribution, sent it to
the *Irish Times*. It was the poem's good luck to be published two days after
the IRA's declaration.'[37] The contribution the poem makes is not what
you might expect to find in a newspaper. There is no glossing over the
pain of the past in a drive to secure peace in the present, but rather an
insistence on it. Longley reorders the lines that he translates so that his
poem ends, not with Priam's and Achilles's admiring mutual stare, nor
with their redemptive common weeping, but with a mention of the
murder that is having to be got past, though it cannot be got over:

> 'I get down on my knees and do what must be done
> And kiss Achilles' hand, the killer of my son.'[38]

'Ceasefire' connects the world lived in by Longley and that imagined by
Homer with a structure like that of a simile. The Troubles left many
people with sons who had been killed; but none of them could kiss the
hand of Achilles. Just as in a simile, both difference and likeness matter;
but the difference fades before the assertion of similarity. As its title
announces, 'Ceasefire' contains an element of didacticism which is, in
the circumstances, not only understandable but praiseworthy. Priam's
action is being offered as an example.[39]

But in the next poem in the volume, 'The Helmet', the likenesses
between here and there, between now and then, are more tentative. The
structure of relation is more like that which is established between Mayo
and Ilium in 'The Campfires': both moments are placed on the same
imaginative landscape but the degree and point of any connection between them is left searchingly undefined. Hector's child is 'terrorised' by
him, a word that leaps into the Northern Irish present; but the poem then
moves on to focus on the 'horse-hair crest' of Hector's helmet, pushing the
scene back into history. Then:

> His daddy laughed, his mammy laughed, and his daddy
> Took off the helmet and laid it on the ground to gleam,
> Then kissed the babbie and dandled him in his arms and
> Prayed that his son might grow up bloodier than him.[40]

Daddy and mammy and babbie feel local and present, but also universal: they are the modern Irish-English words for expressing a relation of tenderness that must always (we like to think) exist between parents and a baby. Then comes the brutal strike of the last line, which is summarized from six lines of Greek—a change of tactic from Longley's first three lines which have been close translation. This might be a drawing back from Homer, a withdrawal of sympathy from the language of honour and respect with which Hector palliates the brutality of his hope. Or it might be an attempt to 'give us Homer', to reveal the violence which—this line of thought would assume—is what the *Iliad* is really about. The line might imply that, surely, such a prayer could not be uttered these days. Or it might suggest that, in the 1980s and 1990s, among the IRA and the loyalist paramilitaries, this is the sort of barbarous wish that was expressed, so different from Hector's elaborate code of valour. By releasing these possibilities, the line searches the gulf between Longley's English and Homer's Greek. The source text here offers no structured landscape to guide the translating imagination's sense of its own activity. Instead, the impression of a distance being recognized, and perhaps in some ways crossed, arises from the various feelings of place and time that attach to the Irish-English words.

This use of diction as a means of echo-location, to probe the space between present and past, is adopted also by the late twentieth century's most vigorous poet-translator of Homer, Christopher Logue. Where Longley is a poet of locality and of domestic milieux, Logue's writing inhabits a mediatized world. His versions respond to Homer's way with landscape no less vividly than Pope's *Iliad* had done. But place and time both figure differently in a culture that includes high-speed travel, TV, radio, and film.

22

Epic Zoom: Christopher Logue's Homer (with Anne Carson's Stesichoros and Seamus Heaney's *Beowulf*)

Logue's scattered, reimagined extracts from the *Iliad*, written, performed, and published piecemeal since 1959, get started, when they are gathered and arranged in the 2001 book *War Music*, with a view:

> Picture the east Aegean sea by night,
> And on a beach aslant its shimmering
> Upwards of 50,000 men
> Asleep like spoons beside their lethal Fleet.[1]

As with Pope, and with Longley, the broad landscape implies a broad timescape. What resources might the average English-language reader have for picturing the East Aegean? Holidays, perhaps, and television pictures; and encounters with other beaches elsewhere. The natural landscape back there in the distance of the landscape of the past is—we have to take it—something we can 'picture'. It cannot have changed: it must be the same as the landscape now. Next comes a hook to a strange particular moment: 'Upwards of 50,000 men'. Yet at once this shock figure is gentled by a familiar simile, 'asleep like spoons'. *OED* shows that 'to spoon', meaning to sleep front to back, has been around since the late nineteenth century; the point of the image here at the beginning of Logue's epic endeavour is precisely that it is ordinary and, usually, tender. A couple will spoon—but 50,000 men? And 50,000 men beside a 'lethal fleet'? Just like Longley's switch from 'babbie' to 'bloodier', Logue's verse sends out oscillating signals, tender and brutal, familiar and strange. Like the sea, it shimmers.

Then: the zoom. Having done our picturing, we are given more imperious imperatives to obey: 'now look along that beach, and see…'. We are to see a wall, a gate, and through it 'a naked man / Run with what seems to break the speed of light' across sand to the luminescent panes, sliding over each other, of the sea:

Then kneel among those panes, burst into tears, and say:

'Mother, ·
You said that you and God were friends.
Over and over when you were at home
You said it. Friends. Good friends. That was your boast. . . .'

Perhaps the man has raised his voice to speak to the sea, though the descriptor is 'say' not 'shout'. But even if he has, we must have zoomed in pretty close to be able to hear him. The sequence of verbs in the passage suggests an even more intimate association: 'Picture', we have been told, then 'look', 'see', 'run', 'kneel', 'burst', 'say'. The imperatives addressed to Logue's readers have morphed into verbs which, to judge from their form, might still be imperatives but which, to judge from their context, must rather be infinitives describing what we are meant to look at: *see him run*. Yet the hint of imperative lingers, and holds out an invitation to readers to think of themselves, too, running and kneeling and bursting into tears, and speaking with the voice of this man whom we have not yet been told is Achilles.

As Logue's readers zoom into scenic and emotional close-up, his verse zooms into verbal proximity with the Greek. The picturing, the running, the kneeling were all Logue's scene-setting extrapolations: but 'Mother' is indisputably word for word. '$\mu\hat{\eta}\tau\epsilon\rho$' Homer had written in the corresponding episode of his Book 1 – so the *Iliad* begins to be quoted at the same time as Achilles.[2] 'Burst into tears', too, is close translation from '$\delta\alpha\kappa\rho\acute{\upsilon}\sigma\alpha\varsigma$', though in Homer that word comes a few lines earlier, just after Briseis has been led away.[3] For the speech of Achilles that follows, Logue goes on picking out details from here and there in the Greek. The bit about Thetis saying that she and God are friends comes from where Homer, forty-four lines after 'Mother', has Achilles remember her boasting 'often, in the halls of his Father', of Zeus's indebtedness to her. Pope, in his version of this scene, was concerned to preserve Achilles's dignity, as we saw in Chapter 19: he described him as 'bath'd in Tears of Anger and Disdain'. But Logue must discern a mummy's boy aspect to Achilles and chooses his words accordingly. He probably pinched 'burst into tears' from an unusual flicker of unstiltedness in one of his cribs, the 1924 Loeb translation by A. T. Murray: 'Achilles forthwith burst into tears, and withdrew apart . . .'.[4] But 'at home' for '$\pi\alpha\tau\rho\grave{o}\varsigma$ $\grave{\epsilon}\nu\grave{\iota}$ $\mu\epsilon\gamma\acute{\alpha}\rho o\iota\sigma\iota\nu$' and 'over and over' for '$\pi o\lambda\lambda\acute{\alpha}\kappa\iota$' are his own modernizing, colloquializing shifts.[5] 'Boast', though, pulls Achilles back towards the register he has traditionally been thought to have in the Greek: it is the

word Lord Derby used at this point, translating 'εὐχομένης'.[6] But then, in
what follows, Logue moves into summary and extrapolation once again.

This zooming in and out of verbal proximity to the Greek is typical of
Logue's way with Homer. Pound once said the *Cantos* were a 'poem
including history':[7] Logue's Homer is a poem including translation.
War Music is subtitled *An Account of Books 1–4 and 16–19 of Homer's*
Iliad, and occasionally Logue gives an 'account' of his source in the precise
monetary sense of telling out word for word. At these moments, he is not
unlike Longley. But the surrounding liberty, the reworking and frank
invention, the collage of striking scenes with large gaps between them,
make blatant an idea that was left implicit in Longley's practice of
microscopic selection: though all the *Iliad* may be translatable into English, and indeed into English lines that look like verse, perhaps it may not,
at present, all be translatable into English poetry. And so Logue also gives
an 'account' in the looser sense of summary, narrative retelling, or musical
performance.[8]

As evidence of the need for Logue's stretching, perhaps rupturing, of
translation, consider what one distinguished translator of the whole work,
Robert Fagles, made of the passage I have been discussing:

> But Achilles wept, and slipping away from his companions,
> far apart, sat down on the beach of the heaving gray sea
> and scanned the endless ocean. Reaching out his arms,
> again and again he prayed to his dear mother: 'Mother!
> You gave me life, short as that life will be,
> so at least Olympian Zeus, thundering up on high,
> should give me honour—but now he gives me nothing.'[9]

And here is another distinguished translator of the whole work, Richmond
Lattimore:

> ... But Achilleus
> weeping went and sat in sorrow apart from his companions
> beside the beach of the grey sea looking out on the infinite water.
> Many times stretching forth his hands he called on his mother:
> 'Since, my mother, you bore me to be a man with a short life,
> therefore Zeus of the loud thunder on Olympos should grant me
> honour at least. But now he has given me not even a little.'[10]

The extracts are typical of both translators; and they leave one struggling
to rebut Logue's complaint that 'they do not write verse. They write
blank-verse prose'.[11] Both are of course closer to the words of the *Iliad*
and both shadow its syntax, while Lattimore does his best to echo, and
Fagles to hint at, Homer's hexameter verse form. But the resulting texture
of language, with its mild, would-be poeticisms ('slipping away', 'scanned',

'stretching forth') so characteristic of everyday translation from the classics, has no connection to the modes and energies of the poetry that was contemporary to it; and neither does it have that stringency in the choice of words and pointedness in their arrangement that poetry of any period requires. 'Olympian Zeus thundering up on high'? 'Sat in sorrow apart from his companions'? No. But now try Logue again: 'then kneel among those panes, burst into tears, and say: / "Mother"'.

Quite apart from whatever may be their shortcomings as writers, Fagles and Lattimore hold themselves—as is necessary given the sort of use and market for which their books are intended—to the metaphor of 'translation rigidly conceived'. As usual, the consequence is that Homer's poetry is not translated into poetry (this usual consequence is not inevitable: as we noted in Chapter 8, Peter Robinson's Luciano Erba is an exception). Dryden and Pope were able to translate, respectively, all the *Aeneid* and all the *Iliad* into verse that drew fully and brilliantly on the poetic resources of their times. As we have seen, they adopted different metaphors of translation – 'opening', 'passion', 'taking a view' – in order to channel and extend the energies of their source texts. But these metaphors allowed them to keep pretty close to the words of those sources, and very close to their narrative structures. Logue gambles that much more vigorous rewriting may be necessary if whatever it is that counts as Homer's 'poetry', as distinct from the readily imitable elements of narrative structure and descriptive meaning that I discussed in Chapter 4, is to be represented in English poetry of the late twentieth to twenty-first centuries. 'I respect translators,' he has said, 'I have no doubt that many texts can be accurately and beautifully translated.' Then comes the intransigent 'but': 'but certain texts, like poetry and some kinds of prose, have special problems'.[12]

For Logue, the special problems posed by the *Iliad* appear to have been: its length, its narrative continuity, its verse form, its cultural distance, and the air of solemnity that comes with classic status. In order to overcome them, he cuts and pastes, grafts in references to other texts (Shakespeare, H. D., Jacques Brel) and modern wars and the modern world (a radio telescope, a taxi).[13] He has also, as he says, 'written new scenes and introduced some new characters'.[14] Ezra Pound's *Cantos* are the authoritative, high-literary precedent for the resulting multiplicitous montage; but more immediate and active analogues for Logue were the common procedures by which written texts are adapted for radio, theatre, and film. These media, of course, are among the vehicles of the cultural changes that made Homer seem difficult to translate. The feeling that a Pope-length *Iliad* was all but out of the question for a late twentieth-century poet must have helped release Michael Longley into the creation of his lyric precipitates: they preserve the classical tradition in a microculture of attentive

reading and rewriting. Logue meets the challenge of his cultural circumstances in the opposite way. In order to write a long poem deriving from
Homer, he adopts the tactics of those media that have helped make a long
poetic translation seem impossible.

Logue's first bash at Homer occurred in 1959 at the invitation of the
classical scholar Donald Carne-Ross, as part of a series of Homer extracts
that were to be read on the radio. 'Achilles and the River' is too straightforward—too narratively consecutive, and too consistent in its loosely penta-
metric verse—to be incorporated into *War Music* (it is collected separately,
under the self-effacing title 'From Book XXI of Homer's *Iliad*', in Logue's
Selected Poems). But it does already manifest two traits that were to become
fundamental in the later, wilder versions. There is a dominant, in fact
domineering, narrative voice: 'You must imagine how a gardener prepares /
To let his stored rainwater out'—which anticipates the many commands in
War Music, starting with 'Picture the east Aegean sea'.[15] And there is (as
David Ricks has noticed)[16] a 'cinematic' quality, as in this invented close-
up shot of Achilles's hand-to-wave combat with the river Scamander:

> He beat it
> With the palm of his free hand, sliced at it,
> At the whorled ligaments of water, yes, sliced at them, Ah!—
> There, there—there, and—*there*—such hatred,
> Scamander had not thought, the woman Prince,
> Scamander had not thought, and now, slice, slice,
> Scamander could not hold the Greek![17]

This writing feels 'cinematic' because of its visual intensity; and because the
past-tense narrative is ambushed by movement which is vividly enacted by the
dashes, italics, and repetitions, and which butts into the present tense as though
it is something we can see (the time warps are created by 'yes', 'Ah!', 'now'). But
of course we cannot see it. 'There, there—there, and—*there*' might be effective
if spoken in a film because there are images to fill out the denotation. The same
words are differently effective on the radio, or on the page, because their visual
counterpart has to be not only imagined (as sights always have to be imagined
from words) but frankly made up by the listener or reader. This early example
heralds complications which will develop, often searchingly, though occasionally rather randomly, in *War Music*. What is meant by 'cinematic', as applied to
a piece of writing, is only loosely comparable to what really goes on in a film. In
particular, such writing tends, paradoxically, to emphasize its lack of the images
and action that it is endeavouring to call to mind. In Logue, this pervasive
hollowness is emphasized by the vehement narrative voice which fades in and
out of 'cinematic' styles of description. It is as though we are being ordered to
imagine a film that cannot be seen.

Logue has talked about how film mattered to him:

> There is no time to waste in a narrative poem. ... Get the stuff on stage.
> Stage the action. ... I think going to the cinema a lot, reading film scripts,
> and writing for cinema, has made this very clear to me.[18]

(Logue wrote the script for the 1965 TV musical, *The End of Arthur's
Marriage* directed by Ken Loach, and *Savage Messiah*, a 1972 biopic of
Gaudier Brzeska directed by Ken Russell.) The connection, though force-
ful, is loose: 'cinema' lumped together with 'stage'. But it persists into
Logue's storyboard method of composition:

> he works on lengths of continuous computer print-out paper to which he
> sticks Post-It notes, building up detail upon detail, image after image. A draft
> page for a section of War Music, therefore, can be five metres long. Portions
> of it get nailed to the wall ... to establish what Logue calls a 'flow chart'.[19]

There is something filmic, too, about how the narrative spine of 'Achilles
and the River' ran through his mind:

> When I walked up to the Gate for a newspaper or as far as Kensington
> Gardens for a stroll, I found myself thinking of Achilles and Scamander,
> running through the events listed as easily as I might the alphabet. More,
> I could reverse the sequence to test its strength overall, as painters hold a
> canvas to a mirror to inspect its composition afresh.[20]

Here again the analogy is not wholly brought into focus: not film, quite,
but a scrolling alphabet; not cinema, exactly, but moving pictures.

Film presses in again when Logue is thinking about point of view. In an
interview he says, of Homer's *Iliad*:

> L: It's nearly all close-ups. There's a few in the middle distance, and one or
> two panoramic views, but not many in so long a work.
> QU: Whereas you do a lot of panoramic shots.
> L: Yes, I do, and I want to vary them all the time.[21]

This varying contributes to the 'vigour and dynamism' that have been
widely praised in reviews.[22] And it allows Logue to bring into his poem-
translations a feeling about Homer that was put into his mind right at the
beginning, by the classicist Xanthe Wakefield:

> 'The Greeks are not humanistic, not Christian, not sentimental. Please try to
> understand that. They are musical. Such music. And Homer ... Homer is
> close to your ear, and at the same time—so distant. He has a passage' –
> giving me the book and line reference—'where he describes the snow falling
> on to the sea at Zeus's will. You feel that Zeus is so far away, so far ...' And
> she looked out of the window.[23]

(The line reference must have been to *Iliad* 12. 284–5.) Wakefield's tactic of describing Homer with lines from his poem is just like Pope's.[24] As Zeus appears in the *Iliad*, so the *Iliad* appears to her. This apprehension lasts and grows, in Logue's poem-translations, into shifts of focus between the glassily distant ('Picture the east Aegean sea') and the throbbingly close ('Mother')—just as Wakefield's appreciation of Greek musicality lasts into the compendium title of Logue's work, *War Music*.

Logue's Homer is, then, the freest of all the poems of translation I consider in this book. But Logue also has hopes in common with the other poet-translators. He echoes Dryden's practice of 'opening' in his ambition 'to get at what is there and to make explicit the thoughts present in Homer's work'. And he is like Pound (as we will see in Chapter 23) when he says 'I think I know how to make the *Iliad*'s voices come alive'. His declaration of fidelity, 'I aim to make my Homer poem true to *my* idea of the *Iliad*', expresses with unusual clarity a truth that we established in Chapter 4: a translator can only ever translate an 'idea' of the source, however thoroughly grounded that might be in scholarly knowledge or popular assumptions.[25] This is why there is a virtue—as well as the obvious shortcoming—to the fact that Logue does not know Greek, and, even more strikingly, seems not to have tried to learn it during the half-century of his involvement with Homer. The labour of calibrating other translations, of imagining poetry out of word-for-word cribs supplied by the classicist Donald Carne-Ross, of consulting other experts, of dipping into published scholarship—all this means that the work of imagining-in which, as we saw in Chapter 4, is vital to the translation of any poetry, however expert the translator's knowledge of the source language, is in Logue's case especially to the fore. He is very obviously not just 'reading' the source, but having to conjure it up. This drive to make the absent present results in an 'idea' of Homer that is intensely visual, auditory, and energetic. Repeatedly, that imperious, mediating narrative voice zooms in on bits of action that are designed to seem vividly seen and heard in real time.

As here, in the duel taken from *Iliad* Book 3, where Menelaos (Logue's spelling) has just avoided Paris's spear-throw:

And

—'Yes!'—

Cried the Greeks, but by that time
Their hero has done more than hurl his own, and

—'Yes!'—

He is running under it, as fast as it, and

—'Yes!'—

As the 18-inch head hits fair Paris' shield
And knocks him backwards through the air
(Bent like a gangster in his barber's chair)
Then thrusts on through that round
And pins it, plus his sword arm, to the sand,
The Greek is over him, sword high, ...[26]

One of Logue's helps towards imagining Homer, the A. T. Murray Loeb, represents the same passage like this:

> Next Atreus' son, Menelaus, rushed upon him with his spear and... [he makes a prayer at this point which Logue has brought forward to a moment earlier] ... poised his far-shadowing spear, and hurled it; and he smote upon the son of Priam's shield, that was well balanced upon every side. Through the bright shield went the mighty spear, and through the corselet, richly dight, did it force its way; and straight on beside his flank the spear shore through his tunic; but he bent aside and escaped black fate. Then the son of Atreus drew his silver-studded sword, and raising himself on high ...[27]

Logue shifts the narrative into the present tense, and casts it in lines that—as in much of the rest of *War Music*—are loosely related to the pentameter, though frequently shorter and quite often interrupted by staccato one-worders. He cuts out the epithets and routine elaborations that have their roots in oral composition ('far-shadowing', 'well balanced upon every side', etc.) and substitutes a bit of technical specificity: 'the 18-inch head'. For Pope in the early eighteenth century, translating Homer into English poetry meant broadening his particularities into a more general language of feeling and valuing; for Logue, in the wake of Pound, it means highlighting—or where necessary inventing—the telling detail. Logue's image of 'a gangster in his barber's chair' is a hook to the modern and especially to cinema—for he must have got the image from a movie like Scorsese's *The Godfather* (1972). The layering of Menelaos's run with the flight of the spear is indebted to the same, or more accurately a similar, medium: it is the sort of thing that happens in animations such as Chuck Jones's *Road Runner* series. And the image of Menelaos standing over the prostrate, pinned Paris has a filmic air to it as well: in Homer Paris is still standing when Menelaos rises on high.

So far, so compellingly, if loosely, 'cinematic'.[28] But a disturbance is introduced by Logue's imagining of an audience whose presence is signalled by their invented and interpolated cries '—"Yes!"—...—"Yes!"—'.

Films have audiences, of course, as does the stage, but in neither case do the observers get quite this involved. "'Off with his cock! Off with his cock!'" shout Hera and Athene when Menelaos starts battering Paris; and, when Menelaos's sword shatters on Paris's helmet:

> A hundred of us pitch our swords to him ...[29]

'Us.' Logue's airy narrator has zoomed in and shifted point of view so as to become one of the cheering crowd. He has not only been, like Pope, 'Hurry'd out of himself' and changed 'in one place to a Hearer, in another to a Spectator'; he has also been transformed into an extra who is, if only in a small way, a participant.

That shocking pronoun, 'us', releases a charge of ambiguity that had been building through the previous lines. Have we been so thrilled as to enter wholly into the narrator's perspective, following gleefully as he in turn enters into the perspective of a soldier, enthusiastically feeling the excitement of the action? Or do we rather refuse to join in this concatenation of butchness, and instead observe the brutal events appraisingly, contemplating that narratorial 'us' from the outside, so that we are an audience watching an audience? In the first case we will relish the 'gangster in his barber's chair', the sword arm pinned to the sand, the Greek standing over Paris, 'sword high'. We will feel that these phrases electrifyingly jump Homer into the present, and we will seem to see with our imagining eyes the film they call to mind. In the second, we will distrust those same phrases for releasing such ready-formatted pictures from the push-button store of our cultural imaginary. The 'cinematic' elements in the text ask readers to share in the illusion that Homer has been made 'present': that we can really see what is happening, even to the point of stepping into the imagined movie, like that narratorial 'us'. But they also lay bare the illusion's artificiality, its reliance on mediatized images that obviously cannot be in Homer.

Another element in *War Music* again puts pressure on the filmic metaphor which energizes but does not encapsulate Logue's poetry of translation. This is the silence which, he insists, surrounds and punctuates the movements that catch his eye. 'No sound', we are told when, in an invented episode from the section titled *GBH*, Merionez strips the body of someone he has killed. 'Silence' before Logue's version, in *Cold Calls* (2005), of the debate between Agamemnon and the other Greek leaders at the start of Book 9; and 'Silence again' and 'Silence again' between the speeches.[30] When Agamemnon summons his army in Book II of Homer's *Iliad*, nine heralds struggle to quieten the men's uproar. In Logue, the army files to the meeting place 'muter than sheep' and sits down 'All still'. Even so, Logue cannot resist retaining one herald to get things even quieter:

Talthibios:

> 'Absolute silence for
> Agamemnon of Mycenae, King of kings'.[31]

This peculiarity of Logue's rendition must owe something to his memories of living through the Second World War as a teenager:

> Though we knew that, far away in Russia, in North Africa, tremendous battles, and the terrifying, overwhelming noise that such battles create, filled the world, here in Bournemouth, over and above its natural climate of repose a mood of silent, immoveable stillness filled the air. It was unnecessary to tell me to keep my voice down.[32]

And something also to his experience of army training during national service: 'split the Platoon . . . No noise . . . ', his sergeant told him by way of advice on how to attack a spur.[33] But the silence that intersperses Logue's flurries of involvement also suggests, and must have been nourished by, the silence in which they were invented, that quiet of the concentrating imagination through which the filmic 'idea' of Homer emerges, its voices coming to be heard and sights to be seen. Illustrated by the blanks of white paper that similarly punctuate the verse, these lapses into silence register the constructed nature of what is on the page. When nothing has been imagined, nothing is there. They are the auditory equivalent of the artificial light with which Logue bathes his scenes, the 'neon' edge of the sea, the 'chromium wash' of fires in the distance.[34] It is 'not necessarily stage or film-set lighting', Logue has said; but 'I think of this "light" as an indication of the non-realistic world my work inhabits'.[35]

The non-realism of *War Music* both enables and excuses Logue's liberties. It makes continually visible the fact that what we are reading does not claim to embody authentic Homer but rather '*my* idea' of him. As the work has progressed, the emphasis of those italics appears to have strengthened: Logue has, he admits, 'moved further away from Homer's actual text'.[36] When the focus on the *Iliad* fades, in the latest instalments *All Day Permanent Red* (2001) and *Cold Calls* (2005), the verse becomes more slack and gestural, with a gathering sense of arbitrariness about the references to twentieth-century warfare, and an encroaching tonality of pastiche as when (in an invented scene) the river Scamander gets excited as Venus walks into him:

> 'And now your knees . . . '
> 'You tickle me . . . '
> 'And now your thighs!'
> 'Oh, oh, go on . . . '
> 'And now your bum!'[37]

It's pretty good fun, but (at the risk of being a latter-day Bentley) it's hard to see much trace of Homer in this 'idea'. Throughout his 'Accounts', Logue's writing has been most taut when most sharply focused on an idea that more seriously is an idea of the *Iliad*: the weakest parts of the collected *War Music* are the passages of expanded or invented conversation. What most energizes his imagination is an endeavour to translate; that is, to pursue his particular mode of the poetry of translation, zooming in on an 'idea' of the *Iliad* while also putting its veracity in question.

How to suggest, for instance, the accumulated traditional wonder that must resound, at the beginning of Book 19, in the lines Murray translates like this: 'Now Dawn the saffron-robed arose from the streams of Oceanus to bring light to immortals and to mortal men'?[38] Logue's 'idea' of it gives rise to this:

> Rat.
> Pearl.
> Onion.
> Honey.
> These colours come before the Sun
> Lifted above the ocean
> Bringing light
> Alike to mortals and immortals.[39]

How to give sufficient energy to the spat, at the start of Book 17, between Menelaos and Euphorbus over the body of Patroclus? Lattimore has Euphorbus say:

> 'Son of Atreus, Menelaos, illustrious, leader of armies:
> give way, let the bloody spoils be, get back from this body . . . '

At which:

> Deeply stirred, Menelaos of the fair hair answered him:
> 'Father Zeus, it is not well for the proud man to glory . . . '[40]

Logue, who has renamed the participants 'Thackta' and 'Merionez' as a flag of his liberty, translates like this:

> 'Cretan, get off my meat.
> I got him first; (a lie) 'his flesh is mine.'
> Smooth as a dish that listens to the void
> Merionez' face swings up.
>   Dear God, he thinks,
> Who is this lily-wristed titch?[41]

The warriors' hunger for control of the corpse is fiercely imagined; and the startling representation of Merionez as a radio telescope recognizes that something tougher and colder might, in the heat of battle, be meant by the Greek '$\mu\acute{\epsilon}\gamma$' $\mathring{o}\chi\theta\acute{\eta}\sigma\alpha\varsigma$'[42] than 'deeply stirred'. There is an obvious cheek in offering both these passages as 'Homer'—as a making explicit of his 'thoughts', as a bringing to life of his 'voices'—rather than as a free response or new creation. Of course all translations differ from their sources, and we have by now explored many various examples: but here the difference is pushed so wide! And yet, what results from that difference is verse that is visually intense and dramatically arresting, Homeric qualities which the straight contemporary translations lack.

Anne Carson, the scholar-poet whose translation of Sappho I touched on in Chapter 16, has made a poem around the Greek lyricist Alkman's Fragment 20, which begins (as she translates): '[?] *made three seasons*'. A little later, her poem turns back to comment that 'Strict philologists will tell you' that Alkman's text as we have it 'is surely a fragment'. Then comes the poet's retort:

> But as you know the chief aim of philology
> is to reduce all textual delight
> to an accident of history.
> And I am uneasy with any claim to know exactly
> what a poet means to say.
> So let's leave the question mark there.[43]

In *Autobiography of Red* (1999), Carson grew a volume out of fragments of the *Geryoneis* of Stesichoros, a post-Homeric poet whose traces are even more exiguous than Alkman's. The book starts with an introductory essay; then follow 'Fragments of Stesichoros'; then appendices on 'The Question of Stesichoros' Blinding by Helen'; then, finally, the volume's title again, now with the subtitle 'A Romance'. There ensues a story of awkward teen passion which takes little from the little that remains of the *Geryoneis* save the names of its protagonists, Geryon's monstrosity, the imposing figure of a mother, and the plot gambit of Herakles doing Geryon harm— though here by breaking his heart rather than by killing him. And in fact the romance of invention extends back into the introductory apparatus. What had at first glance seemed to be a scholarly translation from the fragments turns out to be blatantly otherwise. From fragment VI: 'Athena was looking down through the floor / Of the glass-bottomed boat'.[44]

Carson finds a place for her poetry in the gaps created by the ravages of manuscript transmission. Logue finds a place for his in a less tangible loss: that of so much of the nuance, heft, and spark of the words of Homer whose forms have come safely through to us. Back in 1959, at the start of his work, Logue 'wanted to know *exactly* what it was Homer said in the first instance'. Carne-Ross replied: 'There is no exactly, no first in-stance'.[45] It is nevertheless clear that, in a tradition of interpretation that has ended up with Menelaus 'deeply stirred' and Achilles sitting 'in sorrow apart from his companions', almost as much may have vanished as in the mutilation of the manuscripts of Alkman or Stesichoros. There is a need for such gambles as Logue's, to hazard an 'idea' of what the poetry might have been.

The awarenesses embodied in Logue's zooming technique—of how much has faded into the distance of time, and of how much he may be inventing so as to restore energy—contrast with the assertions of continuity that are so marked a feature of another late twentieth-century translation of an epic, Seamus Heaney's *Beowulf* (1999). Heaney feels, he writes in his 'Introduction', that he is linked to the language of his source by a continuous 'historical heritage'. He thinks he hears in *Beowulf* a 'familiar local voice, one that had belonged to relatives of my father', in whose speech, he goes on, there was 'a kind of foursquareness about the utterance, a feeling of living inside a constantly indicative mood'.[46] Of course, *Beowulf* is not from so many years ago as the *Iliad*, and not from so far away in miles. But it is not certain that it is therefore closer to us culturally. More, probably, is known about ancient Greek culture than about the culture of the Anglo-Saxons; and the fact that Heaney's aunt used the word 'thole', which derives from Old English, is in itself no more freighted with significant continuity than the fact that Logue uses the word 'idea' which derives from Greek. Heaney's layering of cultural history and family nostalgia has given him an idea of *Beowulf* which, as Chris Jones has pointed out, would not be shared by most scholars. In their more expert eyes, *Beowulf* is not 'a bluff, straightforward, speechlike utterance' but rather 'elevated, lofty, and both syntactically complex and compressed'.[47]

Heaney does not take any of Logue's liberties. There are no cuts, reorderings, and inventions; no shock appearances of neon, nor references to twentieth-century history. Rather, he translates in such a way as to play down contrasts between the present and the past, urging readers to join in his belief that 'as a work of art', *Beowulf* 'lives in its own continuous present, equal to our knowledge of reality in the present time'.[48] The metaphors implicit in this practice can be summed up as 'preserving heritage' and 'asserting universal value'. After Grendel's first raid on his hall, King Hrothgar, Heaney tells us, was 'numb with grief' and 'in deep distress', 'humiliated by the loss of his guard, / bewildered and stunned'; and soon Grendel, who was 'malignant by nature', 'struck again with more gruesome murders'.[49] The run of newspaper clichés makes Hrothgar's grief and Grendel's violence seem easily assimilable: the same words could do just as well, or just as badly, for pretty much any murderous attack anywhere. They give no hint that there might be some cultural specificity here which a translator or reader might need to work to grasp. Contrast another translation, Edwin Morgan's (1952), which is done according to a sharp-eyed variant of the metaphor of 'translation as carrying across'. Morgan finds more particularity in Hrothgar's reaction—the fact that it is a special kind of grief, 'Þegn-sorg' (thane-sorrow) that he is feeling, and the strange intensity of his response to Grendel's footprints:

> Bearing, enduring grief, strong
> Sorrow for his soldiers, when they saw the footprint
> Of the hated, of the accursed spirit; that strife
> Was too strong, too long, and too malignant.[50]

Morgan also represents more strictly the terms of understanding in the line which Heaney blurs into 'malignant by nature', 'fæðe ond fyrene; wæs to faest on Þām': 'In hatred, in violence—in these ways too set'. Not 'nature', then, but the stranger, more interesting thought of something akin to habit. Heaney's conviction that *Beowulf* must be 'the embodiment of a knowledge deeply ingrained in the species' leads him to soften the challenging formulations of the source into categories that are not in fact universal to the 'species' but belong instead to late twentieth-century western anglophone modes of imagining.[51] This comforting tactic is what has enabled the work to be so thoroughly commodified as an embodiment of heritage value. As Heaney himself has said of this poem-translation's commercial and critical success: 'it's a part of the phenomenon of a consumer society'.[52]

In *War Music*, grief (the particular grief of Achilles for Patroclus) is represented like this:

> ...forward on your hands and thrust your face into the filth,
> Push filth into your open eyes, and howling, howling,
> Sprawled howling, howling in the filth,
> Ripping out locks of your long redcurrant-coloured hair,
> Trowel up its dogshit with your mouth.[53]

This is fairly close to the Greek of Book 18. 22–7. Nudges in the choice of words, and in the detail of the idea imagined, keep the description strange: 'filth' and 'dogshit' for what Murray calls 'dust'; 'open eyes' and 'mouth' where Murray has 'fair face'.[54] The big alteration is that Homer's narrative past tense becomes, in Logue, imperative. Just as, in the duel of Paris and Menelaus, ' "Yes" ' and 'us' allowed readers the choice of joining in or distantly appraising the excited involvement of the watching crowd, so, here, the imperatives create an involved persona whose relish we can share or be repulsed by. Contrasting perspectives are questioningly superimposed. Then comes a franker strangeness, a representation of the sound made by the 'handmaidens' (Murray) or 'prize shes' (Logue) when (Murray again) they 'shrieked aloud in anguish of heart':

> 'Eeeeeeeeeeeeeeeeeeeeee...'
> 'Eeeeeeeeeeeeeeeeeeeeeeee...'
> 'Eeeeeeeeeeeeeeeeeeeeeeee...'

This is, Logue's narrator tells us, 'a terrifying noise / The like of which, the likes of you and me have never heard'.[55] The explanation is obviously unnecessary, and so seems meant to prompt particular questioning. The letters Logue has written down must be like the sound-idea that he has formed from Homer's phrase: they represent it. And yet that imagined sound is shut off from readers by the silence of the page: the difference between what the author and one reader and another will imagine—always of course present in any bit of any text—is here emphasized. Because those letters are in themselves so utterly alike (innumerable 'e's in a pod) they resist being drawn into the work of calibration by which a reader could make sense of them (high-pitched? low-pitched? multitoned or monotone? continuous or intermittent?). As everywhere in Logue's poem of translation, the vivid assertion is undercut in the act of being made: the likeness is unlike what it is a likeness of. In comparison to this, 'you and me'—not perhaps in fact so very like one another—come to seem alike, 'the likes of you and me', a community face to face with something that we cannot assimilate. We are asked to imagine a sound that we cannot imagine.

On one occasion, *War Music* swaps its usual guiding metaphor of 'zooming in on imagined sights and sounds' for something closer to translation rigidly conceived. It is another scene of grief, where Zeus entrusts to Apollo the body of his beloved son Sarpedon, asking him to 'clarify his wounds with mountain water', and anoint him, and carry him to Lycia:

> Where, playing stone chimes and tambourines,
> The Lycians will consecrate his death,
> Before whose memory the stones shall fade.[56]

In Homer, Zeus's orders are repeated exactly in the narrative of what happens next: Apollo does 'clarify his wounds with mountain water', does anoint him, and so on. Logue, here, translates nearly word for word for longer than anywhere else in his 'Accounts'. As it repeats Homer's repetition, the work relaxes from its usual endeavour to visualize and takes on the feel of a written text that is mediating another written text. It accepts a touch of archaism, in the construction 'his death, / Before whose'. It allows its words to join in a ritual of reiteration, so as to commemorate a life that has died. This tactic of translating so as to create an expressive deadness has been pursued further by other poet-translators, as we will see.

PART V

TRANSLATION AS 'LOSS', AS 'DEATH', AS 'RESURRECTION', AND AS 'METAMORPHOSIS'

23

Ezra Pound: 'My job was to bring a dead man to life'

'We murder to dissect', Wordsworth said of the analysis of nature in science and, more provocatively, 'Art'.[1] People have also murdered to translate. 'A good Poet'—Dryden wrote in the Preface to *Sylvae*— 'is no more like himself, in a dull translation, than his carcass would be to his living body'.[2] Dryden's hope for his own translations, as we saw in Chapter 14, was that they would make dead poets speak as if they had 'been born in *England*, and in this present Age'. The corresponding worry was that a botched rebirth would leave an author, not only as dead as he was already, but deader. Untranslated, the works of Virgil or Ovid would be closed to many English readers; but at least they would still be themselves in their own languages. Their spark could be felt by scholars; it could live on through allusion and influence in the work of poets expert in the classics such as Jonson or Milton or Dryden himself; and it would remain as a goad to possible future good translators, a store of energy with the potential to be re-activated in a new place and time and language. A bad translation wasted that potential. It murdered a work by represent-ing only those elements that tended to count as 'dead'—its narrative structure and the denotations of its words—without reacting to its poetry.

But to Madame Dacier it seemed that a 'carcass' was worth having. She felt something similar to the unease which (as again we saw in Chapter 14) was later to be voiced by Cowper. Since 'voice', 'life', and 'spirit' are difficult attributes to measure and compare, it is hard, perhaps impossible, to be sure that the voice or life or spirit you have embodied in your translation are more the source text's than your own. Opting to translate the *Iliad* into prose, Dacier turned away from key elements of what was thought of as poetic 'life', the sound and movement of verse. The result, she admitted, 'n'est pas Homere vivant & animé' ('is not the living, spirited Homer); 'mais c'est Homere' ('but it is Homer'):

on n'y trouvera pas cette force, cette grace, cette vie, ce charme qui ravit, &
ce feu qui échauffe tout ce qui l'approche, mais on y demeslera tous ses traits,
& la symmetrie admirable de toutes ses parties.[3]

[you will not find there that force, that grace, that life, that charm which
ravishes and that fire which heats everyone who approaches him; but you will
be able to make out his features and the admirable symmetry of all his parts.]

Startlingly, verse does not count as one of Homer's 'traits': the reason is
that, for Dacier, what is most him is not his 'expression' but his 'ideas',
his 'subject', and his 'characters'.[4] It is plain to see how this passage
stimulated Pope: to a degree of emulation, via the metaphor of 'taking a
view'; and to fierce disagreement, via the metaphor of 'passion'. As we
saw in Chapter 19, his verse translation aimed 'above all things to keep
alive that Spirit and Fire'—that is, to do what Madame Dacier had not
done.

When the metaphor of 'adherence' became dominant during the nineteenth century, translators generally committed themselves to achieving
the sort of equivalence that mattered to Madame Dacier: prose translations of verse multiplied and the field became littered —as Dryden would
see it—with carcasses. I explored some artistic consequences of this shift in
Chapter 21; one more was that the imaginative deadness now so strongly
associated with translation became interesting to poets.

An early, small example can be found in Byron's teenage volume *Hours
of Idleness, a Series of Poems, Original and Translated* (1807). The section
of original poems ends with 'Oscar of Alva', a ballad which recounts a
murder and a haunting. Next, a new title-page announces the crossover to
'Translations and Imitations', beginning with 'Adrian's Address to his
Soul, when Dying'. The Latin is given first:

> ANIMULA! vagula, blandula,
> Hospes, comesque, corporis,
> Quae nunc abibis in loca?
> Pallidula, rigida, nudula,
> Nec, ut soles, dabis jocos.

Then, over the page, Byron's English:

> AH! gentle, fleeting, wav'ring sprite,
> Friend and associate of this clay!
>   To what unknown region borne,
> Wilt thou, now, wing thy distant flight?
> No more, with wonted humour gay,
>   But pallid, cheerless, and forlorn.[5]

Whatever may have happened to the actual 'sprite' of Adrian (i.e. the Emperor Hadrian), the spirit of his 'Address' has winged its flight an unforeseen distance into English translation where—the self-referential implication flickers—it cannot but be pallid, cheerless, and forlorn. The sequential arrangement of the texts allows readers to see the transformation happen: Hadrian's plain 'loca' ('place') deliquescing, as it finds its new English co-ordinates over the page, into Byron's numinous 'unknown region'; Hadrian ending on 'jocos' ('joke'), Byron ending on 'forlorn'. The tough, light humour of the Latin subsides into early Byronic plangency. Since it is placed as a hinge between Byron's own 'Poems, Original' and 'Poems...Translated', this layering of Hadrian's original poem and Byron's version suggests a broader feeling about the comparative pallor and cheerlessness of translation. The young Byron holds to the eighteenth-century conception of translation of the 'spirit'; but the spirit which comes across is shown to be sadly changed from what it was.

Many of the translations collected in *Hours of Idleness* have to do with death: there is 'The Episode of Nisus and Euryalus' from *Aeneid* 9 (earlier and famously translated by Dryden—see above, Chapters 12 and 15); there is Domitius Marsus's epitaph on Virgil and Tibullus, and the sad demise of Lesbia's sparrow, and the 'temporary death' which afflicts the lover at the end of Catullus's 'Ad Lesbiam' (a version of the lyric by Sappho which I discussed in Chapters 16 and 17). Byron revels in the afflictions felt by Catullus's and Sappho's speaker while the youth and Lesbia chat so unconcernedly: he invents 'cold dews', 'deadly languour', and the heady thought that (with an echo of his Hadrian) 'life itself is on the wing'. Lesbia's sparrow too is sent to a considerably elaborated end, in a 'devouring grave', 'receptacle of life's decay'.[6] These scenes of demise, when they are re-done in the posthumous medium of translation, give rise, paradoxically, to invention—the reason being that, as we saw in Chapter 18, Byron (or a part of him) feels forlornness to be a very poetical state, and death to be an occasion for the lively expression of feeling. It took Browning, half a century later, to find expressive possibilities in a style of translation that actually feels dead. In the transcript of *Herakles* within *Aristophanes' Apology* (1875), flat word-for-wordism suggests a stunned response to the horrors that are enacted:

> Alas for me! these children, see,
> Stretched, hapless group, before their father—he
> The all-unhappy, who lies sleeping out
> The murder of his sons, a dreadful sleep![7]

And then there is the rebarbative materiality of his *Agamemnon of Aeschylus* which I described in Chapter 5. In *The Ring and the Book* (as we saw in Chapter 21) Browning's conviction that 'the life in me' had abolished 'the death of things' releases an imaginative flight across the Italian landscape as the book in his hand takes on life in his imagination. But Browning also wants to represent the dead letters that are being shucked off during that transformation. In the poem's first chapter, this is done with a snatch of—as he says—'word for word' translation from the title page of the book that is inspiring him:

> Wherein it is disputed if, and when,
> Husbands may kill adulterous wives, yet scape
> The customary forfeit.[8]

The implications folded into this act of translation are complex. First, since it focuses on literal meanings, close translation attaches itself to those 'things' which it is Browning's quest to pass beyond. So, here, the dogged style of word-for-wording grafts itself onto the finickiness of legal discourse. Faced with a human tragedy, the lawyers in the story see nothing moral, nor spiritual, but only an opportunity for dispute according to the letter of the law; and the passage of translation reproduces their line quiescently: it embodies 'the death of things'. Yet, by doing that, it starts a process of interpretive protest, almost of revulsion, which balloons into reimagining. Nevertheless (a further cross-current of suggestion) it continues to function as a kind of tether for the poem's predominant fictionality, a point of contact with the historical record. Browning's commitment to the redemptive power of imagination requires him to believe that something real is being redeemed in the retelling. And so his narrator maintains that the story he offers is not mere fantasy, but an alloy of 'fancy' with 'facts'.[9]

It turns out that this passage is the only instance of actual close translation in *The Ring and the Book*. But what does sometimes appear, as Browning gives himself over to creating voices for the various characters in the drama, is a kind of writing that sounds like word-for-word translation because it calques Italian or Latin constructions into English. The most startling example occurs when 'Tertium Quid', an everyman character known only by that Latin appellation, addresses a cardinal:

> Highness, decide! Pronounce, Her Excellency![10]

'Her' is a more-than-literal translation of the Italian formal pronoun 'Sua', which is feminine so as to agree with the noun 'Eccellenza' (I say 'more-than-literal' because there is no literal counterpart for this grammatical inflexion in English so Browning has to invent one). At the moment when the Cardinal is invited to 'pronounce'—to judge as to the rights and wrongs of the story Tertium Quid has told—readers are made aware that Tertium Quid's own voice, veering between Italian and English, is utterly unpronounceable. We need to imagine a voice if the poetry is to come alive for us; and perhaps in the lines running up to this point we have felt able to do so. But here Tertium Quid falls dead on the page.

The Ring and the Book is a laboratory for investigating both the possibility of imagining voices from the past and the dangers—of appropriation, delusion, and simple failure—by which that enterprise is dogged. At times, as with the wise Pope Innocent or the heroic Caponsacchi, Browning conjures up for his characters what feels like a hearable voice. But elsewhere in the work, the materiality of the foreign languages and the past culture reassert themselves so as to challenge and perhaps destroy our confidence in being able to understand them. The work worries massively at a paradox similar to that which we explored in Part II: the past needs to be imagined if it is to be understood; and yet if it is imagined it is no longer itself. Failures of imaginative resurrection must therefore be recognized no less than successes. The language of *The Ring and the Book* represents what can, and just as importantly what cannot, be brought to imaginative life out of the past.[11]

As I showed in Chapter 21, Browning's writing in and around translation mattered to Pound. Part of what grew in him out of Browning's example was an interest in linguistic deadness. That translation from Andreas Divus's translation of the *Odyssey* which begins the *Cantos* concluded, in an early version, with this: 'Lie quiet Divus, plucked from a Paris stall'.[12] The thought is itself plucked from Browning, who had likewise plucked his source for *The Ring and the Book* from a 'Stall', though in a different, vividly-imagined European city: Florence. In Pound, the voice of Tiresias's shade, summoned by Odysseus, does not come quite fully over into the language of the living, any more than, in Browning, Tertium Quid's had quite fully settled into English:

> "Odysseus
> "Shalt return through spiteful Neptune, over dark seas,
> "Lose all companions."[13]

It would need a pronoun and a little bit more syntax to become a fully articulated English sentence. Pound here picks out phrases from the Latin—Neptune is 'iratus'; 'nigrum pontum' comes a few lines later; 'perdens omnes socios' is over the page—and sticks them together into an utterance which feels interrupted: it suggests, perhaps, the elliptical quality of prophecy, or perhaps the halting utterance of the 'impetuous impotent dead' (as Odysseus calls them); perhaps both.[14] But this interpretation is complicated by the fact that Pound's Odysseus, himself of course alive in the world of the Odyssey, does not speak fully living English either. The accoutrements for his prayer, he says, were:

> As set in Ithaca, sterile bulls of the best
> For sacrifice, heaping the pyre with goods
> A sheep to Tiresias only, black and a bell-sheep.[15]

This keeps continuously close to the Latin: 'profectus in Ithacam sterilem bovem, quae optima esset', and so on.[16] But it is hardly less elliptical and strange than Tiresias's speech. Pound's version of 'The Seafarer: From the Anglo-Saxon' (1912) is commonly said to be a precedent for Canto I, and so it is.[17] But the voice of that earlier poem of translation had, thanks to its alliterative pulse, seemed unequivocally vigorous, as though it were punching through the history of the language. The translation from Divus's translation of Homer is more uneven, and more searching. It is certainly 'alive' in the loose sense of 'compelling'; but what makes it so is its recognition of the difficulties of translation that come between us and Homer's Odysseus, its refusal to pretend that we can abolish 'the death of things'.

This stylistic deadness, created through translation, is at odds with many of Pound's recorded pronouncements. There is his protest, which I discussed in Chapter 7, that Browning in his *Agamemnon of Aeschylus* should have written for Klutaimnestra 'anything, literally anything that can be shouted . . . Anything but a stilted unsayable jargon'. And there are his mission statements for his own translations from Cavalcanti—'to present the vivid personality of Guido Cavalcanti'—and from Propertius: 'my job was to bring a dead man to life, to present a living figure'.[18] As we will see, in his early endeavours to translate the lyrics of Cavalcanti, Pound tried out different tactics for presenting 'a vivid personality'. He came up against a paradox: that it is impossible to achieve vividness without a deadening happening in some other respect. His great poems of translation—in *Cathay* (1915) and *Homage to Sextus Propertius* (1919)—draw energy from the conflict between an explicit metaphor 'translation as bringing to life' and an implicit metaphor by which it is haunted: 'translation as deadening'. Just as with Dryden, the push to achieve life and presence brings with it an awareness of death and loss. But, for Pound, as for Browning, the airs of deadness and of absence which can hang around translation became, not difficulties to be overcome, but possibilities to be activated and explored.

Than Cavalcanti, Pound tells us in the 'Introduction' to his 1912 *Sonnets and Ballate*, 'no psychologist of the emotions is more keen in his understanding, more precise in his expression; we have in him no rhetoric, but always a true delineation'. A translator who wishes to 'present' his 'vivid personality' should therefore work with similar precision, adopting (as Pound went on to explain in a letter to the *TLS*) a 'scholastic method' and 'setting forth' Cavalcanti's 'exact meaning'. This, Pound says, is how his own versions differ from those put out by Dante Gabriel Rossetti in *The Early Italian Poets* (1861): 'he was as avowedly intent on making beautiful verses as I am on presenting an individual'.[19] For instance, Cavalcanti's line 'Ch'a lei s'inchina ogni gentil virtute' means:

> that "she" acts as a magnet for every "*gentil virtute*," that is, the noble spiritual powers, the invigorating forces of life and beauty bend towards her; not [as Rossetti had translated]
> To whom are subject all *things* virtuous.
> The *inchina* implies not the homage of an object but the direction of a force.[20]

Rossetti had too much adapted the verse to modern assumptions, and so had lost the edge of Cavalcanti's individuality.

Not only the key words in that line, but much else in medieval Italian vocabulary—the medium of Cavalcanti's thought—required clarification:

> *Gentile* is 'noble;' 'gentleness in our current sense would be *soavitate*. ... The *spiriti* are the 'senses,' or the 'intelligence of the senses,' perhaps even 'the moods,' when they are considered as 'spirits of the mind.' *Valore* is 'power.' *Virtute*, 'virtue, potency', requires a separate treatise.[21]

Just occasionally—Pound thinks—Cavalcanti's meaning leaps across so as to become present in an English word: '*Valore* is "power."' But more often there is a yawning non-correspondence:

> It is conceivable the poetry of a far-off time or place requires a translation not only of word and of spirit but of 'accompaniment,' that is, that the modern audience must in some measure be made aware of the mental content of the older audience, and of what these others drew from certain fashions of thought and speech. Six centuries of derivative convention and loose usage have obscured the exact significance of such phrases as: 'The death of the heart,' and 'The departure of the soul.'[22]

Those apparently translated phrases are in fact offered as stand-ins for what they have failed to translate. They are readily understandable; but what a reader understands from them is far different from what was meant by their medieval Italian counterparts. Pound is faced with a paradox: to 'present' Cavalcanti means making clear how un-present he actually is. The metaphor of 'presenting a vivid personality' is implicitly shadowed by countervailing metaphors of failure and decay, of something more like exhumation than resurrection. This apprehension comes through, perhaps, in the phrases Pound chooses as examples: 'the death of the heart', 'the departure of the soul'. Cavalcanti's heart, too, may be dead; his soul, no less than Hadrian's, irrevocably departed.

The short-circuit between achieving presence and recognizing absence brings Pound up against those uncertainties which translation theory (as we saw in Chapter 5) usually frames in terms of 'domestication' versus 'foreignization', or 'dynamic' versus 'formal' equivalence. Should one write something understandable (i.e. present to the reader) but misrepresentative?—or something better representative which risks being misunderstood? The forking possibilities goaded Pound to produce multiple versions of one of Cavalcanti's sonnets. 'Chi è questa che vien' ('Who is she that comes') describes the impossibility of describing a particular woman:

> Chi è questa che vien, ch'ogni uom la mira,
> Che fa di clarità l'aer tremare!
> E mena seco Amor, sì che parlare
> Null'uom ne puote, ma ciascun sospira?

Who is she coming, whom all gaze upon, / Who makes the whole air tremulous with light, / And leadeth with her Love, so no man hath / Power of speech, but each one sigheth? (Pound's 1910 translation).[23]

The sonnet has some affinities with Sappho's Fragment 31, whose translation by Catullus was translated by Byron, and whose own fortunes in English I discussed in Chapters 16 and 17. The beloved cannot be described because she provokes inarticulacy in her admirers; so the inarticulacy itself must do as an indication of her excellence. In the Sappho, the beloved's power is suggested by her disruptive effect on the lover's body. But in Cavalcanti it provokes an intellectual response, a series of definitions of her undefinability. This push towards 'true delineation', is what excites Pound:

> Non si potria contar la sua piacenza,
> Ch'a lei s'inchina ogni gentil virtute,
> E la beltate per sua Dea la mostra.[24]

The middle line is the one that detained Pound in his introduction; and 'piacenza', 'beltate', Dea', and 'mostra' might well have been added to his list of difficult words. Here is his first full stab at a translation, from 1910:

> Her charm could never be a thing to tell
> For all the noble powers lean toward her.
> Beauty displays her for an holy sign.*

* "*E la beltate per sua Dea la mostra.*" The metaphysics of this line requires a separate treatise.

The despair implied by the note is amply illustrated in a preliminary draft where there are five different attempts at the line:

> Beauty hath founded her[e?] our cult of Her / Beauty disp[layeth] in her [...] div[inity?] / Beauty shows her for an holy sign / Beauty's godhead is in her displayed / And beauty shows her for her /i.e. beauty's Dea / Goddess.[25]

Selecting 'displays' and 'sign' from this menu, Pound gives a technical feel to his line, and so marks it off from emotional English analogues such as (say) Byron's 'She walks in beauty like the night'. The line, then, is readily grasped even though it feels unusual as a line of poetry—clearer, more straightforward, and therefore (Pound might like to think) so much the more like Cavalcanti. But 'signs' and 'displays' are commonly found outside pubs or in department stores: their conjunction creates an aroma of commerce which Pound's deployment of the adjective 'holy' cannot quite dispel. It may be that, if he noticed the incongruity, Pound would have thought that it might energize readers by making them realize that they are meant to shut it out. The translation was designed to be printed—as Pound's books of Cavalcanti translations always were—in parallel text; and since Italian is semi-comprehensible to most literate English people, the implied reader could look across at the Italian, see the word Dea, realize that it means 'goddess', and then take 'sign' as pointing to a functional, non-misty sense of 'Dea' which might otherwise be missed. Used like this, the translation calibrates the Italian, and is in turn calibrated against it—rather than being read in its place. Readers are to think their way out of 'loose usage' and towards what might be the 'exact significance' of the phrase, to drive their 'perceptions further into the original' than they would otherwise have penetrated (that was the hope Pound expressed for his later translation of Cavalcanti's canzone 'Donna mi prega').[26]

Still, Pound was not wholly satisfied with this translation. In a collection of mainly original poems, *Provença* (1910), he printed a looser version:

> Say, is it Love, that was divinity,
> Who hath left his godhead that his home might be
> The shameless rose of her unclouded heart?[27]

This adopts the 'derivative conventions' of Edwardian verse so as to pass as a poem that could be read without parallel text. But something of the strangeness Pound relishes in Cavalcanti remains, and struggles against the vesture that is here pulled over it. The talk of Love making his 'home' in the woman's heart domesticates Cavalcanti's idea, bringing it too 'home' into bourgeois English preconceptions. But once it appears to have settled down there it starts, or tries to start, a revolution: the word 'shameless' in English has always meant 'without shame', or 'wanton'; but here in Pound's Englishing of Italian it must be meant to mean 'without cause for shame', that is, 'pure'. Cavalcanti's poem asks a question about the woman: 'Chi è questa...?' Pound's poem asks a question about Cavalcanti's poem and the conception of Love which it expresses: is this really love, this state which causes no shame and which, though passionate, is intellectually clear, 'unclouded' by emotionality? What relation does it bear to what is usually meant by 'love' in modern English poetry and culture? Cavalcanti's own bafflement before the woman turns into the imagined bafflement of English culture before Cavalcanti.

When Pound at last published his parallel-text translation of the poem, in *Sonnets and Ballate of Guido Cavalcanti* (1912), he appears to have lost confidence in the provocative power of 'display' and 'sign': he replaced them with one of the more obviously poetical words chosen for the *Provença* version, 'godhead':

> No one could ever tell the charm she hath
> For all the noble powers bend toward her,
> She being beauty's godhead manifest.[28]

'Charm' is carried over from the draft and retains a tart immediacy which works rather in the way 'displays' and 'sign' had done before: Donald Davie, for instance, is shocked by its 'commercialized vulgarity'.[29] But 'godhead', especially in conjunction with 'manifest', is squarely in the idiom of Victorian religiosity: the words appeared side by side in verses by Bishop Christopher Wordsworth printed in *Hymns Ancient and Modern*, and in *The Altar* by the Tractarian Isaac Williams; and they were predictably paganized by Swinburne.[30] In conjunction with the clotted syntax of 'She being', the phrase is certainly dignified, and philosophical; but it suggests nothing of Cavalcanti's strenuous clarity.

So, when he returned to the poem in the late 1920s, Pound tried a startlingly different tactic:

> No one could ever tell all of her plesauntness
> In that every high noble vertu leaneth to herward,
> So Beauty sheweth her forth as her Godhede.[31]

One difference from the 1912 version is—as Davie has pointed out—the metrically free (though rhyming) verse, usually with feminine endings, which replaces the earlier pentameters and better suggests the fluid movement of Cavalcanti's lines. Another is syntactic: 'Beauty' here is made energetic again, put in charge of an active verb as she had been back in 1910 with 'Beauty displays her'. But the consequent push to immediacy is somewhat dissipated by the third big change: the more archaic vocabulary. To Davie, it seems that this 'much heavier archaism' is not employed 'for the sake of loftiness and ornateness'; 'on the contrary, it serves to cleave more closely to the sense as Pound perceives it' (Davie's own archaism, 'cleave', reveals his sympathy with Pound's endeavour). For instance—he goes on—'it is the archaism "to herward" that permits a precision, a hard definiteness of meaning',—for it captures the nuance Pound felt Rossetti had lost, that '*inchina* implies... the direction of a force'.[32] But it has to be admitted that the archaism creates indefiniteness too. Pound said that he hoped, with this diction, to 'reach back to pre-Elizabethan English, of a period when the writers were still intent on clarity and explicitness, still preferring them to magniloquence and the thundering phrase'.[33] But to most modern readers, all that will be explicit about words such as 'pleasauntness' and 'vertu' is that they must mean something other than 'pleasantness' and 'virtue'. All the same, they do open a space in which those other meanings can perhaps achieve some definition. Lawrence Venuti goes so far as to claim that 'Pound's pre-Elizabethan English could do no more than signify the remoteness of Cavalcanti's poetry'; but this loses sight of the work of interpreting and imagining-in which is nevertheless accomplished in the text and held out to its readers.[34] Pound's endeavour to 'present' the 'vivid personality' of Cavalcanti is challenged by the poem-translation's simultaneous recognition of his pastness; but not wholly done away by it.

Pound's turn to archaism in this last version of 'Chi è questa' owes something to the 'Wardour Street English' typical of Victorian translations from the classics (shops in Wardour Street sold antique and reproduction furniture). F. W. Newman, for instance, aimed, in his translation of the *Iliad*, to give his language 'a plausible aspect of moderate antiquity' so as 'to break off mental association with the poetry later than Dryden'.[35] But Pound's practice has a more specific aim: as we have seen, it was the latest in a succession of dictional efforts to 'present' the qualities of the source. This expressive probing of the history of the language harmonizes with the metaphors of 'presenting an individual' and 'bringing to life' much more than with the visual metaphors which we explored in Part IV. When time is conceived as a landscape, translators can think of themselves as walking over it, or flying above. What they are moving towards or away from is, not so much an author or a text, as the events and characters described. A feeling of distance from those events tends to be expressed, not through archaism, but through abstraction, whether moral—as in Pope's 'Love, Duty, Safety, summon us away'—or geographical, as with Logue's 'picture the east Aegean sea by night'.[36] Closeness comes through visual detail (Logue: 'Observe his muscles as they move beneath his skin').[37] Pope, in his Preface, announces his tolerance of 'some *Graecisms* and old Words', and his eschewal of '*modern Terms of War* and *Government*';[38] but his idiom in the poem is not at odds with that of contemporary poetry; and the same is true of Logue's idiom in *War Music*: it is not clouded with historical depth but clear like a lens which keeps in focus as it zooms in, here on a Homeric event, there on a modern point of reference. The style of Logue's poem-translation owes much to Pound in his imagist phase, with his advocacy of 'direct treatment of the "thing"', his idea that 'an "Image" is that which presents an intellectual and emotional complex in an instant of time'.[39] But when Pound was translating Cavalcanti, what was to be made 'present' was a 'personality': a style of thought and corresponding way with language. Pound's words were matched, not against a 'thing' but against other, distant words whose distinctiveness could not be made present without loss. Of all the Cavalcanti sonnets, 'Chi è questa' is the one that most holds and troubles Pound's attention for the reason that becomes all-but explicit in the *Provença* version: it offers him a double of translation. Pound's perplexity before Cavalcanti is like Cavalcanti's before his beloved. And so the poetry of translation sparks.

   Pound justified the dictional strangenesses of his translations from Cavalcanti by calling them 'interpretive': they are designed to guide a reader towards the 'treasure' of the source, by contrast with that '"other sort"' of writing in which 'the "translator" is definitely making a new poem'.[40] In this, they do indeed differ from the freer, apprentice-style versions from Provençal that had preceded them, texts such as 'Sestina: Altaforte' and 'Planh for the Young English King'. But Pound's mature writing in the vein of 'definitely making a new poem' is no less alert than his work on Cavalcanti to the losses that happen in translation and the deadness that can afflict it. *Cathay* (1915)—poems made from Ernest Fenollosa's word-for-ideogram transcripts of classical Chinese—was welcomed by Pound's associate Ford Madox Hueffer (i.e. Ford Madox Ford) as an epitome of the imagist art, of the view that 'poetry consists in so rendering concrete objects that the emotions produced by the objects shall arise in the reader': the comment was repeated with approval by T. S. Eliot.[41] And it is true that *Cathay* does not play with verbal textures in manner of the Cavalcanti translations. There is nothing like the dubious gleam of 'charm' or the puzzling antiquity of 'plesauntness': the words, for the most part, are plain. But there is strangeness in how the words are combined; and the result is that they do not always treat objects directly, nor make emotions present, in the way the Ford-Eliot description implies. Take, for instance, a famous opening line:

Blue, blue is the grass about the river[42]

We are presented with the river and some grass. But: 'blue'? Is this the blue of dusk? Or does it show that the Chinese colour spectrum is divided differently from the English? (Other translations say the grass is 'green'.)[43] Or is it rather because the person represented in the poem is miserable, 'blue' in that figurative sense which, according to the *OED*, goes back at least to the Renaissance? Because it is figurative, this last possibility feels specifically English: a reader is likely to think 'surely the Chinese cannot have that meaning of "blue"—I'd better shut it out'. But, just as with the cheapened connotations of 'display', 'sign', and 'charm' in the Cavalcanti translations, the need to shut a meaning out becomes part of what is created by the poem. The interference produces an awareness that what we mean by blue is somewhat at odds with what must have been meant in the Chinese poem.

Similar fade-outs of understanding happen repeatedly. There are recurrent Chinese place-names ('Jō-rin', 'Ku-tō-en') which must be off most readers' maps. And then there are cultural references which are similarly unplaceable. The speaker of 'Exile's Letter' is sent away to 'South Wai, / smothered in laurel groves', which means: what?—a specially poetic place, if it is smothered in laurels?—or specially sumptuous?—or specially gloomy? 'The City of Chōan' begins: 'The phoenix are at play on their terrace', a statement whose implications are again impossible to gauge. To 'The Jewel Stairs' Grievance' Pound appends an explanatory note: 'Jewel stairs, therefore a palace. ... Gauze stockings, therefore a court lady'— and so on.[44] This makes obvious how much is left unexplained in the other poems.

The puzzling bits in *Cathay* oscillate with lines which do feel readily comprehensible: 'We go slowly, we are hungry and thirsty'; 'I desired my dust to be mingled with yours'.[45] But such expressions do not present an object in order to provoke its concomitant emotion: they tell us what the emotion is. Reading, then, we are moved in and out of feeling that we know what is going on. An appeal for sympathy leaps across at us only then to be obstructed by some incomprehensible particularity in the foreign culture. This happens in a verbal medium arranged into decorous patterns of repetition which imply, as Hugh Kenner has put it, 'syllable by syllable, with cunning governance of pace, an alien poetic'.[46] T. S. Eliot said that through Pound's translation 'we believe...we really at last get the original',[47] and it is true that, in both form and tone, the poems in *Cathay* are closer to their sources than all earlier, and indeed most subsequent versions: Wai-lim Yip goes so far as to ascribe to Pound 'a kind of clairvoyance'.[48] Nevertheless, the poems also include an awareness of what has been lost from their texture; of how much we cannot 'really . . . get'. Hueffer sidelines the poems' translatedness in the opposite way: 'the poems in *Cathay* are things of a supreme beauty. What poetry should be, that they are'.[49] Kenner, too, despite his sensitivity to the book's 'alien poetic', insists that 'its real achievement lay not on the frontier of comparative poetics, but securely within the effort, then going forward in London, to rethink the nature of an English poem'.[50] Both these claims reveal the assumption I have been combating throughout this book: that to admit a poem is also worth thinking about as a translation is to imply that it is something less than a poem, a 'mere' translation. Desiring (and rightly) to praise the work, Kenner feels he has to say that it is 'securely within' Englishness. The poems in *Cathay* differ from the translations of Cavalcanti in that they do not ask to be calibrated against the Chinese (which Pound in any case did not understand), nor against the Fenollosa cribs he worked from. Nevertheless, they ask us not to forget that they are mediating foreign texts, that they are poems of translation, as alert to what cannot, as well as to what can, be understood in the Chinese writing.[51]

As we have come to expect, the contradictory metaphors that are at work in the texture of the writing—of 'translation as presenting' and 'translation as loss'—find doubles in the scenes that are being written about. Repeatedly, the speakers of the poems wonder what will be made of them and their circumstances: 'who will know of our grief?' 'how shall you know the dreary sorrow at the North Gate', 'Who will be sorry for General Rishōgun . . . ?' Times of togetherness and of easy communication are remembered: 'At fourteen I married My Lord you'; 'And she was a courtezan in the old days'; 'we all spoke out our hearts and minds'. But in the moment of the poems' utterance, all this has gone by; separation has intervened, or is about to: 'At sixteen you departed'; 'And she has married a sot, / Who now goes drunkenly out'; 'Our horses neigh to each other / as we are departing'.[52] According to one scholar, 'examination of Fenollosa's notebooks in relation to Pound's "translations" reveals that the Chinese poems Pound selected for *Cathay* were mostly the ones which present sorrowful or lonely figures who speak out as if to overcome their sorrow or loneliness'; she suggests that the choice 'may reflect Pound's own state of mind'.[53] Another concurs with the observation but not the explanation, proposing instead that Pound selected poems to suit his Imagist preferences—even though a few pages later she self-contradictorily admits that it was the nature poems in the Fenollosa manuscripts which most 'closely coincided with Pound's own theory of the Image', and that they were utterly ignored by him.[54] Another points to the 'fundamental importance of gender issues'.[55] The most compelling idea remains Hugh

Kenner's—that the war exerted a pressure on Pound's selection, which
was done

> by a sensibility responsive to torn Belgium and disrupted London; and as
> 'The Jewel Stairs' Grievance' is 'especially prized because she offers no direct
> reproach,' so *Cathay* essays an oriental obliquity of reference to what we are
> to understand as its true theme. . . . The *Cathay* poems paraphrase an elegiac
> war poetry nobody wrote.[56]

But there is another factor. The *Cathay* poem-translations are elegiac
also for their own existence as poems in a culture where they stood a
chance of being fully felt and understood. As with Browning's *Herakles*, it
is this attenuation in their own being which makes them such compelling
responses to the catastrophe that was going on around them. The singer of
'The River Song' knows something of great beauty: 'the gardens at Jō-rin
are full of new nightingales'. His poem ends with a claim:

> Their sound is mixed in this flute,
> Their voice is in the twelve pipes here.[57]

But their voice is not in the words that have been given to English readers.
In her 'Letter', the 'River-Merchant's Wife' imagines a meeting:

> If you are coming down through the narrows of the river Kiang,
> Please let me know beforehand,
> And I will come out to meet you
>   As far as Chō-fū-Sa.[58]

But how far is that? A mad, romantic distance? Or the modest distance
suitable for a decorous wife to travel? Or might it be a practical distance, as
far as can be gone in daylight? English readers cannot come to meet the
poem fully, cannot grasp its point. 'Exile's Letter' recounts a life of
intensely lived companionship:

> And I, wrapped in brocade, went to sleep with my head on his lap,
> And my spirit so high it was all over the heavens.

A life, also, of intermittent separations 'till we had nothing but thoughts
and memories in common'; of travel through a sharply felt landscape,
'roads twisted like sheep's guts', of new pleasures—'eyebrows painted
green are a fine sight in young moonlight'—and new disappointment:
'I went up to the court . . . / And got no promotion'. When all this is listed
in a letter, its presence is evoked and, simultaneously, its passing mourned.
The talking that was so vividly experienced ('we all spoke out our hearts
and minds') has given way to the figurative 'talking' of words on paper:

> What is the use of talking, and there is no end of talking

Talking with the voice is no use because it does not endure; 'talking' with the pen is no use because it cannot bring back the voice. There is no end of talking because there is always more to talk about; and because the voice-talking that has happened is remembered; and because the pen-talking will never achieve presence:

> There is no end of things in the heart.
> I call in the boy,
> Have him sit on his knees here
>   To seal this,
> And send it a thousand miles, thinking.[59]

The 'boy' cannot know what is meant and felt in the letter that he seals but does not read, for he has not yet lived the sort of 'thing' it describes. And how sealed is the Chinese poem to what can be made of it in English, by Pound, or by a reader faced with these English words? Throughout *Cathay*, pronouns are deployed with circumspection: 'we', 'you', 'I', 'here', 'this'. The sequence begins with words, 'Here we are', which establish characters unknown to us in a place where the English reader definitely is not.[60] Sealing 'this', 'here', so as to 'send' it and avert the 'end', the writer of the letter leaves readers wondering how much of what is in his heart can come into theirs through the words of his letter as they have been represented in Rihaku's poem, and then travelled more than a thousand miles to reach Pound, via Fenollosa's crib and 'the decipherings of Professors Mori and Ariga', and been worked over by him into a poem of translation. 'Thinking' (that ambiguously poised last word) no doubt happens all along the line; but what the thinking is, exactly, gets sealed from one stage to the next.

Pound's own next stage in the poetry of translation, *Homage to Sextus Propertius* (1919), ends with a similar glance forward to an uncertain future of interpretation. Imagining that his verse will 'triumph among young ladies of indeterminate character', the speaker lists poets from the previous generation who had sung of women they loved: Varro who had sung of Leucadia (this is Publius Terentius Varro Atacinus, incidentally, not Varro the great scholar and historian), Catullus of Lesbia, Calvus of Quintilia, Gallus of Lycoris:

> And now Propertius of Cynthia, taking his stand among these.[61]

In the Latin from which this comes, Propertius is establishing a genealogy for his own work, at least partly—as Francis Cairns has shown—so as to claim for himself 'the principal elegiac role' in the circle of Maecenas, the great patron of the arts under Augustus.[62] Pound was (barring the lavish patronage) animated by something of the same desire. Propertius, he said in a letter 'began to touch words somewhat as Laforgue did': translating him, Pound takes his own stand among those who can 'touch' words—i.e. pose them ironically so as to release a skittering of nuance and innuendo.[63] 'Logopoeia', he called it, with his ad-man's facility in branding.[64] T.S. Eliot, too, was implicitly of the company as he was much influenced by Laforgue. Yet, since the translation is reiterating words from two millennia earlier, the other aspect of Propertius's claim—not only whom he will be ranked with but for how long he will be known—is brought to the fore. Pound's word 'now' brings to mind its difference from the old 'now' in which Propertius had written. From the point of view of the early twentieth century, to stand next to Catullus is quite something; but to be like Varro or Calvus or Gallus—whose works are all lost—is a good deal less impressive.

Not only in its last line, but also from its first, *Homage to Sextus Propertius* worries at the possibility and modes of literary immortality, and therefore also at the ways in which it might and might not be possible to 'bring a dead man to life, to present a living figure'. The poem begins:

> Shades of Callimachus, Coan ghosts of Philetas,
> It is in your grove I would walk, . . .

> Callimachi Manes et Coi sacra Philetae,
>   in vestrum, quaeso, me sinite ire nemus.[65]

Propertius's 'manes' means 'spirits'; his 'sacra' has much exercised scholars but must mean something like 'the sacred rites by which the poet, as a sort of priest, perpetuates an imaginative tradition'.[66] Pound's 'ghosts' and 'shades' nudge a little further into the open a question which is already implicit in the Latin. What is it that is perpetuated in literary recollection? Is it a 'ghost'? Or is it rather a 'shade'?—a word which, although long standard in translations from the classics as the term for whatever it is that persists in the pagan underworld, is still a touch weaker than 'ghost', and especially so when it appears in conjunction with 'grove' since trees cast 'shade' in an everyday, unspiritual sort of way. (The distinction casts its own shade towards Michael Longley's 'shadow or idea' in one of his lyrics from the *Odyssey* which I discussed above, Chapter 21.) And the plural, 'shades', which is already there in the Latin, layers the issue further. If Callimachus leaves, not 'a shade', but 'shades', then his afterlife will be, not the continuance of an identity, but a proliferation of modes of being, of 'shades of character'—as it was possible to say in Pound's English just as it is now. A few lines later, at the end of his first lyric, Pound's Propertius compares the immortality of literary writing with the bids for remembrance made by the rich and grand, 'expensive pyramids scraping the stars', or 'the monumental effigies of Mausolus'. They are all vulnerable:

> Flame burns, rain sinks into the cracks
> And they all go to rack ruin beneath the thud of the years.
> Stands genius a deathless adornment,
>   a name not to be worn out with the years.

> aut illis flamma aut imber subducet honores,
>   annorum aut ictu pondere victa ruent.
> at non ingenio quaesitum nomen ab aevo
>   excidet: ingenio stat sine morte decus.[67]

Broadly speaking, this is a familiar thought; and in the Latin it appears to have been given a vigorous shine. Propertius's word 'quaesitum' ('obtained', 'won') echoes his request, 'quaeso', from right at the beginning of the lines Pound has translated: he has, it now seems, won full entry to the grove of Callimachus and Philetas, and the result is a confident claim to immortality. Paolo Fedeli notes that, with an echo of Pindar, and the repetition of 'ingenio', this is Propertius's strongest assertion of his own genius ('il più alto elogio del proprio *ingenium*').[68] But look what becomes of it in Pound's translation. Propertius's last word 'decus' ('honour, glory') subsides into 'adornment', a word which sounds odd in conjunction with 'deathless' and so gives a bathetic wobble to a line which seems at its outset to want to be resounding. The repetition of 'ingenio' has given way to a repetition of 'years'; and now it is 'years', not 'decus' that is the last word. The identical rhyme, of 'years' with 'years', creates another counter-current of uncertainty: it is asserted that the name of genius is what survives but it looks as though the years, repeating and enduring, are not to be so easily overcome. Here, just as with the echo of this moment in the *Homage*'s last line ('. . . taking his stand among these'), the fact of the translation bears out the claim made by Propertius's Latin: his name and his words have indeed not perished with time. But the manner of the translation pulls in the opposite direction. Is this really life, really the dead poet's spirit made fully present once more, these 'shades' of Propertius which Pound is summoning up for us? Just as with the soul-summoning that opens the *Cantos*, the loss of tone and meaning is as visible as their continuance. Pound translates so as to show the cracks that the rain has widened also in the monument of verse.

A concern with survival after death is already there in Propertius's Latin. But, as Michael Comber has pointed out, it is greatly focused, not only by Pound's style of translation, but by the lyrics he selected to translate. All are from the second and third of Propertius's four books of elegies, and 'almost all . . . are in some way life/death pieces with the conflict now being played out on the stage of language'.[69] Beyond the figurative life of literary reputation, there is the possibility of dying for love in III and V; in VI a necrophiliac fantasy (from the point of view of the dead person) of 'moving naked over Acheron' while Cynthia places 'the last kiss' on the lips of his corpse; and, in VIII, Cynthia's grave illness which looks likely to result in an 'ornamental death'.[70] As the flicker of similarity between that phrase and the 'deathless adornment' of his own genius suggests, Pound's Propertius traces filaments of connection between the different kinds of demise. When Cynthia seems likely to die, the weather takes on a grimly orgasmic aspect:

> The time is come, the air heaves in torridity,
> The dry earth pants against the canicular heat.[71]

The giving-way that happens in writing, at least in the sort of writing done by Pound's Propertius, is no less sensual (though rather more fun): he touches words alluringly, in a teasingly cross-gendered sort of way. 'My genius is no more than a girl', he says, and: 'this soft book comes into my mouth', where the English suggests an innuendo which appears not to be in the Latin 'meus veniat mollis in ora liber' (at least not according to the *Oxford Latin Dictionary*).[72] Reading too has a sexual frisson:

> And in the meantime my songs will travel,
> And the devirginated young ladies will enjoy them
>   when they have got over the strangeness.
>
> gaudeat in solito tacta puella sono.[73]

The standard prose version of Pound's time, the volume of Latin *Erotica* published in Bohn's Classical Library in 1854, gives 'that my mistress be touched by and pleased with the accustomed sound'—a fairer translation than the saccharine solution offered by our modern Loeb (1990): 'so that my sweetheart is thrilled by the familiar strain'.[74] Pound's 'enjoy' has been touched with the same louche glitter as 'come into my mouth'; and 'devirginated' is his contentious translation of 'tacta', from 'tangere' ('to touch')—a word whose scattering of appearances in the *Elegies* anchors his feeling that Propertius was a poet interested in 'touch' (of more than one variety). In this context of veering erotic suggestiveness, the claims to enduring appeal made by Pound's Propertius—'stands genius a deathless adornment', 'taking his stand among these'—start to bulge with innuendo. The nudge-nudge wink-wink meaning of 'stand' goes back many centuries: the tender care given by Venus to Paris in Thomas Bridges's *Homer Travestie* (1762) offers a helpful analogue to Pound's way with the word:

> She guides his weapon where she list;
> Nay more, a touch of her soft hand,
> If fallen down, will make him stand.[75]

Here too, skilful 'touch' guarantees a 'stand'. The swirling *double entendres* of Pound's 'Propertius' pull two ways. They give the verse a fruity liveliness; but they also bring in the disenchanting, perhaps deadening thought that all the speaker's imaginings of personal and literary immortality may be no more than sublimations of eros.

For Comber, Pound's choice of 'life/death pieces' reveals his wish to prevent the classics from becoming mere objects of scholarship, and thus to keep them alive as a stimulus for poetry. 'The focus'—Comber proposes—'is now on a vital struggle between a dying, fading tradition and a living continuity. "My job," said Pound, "was to bring a dead man to life, to present a living figure." '[76] Pound did certainly feel that he was engaged in such a struggle, more so than earlier poets because, as the twentieth century dawned, Latin was sinking into the unhappy status of a 'dead language'. Dryden's Latin had been as fluent as his English, or nearly so. To make Virgil speak modern English was, for him, less a resurrection than the transfer of a liveliness still present in the Latin: as I suggested at the start of this chapter, it was not so much that the classics were already dead as that they risked being killed by bad translations. The phrase 'a dead language' seems to have gained currency during the eighteenth century when Dr Johnson was one of the people who used it.[77] But he did so (at least on one occasion) when discussing a poem written in Latin by Addison—a sign that Latin was still not yet so very dead; and of course Johnson himself wrote Latin verse. Even for Tennyson and Browning, Latin would have had an air of familiarity which had vanished from the world in which Pound moved.

As Latin faded from literary currency it became more established as an academic discipline. According to Christopher Stray 'between the 1870s and the 1920s, the relaxed classical scholarship of Anglican gentlemen gave way to the specialized, methodic activity of a community of professional scholars'.[78] Pound himself, in an article published a year or so before he started work on the 'Homage', discerned and denounced a hazier change which went back—it seemed to him—much earlier:

> We have long since fallen under the blight of the Miltonic or noise tradition, to a stilted dialect in translating the classics, a dialect which imitates the idiom of the ancients rather than seeking their meaning, a state of mind which aims at 'teaching the boy his Latin' or Greek or whatever it may be, but has long since ceased to care for the beauty of the original.[79]

Pound's feelings about the use of 'stilted dialect' in translation were complex. A couple of years after this essay he criticized Browning's

Agamemnon for being written in 'stilted unsayable jargon' (I discussed the point in Chapter 7); and yet, as we have seen, Browning's way with translation was a strong influence on him and he sometimes had recourse to the stilted and unsayable himself. But his hostility to Milton's syntax, diction, and beliefs was more settled and it leads him to misrepresent the dialect which had in fact become dominant in translations from the classics. Milton exerted his sway over some translators, for instance Henry Francis Cary in his *The Vision: or Hell, Purgatory and Paradise of Dante Alighieri* (1814). But translation from the classics in the nineteenth century was more commonly done either in prose à la Madame Dacier or, if in verse, in a manner inherited from Dryden and Pope. Epic was often translated into couplets; and even lyrics—including those of Propertius—were made over into a broadly Augustan poetic diction. For instance, the lines represented by Pound's 'devirginated young ladies' etc., were translated by Sir Charles Abraham Elton, in his *Tales of Romance* (1810), like this:

> So may the Lycian god my vows approve!
> Now let my verse its wonted sphere regain;
> That, touch'd with sympathies of joy and love,
> The melting nymph may listen to my strain.[80]

This talk of 'sympathies', 'love', and a 'melting nymph' is in a sentimental vein which had flourished in magazine verse throughout much of the previous century. Elton's versions were reprinted in the Bohn Classical Library's volume of *Erotica* (1854), along with similar offerings from John Nott's *Propertii Monobiblos* (1782), to titivate the main prose translation. And if you look into *The Cynthia of Propertius: Being the First Book of his Elegies Done into English Verse* by Seymour Greig Tremenheere, one of H. M. Inspectors of Schools, 1899, or *The Elegies of Propertius Translated into English Verse* by Charles Robert Moore MA, late scholar of Corpus Christi College, Oxford, 1870, you will be met by similar tightly rhymed forms and the same eighteenth-century poetic diction in the bad Coleridgean and Wordsworthian sense of that phrase, all bright cynosures and vulgar throngs.

Pound's pursuit of what he took to be the beauty in Propertius shattered this stucco idiom: the vocabulary of his 'Homage' stretches from 'rack ruin' through 'grove' to 'canicular', and his voice moves rangily in free verse which slightly echoes the cadence of the Latin elegiac couplet.[81] He also pushed against what had become established by scholars as a proper knowledge of Latin. Here is what W. G. Hale, a classicist moved to scorn by early extracts of the 'Homage' published in *Poetry* magazine, had to say about the 'devirginated young ladies' who have to get 'over the strangeness':

> Just possibly, though not probably, Propertius meant 'young ladies' rather than 'my lady'. But there is no hint of the decadent meaning which Mr. Pound read into the passage by misunderstanding *tacta*, and taking the preposition *in* as if it were a negativing part of an adjective *insolito*.[82]

Pound responded to the last point in a private letter:

> Precisely what I do not do is to translate the *in* as if it negatived the *solito*. IF I was translating, I [would] have translated *solito* (accustomed) by a commentary, giving "when they have got over the strangeness" as an equivalent, or rather emphasis of "accustomed." Absolutely the contrary of taking my phrase, as the ass Hale does, for the equivalent of *unaccustomed*. He can't read English.[83]

His conviction is animated, first, by the simple desire to make his own 'Homage' interesting; and, second, by his certainty that Propertius thought of himself as being interesting: it seems to him implausible that Propertius would ever have referred to his writing with a phrase like 'the familiar strain'. And so his eye lights on that suggestive 'in'. He takes it, not as negativing the 'solito', but nevertheless as exerting a pressure on that adjective so as to bring out a latent implication. If you are used to something, you must have got used to it, and so, once upon a time, must not have been. Like 'familiar', or 'usual', or 'accustomed', then, 'solito'—Pound thinks—includes a buried recollection of the unfamiliar, unusual, or unaccustomed.

The magnetic field of 'in' does not stop there. Goaded to write to the *Observer* in response to another precisian attack, this time on the whole 'Homage', Pound scorns the reviewer who can see, in 'gaudeat in solito tacta puella sono', 'no trace of anything save Victorian sentimentality':

> All of which is beautifully academic; the carefully shielded reader, following Professor Mackail's belief that Propertius was a student of Rossetti and Pater, and filled with reminiscences of the Vita Nuova, is asked to read *one* word at a time and one line at a time.[84]

(Professor MacKail was author of *Latin Literature*, a standard handbook that had been through several editions since 1895.) Pound goes on: 'if the division of *in* and *tacta* is *wholly* accidental, then Propertius was the greatest unconscious ironist of all time'.[85] Here again, he sees words connecting outside the pathways laid down for them by grammar. The proximity of 'in' and 'tacta' brings to mind the phrase 'virgo intacta'; and so 'tacta' takes on a corresponding innuendo.

It is impossible to be sure how much this tonal flicker, like many others suggested by the 'Homage', really owes to the Latin. Virginia Woolf's apprehension about Greek, 'we do not know how the words sounded, or where precisely we ought to laugh', or Pope's about Homer 'we are not competent Judges of what Ideas Words might carry in *Homer*'s Time', are as true of Propertius's Latin.[86] For all the scorn with which Pound's 'devirginated young ladies' were greeted on their first outing, they have left at least one more recent classicist at least half convinced. J. P. Sullivan, noting an echo of Catullus 62 (a poem we lit upon in Chapter 17), confesses that the innuendo Pound saw there was 'conceivably intended'.[87] In one of his embattled self-justifications, Pound himself said:

> As for my service to classical scholarship, presumably nil, I shall be quite content if I induce a few Latinists really to look at the text of Propertius instead of swallowing an official 'position' and then finding what the text-books tell them to look for.[88]

The enterprise of bringing a 'dead man to life' and presenting a 'living figure' here modulates into that of bringing a text to life, awakening its ambiguities so that readers realize they need to puzzle at them, even be shocked by them, if they are to gather from them for themselves the 'living figure' of an alert interpretation.

For Pound, then, the life of Propertius's text consisted principally in its poised double meanings: they feel alive because they are not stored in the coffins of dictionaries and grammar books but must be awakened by an imaginative reading. Typically, they are latent in the way words are juxtaposed (hence Pound's hostility to reading only '*one* word at a time'). For instance, *testudo* means a 'tortoise', or 'a tortoise shell used as the sounding-board of a lyre', and so, by synecdoche, simply 'lyre'; while *doctus* means 'learned' or 'expert'.[89] Faced with a description of music made by fingers placed 'docta testudine', Pound thinks there must be at least some hint of incongruity in the collocation of those two words, and translates so as to exaggerate it: not 'upon his skilled lyre', but 'like a trained and performing tortoise'.[90] He brings the dead synecdoche—and the dead tortoise—to life. As we saw with 'in', 'solito', and 'tacta', such juxtapositions can exist independently of the official channels of grammatical agreement. Here is another instance (Pound's Propertius is speaking to his servant Lygdamus):

> Dic mihi de nostra, quae sentis, vera puella.[91]

'Vera' may be an adverb qualifying 'dic' so as to give 'tell me truly': the punctuation of Mueller's edition—used by Pound—appears to support this reading. Or it may more probably (according to Fedeli) attach itself to 'quae sentis' so as to yield the meaning: 'tell me what you think to be true'.[92] Pound opts for the latter possibility; but he sees something else as well. 'Vera'—he thinks—must have an effect on the noun that is next to it and with which it looks as though it might want to agree: 'puella'. And so he shows 'vera' reaching in these two directions at once by translating it twice, as 'truths', and as 'constant':

> Tell me the truths which you hear of our constant young lady.[93]

This tactic of double translation recurs throughout the 'Homage'. One more example:

> And one raft bears our fates
> > on the veiled lake toward Avernus
> Sails spread on cerulean waters, . . .

Both 'veiled' and 'sails' derive from 'velificata', which agrees with 'ratis' ('raft') but is placed next to 'lacus' ('lake'); 'lacus' too is doubly translated as both 'lake' and 'waters'.[94]

In one of his more embattled self-justifications, Pound declared: 'I paid no conscious attention to the grammar of the latin [sic] text'.[95] Perhaps not *no* conscious attention; but he does give at least as much room to flickers and swoons of meaning that do not obey the structures laid out in grammar books. His dress-down 'latin' is more chaotic and more relaxed than its upper-case cousin 'Latin'. He treats the text as though it were itself a veiled lake of signifying potential, a 'Sargasso Sea' like that to which he compared a person's consciousness in an early poem.[96] One current that guides these free-floating possibilities of meaning is verbal proximity; another is his conviction of Propertius's elegant impishness. But there are also swirls of simply what occurs to him. For instance, in the passage I have just quoted, the Latin for 'Cerulean', 'caerula', agrees with 'velificata': the raft is dark-sailed to signify death. But Pound hooks 'caerula' to 'waters' even though the corresponding Latin word is at the opposite end of the line. The reason? Well, presumably it felt better like that, and in any case the waters have to be dark if they are on the way to Avernus. Given this degree of translatorly wilfulness, the boundary between creative alteration and simply making a mistake breaks down. James Laughlin, in a re-appraisal two decades after the event, good-naturedly threw up his hands at:

> The boners, real schoolboy boners, half a dozen of them: 'sitiens' (thirsty)—'sitting'; 'vota' (vows)—'vote'; 'fugantes (putting to flight)—'fleeing'; 'vela' (sails)—'veil'; and the PRIZE, the *grand* prize!

Cimbrorumque minas et benefacta Mari
(roughly: 'the threat of Cimbrian invasion and Marius' public service and the
profit of defeating them')
    Welsh mines and the profit Marus had out of them
Believe it or not!⁹⁷

(The 'vela' that strikes Laughlin comes in the section before our 'velificata'.)

The Romans did mine for lead and gold in Wales, but not until well
after Propertius's death. Pound's 'Welsh mines' are not his only frank
anachronism. There is the 'frigidaire patent' which concludes a cascade of
departures from the source in Section I; a reference to Wordsworth in XII;
an echo of Yeats's 'The Withering of the Boughs' in IV ('because she had
told them her dreams'),⁹⁸ and, in X, a delightful hit at Clive Bell who had
famously launched the phrase 'pure form' in 1914 ('Who has not, once at
least in his life'—he said—'had a sudden vision of landscape as pure
form?'—i.e., 'as lines and colours', freed 'from all casual and adventitious
interest... that it may have acquired from its commerce with human
beings' so that 'he has felt its significance as an end in itself').⁹⁹ Pound's
Propertius comes upon Cynthia alone in her bed:

I had never seen her looking so beautiful
    No, not when she was tunick'd in purple.
Such aspect was presented to me, me recently emerged from my visions,
You will observe that pure form has its value.¹⁰⁰

He feels, no doubt, a vivid appreciation of Cynthia's 'lines'; but perhaps
not 'freed from all casual and adventitious interest'. (The point of the jibe
at Fry, though it feels po-faced to spell it out, is to assert that forms can
never be purified of associations, and that it is only thanks to their
associations that people can respond to them.)

As we saw with Dryden in Chapter 11, and even more so with Logue in
Chapter 22, anachronisms can flourish under the metaphors of 'translation as opening' and 'as zoom'. But, together with Pound's more inventive
interpretations, they create a difficulty for the metaphor of 'bringing a
dead man to life'. In themselves they might well be described as 'lively';
and indeed early reviews, even those hostile to the work, tended to
concede that it had 'at least a live voice', or even was 'very much alive
indeed'.¹⁰¹ The trouble is that this life came at the cost of Propertius's—or
rather, of anything that could seriously be thought of as a presentation
of his 'figure'. In many of his discoverings of tone and innuendo—
'devirginated', 'performing tortoise'—Pound was guided by an idea of
how Propertius might have meant his words to be taken. But Propertius
cannot have had an inkling of Welsh mines or Wordsworth or the
doctrine of pure form. Extrapolating these from the Latin, Pound ascribes

to Propertius's text a 'life' which can emerge only when respect for authorial intentionality (conscious or unconscious) has been abandoned. This second kind of life can only be called 'Propertian' if we manage to accept Daniel M. Hooley's suggestion that 'Pound translates as he feels Propertius might have translated'.[102] The idea does tally with some of what Pound said about his intentions, for instance that the 'Homage' was 'my development of a "germ" of Propertius'—of his 'soul' in the sense of 'that which he has which no other man, god, or creature has'.[103] Just as Pope engaged in sublime translation of Homer's sublimity, so Pound might 'touch' again, in his translation, words that were already 'touched' in the Latin. Propertius translated would be Propertius squared.

Pope's sublime mode of 'translation as passion' can, as we have seen, be quite precisely described. It includes a tendency to increase numbers and sizes, to double similes and metaphors, and to emphasize moments in the narrative when fire is spreading or characters are giving each other inspiration. All this fits the description 'sublime'; and it can be distinguished from the other dominant tendency in Pope's *Iliad* which follows the metaphor of 'taking a view'. Pound's style—or styles—of translating in the 'Homage' can also be delineated, as we have begun to see. There is the discovery (and invention) of innuendo; the tactic of double translation; the deployment of startlingly varied kinds of diction. But the trouble with calling all this a Propertian translation of Propertius is that these verbal tactics have only a very distant (if any) connection to his. The adjective 'Propertian' ends up being pulled a long way away from Propertius. This is a weakness with Pound's self-characterization too. In 'developing' what he takes to be specific in Propertius, 'that which he has which no other man, god, or creature has', he has ended up with something that other writers do in fact share, i.e. a disposition 'to touch words somewhat as Laforgue did'. The stylistic explosion which occurs in the 'Homage' not only 'develops' from an idea of Propertius but at times abandons it. A central question raised by the poem, then, is how far a style can be stretched and still be itself; and therefore, how far (if it all) it is possible 'to bring a dead man to life, to present a living figure'.

For instance, in Section I,

> Annalists will continue to record Roman reputations,
> Celebrities from the Trans-Caucasus will belaud Roman celebrities
> And expound the distensions of Empire,
> But for something to read in normal circumstances?
> For a few pages brought down from the forked hill unsullied?
> I ask a wreath which will not crush my head.

> And there is no hurry about it;
> I shall have, doubtless a boom after my funeral,
> Seeing that long standing increases all things
>   regardless of quality.[104]

After the first three lines, this tracks the Latin quite closely, and so embodies a quality which is 'Propertian' in a precise sense: the mobility of judgement by which something that starts out seeming modest ('a wreath which will not crush my head') gives rise to what sounds like self-congratulation ('a boom after my funeral'), only for the boast to be dissipated utterly by the last full line and languid hemistich ('regardless of quality')—after which an unwritten thought may perhaps still flower: that this disenchantment with false valuations might itself be honestly worth valuing. There is an elegance in the way each claim morphs into its opposite; and also a vulnerability which comes through again in the way some of the words are poised: 'unsullied', for instance, which corresponds to the Latin 'intacta'. In Propertius it is the path down from Mount Helicon that is 'intacta' primarily in the sense of 'previously untrodden'; but Pound's displacement of the word onto the poems ascribes to them—especially given what he does with 'tacta puella' on the next page—the ambivalent quality of innocence, at once a virtue and a shortcoming. 'Long standing' too will be pulled into an unstable web of complexities once 'stands genius' and 'taking his stand' have come into the poem to connect with it.

But the first three lines of this passage are vigorous extrapolations. Here is the Latin, followed by the Bohn Classical Library's prose translation:

> multi, Roma, tuas laudes annalibus addent,
>   qui finem imperii Bactra futura canent.

> there will be many writers, O Rome, to exalt thy glories, and to sing that Bactria is doomed to be the limit of thy empire.[105]

Fedeli points out that Propertius makes a sardonic pun on the word 'annales' which can mean both the official record of a war and its celebration in verse: epic is diminished by being lumped together with clerkly note-taking. He also observes that the idea that Bactra, namely Afghanistan, might become part of the empire was a pious hope, much repeated but never realized: the Parthians were unshiftably in the way.[106] Propertius, then, is giving the pretensions of epic poetry a clear, brisk slap. Pound's version has a similar target, but attacks it in quite a different style, for, with its hifalutin vocabulary and its pompous repetition of 'Celebrities', it goes much further in imitating the traits that it deplores. The 'Homage' is here being pulled away from Propertius by Pound's own hostility to the distensions of the modern British Empire, his hatred of politicians and capitalists such as those he was later to damn in *Cantos* XIV—XV, for sins including a dislike of 'colloquial language'.[107] Clotted as they are with obvious Latinates, his lines look as though they might be awkward word-for-word translation, like Browning's *Agamemnon*, only a little less so. But in fact they veer wildly away from the Latin: the 'celebrities' are invented and the words which do derive from the source are vigorously distorted: 'annalibus' ('to the annals') becomes 'Annalists'; 'laudes' ('praises') becomes 'belaud'. This part of the passage is a sarcastic parody of Pound's bugbear, 'the Miltonic or noise tradition...a dialect which imitates the idiom of the ancients rather than seeking their meaning'. His personal investment in the denunciation is suggested by the signature engraved within it: 'ex*pound*'.

Here at the beginning of the sequence, it seems—just as Michael Comber says—that a conflict between death and life will be 'played out on the stage of language'. On the one hand, an erroneous, pompous, antiquated language associated with institutional inefficiency and violence—a dead language, we might call it, were it not that it continues to play a part in the distensions of empire. On the other, an alive, unpretentious, individual idiom, the voice of Propertius's 'soul', of sharp thought and quick feeling. Two translation metaphors would correspond, and would jostle in the text rather like the two metaphors in Pope's *Iliad*, only more aggressively. On the one hand, translation as the thoughtless perpetuation of verbal bodies: 'translation as deadening'— or even 'zombie translation'—resulting in lines which, though not wholly dead, are definitely not fully alive. On the other hand, translation fulfilling what Pound said to be his aim—'bringing a dead man to life', 'presenting a living figure'.

Throughout the *Homage*, Pound's ways with translation do at times gather themselves into these two opposing orders. But even then—as in the passage we have just been exploring—it is too simple to say that 'life' is fighting a battle against 'death'. After all, the satire on dead language is, as we say, 'lively': as Pound's concealed signature hints, imaginative energy has gone into its creation. Elsewhere, styles that we might be tempted to label 'dead' and 'living' mingle more intricately:

> Midnight, and a letter comes to me from our mistress:
>   Telling me to come to Tibur, *At* once!!
> 'Bright tips reach up from twin towers,
>   Anienian spring water falls into flat-spread pools.'
> What *is* to be done about it?
>   Shall I entrust myself to entangled shadows,
> Where bold hands may do violence to my person?

Yet if I postpone my obedience
        because of this respectable terror
I shall be prey to lamentations worse than a nocturnal assailant.
And I shall be in the wrong,
        and it will last a twelve month,
For her hands have no kindness me-ward.[108]

The third and fourth lines, which appear to be quoted from Cynthia's letter, are in the manner of Imagism. A couple of 'live' lines, then, successfully brought into the idiom of contemporary poetry?—almost, were it not that the insistent alliteration and the tautology 'flat-spread' seem overdone and so create a feeling of pastiche. Held gingerly in the tweezers of their inverted commas, the lines seem to be a specimen, not only of Cynthia's language, but of the sort of thing people usually say about Tibur—Imagism slackened into the language of the postcard. A little further on, primed as we have been by the celebrities from the Trans-Caucasus, we might set out to read the dictional swell that gets going with 'do violence to my person' as an infection of false, 'dead' language: here are many Latinates; here is pomposity; and here, just as with the earlier instance, is very obvious mistranslation, 'respectable terror' being cooked up from 'mandata timore', where 'timore' does mean 'fear' but 'mandata' is a noun meaning 'request'.[109] Perhaps, we might be tempted to think, this is the language of pusillanimity, an impediment that the real living energy of the protagonist needs to cut through. But this endeavour at interpretation will not cohere. 'Respectable terror' and 'lamentations' and 'nocturnal assailant' are not in contradiction with the colloquial blast of '*And* I shall be in the wrong', but join with it in a single curve of thought and feeling. So words that look to be alive turn out to have a falsity about them; and words that seem at first to be zombies turn out to be the vessels of true feeling.

And what of 'me-ward', a swerve into something like archaism, reminiscent of 'to herward' in the Cavalcanti? Where does it fit in the metaphorical scheme we have been developing? It does not. Rather, it is a one-off solution for representing a feeling of bodily tenderness which Pound must discern in 'in me mansuetas non habet illa manus', where the clustering of 'm's and the repeated 'man' creates an eloquent stutter.[110] Not quite a one off, in fact, for here is Pound's Propertius after a night of love:

Me happy, night, night full of brightness;
Oh couch made happy by my long delectations[111]

For Donald Davie, 'Me happy' is 'an expression that has no home in English except in the schoolchild's painful transliteration in the classroom'.[112] But surely it is, like 'me-ward', a phrase that expresses the tender inarticulacy of the body, here sated, verblessly replete with pleasure: 'me happy.' And, here too, simple words are in one expressive texture with a piece of diction that, taken by itself, might seem inescapably pretentious: 'delectations'. Elsewhere in the poem, clotted Latinates are made to express a knot of fear and pain:

> Jove, be merciful to that unfortunate woman
> > Or an ornamental death will be held to your debit[113]

While a clear line, a line—one might think—of ordinary, living English verse, is again made to sound false (this ordinary line is the third one, beginning 'The gentler'):

> There comes, it seems, and at any rate
> > through perils, (so many) and of a vexed life,
> The gentler hour of an ultimate day.

> Io mooed the first year with averted head[114]

Such an obstacle course of prevarications in the first and second lines, all to resist the conclusion that there comes 'The gentler hour of an ultimate day'. That line, whose rhythm is a melodious, rather Tennysonian modulation of the pentameter, is horrifying to Pound's Propertius because, as a platitude, it embodies what it announces: rest. There is no interference in the words, not 'touch', no zest. And so he charges on into a list of examples of metamorphosis; and Pound, translating, charges on with him, not translating 'versa' according to the book as 'transformed', but metamorphosing it into something more expressive: 'averted'. Pound's Propertius is doing everything he can to avert his head from death; and Pound, translating, does likewise, springing surprises out of a dead language.

As we have seen in all the chapters that have gone before, 'translation rigidly conceived' is too narrow a metaphor for the imaginative work that goes on in the practice of poetry translation. The metaphors that have guided my discussion are brought in by poets as more sympathetic shapes for their activities. But all these metaphors, whether left inexplicit (as with Logue's 'zoom') or thoroughly theorized (as with Dryden's 'opening'), are still abstractions from the multifarious processes they partly guide. What is true, to varying degrees, of all the texts I have discussed is made blatant, and revelled in, by Pound in 'Homage to Sextus Propertius'. The explicit metaphors of 'presenting' and 'bringing to life' will do as rough summings-up, or as labels for what was perhaps an initial intention. But when they are brought into contact with the texture of Pound's poetry of translation, they stretch, proliferate, and turn back on themselves. The wish to make 'present' brings with it an awareness of loss. The desire to bring 'a dead man to life' spreads into an enjoyment of kinds of textual 'liveliness' which go beyond and even contradict the personality that was meant to be resurrected.

This variety of the poetry of translation, in which metaphors of translation arise and then disintegrate, allows Pound to explore ideas about selfhood and the passing of time that mattered also to other modernist texts that are not translations. Subjectivity, in the 'Homage', is no less internally divided than in 'The Love Song of J. Alfred Prufrock'; time passes no more consistently than in *Mrs Dalloway*. But cultural circumstances are only part of the explanation. As we have seen, the metaphors of 'opening', 'desire', and 'landscape' (and other, narrower metaphors connected to them) all harmonize with translation because they include an awareness of, respectively, change, absence, and distance. But 'life' and 'presence' are so much at odds with the nature of text, and especially of translated text, that their role as metaphors of translation will inevitably be agonistic: the push to achieve 'life' will come up against the failure to achieve it; what is made 'present' will meet what has been lost. The idea that he was pursuing 'life' and 'presence' helped Pound to be so responsive to Propertius's Latin; but those metaphors gave way before the multifarious suggestiveness of what he found there to respond to. As we are about to see, it is not only in Modernist texts that metaphors of translation fracture and fragment.

24

FitzGerald's *Rubáiyát*: 'a Thing must *live*'

Pound admired FitzGerald's *Rubáiyát of Omar Khayyám* (1859). It was, he wrote in the late 1920s, 'the only good poem of the time that has gone to the people'. What is more, 'it is called, and is to a great extent, a trans- or mistrans-lation': the claim of kinship with his own enterprise of 'trans-or mistrans-lation' is clear.[1] Two decades later, *Rubáiyát* was still with him: its form, and something of its manner, butts in to *Canto* LXXX, written in the prison camp at Pisa and published in 1948.

> Tudor indeed is gone and every rose,
> Blood-red, blanch-white that in the sunset glows
> Cries: "Blood, Blood, Blood!" against the gothic stone
> Of England, as the Howard or Boleyn knows.
>
> Nor seeks the carmine petal to infer;
> Nor is the white bud Time's inquisitor
> Probing to know if its new-gnarled root
> Twists from York's head or belly of Lancaster;
>
> Or if a rational soul should stir, perchance,
> Within the stem ...[2]

Pound innovates by bringing *Rubáiyát* into contact with the Wars of the Roses and Henry VIII's murdered wives: FitzGerald's poem makes no reference to English history, no more than (of course) do the scattered verses by or attributed to the Persian poet and astronomer Omar ibn Ibrahim al-Khayyam (1048–1131) from which it was assembled. But the interest in vegetable life is in the vein of FitzGerald and of Omar, as is the question of what, if anything, might survive from a dead person into a plant.

In the Persian, each set of four lines had been an individual poem, a *ruba'i* which functioned a bit like an English aphorism. Omar ibn Ibrahim al-Khayyam composed many *ruba'iyat* (the standard way of writing the word differs slightly from that adopted by FitzGerald); and they were gathered into collections arranged alphabetically with no continuous thematic or narrative design. Other *ruba'iyat*, by other hands, were interpolated during the centuries that followed. When FitzGerald continued the 'life' of these *ruba'iyat* into English, he also created continuity between them, selecting and—as he put it—tessellating, so as to form 'a very pretty *Eclogue*' out of the 'scattered Quatrains'.[3] When FitzGerald's poem continues into Pound's, so also does this continuity of thinking between quatrains.

Yet, both here and in the texture FitzGerald made from Omar, there is uncertainty within the continuity: the thought metamorphoses as it moves from one quatrain to the next, the syntax shifts orientation as it stretches. In the first stanza, every rose 'cries' most likely in the sense that the elegiac voice of the verse projects the thought of a cry onto their red and white heads: it is not that the plants have become so human that they are really crying. The next stanza continues to obey the known laws of biology as it tells us that the carmine petal does not seek 'to infer' and that the white bud does not probe 'to know'; and yet, as always, the negation of an idea allows it to become a presence in the writing. By the start of the next stanza, there is in the verse, as in the new-gnarled root, a 'twist'. According to the rules of grammar, 'Or if a rational soul' is governed by 'Nor... Probing to know': it is a further example of what plants do not do. And yet, since it is so far away from the controlling hand of that participle, and is given a little extra stir of its own by appearing at the start of its own stanza, the thought bids to turn from negative to positive, or at least into a possibility: a rational soul might stir. The word 'perchance' then seems to accept the change, at which point one's understanding of the whole statement must wobble. Perchance a rational soul does stir, in which case perchance the carmine petal does infer, or the white bud set about probing (just visible in the distance behind this 'perchance' is Hamlet's analogous thought and phrase: 'to sleep, perchance to dream').[4] Or, if they do not, perhaps it is because they have chosen not to rather than because they cannot. Creepily, some sentience seems to have leached from the narrator's thinking into what he is thinking about, just as the blood of York and Lancaster and Catherine Howard and Anne Boleyn seems to have been sucked up into their redness. Tudor is 'gone' into the roses, not in the simple sense of 'vanished', but in a more lingeringly suggestive way, rather as FitzGerald's *Rubáiyát* has 'gone' to the people—including the person who feels it stirring, now, within the stem of his own writing: Pound.

FitzGerald's *Rubáiyát* will have struck Pound as a good medium through which to write about the uncertain continuance of life after death for two reasons: because that is what the poem is about; and because that is what it exemplifies. His imitation has the same duality. The question of how much of York—his aura? his blood? his life?—persists in the red rose finds an echo in the question implicit in Pound's FitzGeraldian writing: how much of FitzGerald stirs in these stanzas of *Cantos*? And the same question is at the heart of the writing that has nourished Pound: how much of Omar lives on in FitzGerald's *Rubáiyát*? None of these questions has a clear answer. Leaving aside their botanical aspect, the continuities (if they are continuities) that occur in translation and imitation must begin in the nebulous space of reading where—as we saw in Chapter 14—your identity to some extent dissolves into the book and the book partially dissolves into you. In consequence—as I showed in Chapter 4—the whatever-it-is that is brought across in translation must first have been found, i.e. partly invented, by the reader-and-translator; and the same is true of the whatever-it-is that is imitated in imitation. For instance, in the stanzas from Pound, the rhyme-scheme is indisputably the same as that of *Rubáiyát*, which is, in turn, indisputably the same as that of Omar's *ruba'iyat*. But the relationship between other aspects of the writing is less clear. Pound's syntax seems kind of FitzGeraldian, kind of not. Might a thought of the Tudors be implicit in FitzGerald even though unmentioned by him (maybe a rose in an English poem will always have some connection to them)?—in which case Pound will have 'opened' it in an interpretative response of the sort we explored in Part II? Or are the Tudors wholly Pound's addition? We are in the same territory as with the adjective 'Propertian', which I discussed in Chapter 23: likenesses which shade into continuities which shade into something new.

In the case of FitzGerald's *Rubáiyát*, the impossibility of quantifying Omar's presence in the poem is made obvious by the fact that the Persian source is incomprehensible to all but a rare English reader (my own sense of it derives from the cribs and commentaries by Edward Heron-Allen and A. J. Arberry). But this does not stop the question of presence from itself being an imaginative presence in the work: on the contrary. FitzGerald's descriptions of his practice are not as developed as Dryden's or Pope's or even Pound's. They consist of fleeting and divergent remarks which appear mainly in letters. Nevertheless, it is possible to trace the metaphors of translation which guided him: as we will see (and as we would expect) they are rooted in the work of Omar's that he translates. In order to show this, I need to look first, and in some detail, at the texture of FitzGerald's *Rubáiyát*, and at its genesis. The picture that will emerge is even more complicated than in the case of Pound. As we saw in the last chapter, Pound's stated guiding metaphor of 'bringing to life' was shadowed and contradicted by metaphors of 'deadening' and 'loss' that were implicit in his practice. What we will discover now is that FitzGerald's metaphors, of 'blowing', and of making a 'Thing... *live*', are in themselves ambivalent. In his practice of translation they sometimes braid and sometimes pull apart. The result is, not perhaps the most achieved, but certainly the most enquiring of all the poems of translation I discuss in this book.

In a passage near the beginning of the poem-translation, FitzGerald's Omar reflects on all that has been lost to time:

> Irám indeed is gone with all its Rose,
> And Jamshýd's Sev'n-ring'd Cup where no one knows;
>   But still the Vine her ancient Ruby yields,
> And still a Garden by the Water blows.[5]

I have to turn to Heron-Allen to discover that there is no 'reference to the Garden of Iram in quatrains attributed to Omar Khayyam".[6] But no comparison with the source is necessary to make us feel that 'Iram' and 'Jamshýd' are gone from the text in front of us, for how many English readers can say to what those names refer? FitzGerald supplies an endnote:

> Irám, planted by King Schedad, and now sunk somewhere in the Sands of Arabia. Jamshyd's Seven-ring'd Cup was typical of the Seven Heavens, 7 Planets, 7 Seas, etc. and was a *Divining Cup*.[7]

This is helpfully unhelpful. One turns back to the poem, not better informed, but more aware of what one does not know: 'King Schedad'? 'the Seven Heavens'? What sort of '*Divining*'? 'Irám' and 'Jamshýd' are not offered by FitzGerald as names that English readers are likely to be able to understand. Rather, they are signs of the absence of their own meaning. Part of the expressive charge of this act of translation comes from what it obviously does not translate.

Heron-Allen notes that this quatrain of FitzGerald's is 'very composite': all of Omar's *ruba'iyat*, indeed all of Persian poetry, 'is filled with references of which we find an echo here'.[8] Placed as it is so early in the poem, this quatrain seems to have been assembled with a particular purpose. It functions something like a key to what follows, for it establishes a contrast between the works of man and of nature, and also an unease with that contrast, which will recur throughout FitzGerald's *Rubáiyát*. 'Irám' and similar constructions are all gone; but still the plant world flourishes, 'still the Vine her ancient Ruby yields'. But where does language sit in this dichotomy of nature and civilization? Language has to be learned, and so in that respect is artificial. But it is, almost as much as air, a medium of human life, a prerequisite of our being. And it endures beyond us. The consequences of this stanza for the work of translation unwind as follows. Omar is gone into the past just like Irám. But his writing has not: it is still giving rise to new *ruba'iyat* just as the vine, in FitzGerald's delicately self-referential phrase, yields 'Ruby'. But then how do FitzGerald's anglicized *ruba'iyat*, his 'Ruby', relate to Omar's? There is no sure answer. No more than the word 'Irám', in an English book, evokes the reality it names? No more (but also no less) than an English 'Garden' is like a garden in Persia?

Gardens, real and imagined, surround and permeate the genesis of the English *Rubáiyát*. In 1857, FitzGerald took momentary refuge from his brief, unhappy marriage by going to stay in Bedfordshire with his adored friend William Browne. He found another 'sort of Consolation' in Omar Khayyam:

> which I could not help looking over in a Paddock covered with Buttercups and brushed by a delicious Breeze, while a dainty racing Filly of W. Browne's came startling up to wonder and snuff about me.[9]

The buttercups, no less than the name W. Browne, sign this as a distinctly English pastoral. But the book FitzGerald is reading opens his mind to influences from further afield than the delicious Bedfordshire breeze, and also from more variously afield than Persia. He translates an Omar *ruba'i* into 'Monkish Latin', done according to the 'Italian value of the Vowels, not the Classical'; Anacreon, Lucretius, Aristophanes and the medieval French poet Olivier Basselin flower in his mind as analogues.[10] Much that has gone can blow again in the garden of writing.

A further mingling of loss and reconnection is latent in these words because FitzGerald is here writing to another dear friend, Edward Cowell, the scholar of Persian who had introduced him to the language and to Omar's *ruba'iyat*, and whose departure to an academic post in Calcutta was perhaps the major stimulus for the creation of the English *Rubáiyát*. Undertaking the translation gave FitzGerald a reason to write long letters of scholarly query and aesthetic appreciation to his absent friend. A month after his encounter with Omar in Browne's paddock, he sent Cowell his first stab at an English version, which had again arisen out of doors:

> a poor Sir W. Jones' sort of Parody which came into my mind walking in the garden here; where the Rose is blowing as in Persia [...] And with this poor little Envoy my Letter shall end. I will not stop to make the Verse better.
>
> > I long for Wine! oh Sáki of my Soul,
> > Prepare thy Song and fill the morning Bowl;
> > For this first Summer Month that brings the Rose
> > Takes many a Sultan with it as it goes.[11]

Sir W. (William) Jones is the eighteenth-century orientalist from whose *Grammar* FitzGerald learned his Persian.[12] The quatrain resembles Jones's verse in the straightforwardness of its syntax and the blandness of some of its diction ('I long for Wine' is the burden of much of *Rubáiyát* but is never said so flatly); and because it is tidied into rhyming couplets. The finished *Rubáiyát*, in contrast, rhyme aaxa, where the unpredictable x-word, which usually does not chime with the rest of the stanza but sometimes does, contributes to that unsureness of continuity, and therefore of identity, which we have begun to explore.

So this stanza is in some respects a false start. But it also begins the real imaginative endeavour of FitzGerald's *Rubáiyát*. There is the transcription of the Persian word *Sáki* (which means someone who pours wine)—an early instance of the 'obvious non-translation' which proliferates in the later work. And it deploys what will become a crucial nexus of rhyme: 'Rose' and 'goes'. In *Rubáiyát*, those words attach themselves to 'blows', here hinted at in the prose of the letter: 'the Rose is blowing as in Persia'. 'To blow' is a key verb for FitzGerald because it hinges achievement and loss: for a rose to 'blow', in long-hallowed poetic diction, means for it to burst into flower; but as soon as it blows it is liable to be 'blown', in the sense of having its petals scattered on the wind. The passages I have already quoted have begun to give us a sense of FitzGerald's way with this chain of rhyme: 'Irám indeed is gone with all his Rose . . . And still a Garden by the Water blows'. The rose that had seemed gone perhaps rises again in the Garden; but if it does it will only be to blow, i.e. to blossom and inevitably thereupon be lost. The same shifty intermingling of ending in beginning, beginning in ending, occurs in the letter to Cowell, where FitzGerald chooses to 'end', as he says, by refusing to 'stop'; and where the last word of the stanza consigns Sultans to the grave while also, as the last word of the letter, starting the process by which something of FitzGerald 'goes' across the sea to Cowell. Pound realized that 'going' had especially to do with FitzGerald's *Rubáiyát*; so did FitzGerald.

'Going', then, with its layered meanings of being lost and being productive, happens through time and also through space, between England and India, or England and Persia. When FitzGerald writes that 'the Rose is blowing' in England 'as in Persia' he employs, in 'as', an interestingly loose term of comparison. It might mean 'in exactly the same way as', or 'in roughly the same way as' (in an earlier letter he had put 'as abundantly as even in Persia'),[13] or just 'at broadly the same time as', since Persian and English seasons overlap. The ambiguity of the simile merges with the ambiguity of what is being compared: is it 'blowing' in the sense of blooming or of being scattered? The result is a comparison which itself blows in both senses of the word, at first flowers into a claim to likeness and then dissipates as one realizes how non-specific the likeness may be. This tentativeness in suggesting kinships between England and Persia recurs in *Rubáiyát*, for instance in the stanza that was to be most echoed by Pound:

> And David's Lips are lockt; but in divine
> High piping Pehleví, with 'Wine! Wine! Wine!
>   *Red* Wine!'—the Nightingale cries to the Rose
> That yellow Cheek of her's to'incarnadine.[14]

Here—English readers must partly feel—there is much that is familiar. In England, as in Persia, there are nightingales and roses; David is a major figure in Christianity as well as in Islam. But what of 'Pehleví'? Here again, as with those other non-translations 'Irám' and 'Jamshýd', we must turn to FitzGerald's end note:

> *Péhlevi*, the old Heroic *Sanskrit* of Persia. Háfiz also speaks of the Night-ingale's *Péhlevi*, which did not change with the People's.[15]

FitzGerald's stanza makes it seem that this changelessness may hold between countries and languages as well as through time. 'Wine! Wine! Wine!' is onomatopoeia for the sound of the nightingale's cry: the mean-ing of the cry emerges naturally from its sound into English just as—we are led to suppose—into Persian. The human word 'Pehleví' may not be translatable in this English poem, but the avian phenomenon it names, the significant cry of the nightingale, is translated with magical fullness. The continuity of nature spans the separation of languages and cultures. Or so it appears until we round the line-end and hit that italicized word '*Red*', which is less amenable than 'Wine' to being taken as onomatopoeia. The italics suggest that the word may come from someone listening to the nightingale: they mark it (like those italics in Bibles which I discussed in Chapter 9) as being an interpretive insertion. But if '*Red*' is in the mind of the listener, perhaps 'Wine' is too; perhaps 'Wine! Wine! Wine!' is as much of a projection onto the nightingale as, in Pound's version, 'Blood, Blood, Blood!' is a projection onto the rose. The doubt may spread to the other elements of what look like 'Pehleví', like signifieds that have been carried across into English without change: the nightingale and the rose (are they really the same in England as in Persia?) and David (surely a different figure in Islam and in the Bible?). The possibility of creating 'Pehleví' across cultures is both raised and put in doubt. Just as in the letter to Cowell, an ideal of achieved presence, of complete communication, flowers and fades. The rose of meaning blows.

The most expert scholar will feel doubts as to what Omar meant and even about which of the many quatrains attributed to him were really his: the textual history of his work is vexed. For FitzGerald, the amateur and the Englishman who, as a recent editor reminds us 'never met a Persian person'—as far as we can tell—'or indeed any Muslim',[16] the uncertain-ties are multiplied. They make themselves felt in the slips and vaguenesses that afflict his commentary—not only the elliptical comment on 'Irám' but the slither of the accent from 'Pehleví' in the verse to '*Péhleví*' in the notes, and the fact that, according to Heron-Allen, 'Pehlevi' (no accent in his rendering) was really 'the language of the ancient Persians of pre-Muhammadan times' so that 'FitzGerald's description of it as "old heroic Sanskrit" is erroneous'.[17] Similar uncertainties appear, though more creatively, in the changes he made to successive editions. In 1867 the French orientalist J. B. Nicolas published *Les quatrains de Khèyam traduits du Persan* which presented Omar as an orthodox Sufi whose apparent hedonism was in fact allegorical—rather in the manner of traditional Christian interpretations of the Song of Songs. FitzGerald was goaded to expand his text in order to contest this interpretation.[18] He also had second thoughts about many of the lines he had already written (the increased clarity and assertiveness of the second edition are reasons for preferring the first as poetry). Third and fourth thoughts followed in the new editions of 1872 and 1879 that were put out to meet the growing demand. For instance, in 1859 FitzGerald had remarked in a note on the 'yellow Cheek' of that rose which (in the stanza about 'Pehleví') the nightingale aims to incarnadine: 'I am not sure if this refers to the Red Rose looking sickly, or the Yellow Rose that ought to be Red'. In 1868, his doubt shifted balance: the rose was given a 'sallow Cheek', thereby part-metamorphosing it into a sickly creature bucked up (or maybe blushing) at the nightingale's adoration. Again, 1859's self-referential line,

> But still the Vine her ancient Ruby yields,

itself yields to a more fulsome claim in 1868 and 1872,

> But still a Ruby gushes from the Vine,

—where 'gushes' hints at ruby port, a suggestion which is in harmony with the franker bibulousness of this edition, a gird at the respectable Nicolas. But in 1879, FitzGerald makes himself a little more respectable:

> But still a Ruby kindles in the Vine,

'Kindles' suggests something less strange than both the earlier versions: a flame of poetic inspiration.

    Words may change in a new edition of any text. But FitzGerald's verbal shuffles are caused especially by the fact that his *Rubáiyát* is a work of translation. As we ascertained in Chapter 10, a translation, since it represents a source, is always provisional: it can always be done again differently. The metaphor of 'translation as paraphrase' spread awareness of this truth—as we saw from Sir John Denham's hope that his translation of Virgil would lead to others, or Richard Baker's canvassing of multiple translations in his *Cato Variegatus*. The successive editions of FitzGerald's *Rubáiyát* are like the *Cato Variegatus* spread out through time. What is even more distinctive to FitzGerald is that the awareness of provisionality revealed by those changes over the years is already implicit, and crucially so, in the text of the first edition.

The names and words that are transliterated—'Pehleví', 'Irám'—feel provisional because they have not been translated. They are place-holders for meaning, and need the further elucidation of commentary. As Herbert Tucker has said, these recurrent nuggets of incomprehensibility 'keep the reader indeterminately suspended between two languages, two cultures, two histories' in a 'delicate balance of managed anxiety'.[19] The balance is wobbled by words that seem provisional for the opposite reason: because they are too English. For instance:

> A Muezzín from the Tower of Darkness cries
> 'Fools! your Reward is neither Here nor There!'[20]

Would a Muezzin really shout a phrase that expresses what feels like such an English quality of not minding and making do? Compare the gentlemanly Dean Winnstay from Charles Kingsley's *Alton Locke* (1850):

> if I had been blest with a son—but that is neither here nor there—it was my intention to have educated him almost entirely as a naturalist.[21]

A distinctive cultural formation of tenderness and its repression bears on this phrase which hints at a depth of feeling but does not reveal it. In FitzGerald's *Rubáiyát*, the Muezzin cannot mean his words in anything like the same way. There has just been talk of 'To-Day' and 'To-Morrow', so his 'Here' must refer to the one and his 'There' to the other.[22] Nevertheless, faced with his significant words, the English reader will be ambushed by the familiar way of saying 'insignificant', just as FitzGerald must have been when faced with the Persian words that Heron-Allen translates exactly like him, and which Arberry translates as 'neither that nor this'.[23] So FitzGerald's text layers a meaning which is close to the Persian with a meaning which is obviously new. This discredits the phrase as 'translation rigidly conceived' but charges it with suggestiveness as a piece of language which straddles two languages and cultures, recognizing what differs between them as well as what they share.

Here is another example:

> Into this Universe, and *why* not knowing,
> Nor *whence*, like Water willy-nilly flowing:
>   And out of it, as Wind along the Waste,
> I know not *whither*, willy-nilly blowing.[24]

Heron-Allen gives: 'He first brought me in confusion into existence' and 'We went away against our will, and we know not what was / The purpose of this coming, and going, and being'.[25] But 'willy-nilly'? The phrase does mean 'willingly or unwillingly' and could still, in FitzGerald's time, be used quite seriously: *OED* gives an example from that most altitudinous of high-brows, Leslie Stephen. But it had also accrued associations with ballad verse and comedy, both of which FitzGerald taps into with his repetition, exaggerated alliteration and feminine rhymes. Compare *Psyche; or, The soul*, a jovial poem by one John Brown of Great Yarmouth (1818):

> From whence it follows, will y' nill y',
> The thought of your's is mighty silly.[26]

Here again FitzGerald translates and at the same time disempowers his act of translation by introducing a note of triviality. In the double sense we have established, his words 'blow'.

When he introduced the seven-volume *Variorum and Definitive Edition of the Poetical and Prose Writings of Edward FitzGerald* (1902–3), Edmund Gosse wrote that FitzGerald's translations 'must never be compared with the original, or treated as translations at all. They should be judged on their own merit as poems'.[27] It is an early example of the sort of claim that (as we saw) was made about Pound's *Cathay*, and which has since become the standard call of critics keen to save work they admire from being thought 'mere translations'—a position whose shortcomings I discussed in general terms in Chapter 8. Most readers have followed Gosse's recommendation; or at least think they have. Few of those many readers to whom, as Pound said, FitzGerald's *Rubáiyát* went out during the late nineteenth and early twentieth centuries can have been able (any more than I) to compare the English with the original, nor are likely to have felt that, in their reading, they were treating the work 'as translation'. Certainly, several recent scholars have felt able to read *Rubáiyát* primarily as an English poem, taking its peculiarities as, for instance, expressions of FitzGerald's desire to efface himself by writing in a way that is difficult to remember, or as evocations of drunkenness inflected by Victorian endeavours towards temperance.[28] No doubt both considerations bear on FitzGerald's part in the work. But, as we have begun to see, the air of provisionality in the writing, its disorienting slips and swerves, the way its meaning 'blows'—all this derives from the work of translation in which it is engaged. When readers come up against these qualities, enjoy them and puzzle them over, it is, whether they realize it or not, the poetry of translation that is affecting them.

It was perhaps just FitzGerald's unassertive disposition that caused him not to explain his own sense of his ways with translation as methodically and fully as Dryden or Pope or Pound. Perhaps, too, he was discouraged by the circumambient intellectual culture which was largely hostile to metaphors of translation, as we saw in Chapters 21 and 23. But he may also have felt some bafflement about how best to define the complex practice of translation that we have begun to explore. For the metaphors which reveal themselves glancingly in prefaces and letters are multiple and in some ways conflicting. There is the idea of friendship with Omar which, as we saw in Chapter 15, veers occasionally into something more exploitative—though FitzGerald's own modesty needs to be mentioned in mitigation: if he called Omar a 'little Fellow' it was in part because he thought himself to be a little fellow too. Then there is the commitment to 'freedom' which arches over all his translations and which I touched on in Chapter 6. Yet, as it bears on *Rubáiyát*, this metaphor is much contested— for instance in a letter to Cowell written when FitzGerald, in 1858, had sent a trial version to *Fraser's Magazine* (it was not rejected, exactly; but it never appeared):

> My Translation will interest you from its *Form*, and also in many respects in its *Detail*: very unliteral as it is. Many Quatrains are mashed together: and something lost, I doubt, of Omar's Simplicity, which is so much a Virtue in him. But there it is, such as it is.[29]

The account is fretted with contradiction. Is Cowell to be interested by the '*Form*' of *Rubáiyát* in the sense of its rhyme-scheme which reproduces Omar's? Or in the sense of the sequential arrangement of the quatrains, which is FitzGerald's invention? Is the '*Detail*' interesting despite the unliteralness of the translation or because of it (this is another instance of FitzGerald's strategic vagueness in the use of 'as'). Even the results of what is most free in FitzGerald's treatment are paradoxical: mash is usually a simple dish; but here the act of mashing reduces Omar's 'Simplicity'. The unclarity of this description suits the complexity of the writing in the *Rubáiyát*; and it suggests that various metaphors blend and jostle in the work of translation that has produced it.

Elsewhere in the letters, one strand of rumination emphasizes the value of fidelity, even literalness. In the early days of his acquaintance with Persian, FitzGerald wrote to Cowell, whose ongoing translation from Háfiz he had been reading:

> Unlike as the two Peoples may be, we English may yet translate, and read in translation, from the Persian Poetry more literally than from Greek and Latin—partly owing indeed to some affinity in the structure of our Languages.[30]

This conviction of FitzGerald's was buttressed by a particular translation which, more than any other (indeed, more than any other book), was at the heart of English culture. Persian poetry, he said:

> should be translated *something* as the Bible is translated, preserving the Oriental Idiom. It should be kept as Oriental as possible, only using the most idiomatic Saxon *words* to convey the Eastern Metaphor.[31]

And again:

> I am more and more convinced of the Necessity of keeping as much as possible to the Oriental *Forms*, and carefully avoiding any that bring one back to Europe and the 19th Century. It is better to be orientally obscure than Europeanly clear . . . I am sure it is *the* rule never to be lost sight of.[32]

These remarks date from a couple of years before he started work on Omar; but the persistence of the belief they expressed can be seen, not only in the recurrence of that italicized '*Forms*' in the later hope that 'my Translation will interest you from its *Form*', but also in his handling of metaphor throughout *Rubáiyát*, nowhere more strikingly than in its opening stanza:

> AWAKE! for Morning in the Bowl of Night
> Has flung the Stone that puts the Stars to Flight:
>   And Lo! the Hunter of the East has caught
> The Sultán's Turret in a Noose of Light.[33]

Just as he had recommended, the Eastern metaphor is conveyed in 'idiomatic Saxon words'. For the metaphor, compare Arberry's crib to the Persian: 'the sun has thrown the lassoo of dawn over the roof; / the emperor of day has thrown the bead in the cup'.[34] And for the diction, note how FitzGerald puts 'stone' for the word which Arberry translates 'bead', 'flung' for 'thrown', 'Noose' for 'lassoo'. The feeling that something strange is here happening in English is flagged by the exclamations—'AWAKE!', 'And Lo!'—which FitzGerald has inserted and which include an element of self-reference: just look at this writing! What FitzGerald admired in the 1611 Bible was that it kept 'so close to almost unintelligible idioms both of Country and Era'—he must have been thinking of phrases like 'keep thy foot when thou goest to the house of God' or 'the fool foldeth his hands together, and eateth his own flesh'.[35] The power of this style, which flourishes especially in the Psalms and the prophetic books of the Old Testament, is its suggestiveness, the way the impact of the image releases numinous possibilities of meaning which linger in the mind, waiting, perhaps, for some event or revelation which will make them clear. It is a style that breeds faith, not certainty.

For Frank Kermode, FitzGerald's *Rubáiyát* was 'exotic without being foreign'. Published at a time when 'people were in the mood for a Persian garden', it formed one of a 'list of approved burgher escape myths'.[36] Kermode does not reveal the rest of his list but it must include orientalist fantasies such as Thomas Moore's *Lalla Rookh* (1817) or Tennyson's 'Recollections of the Arabian Nights' (1830). Yet, as Daniel Karlin has pointed out, 'the designation of Omar Khayyám in the title as "the Astronomer-Poet of Persia" is like a warning not to expect caliphs and harems, genii and giaours, magic carpets or Circassian beauties'.[37] *Rubáiyát*'s language, too, refuses to offer the safe pleasures of the exotic. It eschews the mildly alluring phrases of Sir William Jones, and the '*Drawing-room*' idiom to which FitzGerald objected in Cowell's translations of Háfiz: ' "While all the care of the Rose is *to scatter her faithless smiles*." '[38] An experience of something as 'foreign' rather than 'exotic' must include allowing it to challenge you and perhaps change you. In the helpful formulations of Emmanuel Levinas, you must encounter the 'Other', not as a mere 'cultural signification', nor as 'a simple given' but as an 'interlocutor'.[39] Your sense of who you are must be opened to disruption. This is what happens in the language of *Rubáiyát*. Incomprehensibilities confront us; phrases readers thought they knew, and might have faith in, are twisted out of shape. The canonized strangeness of the Bible gives FitzGerald authority to write like this. And yet his writing pushes to undo the profound domestication to which the Bible has been subjected in the process of becoming the central text of English culture. The challenge comes, not only from the general enterprise of adopting a Biblical idiom to recommend agnostic hedonism, but from such startling particular phrases as these:

> Where the WHITE HAND of Moses on the Bough
> Puts out, and Jesus from the Ground suspires.[40]

A Jesus, not bodily resurrected, but cyclically suspiring from the ground as a life-giving force: it is a startling image. Here we can see why FitzGerald was so concerned to preserve the 'Eastern Metaphor', an ambition which falls between the old categories of word-for-word and sense-for-sense. As we saw in Chapter 6, metaphors connect up different parts of experience and the world so as to create networks of understanding. In *Rubáiyát*, part of an established map of English culture is disarranged. Of course, it is possible to read the poem, as Kermode did, without feeling the full energy of its challenge; and perhaps it has often been read in that way. But it is easy to be disparaging of 'burghers'. Shakespeare, Byron, Dickens: all have been big sellers. The mere fact of *Rubáiyát*'s popularity does not erase its strangeness.

Disruptive, partially transformative metaphors are at work also in the last strand of thought about translation in FitzGerald's letters. A couple of decades after Rubáiyát's first publication he wrote to the American poet James Russell Lowell, about his early translation of Calderón:

> I am persuaded that, to keep *Life* in the Work (as Drama must) the Translator (however inferior to his Original) must re-cast that original in his own Likeness, more or less: the less like his original, so much the worse: but still, the live Dog better than the dead Lion—in Drama, I say.[41]

This in itself shows that there is life yet in the old dog of a familiar sound bite from Ecclesiastes:

> For to him that is joined to all the living there is hope: for a living dog is better than a dead lion.
> For the living know that they shall die: but the dead know not any thing.[42]

Ecclesiastes was also in FitzGerald's mind twenty years earlier just after *Rubáiyát* had been published; but it had itself been strangely re-cast:

> I suppose very few People have ever taken such Pains in Translation as I have: though certainly not to be literal. But at all Cost, a Thing must *live*: with a transfusion of one's own worse Life if one can't retain the Original's better. Better a live Sparrow than a stuffed Eagle.[43]

The sparrow that takes the place of an eagle is a cousin of the speaker of 'Pehleví', the immortal nightingale, whose cry had seemed—at least for a moment—to leap unchanged into English. But this new avian metaphor is very much less heady in its implications for the power and process of translation.

In the later statement (the one I quoted first), the metaphor of 're-casting' is perhaps vaguely industrial but probably more precisely theatrical since plays have to have casts: translating a play, FitzGerald suggests, is like having it performed by a new set of actors. The more tentative image he had found for *Rubáiyát*, 'transfusion', is itself transfused out of earlier discussions of the translation of poetry. FitzGerald would have noticed the word in Dryden, whose Prefaces he much admired, and who talks of transfusion when, in the Preface to *Ovid's Epistles*, he is paying tribute to a precursor in the art of 'translation as paraphrase'. Sir John Denham, he recalls, asserted that 'Poetry is of so subtle a spirit, that in pouring out of one language into another it will all evaporate; and if a new spirit be not added in the transfusion, there will remain nothing but a *caput mortuum*.'[44] The image is from alchemy: a '*caput mortuum*' is a useless residue from a chemical reaction, and a 'spirit' is a key alchemical substance such as quicksilver or brimstone. Yet since Dryden, like Denham, conceives translation also to be a way of making a dead author 'speak', 'spirit' takes on a hint of the human soul as well.

FitzGerald's 'transfusion' is similarly, and more creepily, ambivalent between the spiritual and the material, for his talk of dead and living animals, as well as of his own 'Pains', brings the idea of blood transfusion to the surface of his rumination. 'The experiment of transfusion proves that the blood of one animal will serve for another', observed William Paley, the influential Anglican theologian whose work FitzGerald had been forced to read at Cambridge.[45] Still, no amount of transfusion, whether of blood or spirit, will turn an eagle into a sparrow; and a feeling of doubt as to the re-animating power of translation appears also in his phrase 'a Thing must *live*'. A 'Thing'? This is more ambivalent than Pound's 'my job was to present a living figure', or Dryden's ambition to make Virgil speak as if 'he had been born in *England*, and in this present Age'.

Ecclesiastes's lion and dog are recast as eagle and sparrow not only because of the latent influence of the nightingale but also, and more immediately, because FitzGerald has just been talking about his translation of another Persian text, never published in his lifetime, which he entitled *A Bird's-Eye View of Faríd-Uddín Attar's Bird Parliament*. A bird's-eye view of the *Bird* Parliament?—as so often in the works we have been exploring, a translator's understanding of translation is inflected by the work he is translating. The same goes for this whole strand of thought about the preservation or creation of life through translation: it has been animated, and complicated, by transfusions from Omar's thoughts about re-animation. Fitzgerald brings them together in a sequence of stanzas:

XVIII.

They say the Lion and the Lizard keep
The Courts where Jamshýd gloried and drank deep;
    And Bahrám, that great Hunter—the Wild Ass
Stamps o'er his Head, and he lies fast asleep.[46]

In Ecclesiastes, and in FitzGerald's later letter, a lion is a metaphor: of a person and of the whatever-it-is of a person that continues into a text they have written. Here in *Rubáiyát*, 'the Lion' lives where a human used to, as do 'the Lizard' and 'the Wild Ass'. The main feeling in the stanza is of loss and incongruity. But there is also a countervailing drift: there is life again, or still, in the place where life once was—a continuity of sorts. 'The' before 'Lion', 'Lizard', and 'Wild Ass' shows that these creatures are conceived in general, and assumes that humans are individual to a degree that animals are not. There was only ever one 'Jamshýd', and he is dead; but 'the Lion' is, in a sense, immortal. As in some of those Homeric similes which I discussed in Chapter 20, the linear time of human history is layered with the cyclical time of nature in a way that strangely both emphasizes and mitigates the finality of human death.

Next comes the possibility of a sort of resurrection:

> XIX.
> I sometimes think that never blows so red
> The Rose as where some buried Caesar bled;
> That every Hyacinth the Garden wears
> Dropt in its Lap from some once lovely Head.
> XX.
> And this delightful Herb whose tender Green
> Fledges the River's Lip on which we lean—
> Ah, lean upon it lightly! for who knows
> From what once lovely Lip it springs unseen.[47]

The verse stirs with the semantic counter-currents which recur throughout FitzGerald's *Rubáiyát*: 'wears' against 'dropt'; 'lean' against 'springs'; 'bled' against 'blows'. Both stanzas keep quite close to the Persian, but the second one also has a root in a very English location, the site of the Civil War Battle of Naseby which lay within the FitzGerald family's Northamptonshire estate. In 1842, FitzGerald had explored the site on behalf of Thomas Carlyle, who was writing about Cromwell. He reported in a letter:

All the old names of the localities are in present use . . . 'Lean Leaf' is 'Lean Leys' (I suppose *leys* or *lays* of grass—as people now talk of clover-lays, etcc., and these 'leys' are *lean* enough, as I can testify; of a coarse grass, and marshy) is a slightly rising pasture that reaches *to* the hill: which hill (wonderful to say) has no name in particular, and so may be called Lean Leys Hill.[48]

At Naseby too, something that once was life has sprung (though not unseen) from beneath the surface of the grass:

You will find in the Histories of Naseby how an old man (living in 1792 when the book was written) describes how the dead were buried "very shallow" so that the putrid matter oozed out over the ground several yards, etcc.—he heard it from his Grandfather . . . [49]

Back then, FitzGerald was not satisfied by the thought of leaning lightly on the dead:

Having ordered one of the reputed graves to be opened near Cloisterwell—a soil of animal matter mixed with crumbling jaw-bones, arm-bones, skulls, etc., is found about four feet under the surface. Only the teeth perfect: plenty of them. The Scotchman is digging hard now this late: and proposes the whole matter as a manure for turnips.[50]

The teeth perfect . . . but no sign of a 'once lovely Lip'.

Naseby is a place of resurgence: of putrid bodily matter, of old names. The resurgence of this resurgence in *Rubáiyát* was of course private to FitzGerald and (I would guess) hidden even from his conscious mind. But there is another, public, re-animation here too, of Thomas Gray's famous line from that most English poem, 'Elegy Written in a Country Church-yard': 'Full many a flower is born to blush unseen'.[51] Both echoes tally with the metaphor of 'transfusion of one's own worse Life': they mix a current of Englishness into the flow of imagining which comes mainly from the Persian. This mingling of influences is not domestication: the lines which result are nothing like William Jones's '*scatter her faithless smiles*'; the Persian *ruba'iyat* have not been 're-cast' into FitzGerald's 'Likeness'. The balance is tipped the other way, for elements of the source press strongly into the English version: not only the rhyme-scheme, and not only the startling thought embodied in 'Ah, lean upon it lightly' (translated from words which Arberry renders 'beware you do not set your foot on the verdure contemptuously'),[52] but a particular stylistic signature: the close repetition of a word in two different senses. The Persian for 'lip' is not repeated in the *ruba'i* which FitzGerald here translates. But the pattern does occur often elsewhere, for instance in lines that FitzGerald translates accurately in his second stanza:

> 'Awake, my Little ones, and fill the Cup
> Before Life's Liquor in its Cup be dry'.[53]

The pattern recurs so often as to become the most prominent feature in FitzGerald's likeness of Omar:

> The Bird of Time has but a little way
> To fly—and Lo! the Bird is on the Wing.

> Beside me singing in the Wilderness—
> And Wilderness is Paradise enow.

> Look to the Rose that blows about us—'Lo,
> Laughing', she says, 'into the World I blow':

> Ourselves must we beneath the Couch of Earth
> Descend, ourselves to make a Couch—for whom?

> Dust into Dust

> And many Knots unravel'd by the Road;
> But not the Knot of Human Death and Fate.

> Some little Talk awhile of ME and THEE
> There seem'd—and then no more of THEE and ME.

> How long, how long, in infinite Pursuit[54]

It is tempting to say that one instance of each pair is metaphorical and the other literal; and on some occasions FitzGerald does offer up this structure of understanding ready made: 'the Bird of Time . . . / the Bird'; 'the Couch of Earth/ . . . Couch'. But the insistence of the pattern is such as to loosen one's grasp of which is the literal and which the metaphorical meaning: is not a 'Couch of Earth' the real, original couch from which later couches are metaphorical extrapolations? Is not the 'Bird on the Wing' just an image of the real, most powerful and most fleeting bird, 'the Bird of Time'? The uncertainty spreads to what might seem at first like simple repetitions. Is 'the Knot of Human Death and Fate' the same kind of already-figurative knot as all the other 'many Knots unravel'd by the Road'?—or a different sort of knot entirely, perhaps mystical rather than rational, a metaphor built on a metaphor? Or is it, on the contrary, crucially a literal, material knot in which your body is fatally entrammelled? Is 'Me' still 'Me' when there is no longer any talk of me? Is the second 'how long' the same as the first? Or better? Or worse? Might the 'in' in 'infinite' have some kinship with the 'in' in front of it? Meaning fractures and fades as the words recur.

A couple of years after he had published *Rubáiyát*, FitzGerald sent some letters to *Notes and Queries* on the subject of East Anglian dialect words. One, in particular, was:

worth recording to show what changes a word may go through and come to. A young sailor was telling me how, one blowing night at sea, they had *Composites* on the mastheads. I was beginning to wonder at "Price's Patent" in such a place at such a time, when an older hand corrected us. "Compo-*sants* he mean, Sir;" the meteors that are well known to light on vessels at such seasons. But, then, why *composants*? I then remembered Dampier's telling of a "corpus sant" appearing on *his* masthead, "a Spanish or Portuguese corruption of *corpus sanctum*," he says, and considered by them, as also by those then with him, as a good sign (when seen aloft at least) . . . [55]

(A Price's patent composite was a sort of candle.) The residue of the *Rubáiyát* is present in this passage, not only in the word 'blowing', and not only in the idea of a body ('corpus') that turns into something else, but in FitzGerald's interest, long latent in him and quickened by his experience of translating Omar, in the 'changes a word may go through and come to'. That tic of verbal repetition which he catches from the Persian shows words going through and coming to changes of meaning even when their physical substance as signifiers remains the same. A 'lip' (on a face) may turn into a 'lip' (of a river); the rose that 'blows' (flowers) also 'blows' (is scattered).

Like Pound's *Homage to Sextus Propertius*, FitzGerald's *Rubáiyát* has a liveliness that overflows the metaphors of continuing Omar's 'life' and transfusing FitzGerald's own. Just as with the different liveliness of Pound's text, it arises from the act of translation. The experience of layering English and Persian sensitizes FitzGerald, not only to the openness of English, its ability to express 'Oriental metaphor' and ingest words like 'Pehleví', 'Sáki', and indeed 'Rubáiyát', but also to its internal dividedness: 'lip' need not mean the same as 'lip' any more than 'pain' in English means the same as 'pain' in French. Omar's own imaginings of uncertain continuity—from human life to lion and rose and grass—gave FitzGerald images with which to imagine the uncertain continuity between his writing and the Persian; and Omar's habit of repetition suggested a way of giving the same quality to *Rubáiyát*'s verbal patterning. These textual interactions, just as much as the personal interest FitzGerald felt in Omar, are what lift *Rubáiyát* so much above his other Persian translations, from Jámí and Faríd-Uddín Attar, let alone his versions of Aeschylus and Calderón. The 'life' of this 'Thing' that 'lives' (if 'life' is the right word) is disorienting, questioning, slippery. Incomprehensibilities confront us; familiar words and phrases are twisted from our grasp. It is not only that Omar's *rubai'yat* are translated into English; English shifts and proliferates in reaction to them. The voice in this poem of translation contributes to the unravelling of certainties. In the last passage I quoted, it was FitzGerald who introduced the notes of doubt '*They say* the Lion and the Lizard keep', '*I sometimes think* that never blows so red', '*who knows /* From what once lovely Lip it springs unseen'.

All the metaphors of translation discussed in this book are narrower than the texts that they inhabit. 'Opening' is not the whole story of Dryden's *Aeneis*; 'to bring a dead man to life' was not the sum total of Pound's endeavour in *Homage to Sextus Propertius*. But what is unusual about FitzGerald's *Rubáiyát of Omar Khayyám* is the degree to which it dissolves even those various and fleeting metaphors that were in the environs of its creation. It is neither 'literal' nor 'unliteral'. The metaphor of 'friendship' does not take us very far towards understanding it; and neither does the idea of its being 're-cast' in FitzGerald's 'Likeness'. Its 'transfusions' are multiple and intermingling; it is not even unequivocally 'alive'. More so than better scholars, more so than greater poets, FitzGerald opened his imagination and his language to the stimulus that came to him from Omar and the result asks to be interpreted with the same receptive hesitation. This translation, more than perhaps any other, leaves you wondering what 'translation' means. Do *Rubáiyát* stand to *Ruba'iyat* as Lip to Lip? or Rose to Caesar? Or Lion to Jamshýd? Who knows?—they say ... and yet I sometimes think. ...

25

The *Metamorphoses* of Arthur Golding

FitzGerald's Omar sometimes thinks that 'every Hyacinth the Garden wears / Dropt in its Lap from some once lovely Head'.[1] 'Hyacinth', there, is substituted for a flower in the source which both Arberry and Heron-Allen translate as 'violet'; it has itself dropped in FitzGerald's lap from Ovid, who tells the story of how Hyacinth, loved by Apollo, was killed by a blow from a discus: Hyacinth flowers then grew from the splashes of his blood.[2] In Ovid, the metamorphosis happens; in FitzGerald it is aired as a possibility—and the same tentativeness characterizes the other images in and around *Rubáiyát* which feel close to Ovid: blood perhaps growing into roses and a lip into a lip; a sparrow taking the place of an eagle; and the lion and the lizard keeping the courts of Jamshýd. All are possibly metamorphoses but not certainly; or almost but not quite.

FitzGerald's way with metamorphosis tallies with that general tentativeness in metaphorical self-definition which we explored in the last chapter. It is also likely that metamorphosis struck him as a markedly classical idea which did not entirely suit Omar's own probings of continuity and change. And yet other translators too have resisted adopting metamorphosis as a metaphor of translation even though it might appear to be an obvious candidate: in Ovid's *Metamorphoses*, 'forms', we are told at the beginning, change into 'new bodies' ('In nova ... mutatas ... formas / corpora').[3] Dryden made the link to translation when he re-embodied part of Book XV of Ovid's poem as 'On the Pythagorean Philosophy', published in his *Fables* (1700):

> 'Then to be born, is to begin to be
> Some other thing we were not formerly:
> And what we call to die, is not t'appear
> Or be the thing that formerly we were.
> Those very elements which we partake
> Alive, when dead, some other bodies make;
> Translated grow, have sense, or can discourse;
> But death on deathless substance has no force.'[4]

The first four lines of this stick close to the Latin in which Ovid has imagined Pythagoras's speech. But the second four all emerge from a little generalizing bullet point: 'cum sint huc forsitan illa, / haec translata illuc, summa tamen omnia constant'[5] ('though things may move from there to here and here to there, the sum total remains constant'). Charles Tomlinson has admired the 'audacity, the *sprezzatura*, with which Dryden throws in the word "Translated" here';[6] and the charm of the moment does not diminish when you notice that the word has not been thrown in, exactly, but has continued almost unchanged from Ovid's 'translata'. All around it, the translation has that expansive afflatus whose complexities we explored in Chapter 9. The 'sense' is 'amplified' to the point of perhaps being 'altered'; but this surge of collaborative imagining is guided by Dryden's familiarity with Ovid—his sense of himself as translating an 'Author'—for his talk of 'elements' becoming 'other bodies' derives from the 'formas' and 'nova corpora' of the *Metamorphoses*' first lines. The nugget of word-for-word translation, 'translated', likewise restrains the move to paraphrase, anchoring it, and introducing a flicker of uncertainty about the assumptions on which it is based. What is the 'deathless substance', when it comes to language?—'sense'?—or rather the etymological stuff which develops via derivation, as 'translata' has become 'translated'? We touched on the question in the opening pages of this book, when we saw, in the Wycliffite Bible, a similar translation of translation: 'translationem' into 'translacioun'.

Tomlinson goes on to propose that Dryden here 'wittily incorporates the notion of literary translation into the conception of an ongoing world empowered by the metamorphosis of its own elements—mud and stones into flesh and blood, flesh into trees, human into divine'.[7] Certainly, translation is viewed as one of many kinds of change. Yet the thought that it belongs in such company may also cause unease, as we can see in another passage quoted by Tomlinson from a commendatory poem by Joseph Addison. Dryden had included a translation of Book 1 of the *Metamorphoses* in the anthology *Examen Poeticum* (1693); Addison hopes that he will go on to attempt the rest of the work:

> Then may we wondring read how Human Limbs,
> Have water'd Kingdoms, and dissolv'd in Streams;
> Of those rich Fruits that on the Fertile Mould
> Turn'd yellow by degrees, and ripen'd into Gold:
> How some in Feathers, or a ragged Hide
> Have liv'd a second Life, and different Natures try'd.
> Then will thy *Ovid*, thus transform'd, reveal
> A Nobler Change than he himself can tell.[8]

The transformation of a person into a stream, let alone into a bird or beast, does not offer a very flattering analogy for what Dryden has done to Ovid. The fruit that ripen into gold are a more auspicious vehicle of praise; but they do not in fact appear in the *Metamorphoses* (the nearest thing is a two-line description of the apples thrown by Hippomenes to distract Atalanta in Book 10). Addison must have been helped to mis-remember by his wish to find in Ovid a sort of metamorphosis that would do as an image for what he wanted to say: that Dryden had improved Ovid by translating him. But Addison cannot shut out the reality of the *Metamorphoses* completely—so he has to put in that word 'Nobler' in the last line to keep out the suggestion that Dryden may instead have given Ovid 'Feathers' or a 'ragged Hide'. Translation is brought temptingly close to metamorphosis but is finally held apart from it: the changes wrought by Dryden are 'Nobler' than anything in Ovid.

And in fact Dryden's own writing expresses a similar hesitation. For it matters that the passage in which he lodges that startling word 'translated' comes, not from the description of any particular metamorphosis, but from the philosophical disquisition, attributed to Pythagoras, which appears in the last Book of the *Metamorphoses*. In the rest of the work, stones can indeed, as Tomlinson says, turn 'into flesh and blood, flesh into trees, human into divine'. But the world dreamt of in Pythagoras's philosophy is considerably more ordered than that. On the one hand, forms decay and their constituent matter circulates, gathering into new forms, be they rocks or plants or the bodies of animals or people. On the other, the souls of the dead are reincarnated, but only in bodies that can be animated. A human soul can pass into the body of an animal, and vice versa; but there is no suggestion, here in Book 15, that it might be metamorphosed into a plant or a stone. This is why Pythagoras can advocate vegetarianism with a clear conscience. Eating meat is wrong, for then—as Dryden accurately and ickily translates—'bowels are in other bowels closed'.[9] But there is no danger (as Pythagoras sees it) of biting on a laurel leaf and hurting Daphne. What Dryden thinks similar to translation is, not the full, energetic anarchy of metamorphosis, but the more restrained idea of the transmigration of souls after death: metempsychosis. The detail of his vocabulary implicitly narrows the transformation even further: the elements which 'we' partake, he writes, go to form other bodies which 'translated grow, have sense, or can discourse'. 'We' can only be humans; and the power to discourse is uniquely human too.

This restrained variety of metamorphosis, metempsychosis, had been a possible figure of translation since the late sixteenth century. Theo Hermans has gathered examples, for instance Pierre de Ronsard in 1577 praising Amadis Jamyn's translation of part of the Iliad—'et tu (Homer) as ton ame passee / En Jamyn pour interpreter'—and Ben Jonson admiring Sir Henry Savile's translation from Tacitus (1591):

> If, my religion safe, I durst embrace
> That stranger doctrine of *Pythagoras*,
> I should beleeve, the soule of *Tacitus*
> In thee, most weighty *Savile*, liv'd to us.[10]

Metempsychosis had affinities with the idea of translating an 'Author', and with the preference for 'sense' over 'word', which we explored in Chapters 9 and 14. Yet its adoption by translators themselves, rather than by the authors of poems lauding them, is often only partial and oblique. In the prefatory material to his *Essayes* of Montaigne (1603), John Florio descanted on the barrier to translation raised by the differences between languages, and gestured at a way of getting through it:

> Every language hath it's *Genius* and inseparable forme; without *Pythagoras* his *Metempsychosis* it can not rightly be translated. The Tuscan altiloquence, the *Venus* of the French, the sharp state of the Spanish, the strong significancy of the Dutch cannot from heere be drawne to life.[11]

The old dichotomy of translation of the 'spirit' and of the 'letter' is shadowily in the background here. But Florio's idea of Metempsychosis seems to bear on something different. It is, not the 'spirit' of a piece of writing, but the 'geniuses' of different languages that need to be subjected to a sort of metempsychosis so that the 'altiloquence' of Tuscan Italian, the '*Venus*' quality of French, etc., can be re-embodied in a different tongue. This notion pulls metempsychosis away from the sense it has in Book 15 of the *Metamorphoses*, and gives it a meaning that derives almost wholly from its new context: the imitation of the character of a language. Florio, most flamboyant of translators, deploys the image as a flourish rather than for its shaping, explanatory power. And even this loosened idea of metempsychosis corresponds, not to what translation can do, but to what it cannot. If we had Pythagoras's metempsychosis—Florio says—the genius of a language could be translated; but as things stand, 'it cannot from heere be drawne to life'.

There is a similar disjunction when, eight years later, George Chapman mentions 'transmigration', an old Bible word that had recently been made over into a synonym for metempsychosis. 'Clerks', he says in the prefatory material to his *Iliads*, do not know Greek and Latin well enough to write poetry in them: they are really only able to 'chat-in' those languages,

> Compar'd with what they might say in their owne,
>   Since thither th'other's full soule cannot make
> The ample transmigration to be showne
>   In Nature-loving Poesie.[12]

Here again 'soule' belongs to a language and will not travel 'thither' to a
distant tongue. In a rather entangled chain of comparison, the results of
this failed transmigration are likened to the 'forced' and graceless work of
translating 'word-for-word'; but when Chapman moves on to recommend
the sort of translation that is more congenial to him the idea of transmigration drops back and 'opening' takes over, as we saw in Chapter 9. In his
visionary poem *Euthymiae Raptus; or the Teares of Peace with Interlocutions*
(1609), Chapman encounters the spirit of Homer who tells him that he
had filled his 'bosome... / With such a flood of soule', during the work of
translating, that 'thou didst inherit / My true sense (for the time then) in
my spirit'.[13] But this temporary flush of inspiration is again not quite
metempsychosis. With Chapman, just as with Florio, the idea is brought
into view but is not finally adopted as a metaphor for translation.

   This tussle of attraction and disenchantment must owe something to
the fact that metempsychosis had already become established as a figure
for hazier literary relationships than those created by translation. In 1596,
Edmund Spenser had published a ringing tribute to Chaucer in Book 4 of
The Faerie Queene:

> Then pardon, O most sacred happie spirit,
>   That I thy labours lost may thus reuiue,
>   And steale from thee the meede of thy due merit,
>   That none durst euer whilest thou wast aliue,
>   And being dead in vaine yet many striue:
>   Ne dare I like, but through infusion sweete
>   Of thine owne spirit, which doth in me suruiue,
>   I follow here the footing of thy feete,
> That with thy meaning so I may the rather meete.[14]

Only the transmigration of Chaucer's soul into his can justify Spenser's
confidence that he is on the way to stealing Chaucer's 'meede', or fame.
And here, a couple of years later, is the religious writer, translator and
anthologist Francis Meres:

> As the soule of Euphorbus was thought to live in Pythagoras: so the sweet
> wittie soule of Ovid lives in mellifluous and hony-tongued Shakespeare,
> witness his *Venus and Adonis*, his *Lucrece*, his sugred *Sonnets* among his
> private friends, &c.[15]

Metempsychosis is revealed, not by the structured similarity of translation
but by the fluid connections of influence, inventive recreation, and finally
(with the sonnets) mere fleeting echoes. And so it should be, for why,
reincarnated, would a soul set about writing its former works over again?
Yet even the relation between Spenser and Chaucer, or between Shakespeare and Ovid, is stronger than that envisaged in *Metamorphoses*

15. Pythagoras is certain that he is a reincarnation of Euphorbus, a warrior who fought in the Trojan war. But the claim implies no similarity of character or talent: there is no question of Euphorbus's having been a great philosopher. Memory is all that their one soul gives the two men to have in common: 'My name and lineage I remember well', as Dryden translates: 'And how in fight by Sparta's king I fell'.[16]

Like the figure of friendship which I discussed in Chapter 15, both metamorphosis and metempsychosis look promising as metaphors for translation; but neither quite catches on. They do not achieve that inwardness with the practice of translators, that defining power, which we have traced in other metaphors such as 'opening', 'desire', 'passion', 'view', 'zoom', and 'bringing a dead man to life'. 'Friendship' fails because it is too solid and, finally, too pleasant an idea: it cannot grasp the strangeness, invasiveness and risk that are inherent in a really searching literary translation. 'Metempsychosis', by contrast, is too fluid. In the disquisition of Ovid's Pythagoras, it can occur without creating any discernible similarity between the new identity and the identity left behind. So when it strays into the literary field, it draws its substance from the already-established ideas of 'spirit', 'character', and 'style', which could be used to describe much looser affinities than those established in translation. 'Metamorphosis' is vaguer still, encompassing as it does a universe of kinds of change. Still, even though metamorphosis *per se* may not have sufficient definition to become a metaphor of translation, particular metamorphoses may spark feelings of kinship in a translator, especially one who is translating the *Metamorphoses*. This is what happened in the poem-translation that did much to spread awareness of Ovid (including Pythagoras his metempsychosis) in the Renaissance, *The XV Bookes of P. Ovidius Naso, Entytled Metamorphosis*, translated by 'Arthur Golding Gentleman', published in 1567, and reprinted every decade until it was trumped by George Sandys's tidier version in 1626.

Golding's was one of a multitude of translations which bloomed after the accession of Elizabeth I in 1558: his desire to 'enrich' the 'native language with things not heretofore published in the same' was widely shared.[17] Some translators sought also to enrich the vocabulary of English by anglicizing Latin words; but Golding sided with those, like Thomas Phaer in his *Eneidos* (1558) or John Studley in his *Seventh Tragedie of Seneca, Entitled Medea* (1566), who held themselves to a markedly English idiom. As Gordon Braden has shown, he outdid those allies in his command of 'quirky, vigorous little terms' like 'gnorr', 'snudge', 'chank', and in his readiness to unfold a Latin word into a string of English equivalents: 'hirtus' becomes 'harsh and shirle'; 'pugnes' becomes 'strive, struggle, wrest and writhe'.[18] The world in which the metamorphoses

occur becomes more English too—a transformation which Madeleine
Forey has summed up well in her edition of the poem-translation:

> It is a world of raspberries, hips and haws rather than mountain strawberries
> (1. 119), crabs rather than octopuses (4. 454), lapwings rather than hoopoes
> (6. 853). One encounters witches, pucks, elves and fairies not nymphs
> (*passim*)...Music is provided by pots and pans not clashing cymbals
> (3. 673 et al.), viols not lyres (5. 139 et al.), and shawms not flutes
> (14. 612). The dead are placed in coffins not urns (12. 682).[19]

The pagan trappings of Ovid's world are rendered somewhat Christian:
'temples become churches with spires and are occupied by priests, chap-
lains and mitred bishops; *pietas* is replaced by godliness', and so on; Forey
sees in this a 'pervasive...rewriting of the work's theology'.[20] Yet, though
certainly pervasive, the rewriting does not go very deep. For instance, in
the flood in Book 1:

> Men, beasts, trees, corn and with their gods were churches washed away.[21]

'Churches' that house 'gods' cannot be wholly Christian. Braden catches
the feel of such moments well when he describes the Christianizing
gestures as being 'fairly casual' and as serving 'mainly as part of a general
shifting of ethnic coloration'.[22] This relaxed attitude on Golding's part is
striking in a devoted Puritan whose many other translations were almost
all of protestant theology, principally Calvin.

Golding does preface his translation with admonitory epistles adapted
to the tastes of, respectively, his patron Robert, Earl of Leicester and the
imagined general reader: Leicester is warned that Narcissus (for example)
is 'of scornfulness and pride a mirror clear'; while the 'simple sort' must
bear in mind that Bacchus stands for 'all the meaner trades and handi-
crafts'.[23] In their paradoxical amalgam of dogmatism and flexibility, these
epistles are in the tradition of moralization to which the *Metamorphoses*
had long been subjected:[24] as Marina Warner has said, 'in the Christian
context, metamorphosis exercised a fascination that could only be disciplined and contained by conscientious and elaborate didacticism'.[25] From
the early fourteenth century, the *Metamorphoses* were commonly encountered in the form of the *Ovide Moralisé* and similar paraphrases, in which
Ovid's verse is dissolved in allegorical commentary. Caxton had translated,
but never published, a text of this kind. In *The Fable of Ovid Treating of
Narcissus*, translated by 'T. H.' (1560) and *The Pleasant Fable of Hermaph-
roditus and Salmacis*, translated by Thomas Peend (1565) translation
is again subjugated to moralizing interpretation. Compared to this,

Golding's moralization is surprisingly unobtrusive: it is proportionately much shrunk, and is held apart from the translation itself.

   The reduction in didacticism may, counter-intuitively, owe something to Golding's religious beliefs, for it bears the marks of that anxiety over the distinction between translation and paraphrase of the Bible which we explored in Chapter 9.[26] In his *Metamorphoses*, as with a sacred book, the text is reverenced by being kept as separate as possible from commentary. Certainly, this structure seems to have been a habit with him, for his two works of authorial writing are arranged in the same way. *A Briefe Discourse of the Late Murther of Master George Saunders* (1573) starts by giving 'a playne declaration of the whole matter, according as the same is come to light by open triall of Justice, and voluntarie confession of the parties'; only after this comparatively impartial record of events has concluded are we told 'what is to be gathered of this terrible example, and how we oughte to apply the same to our owne behoofe'.[27] Narrative and interpretation are likewise distinguished, though their order is reversed, in *A Discourse vpon the Earthquake that Hapned throughe this Realme of Englande, and other Places of Christendom, the first of Aprill. 1580, betwene the houres of fiue and six in the euening* (1580). First the pages of admonition ('let vs turne to the Lorde our God wyth harty repentaunce and vnfeyned amendment of life', etc.); and only then 'The reporte of the said Earthquake, and howe it beganne'.[28]

   In his *Metamorphoses*, the arrangement creates a feeling of risk. Readers are given their instructions, and then released into the text of the translation to obey them or perhaps not. The Epistle to Leicester vividly describes both what should happen, and what may go wrong:

> The use of this same book therefore is this: that every man
> (Endeavouring for to know himself as nearly as he can),
> As though he in a chariot sat well ordered, should direct
> His mind by way of reason in the way of virtue and correct
> His fierce affections in the bit of temperance, lest perchance
> They, taking bridle in the teeth, like wilful jades do prance
> Away and headlong carry him to every filthy pit
> Of vice and, drinking of the same, defile his soule with it;
> Or else do headlong harry him upon the rocks of sin
> And, overthrowing forcible the chariot he sits in,
> Do tear him worse than ever was Hippolytus, the son
> Of Theseus, when he went about his father's wrath to shun.[29]

The danger Golding particularly mentions just before this passage is that 'matter lewd' will provoke our minds to wantonness: but clearly we are to be on our guard against all the bad behaviour represented in the

Metamorphoses—Narcissus's 'pride', the Centaurs' 'drunkenness', and so on—and to make sure that they provoke us to improve ourselves rather than to emulate them. 'Direct'—in the passage quoted—is one of many controlling verbs that toll throughout the 'Epistle': we must grasp what Ovid's words 'show' and 'prove' and 'witness' and 'declare' and 'represent' and again 'prove'; we must hold ourselves in the attitude of one who wants to 'learn'. The reader who abandons this 'way of virtue' and opens himself to the text's other stimuli becomes identified with Hippolytus who likewise lost control of his chariot. Yet if we turn to the episode referred to, we will find that little, beyond the presence of rocks, suits the moral that Golding, in the 'Epistle', wants to take from it. Hippolytus has in fact been virtuously resisting the wanton advances of his stepmother; his 'father's wrath' is explicitly said to be 'without cause'; and his horses run wild, not because he fails in 'reason' or 'virtue' but because a horned bull comes charging out of the sea at them.[30] This disparity between text and interpretation illustrates the distance readers must keep from Ovid's words in order to 'reduce their sense to right of Christian law'.[31] The struggle this may involve is suggested, in the passage from the 'Epistle to Leicester', by the movement of Golding's own artistic 'jade', the fourteen-syllable couplet. Golding's way with this form is never exactly masterly: to C. S. Lewis fifty years ago it seemed that 'he uses enjambment not for musical delight but... for mere convenience'.[32] Nevertheless, the verse does often gather into poetic suggestiveness. Here its movement vividly evokes the headlong dash of the horses of textual pleasure, itself veering out of true with its wild enjambments—'correct / ... ', 'perchance / ... ', 'prance / ... '—and rhymes misplaced at the start of lines: 'His... / His... / They... / Away... '. Hippolytus's accident is vigorously refashioned into a puritan vision of sin.

This idea of the *Metamorphoses* as a spiritual test must have helped release Golding into the relaxed responsiveness of his translation: if he is dangerously inward with his material (or so he could tell himself) it is the better to exercise his readers. He does not doggedly reproduce Ovid's rhetorical structures (as Sandys was to do fifty years later) but he does often freely imitate them; and his long, loose lines allow him to introduce animating little additions which are often, but not always, prompted by rhyme. For instance, in the opening account of the creation, some god or other (as Ovid insouciantly puts it) bids the woods be clothed in leaves ('fronde tegi silvas'); Golding gives 'the woods to hide them decently / With tender leaves'. Ovid says that the land of Auster, the south wind, 'is wet with constant fog and rain'; Golding that he 'beareth showers and rotten mists continual in his mouth'. In Ovid, the earth is 'only recently pulled away from the high ether'; in Golding, it is 'as yet / Young, lusty,

fresh and in her flowers, and parted from the sky / But late before'.[33]
Pound praised Golding for embodying the opposite of that 'Miltonic or
noise tradition' which I touched on in Chapter 23: 'he names the thing of
his original author, by the name most germane, familiar, homely, to his
hearers'.[34] All those adjectives are apposite; but Golding does something
else as well, something less consistent than Dryden's 'openings' or Pope's
passionate expansions and moral 'views'. He elaborates with vivifying
sympathy.

Like all the other translators I have discussed, though more mildly
and fleetingly than most, Golding allows his practice as a translator to
be inflected by what he is translating. In the 'Epistle', Echo had been
taken as an example of 'the lewd behaviour of a bawd and his due
punishment'.[35] But she is also liable to strike any translator as a double
of word-for-wording. Golding's version of her episode shows the influence of that recognition, subliminal though it may have remained in his
mind. His English keeps almost line for line with the Latin during her
conversation with Narcissus, and echoes its structure with unusual
accuracy:

> Said, 'Is there anybody nie? Straight *Echo* answered, 'I'.
>
> dixerat: "ecquis adest?" et "adest" responderat Echo.[36]

But the self-adoring Narcissus is the opposite of a translator: translating his
episode, Golding makes clear his feeling of estrangement:

> He feeds a hope without cause why. For, like a foolish noddy,
> He thinks the shadow that he sees to be a living body.
>
> spem sine corpore amat, corpus putat esse, quod umbra est[37]

This intensifies, and brings right up to the beginning of the episode, a
judgement which Ovid saves for later: 'credule'.[38] Golding's narrator
keeps up the same critical attitude throughout. When Narcissus admires
the features of his reflection:

> All these he wond'reth to behold, for which (as I do gather)
> Himself was to be wondered at or to be pitied rather.[39]

The parenthesis in the first line, and the pity in the second, are Golding's
insertions.

As Gordon Braden has shown, Golding's interpolations often give
an 'observer's response' and tend to express—as with 'foolish noddy'—'a
very secular combination of impatience and amusement' rather than the
Christian moralization rolled out in the 'Epistle'.[40] But the absences of
comment are significant too, for they imply a Golding who does not

always stand back from his source but is sometimes drawn into harmony with it—as in the case of Echo. Open to a text, but also wary of it, he is likely to be especially sensitized to characters who are in a similar position. Deucalion and Pyrrha, for instance, sole survivors of the flood, who are told by an oracle that in order to re-people the world they must 'both of you your grandam's bones behind your shoulders cast'. Whereupon they 'stood amazèd', scanning the 'doubtful words' until Deucalion has an idea:

> Well, either in these doubtful words is hid some mystery,
> Whereof the Gods permit us not the meaning to espy,
> Or, questionless, and if the sense of inward sentence deem
> Like as the tenor of the words apparently do seem,
> It is no breach of godliness to do as God doth bid.
> I take our grandam for the earth; the stones within her hid
> I take for bones; these are the bones the which are meanèd here.[41]

Ovid's Deucalion is brusque by comparison: ' "aut fallax" ait "est sollertia nobis, / aut...magna parens terra est..." '[42] ('either my wit'—he said—'is wrong or...our great mother is the earth...'). Golding's insertions—all the puzzling about 'mystery', 'meaning', 'inward sentence', and 'tenor'—hark back to the concerns of the 'Epistle'; but the connection they establish is not clear. Deucalion might be taken to contrast with the Christian interpreter in that he lacks the eye of faith with which to understand the 'mystery' that—he strangely appears to sense—is hidden beyond his ken. On the other hand, the pragmatism of his interpretation is very like what the 'Epistle' recommends: he turns the prophecy to use just as Golding's readers have been told to find 'the use of this book'.

Thanks to an accident of the English language, Golding's Deucalion has an interpretive key that Ovid's has had to manage without. 'Stones' mean 'bones' because the two words rhyme: the 'inward sense' is indeed 'like as the tenor of the words apparently do seem'. Though it corresponds to nothing specific in the Latin, this verbal trick is in harmony with the general playfulness with words in the *Metamorphoses* which has been resourcefully mapped by Frederick Ahl.[43] In Book 5—to take a straight-forward instance—a rude boy mocks the goddess Ceres: she throws a drink full of barley grains in his face, at which he metamorphoses into a spotted lizard. 'It has a name suited to its disgrace', Ovid tells us, 'since its body is starred with multi-coloured spots' ('aptumque pudori / nomen habet variis stellatus corpora guttis').[44] We have to guess that the name is 'stellio'—a gecko—which has an obvious connection to 'stellatus' and which can also mean a treacherous or deceitful person—as Ovid's Renaissance editor Raphael Regius sees it, in the text Golding used, 'ut enim

Stelliones varii sunt & versicolores, ita impostores atque deceptores'[45] (as Stellios are variable and of changeable colours, so also are imposters and deceivers'—Regius was perhaps thinking of chameleons). English gives Golding no resources for matching this onomastic conjuring trick exactly; but he does manage something similar. The boy, he says, is a 'wag', so it is apt that he ends up with 'a wriggling tail'; he is a 'fast boy', so it is apt that he becomes a 'swift' (i.e. a newt).[46]

This instance of name-fulfilment has an admonitory tone. One can imagine the Golding of the 'Epistle' approving the fate of the so-called 'wag' who ends up having to wag for real. Elsewhere in the poem-translation, wordplay is more variously suggestive, for instance in the description of Hecuba when she sees, washed up on the shore, the body of Polydorus, who had been her last remaining son:

> ... She stood astonied, like
> As if she had been stone. One while the ground she stared upon;
> Another while a ghastly look she cast to heaven; anon
> She lookèd on the face of him that lay before her killed.[47]

'Astonied' (i.e. 'astonished') like a 'stone': the clumsiness of it is moving, like a *faux pas* caused by deep sorrow. The stacking of phonemes continues through 'one while', 'upon', 'Another while', 'anon', suggesting the disorientation, the stopped time, that comes upon her. Just as with the wag, this verbal play finds its conclusion in how she ends up: having taken her revenge on Polydorus's murderer, she finds herself barking when she tries to speak and, 'running at a stone, with gnarring seized thereon / And worried it between her teeth'.[48] This time there is no moral aptness, but rather a recognition of the dehumanizing effect of intense grief. There is no comparable play on words in the Latin at this point: the innovation in Golding's text suggests involvement, and sympathy.

In the episode of Deucalion and Pyrrha, the closeness of stones to people is confirmed by the fact that both have 'veins'. After the metamorphosis, the Latin says:

> quae modo vena fuit, sub eodem nomine mansit.[49]

In Golding the homonymy is the more impressive because it continues from Latin into English:

> The part that was a vein before doth still his name retain.[50]

Golding brings the feel of this extra continuity into his English by giving 'vein' a rhyme (which held in the sixteenth century just as now) with 'retain'. For all his devotion to homely English, then, he was alert to verbal connections between Latin and English, and ready to make play with them in his translation. Another instance occurs during the mutilation of Philomela by Tereus:

> But as she yearned and callèd aye upon her father's name
> And strived to haue spoken still, the cruel tyrant came
> And with a pair of pinions fast did catch her by the tongue
> And with his sword did cut it off. The stump whereon it hung
> Did patter still. The tip fell downe and quivering on the ground,
> As though that it had murmurèd it made a certain sound.
> And as an adder's tail cut off doth skip a while, even so
> The tip of Philomela's tongue did wriggle to and fro
> And nearer to her mistressward in dying still did go.[51]

In the Latin, 'her father's name' is 'nomen patris'.[52] Golding's word 'patter' derives from the Latin 'pater': it had started its life in English a century or so earlier when it meant 'to recite the paternoster'.[53] So, having been prevented from calling on her father's name, Philomela can still do something that has the Latin word for father in it: she can still 'patter'. But that meaning was no longer the dominant one by Golding's time: it is not uttered by the word any more than her tongue, which wriggles like an adder's tail, can get through the half-way house of simile into full metamorphosis.

Golding's way with the texture of the language, then, releases meanings which ramify beyond the grasp of Deucalion's pragmatic style of interpretation, let alone the admonitions of the 'Epistle'. They speak of pain and sympathy in the case of Hecuba; in that of Philomela, they embody a horrifying thwartedness. The two trends of Golding's reaction to Ovid, the proliferating verbal play and the discipline of interpretation, come together in his rendering of the episode of Apollo and Daphne. In the Latin, as Ahl has shown, wordplay is 'threatening to Daphne' from the start. The word 'saepe' is reiterated emphatically: it means 'often' but suggests 'saepes', a shrub. And: 'since she asks to be allowed to enjoy (*FRUi*) virginity (1. 486-87), it is ironic that the tree into which she is changed should be a laurel, which does not bear *FRUctus*, fruit'. Furthermore, there is an 'anagrammatic movement from her virginal blushing *RUBOR* to the *ROBUR*, woody hardness of a tree, *ARBOR*'.[54] Golding allows similar hints to flicker in his writing. Daphne is 'chaste'; and then she is pursued in a 'chase' by Apollo. Her father tells her she should find a 'fere' (lover), and Apollo wants her 'to his fere'; but she ends up feeling 'fear'. Apollo is attracted by her 'hair' and hunts her as though she were a 'hare'; he pursues her like a 'grew'nd' (greyhound) and she ends up being swallowed by 'a tender bark'.[55]

When she is metamorphosed into a laurel, Daphne escapes the grasp of
Apollo's body, but not the embrace of his rhetoric. 'Yet shalt thou be my
tree', he declares, and goes on to load her with masculine significance: she
will 'adorn my quiver full of shafts', as Golding puts it (a touch salacious-
ly); she will reward 'noble feats of arms' and guard 'Augustus' palace
door'.[56] But does she agree to take on all this meaning?—

> ... factis modo laurea ramis
> adnuit utque caput visa est agitasse cacumen.[57]

The laurel nodded consentingly with her/its new-made branches and seemed
to move her/its top like a head.

'Adnuit' normally meant, unequivocally, 'nodded consent'; but when it is
done by a tree with its branches there is room for uncertainty. As Alessandro
Barchiesi notes in his edition of the *Metamorphoses*: 'the movement belongs to
the plant ('è della pianta'), is part of its visible nature, but Apollo interprets it
victoriously as a sign of acquiescence ... a cruel ambiguity persists'.[58]

Dryden, in his translation of this episode, agrees with Apollo:

> The grateful tree was pleased with what he said,
> And shook the shady honours of her head.[59]

'Grateful' and 'pleased' are his telling interpolations. Sandys displays the
same allegiance:

> ... The Laurell all allowes:
> In signe whereof her gratefull head shee bowes.[60]

These Apollonian translators, devoted (albeit ambivalently in Dryden's
case) to getting things clear, side with their god. Now here is Golding:

> Now when that Paean of this talk had fully made an end,
> The laurel to his just request did seem to condescend
> By bowing of her new-made boughs and tender branches down
> And wagging of her seemly top, as if it were her crown.

'Just' is his interpolation, and hints obedience to the forces of masculinity,
significance and empire. But 'seem' then pushes in the opposite direction,
and the echo of 'bowing ... in boughs' emphasizes, like Barchiesi, that it is
in the nature of a bough to bow, just as it is in the material substance of
those words to rhyme. A tree is 'tender' when it is young and easily bent: it
does not follow that there is a tender (in the sense of loving) soul within.
The tree's top is 'seemly', beautiful—but the echo of 'seem' keeps in mind
that all this seeming is happening in the eye of an observer; that these
meanings are not inherent in the tree but are being ascribed to it.
'Wagging' her or its top, in kinship with the 'wag' who became a 'stellio',
the laurel may just be having us on.

Golding's translation of this passage keeps open an awareness of the violence done to the metamorphosed woman—something that Sandys and Dryden are blind to, and that it has taken responses to Ovid by twentieth-century women poets to make fully visible. Alice Fulton:

> Of course, he liked her better as a tree. 'Girls *are* trees'
> was his belief. Mediated
> forms pleased him. 'If you can't find a partner, use
> a wooden chair',
> he'd say.

(Chairs can substitute for partners in dance lessons—though the partnering envisaged by Fulton does not stop there.) But the ambivalence of Golding's rendering also epitomizes the resistance of his whole translation to the interpretive violence exercised by Apollo on Daphne, and by his own 'Epistle' on the *Metamorphoses*. Throughout his version, Golding fleetingly allies himself with different metaphors of translation. He interprets Deucalion's act of interpretation, a little bit as Dryden was to 'open' Virgil's 'openings'; and he responds sympathetically to Hecuba, with a hint of how Pope would later respond passionately to Homer. His way with the word 'patter' momentarily creates a deadness, a thwartedness, out of a layering of Latin and English rather as Browning and Pound were, long after, to do so much more comprehensively. He echoes Echo and turns his back on Narcissus. But none of these doubles defines his practice with anything like the stringency of the metaphors of translation we have explored in previous chapters: the interactions are even more faint and partial than those in FitzGerald's *Rubáiyát*.

As we have seen, metaphors of translation release writers from the tyranny of 'translation rigidly conceived'. They open up, and define, different imaginative practices which enable poets to create translations that are poems. One view of what I have been doing in this book might be that I have mapped varieties of translatory 'freedom'. And certainly that is part of it. Dryden's 'translation as opening', Pope's 'translation as passion' and as 'taking a view', Logue's 'zoom', Pound's 'bringing a dead man to life'—in all these cases (and others) I have offered new descriptions of translation practices that have often been called 'free'. And yet, to focus on those metaphors that are explicit in translators' self-definitions, or implicit in their practice, or both, is to reveal something more particular than a series of sub-categories of 'freedom'. A translator who follows a metaphor of 'opening' subjects his practice to some constraints; there are constraints too—but different ones—for a translator who follows a metaphor of 'passion'. While these tactics of translation turn away from some aspects of the source text, they respond to others with precision and discipline. It is a misrepresentation to call these practices 'free'.

Equally, metaphors such as those I have traced can create expressiveness within practices of translation that would usually be called 'literal' or 'close'. Browning's metaphor of 'transcript' is in this bag; as are Pound's of 'presenting the vivid personality' of Cavalcanti, and Natasha Randall's (discussed in Chapter 7) of 'translation as the sharing of sensations'. Metaphors of translation, then, traverse and fracture those descriptive binaries whose shortcomings we discussed in Chapter 5. In comparison to the range of metaphors we have explored, the old pairs of 'free' and 'faithful', 'foreignizing' and 'domesticating', etc., are revealed to be just different metaphors, which do not describe at all precisely the varieties of translational practice that they have for so long been used to name.

Those binaries have typically been conceived in advance of reading: they are brought to translations and imposed on them so as to fit the multi-plicitous texts into a pre-established structure of understanding. The meta-phors that I have pursued have emerged out of the particular translations that we have read. Sometimes a guiding metaphor has been made explicit in a poet's self-description, sometimes not. Often it has been suggested by the text that is being translated. Of course, in identifying and drawing out each metaphor I must have done some interpretive moulding of my own. Nothing I have advanced in this book is 'objective': I am not putting forward what (as we saw in Chapter 5) some scholars of translation think is needed—a 'theory' that can be 'tested' and thereby proved or disproved. Such a theory would inevitably falsify the processes of reading and inter-preting which are matters, not of observation and proof, but of perception, imagining, judgement, and persuasion. What I have above all wished to demonstrate in this book is that poem-translations are not objects to be analysed and categorized but texts that reward the intuitive and responsive activity of reading. To other readers of translations, I have offered, not a theory in the sense of an objectively-testable model, but theoretically-informed tactics of interpretation—metaphors to look out for—which I hope will have seemed persuasive and fruitful.

The picture of the history of translation given by this book has not been straightforward. There have been various organizing contours. The argu-ment has to some extent followed lines of indebtedness from one poet-translator to another: Lowell to Dryden; Pound to Browning. And it has, to some extent, traced successive versions of the same text: the *Iliad* from Pope to Logue. But these particular, partial principles of organization are both subordinate to the larger endeavour, which has been to group the texts discussed according to similarity of guiding metaphor. Lowell echoes Dryden because he too was exercised by the relation between translation and 'opening' or interpretation. Logue follows (I hope) interestingly from Pope because both drew from the *Iliad* guiding metaphors of looking or moving across a landscape.

Clearly, circumambient cultural factors played a part in allowing the different metaphors to flourish when and where they did. On several occasions (Chapters 14, 16, 21, and 22) we have come up against the spread of a metaphor of 'adherence' at the end of the eighteenth century, and have observed the corresponding retreat of other, more searching metaphors of translation. The reasons for this shift are widespread in the culture and must include (for instance) developments arising from copyright law of the sort that have been chronicled by Roger Chartier.[61] In the case of Dryden I did spend some time tracing the cultural roots of his interest in the metaphor of 'opening'. But I am aware that, in my other chapters, I have done little more than gesture towards the historical interrelations that could (and I hope will in future work) be more thoroughly mapped. To pursue them in these pages would have resulted in an impossibly unwieldy book, and would have risked occluding what I take to be the main original emphases of my discussion: the generative potential of the source texts, and its release when those texts interact with the responsive and interpretive imaginations of poet-translators. Nevertheless, the book does—I think—have implications for literary history. I have arranged acts of translation across time, according to a pattern which emerges from them, rather than being brought to them preformatted as chronology. Of course, the texts have figured as they have been taken by translators who are historically situated. But the texts have, in return, exerted their own pressure on each historical situation, changing it. It is in the nature of translation to mess with literary history in this way. Translation allows a text from one culture to become active again—to be written again—in another culture centuries or millennia later. Other works too can take on new life, of course: they can be rediscovered, or exert new influence. But translations have a unique power to create folds in literary space and time.

My choice of texts has been partial in both senses. Obviously, the discussion gives a great deal of space to translations that have long been established as canonical. Part of my aim was to discover what has made these works so imaginatively compelling: my argument, then, can serve as a contribution to understanding the event of their canonization. However, there are some canonical poem-translations that simply do not—so far as I can see—respond to the approach I have pursued. One example is H. F. Cary's translation of Dante (1805) which was much praised throughout the nineteenth century. It is a skilful making-over of the *Commedia* into Miltonic verse, but I have not been able to discover (save for the moment in *Inferno* 5 which I discussed in Chapter 18) that its guiding metaphors evolve out of or interact with the source in the ways that distinguish the poetry of translation. Another instance is Dryden's *Fables Ancient and Modern*, widely taken to be a 'masterpiece' of the translation of poetry.[62] And so it is. Of the texts included in that volume, 'On the Pythagorean Philosophy' includes a flicker of the poetry of translation, as we saw at the start of this chapter; there is another flicker in 'Baucis and Philemon' (also from Ovid) which I have explored elsewhere.[63] The rest of the volume strikes me as, though brilliantly written, not quite entering into the poetry of translation—the work, perhaps, of someone whose earlier anxieties about translation's potential to do harm had settled somewhat, and whose imagination was therefore no longer agonistically involved in the source texts as it had been during the earlier Englishings of Ovid's *Epistles* and Virgil's *Aeneid*. That 'sprezzatura' admired by Tomlinson would be—on this account—not wholly a good thing. Perhaps I am simply blind here; and I look forward to being proved wrong by other readers. But, if I am not, this is evidence in support of a suggestion I made in Chapter 7. The poetry of translation is sporadic: translation creates the conditions for its existence, but it does not always appear. All translations are guided by metaphors; to grasp these metaphors is to abandon the old binaries of 'free', 'literal', etc. But only in some translations do the metaphors of translation interact with doubles in the source text in such a way that the poetry of translation flowers.

Some texts I have neglected because they have been very well discussed already. Pope's *Odyssey* is one of these: it has been beautifully explored by Paul Davis in *Translation and the Poet's Life* (2008) in terms that I could do little except repeat. Others have lost out to my mortal limitations. It seems to me quite likely that the translations of Psalms by Mary Sidney, Countess of Pembroke (*c.*1555–1621) would turn out to be compelling instances of the poetry of translation—but I have felt myself to be not sufficiently equipped in theological or linguistic knowledge to attempt a serious reading. The same goes for the whole tradition of Psalm translation, sampled in Donald Davie (ed.), *The Psalms in English* (1996). All that said, however, the fact remains that the spine of my book is formed by canonical translations into English, largely done by men. To that extent, I have not heeded the call, recently made in the discipline of translation studies, for our understanding of translation to become 'decentered' so as to take account of a multitude of trans-lingual acts between many different cultures—I say 'trans-lingual acts' because the concept of translation is put in question by this approach. And yet I hope that, from another point of view, my book may be seen to harmonize with this endeavour (which I applaud). For my argument too—I hope—reframes and re-energizes the concept of translation, albeit from the centre. One way of showing what poetry-translation is, is to point to some canonical examples. I hope that those examples will look somewhat different as a result of the explorations that we have undertaken.

As I explained in Chapter 7, the metaphorical interaction characteristic of the poetry of translation flourishes especially in the translation of poetry, more than of prose and drama. Nevertheless, I am uneasy about my neglect of those other genres, and it may be that the approach I have followed can be pursued further with them (I have, elsewhere, taken some steps towards doing this with Thomas Carlyle's translation of Goethe's *Wilhelm Meister's Apprenticeship* [1824], and with prose translations published in Victorian penny weeklies such as the *London Journal*).[64] This is the more likely because much of the poetry that I have discussed shares something crucial with much prose fiction: narrative. Again, there are obvious historical reasons why narrative poetry—especially epic—should have provoked intense efforts of translation by major poets. Dryden's Virgil and Pope's Homer were—as their subscription lists attest—vehicles of national prestige. But it is also noticeable that narratives of action are fertile of metaphors of translation because translation is itself an action. 'Opening', 'passion', 'zoom', 'bringing to life', 'various particular metamorphoses'—in each of these cases it is an action narrated in the source that offers a double of the act of translation. In cases of 'desire', such as those from Dryden's Theocritus and Fairfax's Tasso which I discussed in Chapter 16, the metaphor of translation is prompted by something concealed in the source, or left unsaid. But the metaphor is still one of action—of the action of invasion or penetration that the source's coyness seems to court. We have also discussed metaphors drawn, not from actions, but from states: Wyatt's of 'constraint' and 'liberty' in love, Pope's of 'taking a view', and Byron's (in *Don Juan*) of 'secondariness' or 'conventionality'. But they have been fewer, and seem less assertive, than the action kind.

These metaphors, fundamental to translation though they be, are nevertheless all simplifications. They inhere in the imaginative practice of translating, shaping it to a greater degree (as with Dryden's 'opening') or a lesser (as with Golding), but never dominating it completely. They leave their traces in the translated texts that they have helped to form, where critical readings (as mine have done) can build upon them. In one respect, Golding's *Metamorphoses* epitomizes the tendency for metaphors of translation to emerge out of the texts that are being translated and to stimulate, not only poem-translations, but a poetry of translation. It also embodies a contrary trend: for translated texts to elude the grasp of their guiding metaphors.

Golding's light and fluid way with metaphors of metamorphosis owes something (as we have seen) to his religious and imaginative disposition, and something also to the fact that he was writing before the great elaboration of metaphors of translation done by Dryden and his contemporaries. And it derives also from the mobility of the *Metamorphoses* itself, the baffling multitude of doubles which the text holds out to its translator. Nevertheless, all poems of translation include something of the same freely metamorphic responsiveness, an opening of the imagination to the multiplicity of the text that is being translated.

In Ovid, some metamorphoses—like that of the 'fast boy' into the 'stellio'—are very fully governed by metaphor: they embody an obvious meaning. Others—like that of Daphne—are mysterious and multiply suggestive: they elude metaphor's explanatory grasp. As we saw in Part I, much discussion of poetic translation fails to comprehend its variety: this book, by tracing different metaphors, has endeavoured to arrive at a more nuanced understanding than has been available hitherto. But, like all poetry, the nimble, intuitive work of the great poetic translaters outgoes whatever critical categories are brought to bear on it. In summing up, over these last few pages, I have sought to draw out some general points that readers may like to take away with them. But I am also aware that, with my talk of pursuing, my acts of definition, I have been sounding a little bit like Apollo, narrowing the significance of what has happened to Daphne by decreeing what the Laurel will mean. What poems of translation do seems in some cases to be quite readily describable: those works are like the metamorphosis of the 'fast boy'. Others are obviously complex and ambiguous, like the metamorphosis of Daphne. But all of them have a touch of Daphne-the-laurel about them. They flaunt their leaves at their Apollonian interpreters, and wag their seemly tops.

Notes

NOTES TO CHAPTER 1

1. John Lyly, *Euphues: The Anatomy of Wyt* (1578), 5v.
2. Samuel Johnson, *A Dictionary of the English Language: The First and Fourth Editions*, ed. Anne McDermott. CD-ROM (Cambridge, 1996), *ad loc.*
3. *The Holy Bible . . . in the Earliest English Versions made from the Latin Vulgate by John Wycliffe and his Followers*, ed. Rev. Josiah Forshall and Sir Frederic Madden, 4 vols (Oxford, 1850), ii, 403 (Paralipomenon 8.11) and iv, 498 (Hebrews 11.5).
4. Johnson, *A Dictionary*.
5. J. C. Catford, *A Linguistic Theory of Translation: An Essay in Applied Linguistics* (1965), 35, quoting William N. Locke and Andrew D. Booth, *Machine Translation of Languages: Fourteen Essays* (Cambridge, Mass. and New York, 1955), 124.
6. Jacques Derrida, 'Living On / Border Lines', in Harold Bloom et al., *Deconstruction and Criticism* (1979), 93; Kathleen Davis, *Deconstruction and Translation* (Manchester, 2001), 17; Jacques Derrida, *Positions* (Paris, 1972), 31, tr. Gayatry Chakravorti Spivak in Derrida, *Of Grammatology* (1976), lxxxvii.
7. Andrew Marvell, 'To his Coy Mistress', quoted from *The Poems of Andrew Marvell*, ed. James Reeves and Martin Seymour-Smith (1969), 22.
8. *Biblia Sacra Iuxta Vulgatam Versionem*, ed. Robertus Weber OSB (Stuttgart, 1983), 2 Paralipomenon 8.11; Ad Hebraeos 11.5.
9. Douglas Robinson, *The Translator's Turn* (Baltimore and London, 1991), 195.
10. Maria Tymoczko, 'Western Metaphorical Discourses Implicit in Translation Studies', in James St André (ed.), *Thinking Through Translation with Metaphors* (Manchester, 2010), 109–43, 119. Tymoczko's position is expounded further in her *Enlarging Translation, Empowering Translators* (Manchester, 2007) and 'Reconceptualizing Translation Theory: Integrating Non-Western Thought about Translation', in Theo Hermans (ed.), *Translating Others*, 2 vols (Manchester, 2006), i, 13–32.
11. Geoffrey Chaucer, *Amorum Troili et Creseidae libri duo priores Anglico-Latini*, tr. Sir Francis Kinnaston (Oxford, 1635), 4v.
12. 'A Midsummer Night's Dream', III. i. 109, quoted from William Shakespeare, *The Complete Works*, ed. Peter Alexander (London and Glasgow, 1951).
13. John Dryden, *The Poems*, ed. Paul Hammond and David Hopkins, 5 vols (1995–2005), i, 384–5.
14. In John Dryden, *The Works*, ed. E. N. Hooker, H. T. Swedenberg, Jr., et al., 20 vols (Berkeley and London, 1956–2000), v, 63.

15. Samuel Taylor Coleridge, *Biographia Literaria or Biographical Sketches of My Literary Life and Opinions*, ed. James Engell and W. Jackson Bate, 2 vols (vol 7 of the *Collected Works of Samuel Taylor Coleridge*, 1983), 18–19.
16. Antoine Berman, *L'Épreuve de l'étranger: Culture et traduction dans l'Allemagne romantique* (Paris, 1984).
17. William Hazlitt, *Lectures on the English Poets* (1818), 107.
18. Thomas Carlyle, *On Heroes, Hero-Worship, & the Heroic in History*, ed. Michael K. Goldberg et al. (Berkeley and Oxford, 1993), 94.
19. Walter Pater, *Appreciations, with an Essay on Style* (1889), 31.
20. Paul Valéry, *Cahiers*, ed. Judith Robinson, 2 vols (Paris, 1973), i, 105.
21. Sherry Simon, *Gender in Translation: Cultural Identity and the Politics of Transmission* (1996), 134.
22. George Steiner, *After Babel* (1975; 3rd edn 1998), xii, 49.
23. Ibid., 28–9.
24. Ibid., 1.
25. See Max Black, 'More about Metaphor', in Andrew Ortony (ed.), *Metaphor and Thought*, 2nd edn (Cambridge, 1993), 19–41.
26. Ludwig Wittgenstein, *Philosophical Investigations*, tr. G. E. M. Anscombe (Oxford, 1988), 12.

NOTES TO CHAPTER 2

1. Suzanne Romaine, *Language in Society: An Introduction to Sociolinguistics* (Oxford, 1994), 2.
2. Natalia Ginzburg, *Lessico famigliare* (Milan, 1999), 22, 3, 53.
3. Umberto Eco, *Mouse or Rat? Translation as Negotiation* (2003), 128.
4. Charlie Croker (ed.), *Lost in Translation: Misadventures in English Abroad*, with illustrations by Louise Morgan (2006), 45, 28.
5. William Shakespeare, *Ouevres complétes*, ed. Henri Fluchère, 2 vols (Paris, 1959), ii, 666.
6. A. L. Becker, *Beyond Translation: Essays toward a Modern Philology* (Ann Arbor, 1995), 284.
7. Vyvyan Evans, *How Words Mean: Lexical Concepts, Cognitive Models, and Meaning Construction* (Oxford, 2009), 9–11.
8. John Lyons, *Language and Linguistics: An Introduction* (Cambridge, 1981), 151.
9. Theo Hermans, *The Conference of the Tongues* (Manchester, 2007), 23.
10. Charles Dickens, *Oliver Twist*, ed. Peter Fairclough (Harmondsworth, 1985), 100.
11. Ibid., 181.
12. William Barnes, *Poems of Rural Life in the Dorset Dialect: With a Dissertation and Glossary* (1844), 12, 11; 2nd edn (1848), 20.
13. Dryden, *Poems*, v, 80.

NOTES TO CHAPTER 3

1. Eco, *Mouse or Rat?*, 136–7.
2. Dryden, *Poems*, iii, 395, 318.
3. Ibid., i, 384–9.
4. Ibid.
5. Donald Carne-Ross and Kenneth Haynes (eds), *Horace in English*, with an introduction by Donald Carne-Ross (1996), xiv; Clive Scott, *Channel Crossings: French and English Poetry in Dialogue, 1550–2000* (Oxford, 2002), 1.
6. Robert Browning, *Poetical Works*, 16 vols (1888–9), xiii, 261–2.
7. Dryden, *Poems*, iii, 447.
8. Dante Gabriel Rossetti (tr.), *The Early Italian Poets from Ciullo d'Alcamo to Dante Alighieri* (1861), viii.
9. Catford, *A Linguistic Theory of Translation*, 49, 1. In his *Translation and Language: Linguistic Theories Explained* (Manchester, 1997), p. 54 Peter Fawcett quotes Mary Snell-Hornby as saying that Catford's work 'is now generally considered dated and of mere historical interest' (*Translation Studies: An Integrated Approach* [Amsterdam, 1988], 14–15)—an instance of the sort of jibe that rebounds on the one who utters it. Catford is more sympathetically treated in more recent work, for instance by Anthony Pym in 'Natural and Directional Equivalence in Theories of Translation', *Target* 19.2 (2007), 271–94, largely reproduced in his *Exploring Translation Theories* (Abingdon, 2010).
10. John Lyons, *Semantics*, 2 vols (Cambridge, 1977), i, 237–8.
11. Fawcett, *Translation and Language*, 55. Catford himself remarks that 'the question of "sameness" of situation-substance is a difficult one' (*A Linguistic Theory of Translation*, 55).
12. Eugene Nida, 'A Framework for the Analysis and Evaluation of Theories of Translation', in Richard W. Brislin (ed.), *Translation, Application and Research* (New York, 1976), 47–91, quoted in Christiane Nord, *Translating as a Purposeful Activity: Functionalist Approaches Explained* (Manchester, 1997), 5.
13. Quoted in Ibid., 29–30. In 'Skopos and Commission in Translational Action', tr. Andrew Chesterman in Lawrence Venuti (ed.), *The Translation Studies Reader*, 2nd edn (2004), 227–38, Vermeer recognizes objections of roughly the kind I am about to canvas; but he does not rebut them (in my judgement) at all convincingly.
14. Douglas Robinson, *The Translator's Turn* (Baltimore and London, 1991), 3–64.
15. See Mona Baker, *Translation and Conflict: A Narrative Account* (2006), 64–5.
16. M. M. Bakhtin, *The Dialogic Imagination: Four Essays*, ed. Michael Holquist, tr. Caryl Emerson and Michael Holquist (Austin, Tex., 1981), 263.
17. Roman Jakobson, *Language in Literature*, ed. Krystyna Pomorska and Stephen Rudy (Cambridge, Mass. and London, 1987), 69.
18. Scott, *Channel Crossings*, 2.
19. L. G. Kelly, *The True Interpreter: A History of Translation Theory and Practice in the West* (Oxford, 1979), 35.

20. Robert J. Matthews, 'What did Archimedes Mean by "χρυσός"?', in Joseph F. Graham (ed.), *Difference in Translation* (Ithaca, 1985), 149–64, 149–50.
21. Philip Lewis, 'The Measure of Translation Effects', in ibid., 31–62, 59, 43.
22. Maria Tymoczko, *Translation in a Postcolonial Context: Early Irish Literature in English Translation* (Manchester, 1999), 282. This way of thinking is embodied in Tymoczko's key idea—both in that book and in later work—that translation is 'metonymic' rather than 'metaphorical': see her *Enlarging Translation, Empowering Translators*, 127–8.
23. *London Review of Books*, 28.6 (23 March 2006), 6.
24. Brian Friel, *Translations* (1980), 31.

NOTES TO CHAPTER 4

1. Theo Hermans, *The Conference of the Tongues* (Manchester, 2007), 10.
2. Theo Hermans, 'Paradoxes and Aporias in Translation and Translation Studies', in Alessandra Riccardi (ed.), *Translation Studies: Perspectives on an Emerging Discipline* (Cambridge, 2002), 10–23, 11.
3. Hermans, *The Conference of the Tongues*, 91.
4. There is a similar neglect in the sub-discipline of 'Descriptive Translation Studies', for which 'a "translation" will be taken to be any target-language utterance which is presented or regarded as such, on whatever grounds', Gideon Toury, *Descriptive Translation Studies and Beyond* (Amsterdam, 1995), 20: the passive 'is presented or regarded' leaves the door open for absolutely any text to be taken as a translation since, as we saw in Chapter 1, any text—indeed, anything at all—can 'be presented or regarded' as a translation by someone so minded. For discussion, see Anthony Pym, *Exploring Translation Theories* (Abingdon, 2010), 76.
5. Lyons, *Semantics*, i, 238. Lyons's conception is helpfully summarized and updated in Alan Cruse, *Meaning in Language: An Introduction to Semantics and Pragmatics*, 2nd edn (Oxford, 2004), 44–57.
6. Quoted in Hanna Fenichel Pitkin, *The Concept of Representation* (1967), 66.
7. I am indebted here to Steiner's narrative of 'the hermeneutic motion', *After Babel*, 312–16.
8. Dryden, *Poems,* i, 386.
9. Aleksandr Pushkin, *Eugene Onegin: A Novel in Verse*, tr. with a commentary by Vladimir Nabokov, 2 vols, rev. edn (Princeton, NJ, 1975), i, pp. viii–ix.
10. Ezra Pound, *Selected Poems*, ed. T. S. Eliot (1948), 13.
11. Introduction by Christopher Reid, in Christopher Logue, *War Music: An Account of Books 1–4 and 16–19 of Homer's* Iliad (2001), xi–xiii, xi–xii.
12. Derek Mahon, *Adaptations* (Oldcastle, Co. Meath, 2006), cover blurb.
13. Walter Benjamin, *Illuminationen. Ausgewählte Schriften*, vol. 1 (Frankfurt am Main, 1977), 54.
14. Paul Muldoon, 'The Eel', in Jamie McKendrick (ed.), *The Faber Book of Twentieth Century Italian Poems* (2004), 50–1.

15. Eugenio Montale, *L'Opera in Versi*, ed. Rosanna Bettarini and Gianfranco Contini (Milan, 1980), 254.
16. Paul Muldoon, *The End of the Poem: Oxford Lectures in Poetry* (Oxford, 2006), 195.
17. William Blake, *The Complete Poems*, ed. W. H. Stevenson, 2nd edn (1989), 492.
18. Seamus Heaney, *Opened Ground: Poems 1966–96* (1998), 6.

NOTES TO CHAPTER 5

1. Browning, *Poetical Works*, xiii, 262; Vladimir Nabokov, 'The Servile Path', in Reuben A. Brower (ed.), *On Translation* (1959; 1966), 97–110, 97.
2. Browning, *Poetical Works*, xiii, 261.
3. [Alexander Tytler], *Essay on the Principles of Translation* (1791), 13.
4. *Aeschylus: Translated into English Prose*, tr. F. A. Paley, (Cambridge, 1864), v.
5. Browning, *Poetical Works*, xiii, 269.
6. Aeschylus, *Agamemnon*, ed. Eduard Fraenkel, 3 vols (Oxford, 1950), ii, 10.
7. *Aeschylus*, tr. Paley, 131.
8. See Daniel Weissbort and Astradur Eysteinsson (eds), *Translation—Theory and Practice: A Historical Reader* (Oxford, 2006), 205–9.
9. This is one of many instances we will encounter that disprove Lawrence Venuti's contention that 'foreignization' should be defined, not at all by its proximity to aspects of the source text, but only by its difference from norms of writing in the target culture; that 'in translation the foreignness of the foreign text is available only in cultural forms that already circulate in the translating language', so that Pound's translations, for instance, 'signified the foreignness of the foreign text, not because they were faithful or accurate . . . but because they deviated from literary canons in English' (Lawrence Venuti, *The Translator's Invisibility*, 2nd edn (2008), 176, 174–5). Neither 'manly-counselling' nor 'man's-way-planning' were circulating before their appearance in Paley's and Browning's translation; and like much else in both texts they quite clearly came into being through linguistic and cultural interaction with the source. Furthermore, there are many kinds of deviations from literary norms, many of which do not figure as foreign: it follows that deviation alone cannot account for the feeling of foreignness in a text. For an elaboration of these points, see my 'Varifocal Translation in Ciaran Carson's *Inferno*', in Daniella Caselli and Daniella La Penna (eds), *Twentieth-Century Poetic Translation: Literary Cultures in Italian and English* (2008), 71–84; for more on the varied historical context of Paley's and Browning's work, see my 'Principles and Norms of Translation', in Peter France and Stuart Gillespie (gen. eds), *The Oxford History of Literary Translation in English*, 5 vols, vol. 4, ed. Peter France and Kenneth Haynes (Oxford, 2006), iv, 59–84; for an overview of Browning's other interactions with foreign cultures, see my 'Browning and Translationese', *Essays in Criticism* 53.2 (April 2003), 97–128 and my book *The Realms of Verse 1830–1870: English Poetry in a Time of Nation-Building* (Oxford, 2001).

10. Louis Zukofsky, *Complete Short Poetry* (Baltimore and London, 1991), 260.
11. Pushkin, *Eugene Onegin*, tr. Nabokov, i, pp. viii–ix.
12. Ibid., p. x.
13. Aeschylus, *Agamemnon*, ed. Fraenkel, i, 146–7.
14. Browning, *Poetical Works*, xiii, 313.
15. Tymoczko, *Enlarging Translation, Empowering Translators*, 181.
16. Ibid., 182–3.
17. Ibid., 66.
18. Several of these couples are discussed in Pym, *Exploring Translation Theories*, 30–4.

NOTES TO CHAPTER 6

1. Lieven d'Hulst, 'Sur le rôle des métaphores en traductologie contemporaine', *Target* 4.1 (1992), 33–51, 35. There is further discussion of the metaphors used by scholars of translation in several of the contributions to St André (ed.), *Thinking Through Translation with Metaphors* (Manchester, 2010).
2. Charles Tomlinson, *Poetry and Metamorphosis* (Cambridge, 1983).
3. See above, Chapter 4.
4. Jean Starr Untermeyer, *Private Collection* (New York, 1965), 261.
5. Gayatri Chakravorty Spivak, *Outside in the Teaching Machine* (1993), 181.
6. Black, 'More about Metaphor', 33.
7. Edward FitzGerald, *Letters and Literary Remains*, 7 vols (1902–3), vi, 267–8.
8. Ibid., 284, 316.
9. Ibid., 272.
10. Elizabeth Barrett Browning, *Poetical Works* (1904), 553–5, 560.
11. Elizabeth Barrett Browning, *Prometheus Bound Translated from the Greek of Aeschylus. And Miscellaneous Poems by the Translator* (1833), 62.
12. Quoted in Marjorie Stone, *Elizabeth Barrett Browning* (1995), 70.
13. Barrett [Browning], *Prometheus Bound*, 28–9; Barrett Browning, *Poetical Works*, 562. There are some minor differences between the text in *Poetical Works* and that in Barrett Browning's *Poems* (1850): the second version must have been revised slightly for further publication.
14. Aeschylus, *Prometheus Bound*, ed. Mark Griffith (Cambridge, 1983), 56.
15. *The Tragedies of Aeschylus Translated into English Prose* (Oxford, 1827), 20.
16. Quoted in Yopie Prins, 'Elizabeth Barrett, Robert Browning, and the *Différance* of Translation', *Victorian Poetry* 29 (1991), 435–51, 442.
17. George Lakoff and Mark Johnson, *Metaphors We Live By* (1980), 55.
18. Jacques Derrida, *Marges de la philosophie* (Paris, 1972), 267. The passage is translated in *Margins of Philosophy*, tr. Alan Bass, (Brighton, 1982), 224, but I have here given my own version.
19. Cornelia Müller has criticized this assumption of Lakoff and Johnson's in her *Metaphors Dead and Alive, Sleeping and Waking: A Dynamic View* (Chicago and London, 2008), 68.
20. St André (ed.), *Thinking Through Translation with Metaphors*, 9.

21. Gerard Steen, 'From Linguistic to Conceptual Metaphor in Five Steps', in Raymond W. Gibbs JR and Gerard J. Steen (eds), *Metaphor in Cognitive Linguistics* (Amsterdam and Philadelphia, 1999), 57–78, 57, 72.
22. Derrida, *Marges de la philosophie*, 300; I here quote Alan Bass's translation, *Margins of Philosophy* (Brighton, 1982), 251. See also Christopher Ricks's bracing observations in 'The Pursuit of Metaphor' (1997), reprinted in his *Allusion to the Poets* (Oxford, 2002), 241–60—for instance: 'not only is there the difficulty of saying where the literal and the metaphorical meet, there is the difficulty—or rather the recognition of an intractability that passes beyond difficulty into impossibility—that is alive in our using the terms "metaphorical" (or "the metaphor") and "literal" for the opposing constituents of a metaphor' (248).

NOTES TO CHAPTER 7

1. Douglas Robinson, *The Translator's Turn* (Baltimore and London, 1991), 141, 152, 163, 175, 167, 181, 140–1.
2. Ibid., 179.
3. *The Correspondence of Alexander Pope*, ed. George Sherburn, 5 vols (1956), ii, 341; Dryden, *Poems*, iii, 446.
4. Durs Grünbein, *Ashes for Breakfast: Selected Poems*, tr. Michael Hofmann (New York, 2005), xv, 98–9.
5. Ibid., 96–7, 99.
6. Ibid., xv.
7. Ibid., 102–3.
8. Dante Alighieri, *The Inferno*, tr. Ciaran Carson (2002), xi.
9. Ibid., xx.
10. For instance at the start of *Inferno* 1: Dante Alighieri, *La Divina Commedia*, ed. Giorgio Petrocchi (Milan, 1975), 5.
11. *The Inferno*, tr. Carson, 4.
12. *La Divina Commedia*, ed. Petrocchi, 7.
13. Carlyle, *On Heroes, Hero-Worship, & the Heroic in History*, 85; T. S. Eliot, *Selected Essays*, 3rd enlarged edn (1951), 238.
14. Hermans, *The Conference of the Tongues*, 56.
15. Ibid.
16. Lewis, 'The Measure of Translation Effects'.
17. Untermeyer, *Private Collection*, 261.
18. Quoted in Simon, *Gender in Translation*, 15.
19. Yevgeny Zamyatin, *We*, tr. Natasha Randall (New York, 2006), xvii–xviii.
20. Ibid., 8, 3.
21. Ezra Pound, *Literary Essays*, ed. with an introduction by T. S. Eliot (1954), 267–8.
22. Blake Morrison, 'Turning Classical Plays into Contemporary Theatre', a talk given at the Classics Centre, Oxford University, 26 November 2007. See also David Johnston, 'Theatre Pragmatics', in David Johnston (ed.), *Stages of*

Translation (Bristol, 1996), 57–66, 58: 'any translation done with performance in mind must seek to create not a linguistic construct based on the interrogation of authorial intention but a living piece of theatre'.

23. Tony Harrison, *Theatre Works 1973–1985* (1985), 197.
24. Ibid., 223, 216, 222.
25. Tony Harrison, *Plays Four* (2002), 8.
26. Benjamin, *Illuminationen*, 51, 52. The connotations of 'Entfaltung' are discussed in Carol Jacobs, 'The Monstrosity of Translation', *Modern Language Notes*, 90.6 (December 1975), 755–66, 758.
27. Maurice Blanchot, *Friendship*, tr. Elizabeth Rottenberg (Stanford, Calif., 1997), 59.
28. Christopher Ricks, *Allusion to the Poets* (Oxford, 2002), 9.

NOTES TO CHAPTER 8

1. Umberto Eco, *Mouse or Rat? Translation as Negotiation* (2003), 5; Roman Jakobson, *Language in Literature*, ed. Krystyna Pomorska and Stephen Rudy (Cambridge, Mass. and London, 1987), 429; Karl Popper, *Unended Quest: An Intellectual Autobiography* (2002), 21; Raphael Lyne 'Ovid in English Translation', in Philip Hardie (ed.), *The Cambridge Companion to Ovid* (Cambridge, 2002), 249–63, 260; Christianus Brekelmans, Magne Sæbø, and Menahem Haran, *Old Testament: The History of Its Interpretation* (1996), 87.
2. Axel Bühler, 'Translation as Interpretation', in Alessandra Riccardi (ed.), *Translation Studies: Perspectives on an Emerging Discipline* (Cambridge, 2002), 56–74, 60–4, 72.
3. Matthew Arnold, *The Complete Prose Works*, ed. R. H. Super, 11 vols (Ann Arbor, 1960–77), iii, 12–13.
4. Ibid., 13.
5. Jean-Paul Vinay and Jean Darbelnet, *Stylistique comparée du français et de l'anglais: méthode de traduction, c.1958*, tr. Juan C. Sager and Marie-Josée Hamel as *Comparative Stylistics of French and English: A Methodology for Translation* (1995), 8.
6. Shoshana Blum-Kulka, 'Shifts of Cohesion and Coherence in Translation', in Juliane House and Shoshana Blum-Kulka (eds), *Interlingual and Intercultural Communication* (Tübingen, 1986), repr. in Lawrence Venuti (ed.), *The Translation Studies Reader* (2000), 298–313, 302.
7. Hans-Georg Gadamer, *Truth and Method*, tr. W. Glen-Doepel, 2nd edn rev. tr. Joel Weinsheimer and Donald G. Marshall (1989), 384–6.
8. Hans-Georg Gadamer, *Gesammelte Werke*, Bd 1. *Hermeneutik I: Warheit und Methode* (Tübingen, 1990), 388–90.
9. Robert Lowell, *Imitations* (1962; 1971), xi.
10. Elizabeth Bishop and Robert Lowell, *Words in Air: The Complete Correspondence*, ed. Thomas Trevisand with Saskia Hamilton (2008), 356–7.
11. Ibid., 357; Lowell, *Imitations*, 88.

12. Bishop and Lowell, *Words in Air*, 357.
13. Lowell, *Imitations*, xii.
14. Giacomo Leopardi, *Canti*, ed. Giorgio Ficara (Milan, 1987), 112; Lowell, *Imitations*, 25.
15. Eugenio Montale, *L'Opera in Versi*, ed. Rosanna Bettarini and Gianfranco Contini (Turin, 1980),125; Lowell, *Imitations*, 107.
16. Gayatri Chakravorty Spivak, *Outside in the Teaching Machine* (1993), 180; Luciano Erba, *The Greener Meadow: Selected Poems*, tr. Peter Robinson (Princeton, NJ, 1987), x.
17. Erba, *The Greener Meadow*, tr Robinson., ix.
18. Ibid., 50–1.
19. Louis Untermeyer, *Robert Frost* (1964), 18.
20. Nick Laird, *Guardian* (16 August, 2008): http://www.guardian.co.uk/books/ 2008/aug/16/1 (accessed 12 February 2009).
21. Jamie McKendrick, *Crocodiles & Obelisks* (2007), 37; *Catullus, Tibullus, Pervigilium Veneris*, trs Francis Warre Cornish, J. P. Postgate, and J. W. Mackail, 2nd edn, revised by G. P. Goold (Cambridge, Mass. and London, 1962), 16.
22. Catullus, *Poems of Love and Hate*, tr. Josephine Balmer (2004), 84.
23. *Catullus: The Poems*, ed. Kenneth Quinn (1970), 131.

NOTES TO CHAPTER 9

1. 'The now fashionable translations into free or irregular verse' produce 'a sprawl of language, neither faithful nor distinguished, now on stilts now low, as Dryden would say': Lowell, *Imitations*, xi–xii.
2. John Dryden, *The Poems*, ed. Paul Hammond and David Hopkins, 5 vols (1995–2005), i, 384–5.
3. Rita Copeland, *Rhetoric, Hermeneutics and Translation in the Middle Ages: Academic Traditions and Vernacular Texts* (Cambridge, 1991), *passim*.
4. Garth Tissol asks: 'how can a translator amplify without altering?' 'Dryden's Additions and the Interpretive Reception of Ovid', *Translation and Literature* 13.2 (Autumn 2004), 181–93, 181.
5. Dryden, *Poems*, i, 387–8.
6. Ibid., 388.
7. Dryden, *The Works*, ed. E. N. Hooker, H. T. Swedenberg, Jr., et al., 20 vols (Berkeley and London, 1956–2000), v, 329–30; Dryden, *Poems*, iv, 446. Dryden, *Poems*, prints a modernized text; Dryden, *Works*, does not: the difference is especially visible in the practice of capitalization. But this inconsistency in the style of my quotations harmonizes with Dryden's own awareness of the mutability of texts through time: see my essay 'Most Himself', *London Review of Books*, 29.14 (19 July 2007), 11–15.
8. Dryden, *Poems*, i, 390.
9. Robin Sowerby, 'Chapman's Discovery of Homer', *Translation and Literature* 1 (1992), 26–51, 28; Jessica Wolfe, 'Chapman's Ironic Homer', *College Literature*, 35.4 (Fall 2008), 151–86, 158; John Channing Briggs, 'Chapman's

Seaven Bookes of the Iliades: Mirror for Essex', *Studies in English Literature, 1500–1900* 21.1 (Winter 1981), 59–73, 71–3; Colin Burrow, *Epic Romance: Homer to Milton* (Oxford, 1993), 204. For a full discussion, see Tania Demetriou, 'Strange appearance': The Reception of Homer in Renaissance England, Ph. D. thesis 31121, University of Cambridge (2007), 106–224.

10. *The Holy Bible Conteyning the Old Testament, and the New: newly translated out of the originall tongues: & with the former translations diligently compared and reuised, by his Maiesties speciall comandement. Appointed to be read in churches* (1611), [6].

11. A. E. B. Coldiron, 'William Caxton', in Peter France and Stuart Gillespie (gen. eds), *The Oxford History of Literary Translation into English*, 5 vols, vol. 1, ed. Roger Ellis (Oxford, 2008), i, 160–70, 161.

12. *Biblia the Byble, that is, the holy Scrypture of the Olde and New Testament, faithfully translated in to Englyshe*, tr. Miles Coverdale, 3v in 1 (1535), sig + iiii.v.

13. Ibid.

14. *The Holy Bible* (1611), [6].

15. A. C. Partridge, *English Biblical Translation* (1973), 33–101; David Daniell, *The Bible in English: Its History and Influence* (New Haven and London, 2003), 68–156; F. F. Bruce, *The English Bible: A History of Translations from the Earliest English Versions to the New English Bible* (1961), 22–3; Patrick Collinson, *The Reformation* (2003; 2005), 34–40; Diarmaid MacCulloch, *Reformation: Europe's House Divided 1490–1700* (2003), 203–4; Helen Parish, 'England', in Andrew Pettegree (ed.), *The Reformation World* (2000), 225–36, 225–7.

16. Partridge, *English Biblical Translation*, 95–7.

17. Quoted in ibid., 96.

18. Bruce, *The English Bible*, 41; Partridge, *English Biblical Translation*, 41.

19. Brian Cummings, *The Literary Culture of the Reformation: Grammar and Grace* (Oxford, 2002), 192; see also Stephen Greenblatt, *Renaissance Self-Fashioning: From More to Shakespeare* (Chicago and London, 1980), 95.

20. Quoted in David Norton, *A History of the Bible as Literature*, 2 vols (Cambridge, 1993), i, 100.

21. Partridge, *English Biblical Translation*, 41.

22. *The Holy Bible* (1611), [10].

23. Anne Hudson, *The Premature Reformation: Wycliffite Texts and Lollard History* (Oxford, 1988), 238–47.

24. Anne Hudson (ed.) *Selections from English Wycliffite Writings* (Cambridge, 1978), 68.

25. Ibid., 71.

26. David Lawton, 'The Bible', in France and Gillespie (gen. eds), *The Oxford History of Literary Translation into English*, i, 193–233, 223.

27. Lawton, 'The Bible', 223, 200; Hudson, *The Premature Reformation*, 82.

28. *Die gantze Bibel der ursprügliche[n] Ebraischenn unnd Griechischenn warheyt nach, auffs aller treüwlichest verteütschet*, tr. Martin Luther (Zürich, 1530), 527 v.

29. Martin Luther, *Sendbrief vom Dolmetschen*, ed. Karl Bischoff (Tübingen, 1965), 16. This edition reproduces the text printed at Nuremberg in 1530 and so does not capitalize nouns in the manner of modern German.

30. MacCulloch, *Reformation*, 134; see also Collinson, *The Reformation*, 48.

31. Richard Rolle, *The Psalter or Psalms of David and Certain Canticles with a Translation and Exposition in English by Richard Rolle of Hampole*, ed. Rev H. R. Bramley (Oxford, 1884), 4–5. 'Major precursor' is David Lawton's phrase, 'The Bible', 229.

32. Rolle, *The Psalter*, 40.

NOTES TO CHAPTER 10

1. Desiderius Erasmus, *First tome or volume of the Paraphrase of Erasmus vpon the Newe Testamente*, tr. Nicholas Udall et al. (1548) f. xiiii r.

2. Ibid., f. cvi v.

3. Ibid., f. xiiii v.

4. Anon., *A Poem on the Accession of their Royal Highnesses the Prince and Princess of Orange to the Imperial Crown of England being a paraphrase on the 45 Psalm* [1689], 2.

5. Thomas Watson, *Amyntas* (1585), sig. A. 1 ; Thomas Watson, *The Lamentations of Amyntas for the Death of Phyllis, Paraphrastically Translated out of Latin into English Hexameters*, tr. Abraham Fraunce (1587), sig A.1 r.

6. Watson, *Lamentations*, tr. Fraunce, sig A.1 v.

7. Thomas Middleton, *The Wisdome of Solomon Paraphrased* (1597), sig. B. 1 v.

8. George Sandys, *A Paraphrase upon the Divine Poems* (1638), 1.

9. Obadiah Walker, *Paraphrase and Annotations upon all the Epistles of St Paul* (1684), 3.

10. Richard Baker, *Cato Variegatus or Catoes Morall Distichs: Translated and Paraphras'd, with variations of Expressing, in English verse* (1636), ii.

11. Virgil, *The Destruction of Troy, an Essay upon the Second Book of Virgils Aeneis, Written in the year, 1636*, tr. [John Denham] (1656), [ii].

12. Dryden, *Poems*, i, 407.

13. Matthew Stevenson: *The Wits Paraphras'd, or, Paraphrase upon Paraphrase in a Burlesque on the Several Late Translations of Ovids Epistles* (1680), 109.

NOTES TO CHAPTER 11

1. Dryden, *Poems*, i, 385.

2. Paul Davis, *Translation and the Poet's Life: The Ethics of Translating in English Culture, 1646–1726* (Oxford, 2008), 134.

3. Dryden, *Poems*, ii, 128.

4. Ibid., i, 380–1.
5. Ibid., v, 50, 70.
6. Ibid., i, 389.
7. Ibid., v, 67.
8. Ibid., i, 389. There is further discussion of this passage below in Chapter 15.
9. Ovid, *Opera Omnia*, eds Nicolai Heinsii and Borchardi Cnippingii, 3 vols (Lugduni Batavorum, 1670), i, 88. Dryden had quoted 'idem venti vela fidemque ferent' in his Preface as an instance of phrasing that is impossible to translate 'literally' (*Poems*, i, 388).
10. Dryden, *Poems*, i, 406.
11. *Ovids Heroical Epistles, Englished*, tr. John Sherburne (1639), 38.
12. Later in his career, Dryden became more indulgent towards Ovidian witticisms, even inventing some of his own: see Tissol, 'Dryden's Additions and the Interpretive Reception of Ovid', *passim*.
13. Dryden, *Poems*, i, 407. Paul Hammond records the allusion in his editorial notes.
14. Ovid, *Opera*, i, 100.
15. Dryden, *Poems*, i, 411.
16. Stuart Gillespie and Penelope Wilson, 'The Publishing and Readership of Translation', in France and Gillespie (gen. eds), *The Oxford History of Literary Translation in English*, vol. 3, ed. Stuart Gillespie and David Hopkins (Oxford, 2005), iii, 38–51, 47–8.
17. Paul Hammond, *Dryden and the Traces of Classical Rome* (Oxford, 1999), 149.
18. Ovid, *Opera*, i, 142.
19. Dryden, *Poems*, i, 393.
20. Ovid, *Opera*, i, 142–3.
21. *Ovid's Heroical Epistles Englished*, tr. Wye Saltonstall (1636; 5th edn, 1663), 75.
22. Ovid, *Opera*, i, 143.
23. Dryden, *Poems*, i, 393.
24. Ovid, *Opera*, i, 145.
25. Dryden, *Poems*, i, 395.
26. *Ovid's Heroical Epistles*, tr. Sherburne, 64; *Ovid's Heroical Epistles*, tr. Saltonstall, 77; Ovid, *Opera*, i, 145.
27. Ovid, *Opera*, i, 146–7; Dryden, *Poems*, i, 395–6.
28. Ovid, *Opera*, i, 144; Dryden, *Poems*, i, 394.
29. Ovid, *Opera*, i, 148-9.
30. Howard Jacobson, *Ovid's Heroides* (Princeton, 1974), 167.
31. Ovid, *Opera*, i, 148-9.
32. Hammond, *Dryden and the Traces of Classical Rome*, 149.
33. Davis, *Translation and the Poet's Life*, 181.
34. Duncan F. Kennedy 'Epistolarity: the *Heroides*', in Hardie (ed.), *The Cambridge Companion to Ovid*, 217–32, 220.

35. Stuart Gillespie, 'The Early Years of the Dryden–Tonson Partnership: The Background to their Composite Translations and Miscellanies of the 1680s', *Restoration: Studies in English Literary Culture, 1660–1700* 12.1 (Spring 1988), 10–19, 17; Barbara M. Benedict, *Making the Modern Reader: Cultural Mediation in Early Modern Anthologies* (Princeton, NJ, 1996), 99.

36. Gillespie, 'The Early Years', 12; G. F. Papali, *Jacob Tonson, Publisher: His Life and Work (1656–1736)* (Conehunga, Auckland, 1968), 15–16.

37. Ovid, *Opera*, i, 252; *Ovid's Epistles, Translated by Several Hands* (1680), 60.

38. Dryden, *Poems*, i, 390.

39. *Ovid's Epistles*, 99.

40. Ibid., 98.

41. Dryden, *Poems*, i, 390.

42. *Ovid's Epistles*, 112.

43. I am taking as read here the scholarship by Hammond in *Dryden and the Traces of Classical Rome* and Davis in *Translation and the Poet's Life* which draws attention to the strong sense of constraint in Dryden's work as a translator, thereby balancing the emphasis on his 'liberty' which prevailed in criticism during the '1970s and 1980s' (Davis, *Translation and the Poet's Life*, 133).

44. Dryden, *Poems*, i, 405.

45. *Ovid's Heroical Epistles*, tr. Sherburne, 105; Ovid, *Opera*, i, 250.

46. Dryden, *Poems*, i, 405.

47. Richard Tarrant, 'Ovid and Ancient Literary History', in Hardie (ed.), *The Cambridge Companion to Ovid*, 13–33, 25.

48. Ovid, *Opera*, i, 102; *Ovid's Heroical Epistles*, tr. Sherburne, 43.

49. Dryden, *Poems*, i, 411.

50. Dryden, *Works*, v, 300.

51. Dryden, *Poems*, ii, 237–8.

52. Ibid., i, 387.

53. Quoted in Demetriou, *'Strange Likeness': The Reception of Homer in Renaissance England*, 191.

54. Wentworth Dillon, Earl of Roscommon, *An Essay on Translated Verse* (1684), 14.

55. Dryden, *Poems*, i, 237.

56. Roscommon, *An Essay on Translated Verse*, 5.

57. Dryden, *Poems*, i, 236–7.

58. Ibid., 244, 243.

59. Dryden, *Works*, v, 339.

NOTES TO CHAPTER 12

1. Annotation in Dryden, *Poems*, ii, 258; see also Hammond, *Dryden and the Traces of Classical Rome*, 150–6.

2. Annotations in Dryden, *Poems*, ii, 208, 203.

3. Dryden, *Works*, vi, 814.

4. Julia Griffin (ed.), *Selected Poems of Abraham Cowley, Edmund Waller and John Oldham* (1998), 140.

5. As Stuart Gillespie pointed out to me (private correspondence).

6. Dryden, *Works*, v, 319.

7. Quoted in Keith Thomas, *Religion and the Decline of Magic: Studies in Popular Beliefs in Sixteenth and Seventeenth Century England* (1973), 17.

8. Steven N. Zwicker, *Politics and Language in Dryden's Poetry: The Arts of Disguise* (Princeton, NJ, 1984), 177–205; Dryden, *Works*, vi, 870–6; Hammond, *Dryden and the Traces of Classical Rome*, 218–82; John Barnard, 'Dryden, Tonson, and the Patrons of *The Works of Virgil* (1697)', in Paul Hammond and David Hopkins (eds), *John Dryden: Tercentenary Essays* (2000), 174–239.

9. Barnard, 'Dryden, Tonson, and the Patrons', 171, 185, 200.

10. Dryden, *Works* v, 297–8.

11. Ibid., v, 291.

12. Ibid., 282.

13. J. Griffin, 'The Creation of Characters in the *Aeneid*', in Philip Hardie (ed.), *Virgil: Critical Assessments of Classical Authors*, 4 vols (1999), iii, 287–301, 287–9.

14. Dryden, *Works*, v, 302–3.

15. Stephen Harrison (private correspondence).

16. Dryden, *Works*, v, 303.

17. This is an instance of the general truth that 'writers have consistently responded most actively to Aeneas's actions—the episode with Dido in Book 4, or the descent into Hades in 6—when they delay rather than directly advance the main narrative. The history of Virgil's influence suggests that the imaginative drive of the Aeneid lies in its digressions' (Burrow, *Epic Romance*, 47).

18. Ibid., 291.

19. W. S. Anderson, 'Vergil's Second *Iliad*', *Transactions of the American Philological Association* 88 (1957), 17–30, reprinted in Hardie (ed.), *Virgil: Critical Assessments of Classical Authors*, iii, 74–86, 81–2; Virgil, *Aeneid 10: With Introduction, Translation and Commentary*, ed. S. J. Harrison (Oxford, 1991), 206.

20. *Aeneid* 10. 532–6; Dryden, *Aeneis* 10. 739–46 The *Aeneid* is quoted from Virgil, *Opera*, ed. Carolus Ruaeus (1695), whose text, and line numbers, differ from those in modern editions, though only slightly. Dryden's *Aeneis* is quoted from *Works*, v and vi. In both cases my references are now to book and line number rather than volume and page number. The crib translations are drawn from the Loeb Classical Library *Virgil*, 2 vols, tr. H. R. Fairclough, revised edn (Cambridge, Mass. and London, 1935), with occasional adjustments.

21. *Aeneis* 10. 1152–9.

22. Dryden, *Works*, v, 329–30.

23. *Aeneid* 10. 826.

24. *Aeneid* 2. 45; *Aeneis* 2. 58–9.
25. Ibid., 64–9; *Aeneid* 2. 50–4; Virgil, *Opera*, ed. Ruaeus, 207.
26. Dryden, *Works*, v, 329.
27. *Aeneis* 1. 37–9.
28. *Aeneid* 1. 26.
29. *Aeneid*, 1. 262; *Aeneis* 1. 357. The word appears also in one of Dryden's letters where it refers to an ambition of Tonson's for *The Works of Virgil*: 'he has missd of his design in the Dedication: though He had prepard the Book for it: for in every figure of Eneas, he has caused him to be drawn like K. William, with a hookd nose' (*The Letters of John Dryden*, ed. Charles E. Ward [Durham, NC, 1942], 93.)
30. *Aeneis* 1. 378–9; *Aeneid* 1. 282–3.
31. *Aeneis* 1. 109; 2. 62, 70; 1. 591, 651.
32. Dryden, *Works*, v, 326; *Poems*, i, 382.
33. *Aeneid* 2. 683–703; *Aeneis* 2. 932–55.
34. Virgil, *Aeneidos Liber Secundus*, ed. with a commentary by R. G. Austin (1964), 260.
35. *Aeneid* 2. 704; *Aeneis* 2. 956–7.

NOTES TO CHAPTER 13

1. *Aeneis* 1. 928, 964.
2. *Aeneid* 1. 724–5.
3. *Aeneis* 1. 1007–10.
4. Dryden, *Works*, xvii, 14.
5. *Aeneis* 4. 4–5; *Aeneid* 4. 2, 4.
6. *Aeneid* 4. 24.
7. *Aeneis* 4. 30–1.
8. *Aeneid* 4. 75–6.
9. *Aeneis* 4. 105, 104.
10. Ibid., 4. 240.
11. Ibid., 4. 247–56.
12. *Aeneid* 4. 172.
13. *Aeneis* 4. 274–7.
14. Ibid., 281.
15. *Aeneis* 4. 271, 266, 263; *Aeneid* 4. 190, 184–5, 183; *Aeneis* 6. 126–7, 152; *Aeneid* 6. 81, 100.
16. Paul Davis, *Translation and the Poet's Life*, 187.
17. *Aeneis* 1. 122, 126, 120–1; *Aeneid* 1. 86–7, 89, 85–6.
18. *Aeneid* 4. 221, 170.
19. *Aeneis* 4. 323–4.
20. *Aeneid* 4. 289–91.
21. *Aeneis* 4. 417–8.
22. *Aeneis* 4. 419–24; *Aeneid* 4. 291–5.

23. Virgil, *Aeneidos Liber Quartus*, ed. with a commentary by R. G. Austin (1955), 94–5.
24. Dryden, *Poems*, iii, 19.
25. *Aeneis* 4. 427–8.
26. *Aeneidos Liber Quartus*, ed. Austin, 96.
27. *Aeneis* 4. 429–30.
28. *Aeneid* 4. 307, 316; *Aeneis* 4. 444, 454.
29. *Aeneid* 4. 366; *Aeneis* 4. 522, 489–90.
30. *Aeneid* 4. 340; *Aeneis* 4. 492.
31. *Aeneid* 4. 340; *Aeneis* 4. 492.
32. *Aeneis*, 4. 829–32.
33. *Aeneis* 4. 667–74; *Aeneid* 4. 460–3.
34. Edmund Waller, 'Part of the Fourth Book of Virgil, Translated', quoted from *The Poems of Edmund Waller*, ed. G. Thorn Drury (1893), 26–8. Dryden praises Waller in the Preface to *Ovid's Epistles* (*Poems*, i, 385): see Chapter 9 above.
35. *Aeneis* 4. 677, 723, 728, 773, 735.
36. *Aeneis* 5. 5–9; *Aeneid* 5. 4–7.

NOTES TO CHAPTER 14

1. John Dryden, *The Works*, ed. E. N. Hooker, H. T. Swedenberg, Jr., et al., 20 vols (Berkeley and London, 1956–2000), v, 291, 330–1, 339, 324.
2. Virgil, *The Destruction of Troy, an Essay upon the Second Book of Virgils Aeneis, Written in the year, 1636*, tr. [John Denham] (1656), [ii], [iv].
3. Baldassare Castiglione, *The Courtyer of Count Baldessar Castilio*, tr. Thomas Hoby (1561), Sig. A. iii r, B. ii r. Much material on Renaissance translation is usefully gathered in Flora Ross Amos, *Early Theories of Translation* (New York, 1920); F. O. Matthiessen, *Translation: An Elizabethan Art* (Cambridge, Mass., 1931); and C. H. Conley, *The First English Translators of the Classics* (New Haven and London, 1927).
4. Plutarch, *The Lives of the Noble Grecians and Romanes*, tr. Thomas North (1579), 8 r.
5. Lawrence Venuti, *The Translator's Invisibility*, 2nd edn (2008), 35–51, which reiterates material from his '*The Destruction of Troy*: Translation and Royalist Cultural Politics in the Interregnum', *The Journal of Medieval and Renaissance Studies* 23.2 (Spring 1993), 197–219; Paul Davis, *Translation and the Poet's Life: The Ethics of Translating in English Culture, 1646–1726* (Oxford, 2008), 19–39.
6. Virgil, *The Destruction of Troy*, tr. Denham, [ii]—[iii]; Davis, *The Poet's Life*, 29–30; Amos, *Early Theories of Translation*, 147–8. A helpful sampling of early translations of Virgil is in K. W. Grandsden (ed.), *Virgil in English* (Harmondsworth, 1996).
7. Daniel Weissbort and Astradur Eysteinsson (eds), *Translation—Theory and Practice: A Historical Reader* (Oxford, 2006), 134.

8. Quoted in Dryden, *Works*, vi, 961–2.

9. Ibid., v, 330–1, 339.

10. John Dryden, *The Poems*, ed. Paul Hammond and David Hopkins, 5 vols (1995–2005), ii, 240.

11. Ibid., i, 389.

12. Ibid., ii, 238.

13. Louis Kelly, 'Theories of Translation: The Eighteenth Century to Tytler,' in Peter France and Stuart Gillespie (gen. eds), *The Oxford History of Literary Translation in English*, 5 vols, vol. 3, ed. Stuart Gillespie and David Hopkins (Oxford, 2005), iii, 67–78, 72.

14. Homer, *The Iliad and Odyssey of Homer*, tr. William Cowper, 2 vols, (1791), i, pp. viii, xiii.

15. Ibid., i, 3.

16. Dryden, *Poems*, v, 288–9.

17. Garth Tissol has shown that Dryden's apparent liberties with Ovid likewise show him to be 'intimately familiar with and in tune with Ovid's style': 'Dryden's Additions and the Interpretive Reception of Ovid', *Translation and Literature* 13.2 (Autumn 2004), 181–93, 186.

18. *Iliad and Odyssey*, tr. Cowper, i, p. v.

19. Percy Bysshe Shelley, *Shelley's Prose or The Trumpet of a Prophecy*, ed. David Lee Clark (Albuquerque, NM, 1954), 280. I have touched on this passage before in my 'Principles and Norms of Translation', in France and Gillespie (gen. eds), *The Oxford History of Literary Translation in English*, vol. 4, ed. Peter France and Kenneth Haynes (Oxford, 2006), 59–84, 63.

20. [George Moir], 'Glassford's *Lyrical Translations*', *Edinburgh Review* 60 (1835), 353–63, 358; quoted in Reynolds, 'Principles and Norms', 65.

21. Alexander Pope, *The Poems*, ed. John Butt (1963), 153.

22. Alfred, Lord Tennyson, *The Poems*, ed. Christopher Ricks, 3 vols, 2nd edn (1987), i, 246.

23. Robert Browning, *Poetical Works*, 16 vols (1888–9), xiii, 261. For discussion, see Chapter 5 above.

NOTES TO CHAPTER 15

1. Wentworth Dillon, Earl of Roscommon, *An Essay on Translated Verse* (1684), 7.

2. Katherine Philips, 'A Friend', 19–20, 25–7. Philips' verse is quoted from *The Collected Works of Katherine Philips: The Matchless Orinda*, ed. Patrick Thomas, 3 vols (1990–3).

3. Cicero, *De Senectute, De Amicitia, De Divinatione*, tr. William Armistead Falconer (Cambridge, Mass. and London, 1979), 188.

4. Katherine Philips, 'L'amitié: To Mrs M Awbrey', 1–4.

5. Carl Niemeyer, 'The Earl of Roscommon's Academy', *Modern Language Notes* 49.7 (November 1934), 432–7.

6. Samuel Johnson, *The Lives of the Most Eminent English Poets; with Critical Observations on their Works*, ed. Roger Lonsdale, 4 vols (Oxford, 2006), iv, 44: 'this doctrine is in itself pernicious as well as false'.

7. Alexander Pope, *The Twickenham Edition of the Poems*, John Butt (gen. ed.), 10 vols, vol. 7 ed. Maynard Mack (1939–67), vii, 26.

8. Susannah Hester Everett Jones, *Some Literary Treatments of Friendship: Katherine Philips to Alexander Pope*, Ph.D. dissertation, University of Cambridge (1993), 119. See also Jones's 'Pope's Homer: The Shadow of Friendship', in Howard Erskine Hill (ed.), *Alexander Pope: World and Word*, Proceedings of the British Academy 91 (Oxford, 1998), 55–68, where she goes so far as to claim (I think mistakenly) that Pope applies a 'metaphor of friendship' to his 'relation to Homer' (58).

9. Dryden, *Poems*, v, 79–80.

10. Ibid., i, 388–9. For more discussion of this passage, see above, Chapter 11.

11. Ibid., ii, 247. There is some overlap between this disagreement and debates about the ethics of taking decisions on behalf of someone else in circumstances of which they are unaware. See Allen E. Buchanan and Dan W. Brock, *Deciding for Others: The Ethics of Surrogate Decision Making* (Cambridge, 1989), 112.

12. Stuart Gillespie, 'The Early Years of the Dryden–Tonson Partnership: The Background to their Composite Translations and Miscellanies of the 1680s', *Restoration: Studies in English Literary Culture, 1660–1700*, 12.1 (Spring 1988), 10–19.

13. Dryden, *Poems*, ii, 262.

14. Ibid., ii, 265n; Paul Hammond, *Dryden and the Traces of Classical Rome* (Oxford, 1999), 150–6.

15. Dryden, *Poems*, v, 79.

16. Ibid., ii, 238.

17. Ibid., v, 78–9.

18. Earl Miner, 'Chaucer in Dryden's *Fables*', in Howard Anderson and John S. Shea (eds), *Studies in Criticism and Aesthetics, 1660–1800: Essays in Honour of Samuel Holt Monk* (Minneapolis, 1967), 58–72, 68–9.

19. Chaucer is quoted from the text printed at the end of Dryden's *Fables Ancient and Modern* (1700), 580; interesting instances of Dryden's way with Chaucer are at *Poems*, v, 104, 110–11, 117, 119, 124, etc. Maria K. Greenwood's idea that Dryden peddles 'illusory heroic idealisations' in 'Palamon and Arcite' is more suggestive than she makes it seem in her discussion which is remarkably hostile to Dryden ('What Dryden did to Chaucer's *The Knight's Tale*, or Translation as Ideological Input', in Rosalyn Voaden et al. (eds), *The Medieval Translator / Traduire au Moyen Age*, 8 [Turnhout, Belg., 2003], 189–200, 200).

20. Alan Bray, *The Friend* (2003), 197.

21. Warren Chernaik, 'Philips, Katherine (1632–1664)', *Oxford Dictionary of National Biography*, online edn (Oxford, Sept. 2004): http://ezproxy.ouls.ox.ac.uk:2117/view/article/22124 (accessed 11 July 2010).

22. Thomas Francklin, *Translation: A Poem* (1753), 9–10.
23. Roscommon, *Essay on Translated Verse*, 7.
24. Ibid., 12.
25. John Wilmot, Earl of Rochester, *The Complete Works*, ed. Frank H. Ellis (Harmondsworth, 1994), 30.
26. Dryden, *Poems* ii, 335–6.
27. Ibid., 249.
28. Ibid., iii, 447.
29. Ibid., ii, 336–7. I have discussed this passage before in my 'Semi-Censorship in Dryden and Browning', in Francesca Billiani (ed.), *Modes of Censorship and Translation: National Contexts and Diverse Media* (Manchester, 2007), 187–204, 201–2.
30. David Foxon, *Libertine Literature in England, 1660–1745* (1964), 38–9.
31. Ibid., 247.
32. Ibid., v, 49.
33. Edward FitzGerald, *Rubáiyát of Omar Khayyám: A Critical Edition*, ed. Christopher Decker (Charlottesville, Va. and London, 1997), xxii.
34. Edward FitzGerald, *The Letters*, ed. Alfred McKinley Terhune and Annabelle Burdick Terhune, 4 vols (Princeton, NJ, 1980), ii, 267, 305, 261.
35. Jean Starr Untermeyer, *Private Collection* (New York, 1965), 225.
36. Georges Poulet: 'Criticism and the Experience of Interiority', in Richard Macksey and Eugenio Donato (eds), *The Languages of Criticism and the Sciences of Man: The Structuralist Controversy* (1970), 56–72, 57.

NOTES TO CHAPTER 16

1. Theocritus, *Ta Euriskomena* (Oxford, 1676), 39; *Theocritus*, ed. and tr. A. S. F. Gow, 2 vols (Cambridge, 1952), i, 30–1. Earlier treatments of this passage, and of the Richard Duke translation of Ovid which I discuss below, are in my 'Semi-Censorship in Dryden and Browning', 198–9.
2. Dryden, *Poems* ii, 196.
3. Stuart Gillespie, *Dryden's Sylvae: A Study of Dryden's Translations from the Latin in the Second Tonson Miscellany, 1685*, Ph.D. thesis, University of Cambridge (1987), 39.
4. Dryden, *Poems*, ii, 250.
5. Ibid., v, 54.
6. Ovid, *Opera Omnia*, eds Nicolai Heinsii and Borchardi Cnippingii, 3 vols (Lugduni Batavorum, 1670), 326.
7. Ovid, *Heroides: Amores*, tr. Grant Showerman, rev. G. P. Goold (Cambridge, Mass. and London, 1977).
8. *Miscellany Poems* (1684), 114.
9. See above, Chapter 11.
10. Colin Burrow, *Epic Romance: Homer to Milton* (Oxford, 1993), 175–6.
11. Patricia Parker, *Inescapable Romance: Studies in the Poetics of a Mode* (Princeton, NJ, 1979), 4.

12. Charles G. Bell, 'Fairfax's Tasso', *Comparative Literature* 6.1 (Winter 1954), 26–52, 29.
13. Ibid., 52.
14. Torquato Tasso, *Godfrey of Bulloigne: A Critical Edition of Edward Fairfax's Translation of Tasso's Gerusalemme Liberata, Together with Fairfax's Original Poems*, ed. Kathleen M. Lea and T. M. Gang (Oxford, 1981), 163, 121; Torquato Tasso, *Il Goffredo: Novamente Corretto, e Ristampato, Con l'aggiunta de' Cinque Canti del Sig. Camillo Camilli* (Venice, 1583), 17 r, 7 r.
15. Torquato Tasso, *Godfrey of Bulloigne, or The recouerie of Hierusalem*, tr. Richard Carew (1594), iv.
16. Samuel Taylor Coleridge, *Seven Lectures on Shakespeare and Milton*, ed. John Payne Collier (1856), xxxii; quoted in Tasso, *Godfrey*, tr. Fairfax, 15.
17. Bell, 'Fairfax's Tasso', 40.
18. Tasso, *Il Goffredo*, 18 v; 'Her envious vesture', etc.: Tasso, *Godfrey*, tr. Fairfax, 170.
19. This episode is evidence for Colin Burrow's claim that in Fairfax's translation, 'all those erotic forces which Tasso attempted to push to the bottom of his text ... come bouncing back to the surface' (*Epic Romance*, 168).
20. Tasso, *Godfrey*, tr. Fairfax, 106.
21. Tasso, *Il Goffredo*, f. 3 v.
22. Charlotte Smith, *Elegiac Sonnets*, 2nd edn (Chichester, 1784), 21.
23. Francesco Petrarca (Petrarch), *Le Rime*, 2 vols (Londra [i.e., Livorno], 1778), i, 122.
24. Algernon Charles Swinburne, *Notes on Poems and Reviews* (1866), 9.
25. Yopie Prins, *Victorian Sappho* (Princeton, NJ, 1999), 116–7.
26. Algernon Charles Swinburne, *The Poems*, 6 vols (1904), i, 57.

NOTES TO CHAPTER 17

1. Eric Griffiths and Matthew Reynolds (eds), *Dante in English* (Harmondsworth, 2005).
2. Joseph Addison, *The Papers of Joseph Addison, Esq. in the Tatler, Spectator, Guardian and Freeholder. Together with his Treatise on the Christian Religion*, 4 vols (1790), ii, 318.
3. Sappho, *If Not, Winter: Fragments of Sappho*, tr. Anne Carson (2002), 2–3.
4. Addison, *Papers*, ii, 321.
5. Ibid., 332–3.
6. Sappho, *If Not, Winter*, 62–3; Addison, *Papers*, iii, 333.
7. Anne Carson, *Eros the Bittersweet* (1998), 13.
8. Addison, *Papers*, ii, 330–1.
9. Dryden, *Poems*, i. 205.
10. Sir Philip Sidney, *Selected Poems*, ed. Katherine Duncan-Jones (Oxford, 1973), 117, 215.
11. Geoffrey Chaucer, *Troilus and Criseyde: A New Edition of 'The Book of Troilus'*, ed. B. A. Windeatt (1984), 112.

12. Karla Taylor, 'Writers of the Italian Renaissance', in France and Gillespie (gen. eds), *The Oxford History of Literary Translation in English*, vol. 1, ed. Roger Ellis (Oxford, 2008), i, 390–406, 391.

13. Glending Olson, 'Geoffrey Chaucer', in David Wallace (ed.), *The Cambridge History of Medieval English Literature* (Cambridge, 1999), 566–89, 580; Taylor, 'Writers of the Italian Renaissance', 139.

14. Robin Kirkpatrick, *English and Italian Literature from Dante to Shakespeare* (1995), 55.

15. *The Riverside Chaucer*, gen. ed. Larry Benson, 3rd edn (Oxford, 1988), 387; Griffiths and Reynolds, *Dante in English*, 8–9.

16. Barry Windeatt, *Troilus and Criseyde* (Oxford, 1992), 217; John V. Fleming, *Classical Imitation and Interpretation in Chaucer's Troilus* (Lincoln, Nebr., 1990), 183, quoted in William T. Rossiter, *Chaucer and Petrarch* (Cambridge, 2010), 122.

17. Chaucer, *Troilus and Criseyde*, 112.

18. Paul Strohm, *Theory and the Premodern Text* (Minneapolis and London, 2000), 85–6.

19. Thomas M. Greene, *The Light in Troy: Imitation and Discovery in Renaissance Poetry* (New Haven and London, 1982), 242–4; Anthony Pym, 'Natural and Directional Equivalence in Theories of Translation', *Target* 19.2 (2007), 271–294, 273.

20. Reed Way Dasenbrock, 'Wyatt's Transformation of Petrarch', *Comparative Literature* 40.2 (Spring 1988), 122–33, 124.

21. Stephen Greenblatt, *Renaissance Self-Fashioning: From More to Shakespeare* (Chicago and London, 1980), 120; Karla Taylor, 'Writers of the Italian Renaissance', i, 390–406, 400.

22. Greg Walker, *Writing Under Tyranny: English Literature and the Henrician Reformation* (Oxford, 2005), 284.

23. Greenblatt, *Renaissance Self-Fashioning*, 146.

24. Francesco Petrarca, *Le Volgari Opere del Petrarcha con la Espositione di Alessandro Vellutello da Lucca* (Vinegia, 1525), 30 v–31 r; Sir Thomas Wyatt, *The Complete Poems*, ed. R. A. Rebholz (Harmondsworth, 1997), 76. The sources for Wyatt's translations are helpfully reproduced in the *Collected Poems of Sir Thomas Wyatt*, ed. Kenneth Muir and Patricia Thomson (Liverpool, 1969). I am indebted to Thomson's commentary throughout my discussion, though I prefer to quote Wyatt's poem-translations in the modernized text prepared by Rebholz.

25. Wyatt, *Complete Poems*, 77.

26. Petrarca, *Le Volgari Opere del Petrarcha*, 149 v.

27. Jonathan Crewe sees the Latin phrase as representing 'an enviable, presumably masculine, language of eternal power, duration, alterity, and exclusiveness' (*Trials of Authorship: Anterior Forms and Poetic Reconstruction from Wyatt to Shakespeare* [Berkeley, Los Angeles and Oxford, 1990], 40–1).

28. Wyatt, *Complete Poems*, 77.

29. Ibid., 76–7.

30. Ibid., 78.
31. Ibid., 90, 86, 87.
32. Petrarca, *Le Volgari Opere del Petrarcha*, 118r.
33. Colin Burrow, 'Literature and Politics under Henry VII and Henry VIII', in David Wallace (ed.), *The Cambridge History of Medieval English Literature* (Cambridge, 1999), 793–820, 808; Walker, *Writing Under Tyranny*, 351.
34. Alistair Fox, *The English Renaissance: Identity and Representation in Elizabethan England* (Oxford, 1997), 22–3.
35. William Shakespeare, *The Sonnets and A Lover's Complaint*, ed. John Kerrigan (1986), 19.
36. Sidney, *Selected Poems*, 119.
37. Shakespeare, *The Sonnets and A Lover's Complaint*, 141.
38. Ibid., 22.
39. Bell, 'Fairfax's Tasso', 36–8, 48.
40. Tasso, *Il Goffredo*, 13 v.
41. Tasso, *Godfrey*, tr. Fairfax, 147–9.
42. Burrow, *Epic Romance*, 152–3, 149–50.
43. Lodovico (Ludovico) Ariosto, *Orlando Furioso: Nuovamente Adorato di Figure di Rame da Girolamo Porro* (Venice, 1584), 5.
44. Ludovico Ariosto, *Orlando Furioso Translated into English Heroical Verse*, ed. Robert McNulty, tr. Sir John Harington (Oxford, 1972), 24.
45. Ariosto, *Orlando Furioso: Nuovamente Adorato*, 5.
46. Ariosto, *Orlando Furioso*, tr. Harington, 23.
47. Ariosto, *Orlando Furioso: Nuovamente Adorato*, 5; *Orlando Furioso*, tr. Harington, 24.
48. George Gordon, Lord Byron, *The Complete Poetical Works*, ed. Jerome J. McGann, 7 vols (Oxford, 1980–93), iv (1986), 247.
49. Byron, *Complete Poetical Works*, v, 26.

NOTES TO CHAPTER 18

1. *Byron's Letters and Journals*, ed. Leslie A. Marchand, 13 vols (1963–94) vi, 239.
2. Ibid., 215.
3. Ibid., 216.
4. Ibid., 116.
5. Ibid., 110.
6. Ibid., 116.
7. *Catullus: Tibullus: Pervigilium Veneris*, trs Francis Warre Cornish, J. P. Postgate, and J. W. Mackail, 2nd edn, revised by G. P. Goold, (Cambridge, Mass. and London, 1962), 6; Byron, *Complete Poetical Works*, i, 72.
8. *Byron's Letters and Journals*, vi, 110.
9. Ibid., 111.
10. Leslie A. Marchand, *Byron: A Biography*, 3 vols (New York and London, 1957), ii, 775.

11. Ibid., 111, 121; vii, 112.
12. Dante Alighieri, *La Divina Commedia*, ed. Giorgio Petrocchi (Turin, 1975), 22.
13. Ibid., 24.
14. Dante Alighieri, *Opere Minori*, ed. Domenico de Robertis and Gianfranco Contini, vol. 1, part 1 (Milano and Napoli, 1984), 133; see Dante Alighieri, *La Divina Commedia*, ed. Natalino Sapegno, 3 vols, 3rd edn (Florence, 1985), i, 62n.
15. Dante, *La Divina Commedia*, ed. Petrocchi, 22.
16. Teodolinda Barolini, 'Dante and Francesca da Rimini: Realpolitik, Romance, Gender', *Speculum* 75.1 (January 2000), 1–28, 16.
17. Dante Alighieri, *The Vision or Hell, Purgatory, and Paradise*, tr. Henry Francis Cary (Oxford, 1910), 18.
18. On the circumstances of Hunt's freedom, see above, Chapter 16.
19. Griffiths and Reynolds (eds), *Dante in English*, 117–8.
20. Byron, *Complete Poetical Works*, v, 4, 7. On Byron's hostility to cant, see Jerome J. McGann, *Don Juan in Context* (1976), 51–7. Peter Vassallo has found a source for the attack on Plato in the work of the Italian satirical poet Giambattista Casti (*Byron: The Italian Literary Influence* [1984], 77).
21. Byron, *Complete Poetical Works*, 254, 257, 265; Luigi Pulci, *Il Morgante Maggiore* (Florence, 1732), 3, 5.
22. Byron, *Letters and Journals*, vii, 58–9; *Complete Poetical Works* iv, 516n. Jerome J. McGann appears to err when he says that Byron's 'initial plan' was to publish all three texts together (*Complete Poetical Works*, iv, 508n).

NOTES TO CHAPTER 19

1. Lord Byron, *The Complete Miscellaneous Prose*, ed. Andrew Nicholson (Oxford, 1991), 147.
2. Pope, *Twickenham Edition of the Poems*, vii, 4.
3. Ibid., 22.
4. Ibid., 17–18.
5. Pope, *Twickenham Edition*, i, 316.
6. Stuart Gillespie and Robin Sowerby, 'Translation and Literary Innovation', in France and Gillespie (gen. eds), *The Oxford History of Literary Translation in English*, iii, 21–37, 30.
7. 'Longinus', *On the Sublime: The* Peri Hupsous *in Translations by Nicolas Boileaux-Despréaux (1674) and William Smith (1739)* (Delmar, New York, 1975), 5.
8. Ibid., 14–15.
9. Ibid., 33.
10. Ibid., i v.
11. Pope, *Twickenham Edition*, i, 316.
12. 'Longinus', *On the Sublime*, tr. Boileau, 22.

13. 'Longinus', *On the Sublime*, ed. D. A. Russell (Oxford, 1964), 12 (*Iliad* 17. 646).

14. Pope, *Twickenham Edition*, vii, 18.

15. 'Longinus', *On the Sublime*, tr. Boileau, 22.

16. Pope, *Twickenham Edition*, vii, 18.

17. Homer, *L'Iliade d'Homere, traduite en Fançois avec des Remarques*, tr. Madame Dacier, 3 vols (Paris, 1711), i, p. xxx. David Hopkins, following Pope's early editor Gilbert Wakefield, points out the roots of this opinion in Longinus ('"The English Homer": Shakespeare, Longinus, and English "Neoclassicism"', in Charles Martindale and A. B. Taylor [eds], *Shakespeare and the Classics* [Cambridge, 2004] 261–76 , 270–1). But Pope's phrasing shows the intermediary influence of Dacier.

18. *Chapman's Homer: The Iliad*, ed. Allardyce Nicoll (Princeton, NJ, 1956), 66; *Homer his Iliads translated*, tr. John Ogilby (1660), 65; *Homer's Iliads in English*, tr. Thomas Hobbes (1676), 33; *Homerou Ilias kai Odysseia . . . Operâ, studio, & impensis*, 2 vols, ed. Josuae Barnes (Cantabrigiæ, 1711), i, 103; *L'Iliade d'Homere*, tr. Dacier, i, 89.

19. G. S. Kirk (gen. ed.), *The Iliad: A Commentary*, 6 vols, vol. 1 ed. G. S. Kirk (Cambridge, 1985–93), I (1985), 243.

20. Pope, *Twickenham Edition*, vii, 168.

21. Ibid., lv. Pope was later to admire Shakespeare in terms carried over from Longinus: see Hopkins, '"The English Homer"', 271.

22. Longinus, *On the Sublime*, tr. Boileau, 63.

23. Pope, *Twickenham Edition*, vii, 168n–169n.

24. Ibid., lii–iii.

25. Ibid.; Robin Sowerby, *The Augustan Art of Poetry: Augustan Translation of the Classics* (Oxford, 2006), 257–310.

26. In John Barnard (ed.), *Pope: The Critical Heritage* (1973), 135.

27. Samuel Taylor Coleridge, *Biographia Literaria: or, Biographical Sketches of My Literary Life and Opinions*, ed. James Engell and W. Jackson Bate, 2 vols (1983), i. 18.

28. Homer, *Iliad*, 1. 349–50. I quote the Greek from *The Iliad*, with an English translation by A. T. Murray, revised William F. Wyatt, 2 vols, 2nd edn (Cambridge, Mass. and London, 1999) which I have checked against the *Ilias kai Odysseia*, ed. Barnes, a text known to Pope. For the Greek *Iliad* I give book and line number; for Pope's translation I continue to give volume and page since I am often referring to footnotes and other editorial matter.

29. Pope, *Twickenham Edition*, vii, 109.

30. Ibid., viii, 535.

31. Ibid., vii, 109.

32. Alfred C. Ames, 'Early Criticism of Pope's "Night-Piece"', *Modern Language Notes* 60. 4 (April 1945), 265-7; Coleridge, *Biographia Literaria*, i, 39n-40n.

33. Homer, *Iliad*, 8. 555–6.

34. Pope, *Twickenham Edition*, vii, 428.

35. Ibid., n.

36. Coleridge, *Biographia Literaria*, i, 40n.
37. *The Prose Works of Alexander Pope*, ed. Rosemary Cowler, 2 vols (1986), ii, 192.
38. Sir Richard Blackmore, *Prince Arthur: an heroick poem in ten books* (1695), 15–16.
39. See William Frost, '*The Rape of the Lock* and Pope's Homer', *Modern Language Quarterly* 8. 3 (1947), 342–54; Reuben Arthur Brower, *Alexander Pope: The Poetry of Allusion* (Oxford, 1959), 142–62; H. A. Mason, *To Homer Through Pope: An Introduction to Homer's* Iliad *and Pope's* Translation (1972), 143; Howard Erskine-Hill, *Poetry of Opposition and Revolution: Dryden to Wordsworth* (Oxford, 1996), 89–91; Steven Shankman, 'Pope's Homer and his Poetic Career', in Pat Rogers (ed.), *The Cambridge Companion to Alexander Pope* (Cambridge, 2007), 63–75, 64–6.
40. Pope, *Poems*, 229.
41. Alexander Pope, *The Correspondence*, ed. George Sherburn, 5 vols (Oxford, 1956), i, 406–7.
42. Pope, *Twickenham Edition*, vii, 428–9.
43. Kirk (ed.), *The Iliad: A Commentary*, ii, 110–11.
44. *Chapman's Homer: The Iliad*, 123.
45. Pope, *Twickenham Edition*, vii, 297.
46. Homer, *Iliad*, 5. 591; Pope, *Twickenham Edition*, vii, 302.
47. Ibid., 299.
48. Pope, *Twickenham Edition*, viii, 194.
49. Ibid., 207.
50. Homer, *Iliad*, 15. 241.
51. Pope, *Twickenham Edition*, viii, 207.
52. Homer, *Iliad*, 15. 242.
53. Ibid., 212.
54. Ibid., n.
55. Kirk (gen. ed.), *The Iliad: A Commentary*, vol. 4 (1992), ed. Richard Janko, 265. Tania Demetriou points out to me that this crux also exercised the ancient scholiasts: see Hartmut Erbse (ed.), *Scholia Graeca in Homeri Iliadem (Scholia Vetera)*, 7 vols (Berolini, 1969–88), iv, 85.
56. Pope, *Twickenham Edition*, viii, 230.
57. Ibid., 226, 216.
58. Pope, *Correspondence*, i, 408.

NOTES TO CHAPTER 20

1. Alexander Pope, *The Twickenham Edition of the Poems*, gen. ed. John Butt, 11 vols, vol. 7, ed. Maynard Mack et al. (1939–67), vii, 4, 3, 9, 14.
2. Homer, *Iliad*, 1. 6; Henry George Liddell and Robert Scott, *A Greek–English Lexicon*, 9th edn rev. Henry Stuart Jones (Oxford, 1996). I quote Homer's Greek from *Iliad*, with an English translation by A. T. Murray, rev. William F. Wyatt, 2 vols, 2nd edn (Cambridge, Mass. and London, 1999) which I

have checked against *Homerou Ilias kai Odysseia … Operâ, studio, & impensis*, ed. Josuae Barnes, 2 vols (Cantabrigiæ, 1711), a text known to Pope. For the Greek *Iliad* I give book and line number; for Pope's translation I give volume and page since I am often referring to footnotes and other editorial matter.

3. John Barrell, *The Idea of Landscape and the Sense of Place, 1730–1840: An Approach to the Poetry of John Clare* (Cambridge, 1972), 4–5.
4. Mavis Batey, *Alexander Pope: The Poet and the Landscape* (1999), 29.
5. Alexander Pope, *The Poems*, ed. John Butt (1963), 148.
6. Batey observes that the term 'landscape garden' was not coined until later in the century when (however) such gardens were 'inspired' by Pope's ideas (*Alexander Pope: The Poet and the Landscape*, 13.)
7. See above, Chapter 19.
8. Pope, *Twickenham Edition*, vii, 9.
9. Anthony Collins, *A Discourse of Free-Thinking, Occasion'd by the Rise and Growth of a Sect call'd Free-Thinkers* (1713), 8; Richard Bentley, *Remarks upon a Late Discourse of Free-Thinking: in a Letter to F. H. D. D. By Phileleutherus Lipsiensis* (1713), 18; both are quoted in Steven Shankman, *Pope's* Iliad: *Homer in the Age of Passion* (1983), 81–2. For Bentley's remark on Pope's Homer, see above, Chapter 1.
10. Kirsti Simonsuuri, *Homer's Original Genius: Eighteenth-Century Notions of the Early Greek Epic (1688–1798)* (Cambridge, 1979), 20–1.
11. Pope, *Twickenham Edition*, vii, 14.
12. Ibid.
13. Homer, *The Iliad of Homer*, tr. Alexander Pope, 6 vols (1715), vol. 1. I describe the British Library's copy of the subscribers' quarto (ESTC T014925) as reproduced in *Eighteenth Century Collections Online* (*ECCO*), Gale (http://infotrac.galegroup.com/itweb/oxford?db=ECCO [accessed 21 September 2009]): this corresponds to entry no. 39 in Reginald Harvey Griffith, *Alexander Pope: A Bibliography* (Austin, Tex., 1922). I have looked at the copy of the Folio in the Bodleian Library (Griffith, 42) and the one in Harvard University Houghton Library as reproduced in *ECCO* (ESTC N000937): in both, the order of the prefatory material is disrupted: the royal licence is placed right at the beginning, the names of the subscribers come after the 'Preface' and before the 'Essay on the Life, Writings and Learning of Homer'. In the Bodleian copy, the head-pieces from the quarto printing of the 'Essay' are placed together at its end. The publication of Pope's *Iliad* is discussed in David Foxon, *Pope and the Early Eighteenth-Century Book Trade (the Lyell Lectures, Oxford 1975–76)*, rev. and ed. James McLaverty (Oxford, 1991), 52–91.
14. Foxon says that this engraving was designed by Pope's friend Charles Jervas (*Pope and the Early Eighteenth-Century Book Trade*, 71).
15. Pope, *Twickenham Edition*, vii. 28, 43, 65.
16. Maynard Mack, *Alexander Pope: A Life* (New Haven & London, 1985), 267; Foxon, *Pope and the Early Eighteenth-Century Book Trade*, 71. Both scholars show that Pope kept close control over the design and placing of the images.

17. Barrell, *The Idea of Landscape and the Sense of Place*, 11.
18. Pope, *Twickenham Edition*, vii, 82–5.
19. See above, Chapter 19.
20. Pope, *Twickenham Edition*, vii, 173.
21. Ibid., 82.
22. Ibid., 86–7. The 1715 edition of the 'Observation' has 'to command Attention' after 'Appearance of the Priest', and 'to other Planets' for 'to the Planets' (*The Iliad of Homer*, 1. 54.)
23. Homer, *Iliad*, 24. 130–1; Pope, *Twickenham Edition*, viii. 542.
24. Ibid., 543.
25. Peter J. Connelly, 'Pope's *Iliad*: Ut Pictura Translatio', *Studies in English Literature, 1500–1900* 21.3 (Summer 1981), 439–55, 444, 455.
26. Homer, *Iliad*, 6. 58–9, 62.
27. *Chapman's Homer: The Iliad*, ed. Allardyce Nicoll (Princeton, NJ, 1956), 138; *Homer his Iliads translated*, tr. John Ogilby (1660), 143; *Homer's Iliads in English*, tr. Thomas Hobbes (1676), 84.
28. *Ilias kai Odysseia*, ed. Barnes, i, 234.
29. Pope, *Twickenham Edition*, vii, 327.
30. Ibid.
31. Ibid., lvi.
32. Homer, *Iliad*, 2. 136–7; Pope, *Twickenham Edition*, vii, 136.
33. Ibid., viii, 7.
34. Pope, *Twickenham* Edition, vii, lvi; Robin Sowerby, 'Epic', in France and Gillespie (gen. eds), *The Oxford History of Literary Translation in English*, 5 vols, vol. 3, ed. Gillespie and David Hopkins (Oxford, 2005–) iii (2005), 149–72, 160; Reuben A. Brower, *Alexander Pope: The Poetry of Allusion* (Oxford, 1959), 102–3.
35. Howard Erskine-Hill, *Poetry of Opposition and Revolution: Dryden to Wordsworth* (Oxford, 1996), 57–76.
36. *The Correspondence of Alexander Pope*, ed. George Sherburn, 5 vols (Oxford, 1956), i, 246.
37. Ibid., 332.
38. Ibid., 331.
39. *The First Book of Homer's Iliad*, tr. Thomas Tickell (1715), [iii], [v].
40. Steven Shankman, 'Pope's Homer and his Poetic Career', in Pat Rogers (ed.), *The Cambridge Companion to Pope* (Cambridge, 2007), 70.
41. Homer, *Iliad*, 4. 130–1.
42. Richard Buxton, 'Similes and other Likenesses', in Robert Fowler (ed.), *The Cambridge Companion to Homer* (2004), 153.
43. Homer, *Iliad*, 11. 243.
44. Pope, *Twickenham Edition*, viii, 397.
45. Ibid., vii, 398.; Homer, *Iliad*, 8. 52; Pope, *Twickenham Edition*, viii, 194.
46. Pope, *Twickenham Edition*, vii, 202.
47. Homer, *Iliad*, 3. 353; Pope, *Twickenham Edition*, vii, 213.
48. Homer, *Iliad*, 3. 150–1; Pope, *Twickenham Edition*, vii, 200.

49. Pope, *Twickenham Edition*, vii, 204.
50. Ibid., viii, 215.
51. Ibid., 216.
52. Ibid., 228.
53. Homer, *Iliad*, 16. 276–7; Pope, *Twickenham Edition*, viii, 255.
54. Pope, *Twickenham Edition*, viii, 279.
55. Homer, *Iliad*, 1. 70; Pope, *Twickenham Edition*, vii, 91.
56. Homer, *Iliad*, 13. 732–3; Pope, *Twickenham Edition*, viii, 148.
57. Homer, *Iliad*, 3. 109; Pope, *Twickenham Edition*, vii, 198.
58. Homer, *Iliad*, 23. 305, 306, 318; Pope, *Twickenham Edition*, viii, 505–6.
59. Pope, *Twickenham Edition*, vii, 237.
60. Ibid., 238.
61. Ibid., 3.
62. Ibid., 472.; ibid., viii, 71.
63. Ibid., viii, 72.
64. Ibid., 323.
65. Ibid., 325.
66. Ibid., 334–5.
67. Ibid., 398, 454.
68. Ibid., 365.
69. Homer, *Iliad*, 20. 490; Pope, *Twickenham Edition*, viii, 418.

NOTES TO CHAPTER 21

1. *The Iliad and Odyssey of Homer*, tr. William Cowper, 2 vols (1791), i, pp.vi–vii, xiii.
2. Colin Burrow, 'Virgil in English Translation', in Charles Martindale (ed.), *The Cambridge Companion to Virgil* (Cambridge, 1997), 21–37, 31.
3. *The Iliad of Homer*, tr. F. W. Newman (1856), iii–iv.
4. Matthew Arnold, *The Complete Prose Works, vol 1: On the Classical Tradition*, ed. R. H. Super (Ann Arbor, 1960), 120–2.
5. Timothy C. F. Stunt, 'Newman, Francis William (1805–1897)', *Oxford Dictionary of National Biography*, online edn (Oxford, September 2004): http://www.oxforddnb.com/view/article/20019 (accessed 22 July 2010).
6. Arnold, *Complete Prose Works*, i, 182. See Matthew Reynolds, 'Principles and Norms of Translation', in France and Gillespie (gen. eds), *The Oxford History of Literary Translation in English*, vol. 4, ed. France and Kenneth Haynes (Oxford, 2006), iv, 59–84, 67–70; Lawrence Venuti, *The Translator's Invisibility*, 2nd edn (2008), 99–120.
7. *The Iliad of Homer, rendered into English Blank Verse*, tr. Edward, Earl of Derby, 2 vols (1864), i, pp. viii–ix.
8. John Keats, *The Complete Poems*, ed. Miriam Allott, third impression with corrections (1975), 61–2.
9. Ibid., 60n, 62n.

10. Alfred, Lord Tennyson, *The Poems*, ed. Christopher Ricks, 3 vols, 2nd edn (1987), ii, 608.

11. Ibid., 606n.

12. Ibid., i, 625–6, 467–77, 616. For discussion of these poems, see Christopher Ricks, *Tennyson*, 2nd edn (1989), 113–26, 83–6; Herbert F. Tucker, *Tennyson and the Doom of Romanticism* (Cambridge, Mass. and London, 1988), 192–69; Matthew Reynolds, *The Realms of Verse 1830–1870: English Poetry in a Time of Nation-Building* (Oxford, 2001), 248–9, 219–20.

13. Robert Browning, *The Ring and the Book*, ed. Richard D. Altick (Harmondsworth, 1981), 37, 26.

14. Robert Browning, *The Poems*, ed. John Pettigrew, supplemented and completed by Thomas J. Collins, 2 vols (Harmondsworth 1981), ii, 201.

15. There is further discussion in my 'Browning and Translationese', *Essays in Criticism* 53.2 (April 2003), 97–128.

16. Ezra Pound, *The Cantos*, 4th collected edn (1987), 6; Ezra Pound, *Quia Pauper Amavi (Poems)* (1919), 19–20, 31.

17. Pound, *The Cantos*, 5. For Chapman's use of Divus, see above, Chapter 9.

18. Jody Allen Randolph, 'Michael Longley in Conversation', *PN Review* 31. 2 (November–December 2004), 21–7, 26.

19. Peter McDonald, *Mistaken Identities: Poetry and Northern Ireland* (Oxford, 1997), 140.

20. Michael Longley, *Collected Poems* (2006), 190.

21. Ibid., 184.

22. Ibid., 182.

23. Ibid., 183.

24. Lorna Hardwick hints at this when she notes 'the centrality of *anagnorisis* and *peripeteia*' in what she calls Longley's 'receptions' of Homer: '"Shards and Suckers": Contemporary Receptions of Homer', in Robert Fowler (ed.), *The Cambridge Companion to Homer* (Cambridge, 2004), 344–62, 360.

25. Fran Brearton suggests that the rhythms and rhymes in this poem-translation 'encompass the condition of both immediate recovery and imminent loss' (*Reading Michael Longley* [Tarset, Northumberland, 2006], 166).

26. Homer, *Odyssey*, 11. 207. Quoted from Homer, *Odyssey*, 2nd edn reprinted with corrections, with an English translation by A. T. Murray, revised George E. Dimock (Cambridge, Mass. and London, 1998).

27. Ibid., 194.

28. Homer, *Odyssey*, 24. 10.

29. Ibid., 14.

30. Fran Brearton, *The Great War in Irish Poetry: W. B. Yeats to Michael Longley* (Oxford, 2000), 275.

31. Longley, *Collected Poems*, 225.

32. Ibid., 226.

33. Ibid., 224.

34. Homer, *Iliad*, 8. 553.

35. Victor Shklovsky, 'Art as Technique', tr. Lee T. Lemon and Marion J. Reis, in David Lodge (ed.), *Modern Criticism and Theory: A Reader* (1988), 16–30, 19–20.
36. Longley, *Collected Poems*, 224.
37. Michael Longley, 'Memory and Acknowledgement', *The Irish Review* 17–18 (Winter 1995), 153–9, 158.
38. Longley, *Collected Poems*, 225. Hardwick observes that since 'Achilles and Priam are to die . . . The resonances for the modern equivalent, the truce that had been negotiated in the Troubles in the North of Ireland, remain dark': '"Shards and Suckers": Contemporary Receptions of Homer', 360.
39. Longley himself later expressed misgivings about this aspect of the poem: 'in my poem as in my political attitude, was I pressurising those who had been bereaved or maimed to forgive before they were ready to forgive?' (quoted in Brearton, *Reading Michael Longley*, 212).
40. Longley, *Collected Poems*, 226.

NOTES TO CHAPTER 22

1. Christopher Logue, *War Music: An Account of Books 1–4 and 16–19 of Homer's* Iliad (2001), 7.
2. Homer, *Iliad*, 1. 352.
3. Ibid., 349.
4. Homer, *Iliad*, with an English Translation by A. T. Murray, 2 vols (Cambridge, Mass. and London, 1924), i, 33.
5. Homer, *Iliad*, 1. 396.
6. *The Iliad of Homer*, tr. Derby, i, 22; Homer, *Iliad.*, 1. 397.
7. Hugh Kenner, *The Pound Era* (1991), 360.
8. *OED* gives the following illustrative quotation from 1983: 'Roger Norrington conducted a fizzing account of Offenbach's score'.
9. *The Iliad of Homer*, tr. Robert Fagles, introduction and notes by Bernard Knox (1991), 89.
10. *The Iliad of Homer*, tr. Richmond Lattimore, drawings by Leonard Baskin (1962), 68.
11. Christopher Logue, 'Christopher Logue: The Art of Poetry LXVI.' *Paris Review* 127 (1993) 238–64, 254–5.
12. Ibid., 255.
13. Logue, *War Music*, 211–12, 170; Logue, *Cold Calls: War Music Continued* (2005), 3.
14. Logue, 'Christopher Logue: The Art of Poetry LXVI', 255.
15. Christopher Logue, *Selected Poems* (1996), 137.
16. David Ricks, 'On Looking into the First Paperback of Pope's Homer', *Classics Ireland* 4 (1997), 97–120, 115.
17. Logue, *Selected Poems*, 139.
18. Christopher Logue, 'The Shortest Long Poem Ever Written: An Interview with Christopher Logue', *Areté* 13 (Winter 2003), 117–36, 118–19.

19. James Campbell, 'Classic Upstart', *Guardian* (17 November 2001): http://www.guardian.co.uk/books/2001/nov/17/poetry.books (accessed 1 September 2010).

20. Christopher Logue, *Prince Charming: A Memoir* (1999), 222.

21. Logue, 'The Shortest Long Poem Ever Written', 126.

22. Charles Bainbridge, 'The War in Heaven', *Guardian* (8 October 2005): http://www.guardian.co.uk/books/2005/oct/08/poetry.homer (accessed 1 September 2010).

23. Logue, *Prince Charming*, 209–10.

24. See above, Chapter 19.

25. Logue, 'Christopher Logue: The Art of Poetry LXVI', 255.

26. Logue, *War Music*, 118–19.

27. *Iliad*, tr. Murray, i, 143.

28. My own use of the word 'zoom' has a metaphorical bagginess which I take to be apt to Logue's strong but imprecise notion of film. In cinema, a zoom – strictly speaking – is when the camera stays still and the degree of magnification increases: the technique started to be used in the late 1960s and was much in vogue through to the mid-1970s, flourishing in the work of directors such as Claude Chabrol and Robert Altman. But there are other ways of moving into close-up, using pans, cranes, dollys, or tracking shots, any or all of which could be employed if someone were trying to make a film version of the scenes that Logue has written down. Distinctions between these techniques are crucial in the analysis of film but they cannot readily be transferred to written texts; at least, not to the passages I discuss here. For some reflections on zoom in the cinema, see John Belton, 'The Bionic Eye: Zoom Esthetics', *Cineaste* 11.1 (Winter 1980–1), 20–7. I am grateful to the film scholar Andrew Klevan for sharing his expertise in this area.

29. Logue, *War Music*, 118–19.

30. Logue, *War Music*, 171; Logue, *Cold Calls*, 35–6.

31. Homer, *Iliad*, 2. 96–100; Logue, *War Music*, 65.

32. Logue, *Prince Charming*, 39.

33. Ibid., 54.

34. Logue, *War Music*, 7, 12.

35. Logue, 'The Shortest Long Poem Ever Written', 131.

36. Christopher Logue, 'Interview with Christopher Logue', *Thumbscrew* 1 (1994–5): http://www.poetrymagazines.org.uk/magazine/print.asp?id=5237 (accessed 15 July 2009).

37. Logue, *Cold Calls*, 23.

38. *Iliad*, tr. Murray, ii, 337.

39. Logue, *War Music*, 195.

40. *The Iliad of Homer*, tr. Lattimore, 354.

41. Logue, *War Music*, 170.

42. Home, *Iliad*, 17. 18.

43. Anne Carson, *Men in the Off Hours* (2000), 33–4.

44. Anne Carson, *Autobiography of Red* (1999), 11.

45. Logue, *Prince Charming*, 223.
46. *Beowulf*, tr. Seamus Heaney (1999), xxv–xxvii.
47. Chris Jones: *Strange Likeness: The Use of Old English in Twentieth-Century Poetry* (2006), 234.
48. *Beowulf*, tr. Heaney, ix.
49. Ibid., 7.
50. *Beowulf: A Verse Translation into Modern English*, tr. Edwin Morgan (Manchester, 2002), 6.
51. *Beowulf*, tr. Heaney, xix.
52. Quoted in Daniel Weissbort and Astradur Eysteinsson (eds), *Translation – Theory and Practice: A Historical Reader* (Oxford, 2006), 606.
53. Logue, *War Music*, 184.
54. *Iliad*, tr. Murray, ii, 291.
55. Logue, *War Music*, 186.
56. Ibid., 160.

NOTES TO CHAPTER 23

1. William Wordsworth, *The Poems*, ed. John O. Hayden, 2 vols (Harmondsworth, 1977), i, 357.
2. John Dryden, *The Poems*, ed. Paul Hammond and David Hopkins, 5 vols (1995–2005), ii, 239.
3. *L'Iliade d'Homere, traduite en François avec des Remarques*, tr. Madame Dacier, 3 vols (Paris, 1711), i, p. xxxvii.
4. Ibid., xxxv.
5. George Gordon, Lord Byron, *Hours of Idleness, a Series of Poems, Original and Translated* (1807), 71–2.
6. Ibid., 74, 77.
7. Robert Browning, *The Poems*, 2 vols, ed. John Pettigrew, Supplemented & Completed by Thomas J. Collins (Harmondsworth 1981), ii, 303.
8. Robert Browning, *The Ring and the Book*, ed. Richard D. Altick (Harmondsworth, 1981), 26.
9. Ibid., 41.
10. Ibid., 189.
11. Further discussion is in Matthew Reynolds, 'Browning and Translationese', *Essays in Criticism* 53.2 (April 2003), 97–128.
12. Ezra Pound, *Quia Pauper Amavi (Poems)* (1919), 31
13. Ezra Pound, *The Cantos*, 4th collected edn (1987), 4–5.
14. Homer, *Odyssea*, tr. Andrea Divo Iustinopolitano (Lugduni, 1538), 94r, 95v.
15. Pound, *Cantos*, 3.
16. Homer, *Odyssea*, tr. Divo, 93r.
17. Hugh Kenner, *The Pound Era* (1991), 161, 361.
18. Ezra Pound, *Pound's Cavalcanti: An Edition of the Translations, Notes, and Essays*, ed. David Anderson (Princeton, NJ, 1983), xviii; Ezra Pound, *The Selected Letters of Ezra Pound, 1907–1941*, ed. D. D. Paige (1971), 149.

19. *Pound's Cavalcanti*, 12, xviii.
20. Ibid., 14.
21. Ibid., 12.
22. Ibid.
23. Ibid., 42–3.
24. Ibid.
25. Ibid.
26. Ibid., xxi–xii.
27. Ibid., 44.
28. Ibid., 45.
29. Donald Davie, *Studies in Ezra Pound* (Manchester, 1991), 93.
30. Hymn 81 ('Songs of thankfulness and praise'), in *Hymns Ancient and Modern* (1889), 102; Isaac Williams, *The Altar* (1849), 404; Algernon Charles Swinburne, 'Grand Chorus of Birds from Aristophanes *The Birds*', in *The Poems of Algernon Charles Swinburne*, 6 vols (1905), v, 45. All found in Chadwick Healey's *Literature Online* (http://lion.chadwyck.co.uk/ [accessed 4 September 2009]).
31. *Pound's Cavalcanti*, 46.
32. Davie, *Studies*, 96.
33. *Pound's Cavalcanti*, 250.
34. Lawrence Venuti, *The Translator's Invisibility*, 2nd edn (2008), 173. Venuti reads the successive versions of 'Chi è questa che vien' as illustrating a 'basic archaizing strategy' which 'did not alter'. Its point, he thinks, is to proclaim 'the impossibility of finding any exact linguistic and literary equivalent' to the source (170, 173). But that impossibility is a trivial truth, well-known to translators—as this book makes plain throughout.
35. *The Iliad of Homer*, tr. F. W. Newman (1856), x; *The Iliad of Homer*, tr. F. W. Newman, 2nd edn (1871), viii.
36. See above, Chapters 20 and 22.
37. Christopher Logue, *War Music; An Account of Books 1–4 and 16–19 of Homer's* Iliad (2001), 100.
38. Alexander Pope, *The Twickenham Edition of the Poems*, gen. ed. John Butt, 11 vols (1939–67), vii, 19.
39. Quoted in Kenner, *The Pound Era*, 178, 185.
40. *Pound's Cavalcanti*, 251.
41. J. P. Sullivan (ed.), *Ezra Pound: A Critical Anthology* (1970), 79.
42. Ezra Pound, *Collected Shorter Poems* (1984), 128.
43. See Kenner, *The Pound Era*, 195.
44. Pound, *Collected Shorter Poems*, 130, 134, 138, 132.
45. Ibid., 127, 130.
46. Kenner, *The Pound Era*, 195.
47. Ezra Pound, *Selected Poems*, ed. T. S. Eliot (1928), 14.
48. Wai-lim Yip, *Ezra Pound's* Cathay (New Jersey, 1969), 88.
49. Eric Homberger (ed.), *Ezra Pound: The Critical Heritage* (1972), 108.
50. Kenner, *The Pound Era*, 199.

51. Steven G. Yao points out that the complicated process of transmission culminating in *Cathay* was announced on the title page of the first edition: TRANSLATIONS BY EZRA POUND / FOR THE MOST PART FROM THE CHINESE / OF RIHAKU, / FROM THE NOTES OF THE / LATE ERNEST FENOLLOSA, AND / THE / DECIPHERINGS OF THE / PROFESSORS MORI / AND ARIGA (*Translation and the Languages of Modernism: Gender, Politics, Language* [New York and Basingstoke, 2002], 31.

52. Pound, *Collected Shorter Poems*, 127, 133, 139, 130, 128, 134, 130, 128, 137.

53. Kodama Sannehide, 'Pound and Fenollosa's Notebooks', *Paideuma* 11. 2 (1982), 207–40, 214.

54. Anne S. Chapple, 'Ezra Pound's *Cathay*: Compilation from the Fenollosa Notebooks', *Paideuma* 17. 2–3 (1988), 9–46, 11, 23.

55. Yao, *Translation and the Languages of Modernism*, 33.

56. Kenner, *The Pound Era*, 202.

57. Pound, *Collected Shorter Poems*, 130.

58. Ibid., 131.

59. Ibid., 134–6.

60. Ibid., 127.

61. *Homage to Sextus Propertius*, quoted from the edition, which is printed in parallel with the Latin text Pound used, in J. P. Sullivan, *Ezra Pound and Sextus Propertius* (1965), 169–71.

62. Francis Cairns, *Sextus Propertius: The Augustan Elegist* (Cambridge, 2006), 319.

63. Pound, *Selected Letters*, 178.

64. Ezra Pound, *Literary Essays*, ed. with an introduction by T. S. Eliot (1954), 25.

65. Sullivan, *Ezra Pound and Sextus Propertius*, 114–15.

66. See Propertius, *Properzio: Il Libro Terzo delle Elegie*, ed. Paolo Fedeli (Bari, 1985), 42–4.

67. Sullivan, *Ezra Pound and Sextus Propertius*, 118–19.

68. Propertius, *Properzio: Il Libro Terzo*, 107.

69. Michael Comber, 'A Book Made New: Reading Propertius Reading Pound. A Study in Reception', *Journal of Roman Studies* 88 (1998) 37–55, 54.

70. Sullivan, *Ezra Pound and Sextus Propertius*, 139, 147.

71. Ibid., 147.

72. Ibid., 134–5.

73. Ibid., 116–17.

74. *Erotica: The Elegies of Propertius, the Satyricon of Petronius Arbiter, and the Kisses of Johannes Secundus. To which are Added the Love Epistles of Aristaenetus*, ed. Walter K. Kelly (Bohn's Classical Library, 1854), 76; Propertius, *Elegies*, ed. and tr. G. P. Goold, rev. edn (Cambridge, Mass. and London, 1999), 225.

75. Thomas Bridges, *Homer Travestie: being a new translation of the four first books of the Iliad* (1762), 189.

76. Comber, 'A Book Made New', 54.

77. *Oxford English Dictionary, ad loc.*

78. Christopher Stray, *Classics Transformed: Schools, Universities, and Society in England, 1830–1960* (Oxford, 1998), 2.
79. Ezra Pound, 'Notes on Elizabethan Classicists' (1917–18), in *Literary Essays of Ezra Pound*, ed. with an introduction T. S. Eliot (1954), 227–48, 232.
80. Charles A. Elton, *Tales of Romance, with Other Poems, including Selections from Propertius* (1810), 131.
81. Sullivan, *Ezra Pound and Sextus Propertius*, 119, 115, 147.
82. Eric Homberger (ed.), *Ezra Pound: The Critical Heritage* (1972), 157.
83. Pound, *Selected Letters*, 149.
84. Homberger (ed.), *Ezra Pound: The Critical Heritage*, 169–70.
85. Ibid., 170.
86. Virginia Woolf, 'On Not Knowing Greek', quoted in Jennifer Wallace, 'Elizabeth Barrett Browning: Knowing Greek', *Essays in Criticism* 50. 4 (2000) 329–53, 346; for Pope's remark, see above, Chapter 20.
87. Sullivan, *Ezra Pound and Sextus Propertius*, 100.
88. Homberger (ed.), *Ezra Pound: The Critical Heritage*, 164.
89. *Oxford Latin Dictionary, ad loc.*
90. Sullivan, *Ezra Pound and Sextus Propertius*, 170–1.
91. Ibid., 128.
92. Propertius, *Properzio: Il Libro Terzo*, 207–8.
93. Sullivan, *Ezra Pound and Sextus Propertius*, 129.
94. Ibid., 150–1.
95. Homberger (ed.), *Ezra Pound: The Critical Heritage*, 169.
96. Pound, *Collected Shorter Poems*, 61.
97. Homberger (ed.), *Ezra Pound: The Critical Heritage*, 321.
98. Sullivan, *Ezra Pound and Sextus Propertius*, 119, 169, 129 (compare Yeats, 'The Withering of the Boughs', 8: 'The boughs have withered because I have told them my dreams.')
99. Clive Bell, *Art* (1914), 53.
100. Sullivan, *Ezra Pound and Sextus Propertius*, 157.
101. Ibid., 167, 161.
102. Daniel M. Hooley, *The Classics in Paraphrase: Ezra Pound and Modern Translators of Latin Poetry* (1988), 48.
103. Homberger (ed.), *Ezra Pound: The Critical Heritage*, 163.
104. Sullivan, *Ezra Pound and Sextus Propertius*, 115
105. Ibid., 114; *Erotica*, ed. Kelly, 75.
106. Propertius, *Properzio: Il Libro Terzo*, 66.
107. Pound, *Cantos*, 61.
108. Sullivan, *Ezra Pound and Sextus Propertius*, 125.
109. Ibid., 124.
110. Ibid.
111. Ibid., 143.
112. Davie, *Studies*, 79.
113. Sullivan, *Ezra Pound and Sextus Propertius*, 147.
114. Ibid.

NOTES TO CHAPTER 24

1. Pound, *Literary Essays*, 34.
2. Pound, *Cantos*, 530.
3. Edward FitzGerald, *The Letters of Edward FitzGerald*, ed. Alfred McKinley Terhune and Annabelle Burdick Terhune, 4 vols (Princeton, NJ, 1980), ii, 294.
4. William Shakespeare, *Hamlet*, 3. 1, 65, quoted from *The Complete Works*, ed. Peter Alexander (London and Glasgow, 1951).
5. Edward FitzGerald, *Letters and Literary Remains* (cited as '*Remains*' hereafter), 7 vols (1902–3), vii, 18.
6. *Edward FitzGerald's Rubâ'iyât of Omar Khayyam with Their Original Persian Sources Collated from his own MSS., and Literally Translated*, tr. Edward Heron-Allen (1899), 13.
7. FitzGerald, *Remains*, vii, 34.
8. FitzGerald, *Rubâ'iyât*, ed. Heron-Allen, 13.
9. FitzGerald, *Letters*, ii, 273; Robert Bernard Martin, *With Friends Possessed: A Biography of Edward FitzGerald* (1985), 199.
10. FitzGerald, *Letters*, ii, 273.
11. Ibid., ii, 289.
12. Ibid., 110.
13. Ibid., 281.
14. FitzGerald, *Remains*, vii, 18.
15. Ibid., 34.
16. Edward FitzGerald, *Rubáiyát of Omar Khayyám*, ed. Daniel Karlin (2009), xxix.
17. FitzGerald, *Rubâ'iyât*, ed. Heron-Allen, 15n.
18. Edward FitzGerald, *Rubáiyát of Omar Khayyám: A Critical Edition*, ed. Christopher Decker (Charlottesville, Va. and London, 1997), xxxvi–xxxvii.
19. Herbert F. Tucker, 'Metaphor, Translation, and Autoekphrasis in FitzGerald's Rubáiyát', *Victorian Poetry* 46.1 (Spring 2008), 69–86, 77.
20. FitzGerald, *Remains*, vii, 22.
21. Charles Kingsley, *Alton Locke, Tailor and Poet: An Autobiography* (1876), 131.
22. FitzGerald, *Remains*, vii, 22.
23. FitzGerald, *Rubâ'iyât*, ed. Heron-Allen, 43; Edward FitzGerald, *The Romance of the Rubáiyát: Edward FitzGerald's First Edition Reprinted with Introduction and Notes*, ed. A. J. Arberry (1959), 207.
24. FitzGerald, *Remains*, vii, 23.
25. FitzGerald, *Rubâ'iyât*, ed. Heron-Allen, 49; see also FitzGerald, *The Romance*, ed. Arberry, 209.
26. John Brown, *Psyche; or, The soul, a Poem in Seven Cantos* (1818), 121.
27. Edward FitzGerald, *The Variorum and Definitive Edition of the Poetical and Prose Writings*, ed. George Bentham, with an introduction by Edmund Gosse, 7 vols (New York, 1902–3), i, p. xxviii.

28. Erik Gray, *The Poetry of Indifference: From the Romantics to the Rubáiyát* (Amherst and Boston, 2005), 101; Robert Douglas-Fairhurst, *Victorian Afterlives: The Shaping of Influence in Nineteenth-Century Literature* (Oxford, 2002), 304–8.

29. FitzGerald, *Letters*, ii, 318.

30. Ibid., 164.

31. Ibid., 119.

32. Ibid., 164.

33. FitzGerald, *Remains*, vii, 17.

34. FitzGerald, *The Romance*, ed. Arberry, 192.

35. FitzGerald, *Letters*, ii, 164; Ecclesiastes 5. 1; 4. 5 (quoted from *The Holy Bible Conteyning the Old Testament, and the New* [1611]).

36. Frank Kermode, 'Allusions to Omar', in his *Continuities* (1968), 56–61, 61, 58.

37. FitzGerald, *Rubáiyát*, ed. Karlin, xxxii.

38. FitzGerald, *Letters*, ii, 180.

39. Emmanuel Levinas, *Humanism of the Other*, tr. Nidra Poller, with an introduction by Richard A. Cohen (Urbana and Chicago, 2006), 30.

40. FitzGerald, *Remains*, vii, 18.

41. FitzGerald, *Letters*, iv, 167–8.

42. Ecclesiastes 9. 4–5.

43. FitzGerald, *Letters*, ii, 335.

44. Dryden, *The Poems*, i, 388.

45. Quoted in *Oxford English Dictionary* under 'transfusion', sense 2.

46. FitzGerald, *Remains*, vii, 20.

47. Ibid., 21.

48. FitzGerald, *Letters*, i, 352–3.

49. Ibid., 354.

50. Ibid., 355.

51. *The Poems of Thomas Gray, William Collins, Oliver Goldsmith*, ed. Roger Lonsdale (1969), 127.

52. FitzGerald, *The Romance*, ed. Arberry, 204.

53. FitzGerald, *Remains*, vii, 17.

54. Ibid., 18, 19, 20, 21, 22, 23, 25.

55. FitzGerald, *Letters*, ii, 386.

NOTES TO CHAPTER 25

1. FitzGerald, *Remains*, vii, 21.

2. FitzGerald, *Rubá'iyât*, ed. Heron-Allen, 35; FitzGerald, *The Romance*, ed. Arberry, 204.

3. '"In nova . . . mutatas . . . formas / corpora"': Ovid, *Metamorphoses*, 1, 1-2. For convenience I give references (book and line) to the Loeb Classical Library edition, tr. Frank Justus Miller, rev. G. P. Goold, 3rd edn (Cambridge, Mass. and London, 1977). I have checked this text against one available to Golding

and Dryden, *Metamorphoseos Libri Quindecim, cum commentariis Raphaelis Regii. Adiectis Annotationibus Iacoby Micylli nunc primum in lucem editis* (Basileae, 1543): any substantial differences are noted.

4. Dryden, *The Poems*, v, 541.

5. Ovid, *Metamorphoses*, 15. 257–8.

6. Charles Tomlinson, *Poetry and Metamorphosis* (Cambridge, 1983), 102.

7. Ibid.

8. Joseph Addison, 'To Mr Dryden', *Examen Poeticum* (1693), 249.

9. Dryden, *The Poems*, v, 527.

10. Quoted in Theo Hermans, 'Images of Translation: Metaphor and Imagery in the Renaissance Discourse of Translation', in Theo Hermans (ed.), *The Manipulation of Literature: Studies in Literary Translation* (1985), 103–35, 127.

11. Michel de Montaigne, *The Essayes or Morall, Politike and Millitarie Discourses*, tr. John Florio (1603).

12. Homer, *Chapman's Homer: The Iliad*, ed. Allardyce Nicoll (Princeton, NJ, 1956), 9.

13. George Chapman, *Euthymiae Raptus; or The Teares of Peace with Interlocutions* (1609), sig A 4 r-v.

14. Edmund Spenser, *The Faerie Queene*, ed. A. C. Hamilton (1977), 440. For discussion, see Stuart Gillespie, 'Literary Afterlives: Metempsychosis from Ennius to Jorge Luis Borges', in Philip Hardie and Helen Moore (eds), *Classical Literary Careers and their Reception* (Cambridge, forthcoming).

15. Francis Meres, 'A Comparative Discourse of our English Poets with the Greek, Latine and Italian Poets', in G. Gregory Smith (ed), *Elizabethan Critical Essays*, 2 vols (Oxford, 1904), ii. 314–24, 317–18; quoted in Jonathan Bate, *Shakespeare and Ovid* (Oxford, 1993), 2.

16. Dryden, *The Poems*, v, 532.

17. *Ovid's Metamorphoses*, ed. Madeleine Forey, tr. Arthur Golding (2002), 3. Three groundbreaking surveys are still useful: Flora Ross Amos, *Early Theories of Translation* (New York, 1920); C. H. Conley, *The First English Translators of the Classics* (New Haven and London, 1927); F. O. Matthiessen. *Translation: An Elizabethan Art* (Cambridge, Mass., 1931).

18. Gordon Braden, *The Classics and English Renaissance Poetry: Three Case Studies* (New Haven and London, 1978), 16–17.

19. *Ovid's Metamorphoses*, tr. Golding, xxiii.

20. Ibid., xvi.

21. Ibid., 40.

22. Braden, *The Classics and English Renaissance Poetry*, 13.

23. Ibid., 8, 25.

24. Leonard Barkan, *The Gods Made Flesh: Metamorphosis and the Pursuit of Paganism* (New Haven and London, 1986), 114.

25. Marina Warner, *Fantastic Metamorphoses, Other Worlds: Ways of Telling the Self* (Oxford, 2002), 42.

26. Other aspects of the religious context are sketched in Liz Oakley-Brown, 'Translating the Subject: Ovid's *Metamorphoses* in England, 1560–7', in Roger Ellis and Liz Oakley-Brown (eds), *Translation and Nation: Towards a Cultural Politics of Englishness* (Clevedon, 2001), 48–84.

27. Arthur Golding, *A Briefe Discourse of the Late Murther of Master George Saunders, a Worshipful Citizen of London and of the Apprehension, Arreignement, and Execution of the Principall and Accessaries of the Same* (1573), sig A. 2v, C. 2v.

28. Arthur Golding, *A Discourse vpon the Earthquake that Hapned throughe this Realme of Englande, and other Places of Christendom, the first of Aprill. 1580, betwene the houres of fiue and six in the euening* (1580), sig. C. iv. r, D. 1. r.

29. *Ovid's Metamorphoses*, tr. Golding, 20–1.

30. Ibid., 450–1.

31. Ibid., 14.

32. C. S. Lewis, *English Literature in the Sixteenth Century Excluding Drama* (Oxford, 1954), 251.

33. '"fronde tegi silvas"', etc: Ovid, *Metamorphoses* 1. 44, 66, 80–1; *Ovid's Metamorphoses*, tr. Golding, 24–5.

34. Pound, *Literary Essays*, 239.

35. *Ovid's Metamorphoses*, tr. Golding, 8.

36. Ibid., 106; Ovid, *Metamorphoses*, 3. 380.

37. *Ovid's Metamorphoses*, tr. Golding, 108; Ovid, *Metamorphoses*, 3. 417.

38. Ovid, *Metamorphoses*, 3. 432.

39. *Ovid's Metamorphoses*, tr. Golding, 108.

40. Braden, *The Classics and English Renaissance* Poetry, 14, 41.

41. *Ovid's Metamorphoses*, tr. Golding, 44.

42. Ovid, *Metamorphoses*, 1. 391–3.

43. Frederick Ahl, *Metaformations: Soundplay and Wordplay in Ovid and other Classical Poets* (1985).

44. Ovid, *Metamorphoses*, 5. 461.

45. Ovid, *Metamorphoseos Libri Quindecim*, 120.

46. *Ovid's Metamorphoses*, tr. Golding, 167.

47. Ibid., 389.

48. Ibid., 390.

49. Ovid, *Metamorphoses*, 1. 410.

50. *Ovid's Metamorphoses*, tr. Golding, 45.

51. Ibid., 195.

52. Ovid, *Metamorphoses*, 6. 555.

53. *Oxford English Dictionary*, ad loc.

54. Ahl, *Metaformations*, 134.

55. *Ovid's Metamorphoses*, tr. Golding, 47–50.

56. Ibid., 50–51.

57. Ovid, *Metamorphoses*, 1. 566-7.

58. Ovid, *Metamorfosi*, ed. Alessandro Barchiesi (Milan, 2005–), i, 214–15.

59. Dryden, *The Poems*, iv, 269.

60. *Ovid's Metamorphoses Englished by G. S.*, tr. George Sandys (1626), 15.
61. Polemics in the last three decades of the eighteenth century, Chartier suggests, 'resulted in a new definition of the work, now no longer characterized by the ideas that it embodies (since ideas cannot be the object of individual appropriation) but by its *form*—that is, by the particular way in which an author produces, assembles, expresses, and presents concepts' (Roger Chartier, *The Order of Books: Readers, Authors, and Libraries in Europe between the Fourteenth and Eighteenth Centuries*, tr. Lydia G. Cochrane [1994], 36).
62. Peter France and Stuart Gillespie (gen. eds), *The Oxford History of Literary Translation in English*, 5 vols (Oxford, 2005–   ), iii, 396.
63. Matthew Reynolds, 'Most Himself', *London Review of Books* 29.14 (19 July 2007), 11–15. http://www.lrb.co.uk/v29/n14/matthew-reynolds/most-himself (accessed 24 January 2011).
64. Matthew Reynolds, 'Principles and Norms of Translation', in France and Gillespie (gen. eds), *The Oxford History of Literary Translation in English*, vol. 4, ed. Peter France and Kenneth Haynes (Oxford), iv, 59–82.

Works Cited

Place of publication is London unless otherwise stated. Different volumes by the same author are listed in chronological rather than alphabetical order.

Addison, Joseph, 'To Mr Dryden', *Examen Poeticum* (1693), 249.

—— *The Papers of Joseph Addison, Esq. in the Tatler, Spectator, Guardian and Freeholder. Together with his Treatise on the Christian Religion*, 4 vols (1790).

Aeschylus, *The Tragedies of Aeschylus Translated into English Prose* (Oxford, 1827).

—— *Aeschylus: Translated into English Prose*, tr. F. A. Paley (Cambridge, 1864).

—— *Agamemnon*, ed. Eduard Fraenkel, 3 vols (Oxford, 1950).

—— *Prometheus Bound*, ed. Mark Griffith (Cambridge, 1983).

Ahl, Frederick, *Metaformations: Soundplay and Wordplay in Ovid and other Classical Poets* (1985).

Ames, Alfred C., 'Early Criticism of Pope's "Night-Piece"', *Modern Language Notes* 60. 4 (April 1945), 265–7.

Amos, Flora Ross, *Early Theories of Translation* (New York, 1920).

Anderson, W. S., 'Vergil's Second *Iliad*', *Transactions of the American Philological Association* 88 (1957), 17–30, reprinted in Philip Hardie (ed.), *Virgil: Critical Assessments of Classical Authors*, 4 vols (1999), iii, 74–86.

Anon., *A Poem on the Accession of their Royal Highnesses the Prince and Princess of Orange to the Imperial Crown of England being a paraphrase on the 45 Psalm* [1689].

Ariosto, Ludovico, *Orlando Furioso: Nuovamente Adorato di Figure di Rame da Girolamo Porro* (Venice, 1584).

—— *Orlando Furioso Translated into English Heroical Verse*, ed. Robert McNulty, tr. Sir John Harington (Oxford, 1972).

Arnold, Matthew, *The Complete Prose Works*, ed. R. H. Super, 11 vols (Ann Arbor, 1960–77).

Bainbridge, Charles, 'The War in Heaven', *Guardian* (8 October 2005): http://www.guardian.co.uk/books/2005/oct/08/poetry.homer (accessed 1 September 2010).

Baker, Mona, *Translation and Conflict: A Narrative Account* (2006).

Baker, Richard, *Cato Variegatus or Catoes Morall Distichs: Translated and Paraphras'd, with variations of Expressing, in English verse* (1636).

Bakhtin, M. M., *The Dialogic Imagination: Four Essays*, ed. Michael Holquist, tr. Caryl Emerson and Michael Holquist (Austin, Tex., 1981).

Barkan, Leonard, *The Gods Made Flesh: Metamorphosis and the Pursuit of Paganism* (New Haven and London, 1986).

Barnard, John (ed.), *Pope: The Critical Heritage* (1973).

Barnard, John. 'Dryden, Tonson, and the Patrons of *The Works of Virgil* (1697)', in Paul Hammond and David Hopkins (eds), *John Dryden: Tercentenary Essays* (2000), 174–239.

Barnes, William, *Poems of Rural Life in the Dorset Dialect: With a Dissertation and Glossary* (1844; 2nd edn 1848).

Barolini, Teodolinda, 'Dante and Francesca da Rimini: Realpolitik, Romance, Gender', *Speculum* 75.1 (January 2000), 1–28.

Barrell, John, *The Idea of Landscape and the Sense of Place 1730–1840: An Approach to the Poetry of John Clare* (Cambridge, 1972).

Bartlett, Phyllis, 'Chapman's Revisions in his *Iliads*', *English Literary History* 2.1 (April 1935), 92–114.

Bate, Jonathan, *Shakespeare and Ovid* (Oxford, 1993).

Batey, Mavis, *Alexander Pope: The Poet and the Landscape* (1999).

Becker, A. L., *Beyond Translation: Essays toward a Modern Philology* (Ann Arbor, 1995).

Bell, Clive, *Art* (1914).

Bell, Charles G., 'Fairfax's Tasso', *Comparative Literature* 6.1 (Winter 1954), 26–52.

Belton, John, 'The Bionic Eye: Zoom Esthetics', *Cineaste* 11.1 (Winter 1980–1), 20–7.

Benedict, Barbara M., *Making the Modern Reader: Cultural Mediation in Early Modern Anthologies* (Princeton, NJ, 1996).

Benjamin, Walter, *Illuminationen. Ausgewählte Schriften*, vol. 1 (Frankfurt am Main, 1977).

Bentley, Richard, *Remarks upon a Late Discourse of Free-Thinking: in a Letter to F. H. D. D. By Phileleutherus Lipsiensis* (1713).

Beowulf, tr. Seamus Heaney (1999).

Beowulf: A Verse Translation into Modern English, tr. Edwin Morgan (Manchester, 2002).

Berman, Antoine, *L'Épreuve de l'étranger: Culture et traduction dans l'Allemagne romantique* (Paris, 1984).

Biblia the Byble, that is, the holy Scrypture of the Olde and New Testament, faithfully translated in to Englyshe, tr. Miles Coverdale, 3 vols in 1 (1535).

Biblia Sacra Iuxta Vulgatam Versionem, ed. Robertus Weber OSB (Stuttgart, 1983).

Die gantze Bibel der ursprügliche[n] Ebraischenn und Griechischenn warheyt nach, auffs aller treüwlichest verteütschet, tr. Martin Luther (Zürich, 1530).

The Holy Bible Conteyning the Old Testament, and the New: newly translated out of the originall tongues: & with the former translations diligently compared and reuised, by his Maiesties speciall comandement. Appointed to be read in churches (1611).

The Holy Bible . . . in the Earliest English Versions made from the Latin Vulgate by John Wycliffe and his Followers, ed. Rev. Josiah Forshall and Sir Frederic Madden, 4 vols (Oxford, 1850).

Bishop, Elisabeth and Lowell, Robert, *Words in Air: The Complete Correspondence*, ed. Thomas Trevisand with Saskia Hamilton (2008).

Black, Max, 'More about Metaphor', in Andrew Ortony (ed.), *Metaphor and Thought*, 2nd edn (Cambridge, 1993), 19–41.

Blackmore, Sir Richard, *Prince Arthur: an heroick poem in ten books* (1695).

Blake, William, *The Complete Poems*, ed. W. H. Stevenson, 2nd edn (1989).

Blanchot, Maurice, *Friendship*, tr. Elizabeth Rottenberg (Stanford, Calif., 1997).

Blum-Kulka, Shoshana, 'Shifts of Cohesion and Coherence in Translation', in Juliane House and Shoshana Blum-Kulka (eds), *Interlingual and Intercultural Communication* (Tübingen, 1986), repr. in Venuti (ed.), *The Translation Studies Reader* (2000).

Braden, Gordon, *The Classics and English Renaissance Poetry: Three Case Studies* (New Haven and London, 1978).

Bray, Alan, *The Friend* (2003).

Brearton, Fran, *The Great War in Irish Poetry: W. B. Yeats to Michael Longley* (Oxford, 2000).

——*Reading Michael Longley* (Tarset, Northumberland, 2006).

Brekelmans, Christianus, Sæbø, Magne, and Haran, Menahem, *Old Testament: The History of Its Interpretation* (1996).

Bridges, Thomas, *Homer Travestie: being a new translation of the four first books of the Iliad* (1762).

Briggs, John Channing, 'Chapman's *Seaven Bookes of the Iliades*: Mirror for Essex', *Studies in English Literature, 1500–1900* 21.1 (Winter 1981), 59–73.

Brower, Reuben A. (ed.), *On Translation* (1959; 1966).

——*Alexander Pope: The Poetry of Allusion* (Oxford, 1959).

Brown, John, *Psyche; or, The soul, a Poem in Seven Cantos* (1818).

Browning, Elizabeth Barrett, *Prometheus Bound Translated from the Greek of Aeschylus. And Miscellaneous Poems by the Translator* (1833).

——*Poems* (1850).

——*Poetical Works* (1904).

Browning, Robert, *Poetical Works*, 16 vols (1888–9).

——*The Poems*, ed. John Pettigrew, supplemented and completed by Thomas J. Collins, 2 vols (Harmondsworth, 1981).

——*The Ring and the Book*, ed. Richard D. Altick (Harmondsworth, 1981).

Bruce, F. F., *The English Bible: A History of Translations from the Earliest English Versions to the New English Bible* (1961).

Buchanan, Allen E. and Brock, Dan W., *Deciding for Others: The Ethics of Surrogate Decision Making* (Cambridge, 1989).

Bühler, Axel, 'Translation as Interpretation', in Alessandra Riccardi (ed.), *Translation Studies: Perspectives on an Emerging Discipline* (Cambridge, 2002).

Burrow, Colin, *Epic Romance: Homer to Milton* (Oxford, 1993).

——'Virgil in English Translation', in Charles Martindale (ed.), *The Cambridge Companion to Virgil* (Cambridge, 1997), 21–37.

——'Literature and Politics under Henry VII and Henry VIII', in David Wallace (ed.), *The Cambridge History of Medieval English Literature* (Cambridge, 1999), 793–820.

Buxton, Richard, 'Similes and other Likenesses', in Robert Fowler (ed.), *The Cambridge Companion to Homer* (2004), 139–55.

Byron, George Gordon, Lord, *Hours of Idleness, a Series of Poems, Original and Translated* (1807).

——*Byron's Letters and Journals*, ed. Leslie A. Marchand, 13 vols (1963–94).

——*The Complete Poetical Works*, ed. Jerome J. McGann, 7 vols (Oxford, 1980–93).

——*The Complete Miscellaneous Prose*, ed. Andrew Nicholson (Oxford, 1991).

Cairns, Francis, *Sextus Propertius: The Augustan Elegist* (Cambridge, 2006).

Campbell, James, 'Classic Upstart', *Guardian* (17 November 2001): http://www.guardian.co.uk/books/2001/nov/17/poetry.books (accessed 1 September 2010).

Carlyle, Thomas, *On Heroes, Hero-Worship, & the Heroic in History*, ed. Michael K. Goldberg et al. (Berkeley and Oxford, 1993).

Carne-Ross, Donald and Haynes, Kenneth (eds), *Horace in English*, with an introduction by Donald Carne-Ross (1996).

Carson, Anne, *Eros the Bittersweet* (1998).

——*Autobiography of Red* (1999).

——*Men in the Off Hours* (2000).

Castiglione, Baldassare, *The Courtyer of Count Baldessar Castilio*, tr. Thomas Hoby (1561).

Catford, J. C., *A Linguistic Theory of Translation: An Essay in Applied Linguistics* (1965).

Catullus, *Poems of Love and Hate*, tr. Josephine Balmer (2004).

Catullus: The Poems, ed. Kenneth Quinn (1970).

Catullus, Tibullus, Pervigilium Veneris, trs Francis Warre Cornish, J. P. Postgate, and J. W. Mackail, 2nd edn, revised by G. P. Goold (Cambridge, Mass. and London, 1962).

Chapman, George, *Euthymiae Raptus; or The Teares of Peace with Interlocutions* (1609).

Chapple, Anne S., 'Ezra Pound's *Cathay*: Compilation from the Fenollosa Notebooks', *Paideuma* 17. 2–3 (1988), 9–46.

Chartier, Roger, *The Order of Books: Readers, Authors, and Libraries in Europe between the Fourteenth and Eighteenth Centuries*, tr. Lydia G. Cochrane (1994).

Chaucer, Geoffrey, *Amorum Troili et Creseidae libri duo priores Anglico-Latini*, tr. Sir Francis Kinnaston (Oxford, 1635).

—— *Troilus and Criseyde: A New Edition of 'The Book of Troilus'*, ed. B. A. Windeatt (1984).

—— *The Riverside Chaucer*, gen. ed. Larry Benson, 3rd edn (Oxford, 1988).

Chernaik, Warren, 'Philips, Katherine (1632–1664)', *Oxford Dictionary of National Biography*, online edn (Oxford, 2004): http://ezproxy.ouls.ox.ac.uk:2117/view/article/22124 (accessed 11 July 2010).

Cicero, *De Senectute, De Amicitia, De Divinatione*, tr. William Armistead Falconer (Cambridge, Mass. and London, 1979).

Coldiron, A. E. B., 'William Caxton', in France and Gillespie (gen. eds), *The Oxford History of Literary Translation into English*, 5 vols, vol. 1, ed. Roger Ellis (Oxford, 2008), i, 160–70.

Coleridge, Samuel Taylor, *Seven Lectures on Shakespeare and Milton*, ed. John Payne Collier (1856).

—— *Biographia Literaria or Biographical Sketches of My Literary Life and Opinions*, ed. James Engell and W. Jackson Bate, 2 vols (vol. 7 of the *Collected Works of Samuel Taylor Coleridge*, 1983).

Collins, Anthony, *A Discourse of Free-Thinking, Occasion'd by the Rise and Growth of a Sect call'd Free-Thinkers* (1713).

Collinson, Patrick, *The Reformation* (2003; 2005).

Comber, Michael, 'A Book Made New: Reading Propertius Reading Pound. A Study in Reception', *Journal of Roman Studies* 88 (1998), 37–55.

Conley, C. H., *The First English Translators of the Classics* (New Haven and London, 1927).

Connelly, Peter J., 'Pope's *Iliad*: Ut Pictura Translatio', *Studies in English Literature, 1500–1900* 21.3 (Summer 1981), 439–55.

Copeland, Rita, *Rhetoric, Hermeneutics and Translation in the Middle Ages: Academic Traditions and Vernacular Texts* (Cambridge, 1991).

Crewe, Jonathan, *Trials of Authorship: Anterior Forms and Poetic Reconstruction from Wyatt to Shakespeare* (Berkeley, Los Angeles and Oxford, 1990).

Croker, Charlie (ed.), *Lost in Translation: Misadventures in English Abroad*, with illustrations by Louise Morgan (2006).

Cruse, Alan, *Meaning in Language: An Introduction to Semantics and Pragmatics*, 2nd edn (Oxford, 2004).

Cummings, Brian, *The Literary Culture of the Reformation: Grammar and Grace* (Oxford, 2002).

Daniell, David, *The Bible in English: Its History and Influence* (New Haven and London, 2003).

Dante Alighieri, *The Vision or Hell, Purgatory, and Paradise*, tr. Henry Francis Cary (Oxford, 1910).

—— *La Divina Commedia*, ed. Giorgio Petrocchi (Turin, 1975).

—— *Opere Minori*, ed. Domenico de Robertis and Gianfranco Contini, vol. 1, part 1 (Milan and Naples, 1984).

Dante Alighieri, *La Divina Commedia*, ed. Natalino Sapegno, 3 vols, 3rd edn (Florence, 1985).

—— *The Inferno*, tr. Ciaran Carson (2002).

Dasenbrock, Reed Way, 'Wyatt's Transformation of Petrarch', *Comparative Literature* 40.2 (Spring 1988), 122–33.

Davie, Donald, *Studies in Ezra Pound* (Manchester, 1991).

Davis, Kathleen, *Deconstruction and Translation* (Manchester, 2001).

Davis, Paul, *Translation and the Poet's Life: The Ethics of Translating in English Culture, 1646–1726* (Oxford, 2008).

Demetriou, Tania, *'Strange appearance': The Reception of Homer in Renaissance England*, Ph.D. thesis 31121, University of Cambridge (2007).

Derrida, Jacques, *Marges de la philosophie* (Paris, 1972).

—— *Positions* (Paris, 1972).

—— *Of Grammatology* (1976), tr. Gavatry Chakravorti Spivak.

—— 'Living On / Border Lines', in Harold Bloom, Paul de Man, Jacques Derrida, J. Hillis Miller, and Geoffrey H. Hartman, *Deconstruction and Criticism* (1979), 75–176.

—— *Margins of Philosophy*, tr. Alan Bass (Brighton, 1982).

d'Hulst, Lieven, 'Sur le rôle des métaphores en traductologie contemporaine', *Target* 4.1 (1992), 33–51.

Dickens, Charles, *Oliver Twist*, ed. Peter Fairclough (Harmondsworth, 1985).

Douglas-Fairhurst, Robert, *Victorian Afterlives: The Shaping of Influence in Nineteenth-Century Literature* (Oxford, 2002).

Dryden, John, *Fables Ancient and Modern* (1700).

—— *The Letters of John Dryden*, ed. Charles E. Ward (Durham, NC, 1942).

—— *The Works*, ed. E. N. Hooker, H. T. Swedenberg, Jr., et al., 20 vols (Berkeley and London, 1956–2000).

—— *The Poems*, ed. Paul Hammond and David Hopkins, 5 vols (1995–2005).

Eco, Umberto, *Mouse or Rat? Translation as Negotiation* (2003).

Eliot, T. S. *Selected Essays*, 3rd enlarged edn (1951).

Elton, Charles A., *Tales of Romance, with Other Poems, including Selections from Propertius* (1810).

Erasmus, Desiderius, *First tome or volume of the Paraphrase of Erasmus vpon the Newe Testamente*, tr. Nicholas Udall et al. (1548).

Erba, Luciano, *The Greener Meadow: Selected Poems*, tr. Peter Robinson (Princeton, NJ, 1987).

Erbse, Hartmut (ed.), *Scholia Graeca in Homeri Iliadem (Scholia Vetera)*, 7 vols (Berolini, 1969–88).

Erskine-Hill, Howard, *Poetry of Opposition and Revolution: Dryden to Wordsworth* (Oxford, 1996).

Evans, Vyvyan, *How Words Mean: Lexical Concepts, Cognitive Models, and Meaning Construction* (Oxford, 2009).

Fawcett, Peter, *Translation and Language: Linguistic Theories Explained* (Manchester, 1997).

FitzGerald, Edward, *Edward FitzGerald's Rubá'iyát of Omar Khayyam with Their Original Persian Sources Collated from his own MSS., and Literally Translated*, tr. Edward Heron-Allen (1899).

—— *Letters and Literary Remains*, 7 vols (1902–3).

—— *The Variorum and Definitive Edition of the Poetical and Prose Writings*, ed. George Bentham, with an introduction by Edmund Gosse, 7 vols (New York, 1902–3).

—— *The Romance of the Rubáiyát: Edward FitzGerald's First Edition Reprinted with Introduction and Notes*, ed. A. J. Arberry (1959).

—— *The Letters*, ed. Alfred McKinley Terhune and Annabelle Burdick Terhune, 4 vols (Princeton, NJ, 1980).

—— *Rubáiyát of Omar Khayyám: A Critical Edition*, ed. Christopher Decker (Charlottesville, Va. and London, 1997).

—— *Rubáiyát of Omar Khayyám*, ed. Daniel Karlin (2009).

Fleming, John V., *Classical Imitation and Interpretation in Chaucer's Troilus* (Lincoln, Nebr., 1990).

Fowler, Robert (ed.), *The Cambridge Companion to Homer* (Cambridge, 2004).

Fox, Alistair, *The English Renaissance: Identity and Representation in Elizabethan England* (Oxford, 1997).

Foxon, David, *Libertine Literature in England, 1660–1745* (1964).

—— *Pope and the Early Eighteenth-Century Book Trade (the Lyell Lectures, Oxford 1975–76)*, rev. and ed. James McLaverty (Oxford, 1991).

France, Peter and Gillespie, Stuart (gen. eds), *The Oxford History of Literary Translation in English*, 5 vols (Oxford, 2005–).

Francklin, Thomas, *Translation: A Poem* (1753).

Friel, Brien, *Translations* (1980).

Frost, William, '*The Rape of the Lock* and Pope's Homer', *Modern Language Quarterly* 8. 3 (1947), 342–54.

Fulton, Alice, 'Daphne and Apollo', in Hofmann, Michael and James Lasdun (eds), *After Ovid: New Metamorphoses* (1994), 28–58.

Gadamer, Hans-Georg, *Truth and Method*, tr. W. Glen-Doepel, 2nd edn, rev. tr. Joel Weinsheimer and Donald G. Marshall (1989).

—— *Gesammelte Werke*, Bd 1. *Hermeneutik I: Warheit und Methode* (Tübingen, 1990).

Gillespie, Stuart, *Dryden's Sylvae: A Study of Dryden's Translations from the Latin in the Second Tonson Miscellany, 1685*, Ph.D. thesis, University of Cambridge (1987).

—— 'The Early Years of the Dryden–Tonson Partnership: The Background to their Composite Translations and Miscellanies of the 1680s', *Restoration: Studies in English Literary Culture, 1660–1700* 12.1 (Spring 1988), 10–19.

Gillespie, Stuart, 'Literary Afterlives: Metempsychosis from Ennius to Jorge Luis Borges', in Philip Hardie and Helen Moore (eds), *Classical Literary Careers and their Reception* (Cambridge, forthcoming).

——and Sowerby, Robin, 'Translation and Literary Innovation', in France and Gillespie (gen. eds), *The Oxford History of Literary Translation in English*, vol. 3, ed. Stuart Gillespie and David Hopkins (Oxford, 2005–), 21–37.

——and Wilson, Penelope, 'The Publishing and Readership of Translation', in France and Gillespie (gen. eds), *The Oxford History of Literary Translation in English*, vol. 3, ed. Stuart Gillespie and David Hopkins (Oxford, 2005–), 38–51.

Ginzburg, Natalia, *Lessico famigliare* (Milan, 1999).

Golding, Arthur, *A Briefe Discourse of the Late Murther of Master George Saunders, a Worshipful Citizen of London and of the Apprehension, Arreignement, and Execution of the Principall and Accessaries of the Same* (1573).

——*A Discourse vpon the Earthquake that Hapned throughe this Realme of Englande, and other Places of Christendom, the first of Aprill. 1580, betwene the houres of fiue and six in the euening* (1580).

Graham, Joseph F. (ed.), *Difference in Translation* (Ithaca, 1985).

Grandsden, K. W. (ed.), *Virgil in English* (Harmondsworth, 1996).

Gray, Erik, *The Poetry of Indifference: From the Romantics to the Rubáiyát* (Amherst and Boston, 2005).

Gray, Thomas et al., *The Poems of Thomas Gray, William Collins, Oliver Goldsmith*, ed. Roger Lonsdale (1969).

Greenblatt, Stephen, *Renaissance Self-Fashioning: From More to Shakespeare* (Chicago and London, 1980).

Greene, Thomas M., *The Light in Troy: Imitation and Discovery in Renaissance Poetry* (New Haven and London, 1982).

Greenwood, Maria K., 'What Dryden did to Chaucer's *The Knight's Tale*, or Translation as Ideological Input', *The Medieval Translator / Traduire au Moyen Age*, 8 (Turnhout, Belg., 2003), 189–200.

Griffin, J., 'The Creation of Characters in the *Aeneid*', in Philip Hardie (ed.), *Virgil: Critical Assessments of Classical Authors*, 4 vols (1999), iii, 287–301.

Griffin, Julia (ed.), *Selected Poems of Abraham Cowley, Edmund Waller and John Oldham* (1998).

Griffith, Reginald Harvey, *Alexander Pope: A Bibliography* (Austin, Tex., 1922).

Griffiths, Eric and Reynolds, Matthew (eds), *Dante in English* (Harmondsworth, 2005).

Grünbein, Durs, *Ashes for Breakfast: Selected Poems*, tr. Michael Hofmann (New York, 2005).

Hammond, Paul, *Dryden and the Traces of Classical Rome* (Oxford, 1999).

Hardie, Philip (ed.), *Virgil: Critical Assessments of Classical Authors*, 4 vols (1999).

——(ed.), *The Cambridge Companion to Ovid* (Cambridge, 2002).

Hardwick, Lorna, ' "Shards and Suckers": Contemporary Receptions of Homer', in Robert Fowler (ed.), *The Cambridge Companion to Homer* (Cambridge, 2004), 344–62.

Harrison, Tony, *Theatre Works 1973–1985* (1985).

——*Plays Four* (2002).

Hazlitt, William, *Lectures on the English Poets* (1818).

Heaney, Seamus, *Opened Ground: Poems 1966–96* (1998).

Hermans, Theo, 'Images of Translation: Metaphor and Imagery in the Renaissance Discourse of Translation', in Theo Hermans (ed.), *The Manipulation of Literature: Studies in Literary Translation* (1985), 103–35.

——'Paradoxes and Aporias in Translation and Translation Studies', in Alessandra Riccardi (ed.), *Translation Studies: Perspectives on an Emerging Discipline* (Cambridge, 2002), 10–23.

——*The Conference of the Tongues* (Manchester, 2007).

Homberger, Eric (ed.), *Ezra Pound: The Critical Heritage* (1972).

Homer, *Odyssea*, tr. Andrea Divo Iustinopolitano (Lugduni, 1538).

——*Homer his Iliads translated*, tr. John Ogilby (1660).

——*Homer's Iliads in English*, tr. Thomas Hobbes (1676).

——*L'Iliade d'Homere, traduite en François avec des Remarques*, tr. Madame Dacier, 3 vols (Paris, 1711).

——*Ilias kai Odysseia... Operâ, studio, & impensis*, ed. Josuæ Barnes, 2 vols (Cantabrigiæ, 1711).

——*The Iliad of Homer*, tr. Alexander Pope, 6 vols (1715–20).

——*The First Book of Homer's Iliad*, tr. Thomas Tickell (1715).

——*The Iliad and Odyssey of Homer*, tr. William Cowper, 2 vols (1791).

——*The Iliad of Homer*, tr. F. W. Newman (1856).

——*The Iliad of Homer, rendered into English Blank Verse*, tr. Edward, Earl of Derby, 2 vols (1864).

——*The Iliad of Homer*, tr. F. W. Newman, 2nd edn (1871).

——*Iliad*, with an English Translation, A. T. Murray, 2 vols (Cambridge, Mass. and London, 1954).

——*Chapman's Homer: The Iliad*, ed. Allardyce Nicoll (Princeton, NJ, 1956).

——*The Iliad of Homer*, tr. Richmond Lattimore, drawings by Leonard Baskin (1962).

——*The Iliad of Homer*, tr. Robert Fagles, intro. and notes by Bernard Knox (1991).

——*Odyssey*, 2nd edn reprinted with corrections, with an English translation by A. T. Murray, revised George E. Dimock (Cambridge, Mass. and London, 1998).

——*Iliad*, with an English translation by A. T. Murray, revised William F. Wyatt, 2 vols, 2nd edn (Cambridge, Mass. and London, 1999).

Hooley, Daniel M., *The Classics in Paraphrase: Ezra Pound and Modern Translators of Latin Poetry* (1988).

Hopkins, David, ' "The English Homer": Shakespeare, Longinus, and English "Neoclassicism" ', in Charles Martindale and A. B. Taylor (eds), *Shakespeare and the Classics* (Cambridge, 2004), 261–76.

Hudson, Anne (ed.), *Selections from English Wycliffite Writings* (Cambridge, 1978).

—— *The Premature Reformation: Wycliffite Texts and Lollard History* (Oxford, 1988).

Hymns Ancient and Modern (1889).

Jacobs, Carol, 'The Monstrosity of Translation', *Modern Language Notes* 90.6 (December 1975), 755–66.

Jacobson, Howard, *Ovid's Heroides* (Princeton, NJ, 1974).

Jakobson, Roman, *Language in Literature*, ed. Krystyna Pomorska and Stephen Rudy (Cambridge, Mass. and London, 1987).

Johnson, Samuel, *A Dictionary of the English Language: The First and Fourth Editions*, ed. Anne McDermott, CD-ROM (Cambridge, 1996).

—— *The Lives of the Most Eminent English Poets; with Critical Observations on their Works*, ed. Roger Lonsdale, 4 vols (Oxford, 2006).

Johnston, David, 'Theatre Pragmatics', in David Johnston (ed.), *Stages of Translation* (Bristol, 1996), 57–66.

Jones, Chris, *Strange Likeness: The Use of Old English in Twentieth-Century Poetry* (2006).

Jones, Hester, 'Pope's Homer: The Shadow of Friendship', in Howard Erskine Hill (ed.), *Alexander Pope: World and Word*, Proceedings of the British Academy 91 (Oxford, 1998), 55–68.

—— (as Jones, Susannah Hester Everett), *Some Literary Treatments of Friendship: Katherine Philips to Alexander Pope*, Ph.D. dissertation, University of Cambridge (1993), 119.

Keats, John, *The Complete Poems*, ed. Miriam Allott, third impression with corrections (1975).

Kelly, L. G. (Louis), *The True Interpreter: A History of Translation Theory and Practice in the West* (Oxford, 1979).

—— 'Theories of Translation: The Eighteenth Century to Tytler,' in France and Gillespie (gen. eds), *The Oxford History of Literary Translation in English*, vol. 3, ed. Gillespie and David Hopkins (Oxford, 2005–), 67–78.

Kennedy, Duncan F. 'Epistolarity: the *Heroides*', in Philip Hardie (ed.), *The Cambridge Companion to Ovid* (Cambridge, 2002), 217–32.

Kenner, Hugh, *The Pound Era* (1991).

Kermode, Frank, *Continuities* (1968).

Kingsley, Charles, *Alton Locke, Tailor and Poet: An Autobuigraphy* (1876).

Kirk, G. S. (gen. ed.), *The Iliad: A Commentary*, 6 vols (Cambridge, 1985–93).

Kirkpatrick, Robin, *English and Italian Literature from Dante to Shakespeare* (1995).

Laird, Nick, 'Author, Author: Lost in Translation?', *Guardian* (16 August 2008): http://www.guardian.co.uk/books/2008/aug/16/1 (accessed 12 February 2009).

Lakoff, George and Johnson, Mark, *Metaphors We Live By* (1980).

Lawton, David, 'The Bible', in France and Gillespie (gen. eds), *The Oxford History of Literary Translation in English*, vol. 1, ed. Roger Ellis (Oxford, 2008), 193–233.

Lefevere, André, *Translating Poetry: Seven Strategies and Blueprint* (Assen, 1975).

Leopardi, Giacomo, *Canti*, ed. Giorgio Ficara (Milan, 1987).

Levinas, Emmanuel, *Humanism of the Other*, tr. Nidra Poller, with an introduction by Richard A. Cohen (Urbana and Chicago, 2006).

Lewis, C. S. *English Literature in the Sixteenth Century Excluding Drama* (Oxford, 1954).

Lewis, Philip, 'The Measure of Translation Effects', in Graham (ed.), *Difference in Translation*, 31–62.

Liddell, Henry George and Scott, Robert, *A Greek–English Lexicon*, 9th edn revised by Henry Stuart Jones (Oxford, 1996).

Locke, William N. and Booth, Andrew D., *Machine Translation of Languages: Fourteen Essays* (Cambridge, Mass. and New York, 1955).

Logue, Christopher, 'Christopher Logue: The Art of Poetry LXVI', *Paris Review* 127 (1993), 238–64.

——'Interview with Christopher Logue', *Thumbscrew* 1 (1994–5): http://www.poetrymagazines.org.uk/magazine/print.asp?id=5237 (accessed 15 July 2009).

——*Selected Poems* (1996).

——*Prince Charming: A Memoir* (1999).

——*War Music: An Account of Books 1–4 and 16–19 of Homer's* Iliad (2001).

——'The Shortest Long Poem Ever Written: An Interview with Christopher Logue', *Areté* 13 (Winter 2003), 117–36.

——*Cold Calls: War Music Continued* (2005).

'Longinus', *On the Sublime*, ed. D. A. Russell (Oxford, 1964).

——*On the Sublime: The* Peri Hupsous *in Translations by Nicolas Boileaux-Despréaux (1674) and William Smith (1739)* (Delmar, NY, 1975).

Longley, Michael, 'Memory and Acknowledgement', *The Irish Review* 17–18 (Winter 1995), 153–9.

——*Collected Poems* (2006).

Lowell, Robert, *Imitations* (1962; 1971).

Luther, Martin, *Sendbrief vom Dolmetschen*, ed. Karl Bischoff (Tübingen, 1965).

Lyly, John, *Euphues: The Anatomy of Wyt* (1578).

Lyne, Raphael, 'Ovid in English Translation', in Philip Hardie (ed.), *The Cambridge Companion to Ovid* (Cambridge, 2002), 249–63.

Lyons, John, *Semantics*, 2 vols (Cambridge, 1977).

——*Language and Linguistics: An Introduction* (Cambridge, 1981),

MacCulloch, Diarmaid, *Reformation: Europe's House Divided 1490–1700* (2003).

McDonald, Peter, *Mistaken Identities: Poetry and Northern Ireland* (Oxford, 1997).

McGann, Jerome J., *Don Juan in Context* (1976).

McKendrick, Jamie, 'The Napkin Lifter (Catullus xii)', in *Crocodiles & Obelisks* (2007), 37.

Mack, Maynard, *Alexander Pope: A Life* (New Haven and London, 1985).

Magrelli, Valerio, 'Four Poems', tr. Jamie McKendrick, *London Review of Books* 28.6 (23 March 2006), 6.

Mahon, Derek, *Adaptations* (Oldcastle, Co. Meath, 2006).

Marchand, Leslie A., *Byron: A Biography*, 3 vols (New York and London, 1957).

Martin, Robert Bernard, *With Friends Possessed: A Biography of Edward FitzGerald* (1985).

Marvell, Andrew, *The Poems of Andrew Marvell*, ed. James Reeves and Martin Seymour-Smith (1969).

Mason, H. A., *To Homer Through Pope: An Introduction to Homer's* Iliad *and* Pope's Translation (1972).

Matthews, Robert J. 'What did Archimedes Mean by "χρυσός"?', in Joseph F. Graham (ed.), *Difference in Translation* (Ithaca, 1985), 149–64.

Matthiessen, F. O., *Translation: An Elizabethan Art* (Cambridge, Mass., 1931).

Meres, Francis, 'A Comparative Discourse of our English Poets with the Greek, Latine and Italian Poets', in G. Gregory Smith (ed.), *Elizabethan Critical Essays*, 2 vols (Oxford, 1904), ii, 314–24.

Middleton, Thomas, *The Wisdome of Solomon Paraphrased* (1597).

Miner, Earl, 'Chaucer in Dryden's *Fables*', in Howard Anderson and John S. Shea (eds), *Studies in Criticism and Aesthetics, 1660–1800: Essays in Honour of Samuel Holt Monk* (Minneapolis, 1967), 58–72.

Miscellany Poems (1684).

[Moir, George], 'Glassford's *Lyrical Translations*', *Edinburgh Review* 60 (1835), 353–63.

Montaigne, Michel de, *The Essayes or Morall, Politike and Millitarie Discourses*, tr. John Florio (1603).

Montale, Eugenio, *L'Opera in Versi*, ed. Rosanna Bettarini and Gianfranco Contini (Turin, 1980).

Morrison, Blake, 'Turning Classical Plays into Contemporary Theatre', a talk given at the Classics Centre, Oxford University, 26 November 2007.

Muldoon, Paul, 'The Eel', in Jamie McKendrick (ed.), *The Faber Book of 20th-Century Italian Poems* (2004), 50–1.

——— *The End of the Poem: Oxford Lectures in Poetry* (Oxford, 2006).

Müller, Cornelia, *Metaphors Dead and Alive, Sleeping and Waking: A Dynamic View* (Chicago and London, 2008).

Nabokov, Vladimir, 'The Servile Path', in Reuben A. Brower (ed.), *On Translation* (1959; 1966), 97–110.

Nida, Eugene, 'A Framework for the Analysis and Evaluation of Theories of Translation', in Richard W. Brislin (ed.), *Translation, Application and Research* (New York, 1976), 47–91.

Niemeyer, Carl, 'The Earl of Roscommon's Academy', *Modern Language Notes* 49.7 (November 1934), 432–7.

Nord, Christiane, *Translating as a Purposeful Activity: Functionalist Approaches Explained* (Manchester, 1997).

Norton, David, *A History of the Bible as Literature*, 2 vols (Cambridge, 1993).

Oakley-Brown, Liz, 'Translating the Subject: Ovid's *Metamorphoses* in England, 1560–7', in Roger Ellis and Liz Oakley-Brown (eds), *Translation and Nation: Towards a Cultural Politics of Englishness* (Clevedon, 2001), 48–84.

Olson, Glending, 'Geoffrey Chaucer', in David Wallace (ed.), *The Cambridge History of Medieval English Literature* (Cambridge, 1999), 566–89.

Ortony, Andrew (ed.), *Metaphor and Thought*, 2nd edn (Cambridge, 1993).

Ovid, *Metamorphoseos Libri Quindecim, cum commentariis Raphaelis Regii. Adiectis Annotationibus Iacoby Micylli nunc primum in lucem editis* (Basileae, 1543).

——*Ovid's Metamorphoses Englished by G. S.*, tr. George Sandys (1626).

——*Ovids Heroical Epistles, Englished*, tr. John Sherburne (1639).

——*Ovid's Heroical Epistles Englished*, tr. Wye Saltonstall (1636; 5th edn, 1663).

——*Opera Omnia*, eds Nicolai Heinsii and Borchardi Cnippingii, 3 vols (Lugduni Batavorum, 1670).

——*Ovid's Epistles, Translated by Several Hands* (1680).

——*Heroides: Amores*, tr. Grant Showerman, rev. G. P. Goold (Cambridge, Mass. and London, 1977).

——*Metamorphoses*, tr. Frank Justus Miller, rev. G. P. Goold, 3rd edn (Cambridge, Mass. and London, 1977).

——*Ovid's Metamorphoses*, ed. Madeleine Forey, tr. Arthur Golding (2002).

——*Metamorfosi*, ed. Alessandro Barchiesi (Milan, 2005–), vol. 1.

Papali, G. F., *Jacob Tonson, Publisher: His Life and Work (1656–1736)* (Conehunga, Auckland, 1968).

Parish, Helen, 'England', in Andrew Pettegree (ed.), *The Reformation World* (2000), 225–36.

Parker, Patricia, *Inescapable Romance: Studies in the Poetics of a Mode* (Princeton, NJ, 1979).

Partridge, A. C., *English Biblical Translation* (1973).

Pater, Walter, *Appreciations, with an Essay on Style* (1889).

Petrarca, Francesco (Petrarch), *Le Volgari Opere del Petrarcha con la Espositione di Alessandro Vellutello da Lucca* (Vinegia, 1525).

——*Le Rime*, 2 vols (Londra [i.e., Livorno], 1778).

Philips, Katherine, *The Collected Works of Katherine Philips: The Matchless Orinda*, ed. Patrick Thomas, 3 vols (1990–3).

Pitkin, Hanna Fenichel, *The Concept of Representation* (1967).

Plutarch, *The Lives of the Noble Grecians and Romanes*, tr. Thomas North (1579).

Pope, Alexander, *The Prose Works of Alexander Pope*, ed. Norman Ault and Rosemary Cowler, 2 vols (1936–86).

—— *The Twickenham Edition of the Poems*, John Butt (gen. ed.), 10 vols (1939–67).

—— *The Correspondence of Alexander Pope*, ed. George Sherburn, 5 vols (1956).

—— *The Poems*, ed. John Butt (1963).

Popper, Karl, *Unended Quest: An Intellectual Autobiography* (2002).

Poulet, Georges, 'Criticism and the Experience of Interiority', in Richard Macksey and Eugenio Donato (eds), *The Languages of Criticism and the Sciences of Man: The Structuralist Controversy* (1970), 56–72.

Pound, Ezra, *Quia Pauper Amavi (Poems)* (1919).

—— *Selected Poems*, ed. T. S. Eliot (1928).

—— *Literary Essays*, ed. with an introduction by T. S. Eliot (1954).

—— *A Critical Anthology*, ed. J. P. Sullivan (1970).

—— *The Selected Letters of Ezra Pound, 1907–1941*, ed. D. D. Paige (1971).

—— *Pound's Cavalcanti: An Edition of the Translations, Notes, and Essays*, ed. David Anderson (Princeton, NJ, 1983).

—— *Collected Shorter Poems* (1984).

—— *The Cantos*, 4th collected edn (1987).

Prins, Yopie, 'Elizabeth Barrett, Robert Browning, and the *Différance* of Translation', *Victorian Poetry* 29 (1991), 435–51.

—— *Victorian Sappho* (Princeton, NJ, 1999).

Propertius, *Properzio: Il Libro Terzo delle Elegie*, ed. Paolo Fedeli (Bari, 1985).

—— *Elegies*, ed. and tr. G. P. Goold, rev. edn (Cambridge, Mass. and London, 1999).

—— *Erotica: The Elegies of Propertius, the Satyricon of Petronius Arbiter, and the Kisses of Johannes Secundus. To which are Added the Love Epistles of Aristaenetus*, ed. Walter K. Kelly (Bohn's Classical Library, 1854).

Pulci, Luigi, *Il Morgante Maggiore* (Florence, 1732).

Pushkin, Alexandr, *Eugene Onegin: A Novel in Verse*, tr. with a commentary by Vladimir Nabokov, 2 vols, rev. edn (Princeton, NJ, 1975).

Pym, Anthony, 'Natural and Directional Equivalence in Theories of Translation', *Target* 19.2 (2007), 271–94.

—— *Exploring Translation Theories* (Abingdon, 2010).

Randolph, Jody Allen, 'Michael Longley in Conversation', *PN Review* 31. 2 (November–December 2004), 21–7.

Reynolds, Mattthew, *The Realms of Verse 1830–1870: English Poetry in a Time of Nation-Building* (Oxford, 2001).

—— 'Browning and Translationese', *Essays in Criticism* 53.2 (April 2003), 97–128.

—— 'Principles and Norms of Translation', in France and Gillespie (gen. eds), *The Oxford History of Literary Translation in English*, vol. 4, ed. Peter France and Kenneth Haynes (Oxford, 2006), 59–82.

——'Most Himself', *London Review of Books* 29.14 (19 July 2007), 11–15. http://www.lrb.co.uk/v29/n14/matthew-reynolds/most-himself (accessed 24 January 2011).

——'Semi-Censorship in Dryden and Browning', in Francesca Billiani (ed.), *Modes of Censorship and Translation: National Contexts and Diverse Media* (Manchester, 2007), 187–204.

——'Varifocal Translation in Ciaran Carson's *Inferno*', in Daniela Caselli and Daniela La Penna (eds), *Twentieth-Century Poetic Translation: Literary Cultures in Italian and English* (2008).

Riccardi, Alessandra (ed.), *Translation Studies: Perspectives on an Emerging Discipline* (Cambridge, 2002).

Ricks, Christopher, *Tennyson*, 2nd edn (1989).

——*Allusion to the Poets* (Oxford, 2002).

Ricks, David, 'On Looking into the First Paperback of Pope's Homer', *Classics Ireland* 4 (1997), 97–120.

Ritchie, David, ' "*ARGUMENT IS WAR*" – Or is it a Game of Chess? Multiple Meanings in the Analysis of Implicit Metaphors', *Metaphor and Symbol* 18.2 (2003), 125–46.

Robinson, Douglas, *The Translator's Turn* (Baltimore and London, 1991).

Rochester, John Wilmot, Earl, *The Complete Works*, ed. Frank H. Ellis (Harmondsworth, 1994).

Rolle, Richard, *The Psalter or Psalms of David and Certain Canticles with a Translation and Exposition in English by Richard Rolle of Hampole*, ed. H. R. Bramley (Oxford, 1884).

Romaine, Suzanne, *Language in Society: An Introduction to Sociolinguistics* (Oxford, 1994).

Roscommon, Wentworth Dillon, Earl of, *An Essay on Translated Verse* (1684).

Rossetti, Dante Gabriel (tr.), *The Early Italian Poets from Ciullo d'Alcamo to Dante Alighieri* (1861).

Rossiter, William T., *Chaucer and Petrarch* (Cambridge, 2010).

Sandys, George, *A Paraphrase upon the Divine Poems* (1638).

Sannehide, Kodama, 'Pound and Fenollosa's Notebooks', *Paideuma* 11. 2 (1982), 207–40.

Sappho, *If Not, Winter: Fragments of Sappho*, tr. Anne Carson (2002).

Scott, Clive, *Channel Crossings: French and English Poetry in Dialogue, 1550–2000* (Oxford, 2002).

Shakespeare, William, *The Complete Works*, ed. Peter Alexander (London and Glasgow, 1951).

——*Ouevres complètes*, ed. Henri Fluchère, 2 vols (Paris, 1959).

——*The Sonnets and A Lover's Complaint*, ed. John Kerrigan (1986).

Shankman, Steven, *Pope's* Iliad: *Homer in the Age of Passion* (1983).

——'Pope's Homer and his Poetic Career', in Pat Rogers (ed.), *The Cambridge Companion to Alexander Pope* (Cambridge, 2007), 63–75.

Shelley, Percy Bysshe, *Shelley's Prose or The Trumpet of a Prophecy*, ed. David Lee Clark (Albuquerque, NM, 1954).

Shklovsky, Victor, 'Art as Technique', tr. Lee T. Lemon and Marion J. Reis, in David Lodge (ed.), *Modern Criticism and Theory: A Reader* (1988), 16–30.

Sidney, Sir Philip, *Selected Poems*, ed. Katherine Duncan-Jones (Oxford, 1973).

Simon, Sherry, *Gender in Translation: Cultural Identity and the Politics of Transmission* (1996).

Simonsuuri, Kirsti, *Homer's Original Genius: Eighteenth-Century Notions of the Early Greek Epic (1688–1798)* (Cambridge, 1979).

Smith, Charlotte, *Elegiac Sonnets*, 2nd edn (Chichester, 1784).

Smith, G. Gregory (ed.), *Elizabethan Critical Essays*, 2 vols (Oxford, 1904).

Snell-Hornby, Mary, *Translation Studies: An Integrated Approach* (Amsterdam, 1988).

Sowerby, Robin, 'Chapman's Discovery of Homer', *Translation and Literature* 1 (1992), 26–51.

——'Epic', in France and Gillespie (gen. eds), *The Oxford History of Literary Translation in English*, vol. 3, ed. Stuart Gillespie and David Hopkins (Oxford 2005–), iii, 149–72.

—— *The Augustan Art of Poetry: Augustan Translation of the Classics* (Oxford, 2006).

Spenser, Edmund, *The Faerie Queene*, ed. A. C. Hamilton (1977).

Spivak, Gayatri Chakravorty, *Outside in the Teaching Machine* (1993).

St André, James (ed.), *Thinking Through Translation with Metaphors* (Manchester, 2010).

Steen, Gerard, 'From Linguistic to Conceptual Metaphor in Five Steps', in Raymond W. Gibbs Jr. and Gerard J. Steen (eds), *Metaphor in Cognitive Linguistics* (Amsterdam and Philadelphia, 1999), 57–78.

Steiner, George, *After Babel* (1975; 3rd edn 1998).

Stevenson, Matthew, *The Wits Paraphras'd, or, Paraphrase upon Paraphrase in a Burlesque on the Several Late Translations of Ovids Epistles* (1680).

Stone, Marjorie, *Elizabeth Barrett Browning* (1995).

Stray, Christopher, *Classics Transformed: Schools, Universities, and Society in England, 1830–1960* (Oxford, 1998).

Strohm, Paul, *Theory and the Premodern Text* (Minneapolis and London, 2000).

Stunt, Timothy C. F., 'Newman, Francis William (1805–1897)', *Oxford Dictionary of National Biography*, online edn (Oxford, September 2004): http://www.oxforddnb.com/view/article/20019 (accessed 22 July 2010).

Sullivan, J. P., *Ezra Pound and Sextus Propertius* (1965).

——(ed.), *Ezra Pound: A Critical Anthology* (1970).

Swinburne, Algernon Charles, *Notes on Poems and Reviews* (1866).

—— *The Poems*, 6 vols (1904).

Tarrant, Richard, 'Ovid and Ancient Literary History', in Philip Hardie (ed.), *The Cambridge Companion to Ovid* (Cambridge, 2002), 13–33.

Tasso, Torquato, *Il Goffredo: Novamente Corretto, e Ristampato, Con l'aggiunta de' Cinque Canti del Sig. Camillo Camilli* (Venice, 1583).

——*Godfrey of Bulloigne, or The recouerie of Hierusalem*, tr. Richard Carew (1594).

——*Godfrey of Bulloigne: A Critical Edition of Edward Fairfax's Translation of Tasso's Gerusalemme Liberata, Together with Fairfax's Original Poems*, ed. Kathleen M. Lea and T. M. Gang (Oxford, 1981).

Taylor, Karla, 'Writers of the Italian Renaissance', in France and Gillespie (gen. eds), *The Oxford History of Literary Translation in English*, 5 vols, vol. 1, ed. Roger Ellis (Oxford, 2008), i, 390–406.

Tennyson, Alfred Lord, *The Poems*, ed. Christopher Ricks, 3 vols, 2nd edn (1987).

Theocritus, *Ta Euriskomena* (Oxford, 1676).

Theocritus, ed. and tr. A. S. F. Gow, 2 vols (Cambridge, 1952).

Thomas, Keith, *Religion and the Decline of Magic: Studies in Popular Beliefs in Sixteenth- and Seventeenth- Century England* (1973).

Tissol, Garth, 'Dryden's Additions and the Interpretive Reception of Ovid', *Translation and Literature* 13.2 (Autumn 2004), 181–93.

Tomlinson, Charles, *Poetry and Metamorphosis* (Cambridge, 1983).

Toury, Gideon, *Descriptive Translation Studies and Beyond* (Amsterdam, 1995).

Tucker, Herbert F., *Tennyson and the Doom of Romanticism* (Cambridge, Mass. and London, 1988).

——'Metaphor, Translation, and Autoekphrasis in FitzGerald's Rubáiyát', *Victorian Poetry* 46.1 (Spring 2008), 69–86.

Tymoczko, Maria, *Translation in a Postcolonial Context: Early Irish Literature in English Translation* (Manchester, 1999).

——'Reconceptualizing Translation Theory: Integrating Non-Western Thought about Translation', in Theo Hermans (ed.), *Translating Others*, 2 vols (Manchester, 2006), i, 13–32

——*Enlarging Translation, Empowering Translators* (Manchester, 2007).

——'Western Metaphorical Discourses Implicit in Translation Studies', in James St André (ed.), *Thinking Through Translation with Metaphors* (Manchester, 2010), 109–43.

[Tytler, Alexander], *Essay on the Principles of Translation* (1791).

Untermeyer, Jean Starr, *Private Collection* (New York, 1965).

Untermeyer, Louis, *Robert Frost* (1964).

Valéry, Paul, *Cahiers*, ed. Judith Robinson, 2 vols (Paris, 1973).

Vassallo, Peter, *Byron: The Italian Literary Influence* (1984).

Vermeer, Hans, 'Skopos and Commission in Translational Action', tr. Andrew Chesterman, in Lawrence Venuti (ed.), *The Translation Studies Reader* (2000), 221–32.

Venuti, Lawrence, '*The Destruction of Troy*: Translation and Royalist Cultural Politics in the Interregnum', *The Journal of Medieval and Renaissance Studies* 23.2 (Spring 1993), 197–219.

—— *The Scandals of Translation: Towards an Ethics of Difference* (1998).

——(ed.), *The Translation Studies Reader*, 2nd edn (2004).

—— *The Translator's Invisibility* (1995; 2nd edn 2008).

Vinay, Jean-Paul and Darbelnet, Jean, *Stylistique comparée du français et de l'anglais: méthode de traduction* (*c.*1958), tr. Juan C. Sager and Marie-Josée Hame as *Comparative Stylistics of French and English: A Methodology for Translation* (1995).

Virgil, *The Destruction of Troy, an Essay upon the Second Book of Virgils Aeneis, Written in the year, 1636*, tr. [John Denham] (1656).

—— *Opera*, ed. Carolus Ruaeus (1695).

—— *Aeneidos Liber Quartus*, ed. with a commentary by R. G. Austin (1955).

—— *Aeneidos Liber Secundus*, ed. with a commentary by R. G. Austin (1964).

—— *Aeneid 10: With Introduction, Translation and Commentary*, ed. S. J. Harrison (Oxford, 1991).

Virgil, 2 vols, tr. H. R. Fairclough, revised edn (Cambridge, Mass. and London, 1935).

Walker, Greg, *Writing Under Tyranny: English Literature and the Henrician Reformation* (Oxford, 2005).

Walker, Obadiah, *Paraphrase and Annotations upon all the Epistles of St Paul* (1684).

Wallace, Jennifer, 'Elizabeth Barrett Browning: Knowing Greek', *Essays in Criticism* 50.4 (2000), 329–53.

Waller, Edmund, *The Poems of Edmund Waller*, ed. G. Thorn Drury (1893).

Warner, Marina, *Fantastic Metamorphoses, Other Worlds: Ways of Telling the Self* (Oxford, 2002).

Watson, Thomas, *Amyntas* (1585).

—— *The Lamentations of Amyntas for the Death of Phyllis, Paraphrastically Translated out of Latin into English Hexameters*, tr. Abraham Fraunce (1587).

Weissbort, Daniel and Eysteinsson, Astradur (eds), *Translation – Theory and Practice: A Historical Reader* (Oxford, 2006).

Williams, Isaac, *The Altar* (1849).

Windeatt, Barry, *Troilus and Criseyde* (Oxford, 1992).

Wittgenstein, Ludwig, *Philosophical Investigations*, tr. G. E. M. Anscombe (Oxford, 1988).

Wolfe, Jessica, 'Chapman's Ironic Homer', *College Literature* 35.4 (Fall 2008), 151–86.

Wordsworth, William, *The Poems*, ed. John O. Hayden, 2 vols (Harmondsworth, 1977).

Wyatt, Thomas, *Collected Poems of Sir Thomas Wyatt*, ed. Kenneth Muir and Patricia Thomson (Liverpool, 1969).

—— *The Complete Poems*, ed. R. A. Rebholz (Harmondsworth, 1997).

Yao, Steven G., *Translation and the Languages of Modernism: Gender, Politics, Language* (New York and Basingstoke, 2002).

Yip, Wai-lim, *Ezra Pound's* Cathay (New Jersey, 1969).

Zamyatin, Yevgeny, *We*, tr. Natasha Randall (New York, 2006).

Zukofsky, Louis, *Complete Short Poetry* (Baltimore and London, 1991).

Zwicker, Steven N., *Politics and Language in Dryden's Poetry: The Arts of Disguise* (Princeton, NJ, 1984).

Index

Printed and bound by CPI Group (UK) Ltd, Croydon, CR0 4YY